# MAGNIFICENT OBSESSION

# MAGNIFICENT OBSESSION

Victoria, Albert and the Death that
Changed the Monarchy

Helen Rappaport

**WINDSOR**
**PARAGON**

First published 2011
by Hutchinson
This Large Print edition published 2012
by AudioGO Ltd
by arrangement with
The Random House Group Ltd

Hardcover        ISBN: 978 1 445 89404 1
Softcover        ISBN: 978 1 445 89405 8

British Library Cataloguing in Publication Data available

Printed and bound in Great Britain by
MPG Books Group Limited

For Charlie Viney

# Contents

Preface & Acknowledgements     xi

List of Illustrations     xvii

Prologue: Christmas 1860     1

Part One: Albert the Good

  1 'The Treadmill of Never-Ending Business'     17

  2 'The First Real Blow of Misfortune'     42

  3 'Fearfully in Want of a True Friend'     62

  4 'Our *Most* Precious Invalid'     86

  5 'Day Turned into Night'     113

  6 'Our Great National Calamity'     131

  7 'Will They Do Him Justice Now?'     160

  8 'How Will the Queen Bear It?'     180

Part Two: The Broken-Hearted Widow

  9 'All Alone!'

10 'The Luxury of Woe'     197

11 'A Married Daughter I *Must* Have Living with Me'     224, 247

12 'God Knows How I Want So Much to be Taken Care Of'     271

13 'The Queen Is Invisible'     300

14 'Heaven Has Sent Us This
   Dispensation to Save Us'                    327
15 Albertopolis                               356
Epilogue: Christmas 1878                      373

Appendix: What Killed Prince
   Albert?                                    382
Notes                                         401
Bibliography                                  461

Peel cut down my income, Wellington refused me rank, the Royal Family cried out against the foreign interloper, the Whigs in office were inclined to concede me just as much space as I could stand upon. The Constitution is silent as to the Consort of the Queen . . . and yet there he was, not to be done without.

Prince Albert, letter to Baron Stockmar,<br>24 January 1854[1]

He conquered my heart; so that I could not choose but to love him—there was an indescribable *something* about him—an elevation, an humility, a power and simplicity, a thorough *genuineness* of character, a style and tone in his whole manner, opinions . . . which made him to me my very ideal of a *Christian* Prince! What a Godfearing man he was! What a sense of duty he had.

Reverend Norman Macleod,<br>28 December 1861[2]

For me, life came to an end on 14 December. My life was dependent on his, I had no thoughts except of him; my whole striving was to please him, to be less unworthy of him!

Queen Victoria, letter to King of Prussia,<br>4 February 1862[3]

# Preface & Acknowledgements

Queen Victoria is one of the most written-about women in British—if not world—history. Her consort Prince Albert has also been the subject of several biographies, as well as studies of his contribution to the arts and British culture. This book is neither a biography of the Queen nor of Prince Albert. Instead it focuses on what is, I argue, a crucial period in her life, one that completely changed the course her reign took for the next forty years and had a profound impact on Britain: the lost ten years from Albert's death at the end of 1861 to the beginning of her re-emergence from deep mourning in 1872.

Much has been written about Queen Victoria's later years as the gloomy, humourless, reclusive widow at Windsor, but virtually no attempt has been made to explore the nature of her grief or to describe the circumstances leading up to Prince Albert's death in December 1861 and its catastrophic impact on her. This book seeks to understand why the Queen reacted in the extreme way she did, by explaining her obsessive love for her husband and her total and utter reliance on him. The second half of the book considers Queen Victoria's untiring memorialisation of her dead husband—in biography, art and architecture—at a time when criticism of her withdrawal from public life was mounting.

Prince Albert's death, funeral and the public response to it have been paid surprisingly little attention to date; recent accounts tend to stop abruptly at his deathbed or fast-forward to the Queen's life thereafter. This book sets out to describe the effect that death had both on Prince Albert's contemporaries and on the nation at large. With this objective in mind, I have sought out unpublished, forgotten and neglected sources that comment on the Prince's declining health, his death and funeral and the Queen's reaction to it. In Britain we are blessed with a wealth of published letters, diaries and memoirs from the Victorian period, many of them by personalities who have long since been forgotten and consigned to obscurity, but which nevertheless contain valuable testimony on the impact of Prince Albert's death. It has been a pleasure to rediscover these now-neglected Victorian letter-writers and diarists, who have enlightened and enlivened my research and impressed me with their wonderfully perceptive comments about the Queen, Prince Albert and the true nature of their relationship.

A key resource in the writing of this book has been the Royal Archives in the Round Tower at Windsor Castle. I am indebted to their registrar, Pamela Clark, and her staff for making a range of fascinating material available to me during my research there, and for the permission of Her Majesty Queen Elizabeth II to quote from it, as well as use photographs and illustrations from the Royal Collection. My thanks also go to Sophie Gordon for her assistance in this latter respect.

From Germany, I was able to obtain copies of letters written at the time of Prince Albert's death by the Crown Prince of Prussia and Princess Alice of Great Britain. I am indebted to Christine

Klössel at the Arkhiv der Hessischen Hausstiftung, Schloss Fasanerie, Eichenzell, for providing me with transcripts for those of the Crown Prince; and to Professor Eckhart G. Franz at the Staatsarchiv Darmstadt for making available digital images of the original letters by Princess Alice. Quotations from these letters are included with the gracious permission of Prince Donatus von Hessen. I am greatly indebted to Hannah Veale for translating both sets of letters from German, and in particular for her enormous patience in deciphering Princess Alice's difficult handwriting.

I would also like to thank a number of British archivists who provided valuable help and access to material: Alan Tadiello at Balliol College, Oxford, for the Queen's letters to General Peel in the Morier Family Papers; Nick Mays, at *The Times* Archive, News International Archive, for those of John Delane and Lord Torrington; Caroline Picco at Cheshire Archives, for providing a photocopy of the 'Descriptions of the Death of the Prince Consort, 1861' by Arthur Penrhyn Stanley, and for the permission of the present Lord Stanley to quote from it; the British Library, for permission to quote from the Duchess of Sutherland's letters in the Gladstone Papers and from Queen Victoria's 'Album Consolativum'; Colin Harris at the Bodleian Library Special Collection, for making available to me the diaries of Katharine Clarendon, John Rashdall and Charles Pugh and the Bodleian Library, University of Oxford for permission to quote from them; Briony Hudson at the Royal Pharmaceutical Society of Great Britain, for allowing me to access the account books of Peter Squire; Phil Tomaselli, for obtaining material for me from the Lord Chamberlain's papers at the National Archives, Kew; Helen Burton at Keele University Library, for information on Sarah Hildyard; and Ian Shapiro at Argyll Etkin, for allowing me access to the MS diaries of Sir John Cowell in his collection, as well as providing other materials for my research.

Many other people offered invaluable support, advice and information along the way: Denise Hesselroth alerted me to the underrated diaries of Lady Lucy Cavendish; Paul Frecker provided information on Victorian *cartes de visite* and images for this book; Kevin Brady shared his research on Princess Alice and her family; Marianne Kouwenhoven in The Hague investigated sources in the archives of Queen Sophie of the Netherlands; Geoffrey Munn at Wartskis kindly showed me items of jewellery relating to the Queen, Prince Albert and John Brown from their private collection; fellow historians David Waller, Matthew Dennison and Hugo Vickers answered my queries and suggested sources. Nicholas Janni and Juliet Grayson suggested sources on death and bereavement, and my dear friend Linda Blair gave me her invaluable views on the same, read sections of the manuscript relating to the Queen's grieving and offered insightful comments. Among royalty buffs, Sue Woolmans, Richard Thornton and members of the Royalty Weekend annual conference held at Ticehurst offered valuable support for, and interest in, this project. On a memorable research trip to Whitby to investigate the jet industry, Lynne and George provided a home-from-home at the No. 7 Guest House; Rachel Jones and Matt

Hatch at Hamond's Jewellers on Church Street responded generously to my passion for Whitby jet; Peter Hughes, custodian of the wonderfully idiosyncratic Whitby Museum, which has an extraordinary collection of jet jewellery and artefacts, offered valuable background information.

The arguments contained in the Appendix to this book—'What Killed Prince Albert'—are my own, based on extensive research and much deliberation. I arrived at my conclusions thanks to the assistance of doctors Simon Travis (Consultant Gastroenterologist) and Chris Conlon (Consultant in Infectious Diseases), who read my draft and offered their comments and observations. Professors Ronald Chaplain (Consultant Oncologist) and Neil Mortensen (Consultant Colorectal Surgeon) also offered valuable advice, as did Dr Anne Hardy on the incidence of typhoid fever in the Victorian period. But, in the end, the conclusions are mine. I would welcome comments and feedback on this book, to my website www.helenrappaport.com

Finally, my thanks as always go to my family for their support in all my work, in particular to my brothers Peter and Christopher, and also to my friend and fellow writer Christina Zaba, for her generous and unstinting encouragement in all my literary endeavours. My agent Charlie Viney, to whom this book is dedicated, has been a wonderful friend and guide over the last six years and will I hope support my efforts on many more books to come. I count myself enormously fortunate in having wonderfully supportive and sympathetic commissioning editors and friends, in Caroline

Gascoigne at Hutchinson in the UK and Charlie Spicer at St Martin's Press in the USA.

Helen Rappaport
Oxford, August 2011

# List of Illustrations

First section

Albert by Camille Silvy (Photo by Camille Silvy/ Mansell/Time Life Pictures/Getty Images)
Albert engraving (From the author's collection)
Thanksgiving dress (Photo by W. & D. Downey/ Getty Images)
Augusta Stanley (Copyright: Dean and Chapter of Westminster)
Princess Beatrice (Photo by Hulton Archive/Getty Images)
Grief-stricken Bertie (From the author's collection)
Funeral engravings (two pictures) (From the author's collection)
William Jenner (Photo by Hulton Archive/Getty Images)
Henry Ponsonby (Photo by Popperfoto/Getty Images)
Sir James Clark (From the author's collection)
Alfred Tennyson (Photo by Hulton Archive/Getty Images)
John Brown (Photo by SSPL/Getty Images)
Victoria & Brown cartoon (From the author's collection)
*Tomahawk* cartoon (From the author's collection)
Jay's Mourning Warehouse ©Amoret Tanner
Mourning dress ©Amoret Tanner
Concerned crowd © The Print Collector / Heritage-

Images / Imagestate

Blackfriars © Illustrated London News Ltd/Mary Evans

Disraeli (Popperfoto / Getty Images)

Gladstone (Photo by John Jabez Edwin Mayall/ Henry Guttmann/Getty Images)

Second section

Windsor Castle East Terrace (From the author's collection)

Windsor Castle Christmas (Photo by Hulton Archive/Getty Images)

Design for the interior decorations of the Royal Mausoleum at Frogmore (From the author's collection)

Deathbed cut-out (From the author's collection)

Bertie (Photo by John Jabez Edwin Mayall/Hulton Archive/Getty Images)

Princess Louise (Photo by SSPL/Getty Images)

Princess Alice (Photo by Hulton Archive/Getty Images)

Commemorative pot lid (From the author's collection)

A Nation Mourns (Mary Evans Picture Library)

Framed mourning card (V&A Images/Victoria and Albert Museum)

Whitby Jet Factory © Frank Meadow Sutcliffe / Sutcliffe Gallery

The Royal Albert Hall (Monkey Business/Rex Features)

Wolverhampton Memorial © Spectrum Colour
  Library / Heritage-Images / Imagestate
Albert Memorial (Latitudestock/Getty Images)
Thanksgiving (Mary Evans Picture Library)

# PROLOGUE

## Christmas 1860

It was the coldest Christmas for fifty years, so they said, a bitter winter having followed hard on the heels of a chilly and sunless summer. So cold was it that country people talked of the birds frozen on the trees and song thrushes dying in their thousands; so cold that the legs of waterfowl stuck hard to the ice on the surface of lakes and ponds. Londoners got the best of it—the ice on the Serpentine in Hyde Park was thirteen inches thick, providing welcome Christmastide recreation to the hundreds who skated there well into the night by torchlight. Indeed, such had been the unprecedented cold that year that there was talk of reviving the old seventeenth-century frost fair on the Thames.[1]

Out at Windsor, twenty-one miles west of London and south of the Great Western Railway junction at Slough, a heavy frost had descended across the bare chestnut trees of the park, above which Windsor Castle rose in all its magnificence. A great impregnable stone fortress of history and tradition, dating back to an original wooden structure built after the Norman Conquest, it was reached by climbing the hill from the King Henry VIII Gate down in the little town of Windsor below, and passing through the narrow archway of the Norman Gate that separates the Lower from the Upper Ward of the castle.

The week before Christmas the royal family had transferred from Buckingham Palace to their

1

private apartments here in the Upper Ward for the festive season. In the 1840s the interior of the castle had been extensively remodelled to accommodate the rapidly growing royal family, and from their apartments on the first floor they could look out over the East Terrace, across the ornamental garden and fountain to the dry moat, and beyond it the open grassy swathes of Windsor Home Park. Outside, in the paved quadrangle, soldiers in bearskins perpetually on guard paced back and forth below their windows within sight of a bronze equestrian statue of Charles II.

A labyrinth of staircases and carpeted corridors greeted anyone venturing inside the apartments of the East Terrace, the interior shadowy on dark winter days until it was lit at four in the afternoon by huge lamps that were left to burn all night.[2] The royal family's rooms here—including the Oak Room, where they took informal meals, and a larger Dining Room and the White and Crimson Drawing Rooms for more formal events—were connected along a Grand Corridor, which stretched from Queen Victoria's rooms in the King's Tower at one end to the state rooms and the Prince of Wales's Tower at the far end. The Grand Corridor itself was a place of recreation and association for members of the royal household as they went about their duties, its walls hung with paintings and its length interspersed with white marble busts on pedestals, bronzes, fine inlaid cabinets and choice pieces of furniture. At regular intervals between them huge doors decorated with gilding opened into the royal apartments and guest rooms beyond.[3]

Despite the attractiveness of its interior, Queen Victoria had never found Windsor congenial, remarking that she hoped that 'this fine, old dull place' would never hold her bones. To return there from the more cosy, purpose-built family homes at Osborne and Balmoral that she and her husband so loved was always a wrench. 'I have no feeling for Windsor,' she once wrote, 'I admire it, I think it a grand, splendid place—but without a particle of anything which causes me to love it.'[4] Nevertheless, the royal couple had spent all their Christmases at Windsor since the birth of their first child, the Princess Royal, in November 1840 and, with Prince Albert's encouragement, the royal apartments each Christmas gave pride of place to a host of Christmas trees.

Windsor Castle came into its own at this festive time of year. The silence along its Grand Corridor, where noise was muffled by the red carpets and huge damask curtains that hung at the tall, arched windows looking directly into the quadrangle, was broken by the happy sound of laughter and children's voices. Games of hide-and-seek along the corridors and in the towers and staircases of the castle by the royal children ensured that it had a happy family atmosphere. Fires were kept blazing with beech logs in all the reception rooms—the Queen did not like the smell of coal, although her pathological intolerance of heat was such that she ordained that the rooms should be kept at a temperature of only sixty degrees and she had thermometers in ivory cases mounted on every chimneypiece in order to check that her directive was adhered to. Victoria liked the old way of things: she refused to concede to gas lighting, which had been introduced into the official state rooms at Windsor, insisting that her private apartments were lit only by candles. Such stubbornness might have been an inconvenience, but at Christmas time the softly flickering candlelight throughout the royal apartments lent a particularly romantic atmosphere to the surroundings.[5]

For the first half of December the rain had come down in torrents, but now in the final days before Christmas fine, cold weather and a sharp frost had arrived and would persist right through the holiday. From 5 p.m. on the afternoon of the 20th it had begun snowing and continued till midnight, the snow piling in drifts around the castle, as it rose up like a fairytale citadel in the dazzling white of the surrounding landscape. Prince Albert had always loved 'the dear Christmas Eve' and took great pleasure in his children's 'happy wonder at the German Christmas tree and its radiant candles'.[6] Christmas was a profoundly nostalgic time for him, reminding him of those he had spent with his brother as children. Separated from the home at Coburg that he so loved, he now had to 'seek in the children an echo of what Ernest and I were in the old time', as he mused to his stepmother.[7] By 1860 he and Queen Victoria had nine children, ranging from Vicky (aged twenty) to Beatrice the youngest, who was only three. Yet already, young though they were, the royal children had begun to fly the nest. Vicky, Albert's much-adored favourite, had been married at seventeen to the Crown Prince of Prussia, the first stage in a personal project nurtured by her parents to secure a united, democratic Germany under Prussian leadership. Already the mother of two children, Vicky was now resigned to having to spend Christmas isolated from her family at her palace in Berlin. Her sister

Alice—Victoria and Albert's third child and second daughter—would be the next to marry. At the end of November she had become engaged to Prince Louis of Hesse; he was rather dull, but Alice had fortunately fallen in love with him, and Louis was visiting Windsor that Christmas in anticipation of their marriage in a year or so's time. Victoria and Albert had similar plans for their son and heir Albert Edward, better known as Bertie in the family, who had just returned from an official tour—his first on their behalf—to Canada and the USA. He had acquitted himself well, demonstrating his popular touch and natural social skills, although at a dance in his honour at Pike's Opera House in Cincinnati he had looked with rather too much pleasure on the 'vast array of beauties' lined up for him.[8] Such reports discomfited his parents; Bertie must be married off, and soon, in Albert's view.

It was an unusually large family gathering that year. The days before Christmas were full of laughter and activity as the family was reunited with Affie (Prince Alfred) who, having joined the navy at the age of only twelve, was home from sea, much to his mother's delight. Everyone busied themselves with present-wrapping in between frequent trips down the hill to skate on the frozen pond on the Slopes below the north-east side of the castle. On the 23rd Victoria was delighted to see that the severe frost persisted. Despite the freezing weather, everyone eagerly walked down to the pond again to skate, returning for an intimate family supper, after which, like any ordinary family, 'albums were looked at and Albert played at chess with Affie'.[9]

That particular Christmas, John Delane, editor

5

of *The Times*, was fortunate to receive an insider's view of the royal family at their leisure, thanks to his friend at court, Lord Torrington—'that arch gossip of gossips'.[10] Torrington had been a permanent lord-in-waiting to Queen Victoria since 1859 and, in a private joke with Delane, with whom he frequently corresponded, described himself as 'your Windsor special'.[11] In letters written that Christmas to Delane, Torrington vividly captured the happy and relaxed atmosphere at Windsor: how he played billiards with the two young princes, Arthur and Alfred, and had sat and chatted informally with the Queen and Prince Albert. On Christmas Eve he had ventured down to the castle's cavernous kitchens to see the great baron of beef—all 360 pounds in weight—that was being cooked on a huge spit with great iron chains, constantly attended by four men.[12] Elsewhere in the vast Windsor kitchen with its twelve ranges, other huge fires had roasts suspended in front of them— one alone had fifty turkeys. Yet everywhere the greatest calm and order prevailed among the kitchen's legion of white-jacketed and white-capped cooks.

Everyone was delighted to wake on the 24th to 'true Xmas weather, snow on the ground and sharp frost', as Victoria recorded. In the heart of his family and away from the limelight of public scrutiny and onerous official duty, Prince Albert took an almost childish delight in the pleasures of the Christmas season. In the morning he and the young princes went out for some invigorating shooting, while the others once more went down to the skating pond. The ice lured them all back in the afternoon to enjoy a game of ice-hockey, in which Victoria was delighted to see that the shy and nervous Louis 'joined with great spirit'. Back in their apartments after 4 p.m. as the dark of Christmas Eve drew in, the family set about arranging their many gifts to each other on the present tables. It was, recalled Victoria, 'most bewildering' sorting them all out, but with her husband's 'great indefatigability' they succeeded.[13]

At 6 p.m. everyone in the royal household gathered in the Oak Room for the exchange of presents. Here they were greeted by the Queen and Prince Albert standing by a large table covered with a white damask cloth, in the middle of which stood a decorated fir tree surrounded by presents and handwritten cards for them. In addition, three artificial fir trees about eight feet in height had been specially put in place in each of the Queen's three private sitting rooms—one each for herself, the Prince and the Duchess of Kent—with another tree for the children in the nursery. Smaller fir trees imported specially from Prince Albert's childhood home at Coburg were on display elsewhere in the castle.[14] The chandeliers had to be taken down specially to accommodate the larger ornamental trees, which were securely suspended from the ceiling, their bases resting on the table. The ten rows of symmetrical branches of these trees were decorated with edible fancies: sweetmeats, little cakes, fancy French bonbons, gilt walnuts—and gingerbreads whose delicious aroma filled the air—the effect completed with coloured ribbons and wax tapers and a frosting of artificial snow and icicles. At each tree-top stood a Christmas angel of Nuremberg glass, its outstretched wings holding a wreath in each hand.

Lord Torrington watched as the family exchanged their presents. The largest drawing room was like an Aladdin's cave, 'fitted up with everything that was handsome, various, and in good taste', he wrote. 'Each member gave a present to one another, so that, including the Prince Louis of Hesse and the Duchess of Kent, [everyone] gave and received thirteen presents.' It was a most joyful sight, none more so than that of ten-year-old Prince Arthur—'the flower of the flock' in Torrington's opinion—who 'speedily got into a volunteer uniform, which, with endless other things, including a little rifle, fell to his lot, took a pot-shot at his papa, and then presented arms'. Torrington could not help noticing how carefully chosen all the presents were, how 'beautiful in taste and suited to the receiver'. Those chosen by the children for their parents were selected with great care, so that 'even the Queen might find use for them'. Victoria was delighted with the gift of a bracelet containing small hand-coloured photographs of Louis and Alice. 'All the dear children worked me something,' she recorded with delight in her journal.[15]

After the family had exchanged their own presents, the Queen handed out gifts to the royal household. Torrington wondered whether the Prince Consort had 'had a quiet joke in his mind' in the selection of somewhat quirky presents for gentlemen members of the household— Charles Phipps (Keeper of Prince Albert's Privy Purse), Thomas Biddulph (Master of the Queen's Household), General Charles Grey (Prince Albert's Private Secretary), and General Bruce (Governor to the Prince of Wales):

Phipps had salt cellars resting on little fish with their mouths open, Biddulph a bread basket, Grey a sugar basin, and Bruce a claret jug; but at any rate, the four articles were somewhat true emblems of the loaves and fishes. The parties concerned have not observed the possible joke, nor have I suggested the idea.[16]

Torrington himself was delighted to receive 'a supply of studs, sleeve buttons, and waistcoat ditto, handsome, plain gold; a pocket-book'. In addition, everyone was presented with 'a large cake of Nuremburg gingerbread'. That day at Windsor, he confided to Delane, he had never seen 'more real happiness than the scene of the mother and all her children'. Even Prince Albert, notorious for his reserve, had 'lost his stiffness' and had allowed himself to rest and relax for once. All in all, 'your Windsor special had much cheerful and friendly conversation with them both'. It was, he concluded, 'a sight I should have liked you to have seen'. The Queen concurred in her journal that evening: 'As usual such a merry happy night with all the Children, and not the least happy, dear Alice and Louis.'[17]

On Christmas Day the family awoke to intense cold of minus two degrees Centigrade and an icy fog hanging across Windsor Home Park. 'The windows were frozen, the trees all white with frost,' wrote the Queen. After breakfast everyone gathered round to look at all the unwrapped presents laid out round the Christmas trees on the tables. Then once more they went down to the pond to skate. It was such a wonderful fine day, the church bells echoing Christmas joy across the crisp morning air, as the Queen recalled. The sound made 'such a beautiful effect' as they walked down the hill to St George's Chapel in the Lower Ward for morning service.[18]

Christmas Dinner was a grand affair, once more enjoyed by the entire royal household. 'How I live to tell the tale I don't know,' Torrington told Delane, such was the vast banquet placed before them, the centrepiece of which was the great baron of beef he had seen cooking the previous day, surrounded by dozens of capons, turkeys, pea-hens and Cochin China pullets. The two youngest children, Beatrice and Leopold, had been allowed down from the nursery to join the family for dessert, and after lunch Prince Albert played happily with his little daughter, who had brought some joy back into his life after the departure of Vicky—swinging her back and forth in a large table napkin to shrieks of delight.[19] Altogether it was a most 'jolly' day of relaxed informal conversation with the Queen and Prince Albert and family games of chess, pool and billiards.[20]

On Boxing Day, Prince Albert again took his sons out shooting while the Queen, Prince Louis and Princess Alice and the girls went down the hill to skate. Snow fell all that night and the following day, the 27th. As the candles on the Christmas tree were lit for the last time in the drawing room at 7 p.m. (all the trees in the royal apartments would be lit up again on New Year's Day and Twelfth Night), everyone gathered to dine *en famille*. 'All were very gay,' the Queen recalled, 'and telling many stories.'[21] The happiness and informality of that memorable Christmas continued into the 28th, when everyone piled into sledges and took one last

10

turn across the snowscape of Windsor Home Park before the time came to bid farewell to Prince Louis.

*　　　　*　　　　*

No one who was at Windsor that Christmas of 1860 could have failed to be impressed and moved by the conviviality of the British royal family at home. 'Even as in a public bazaar, where people jostle one another, so lords, grooms, Queen, and princes laughed and talked, forgot to bow, and freely turned their backs on one another,' Torrington told Delane. 'Little princesses, who on ordinary occasions dare hardly to look at a gentleman-in-waiting, in the happiest manner showed each person they could lay hands on the treasures they had received.'[22]

For Torrington, as for the vast majority of the British people, the royal family basked in a halo of sentimentality that reflected the affection that it was now increasingly enjoying as the model British family. No matter that the aristocracy had persisted in disliking Prince Albert and what they perceived as his disdainful and reserved German manner; he and Victoria—the virtuous and devoted couple with their nine pretty children—were idolised by the respectable classes as the epitome of the reassuringly bourgeois, Victorian domestic ideal. More importantly, their happy married life was confirmation of the stability and continuity of the British monarchy itself as a working monarchy, focused on the family and with pride in its material and social achievements. 'The more I see of the Royal domestic life, the more I am in admiration

11

of it,' General Grey had written in 1849. He was convinced that 'so pure and exemplary a Court never before existed'.[23] Two years later the youthful Eleanor Stanley, who had been in waiting at Windsor that Christmas, had told her parents, 'you can't think how simple and happy all the Royalty looked, just like any other family, of the most united and domestic tastes'.[24] This reputation for informal happy domesticity was one that Prince Albert had worked hard to establish and was determined to maintain, as the archetypal paterfamilias. Torrington's admiration was much the same in 1860. There was no doubting the esteem in which Victoria and Albert were held, he told Delane. He had never seen 'a more agreeable sight' that Christmas: 'It was royalty putting aside its state and becoming in words, acts, and deeds one of ourselves, no forms and not a vestige of ceremony.'[25]

At the end of that year the royal family was at the height of its popularity, at a time of political stability and economic progress in Britain. After riding out much hostility in the early years of his marriage and a storm of controversy over his perceived meddling in foreign affairs during the Crimean War of 1854–6, Prince Albert was finally beginning to receive some grudging acknowledgement for his many contributions to the cultural, scientific and intellectual life of the country, for the efficient way in which he conducted official business and for the strict moral code he maintained in his family life.

Victoria herself had enjoyed twenty years of happy marriage, secure in her husband's love and fidelity. That in itself was a rarity, in an age when princesses had little choice in their life partners and were too often consigned to loveless marriages of dynastic necessity. For Britain's queen adored her husband with a fierce and unquestioning devotion that none dared criticise and nothing could dim. Quite simply, he was all in all to her: surrogate father, husband, best friend, wise counsel, amanuensis and teacher—King in all but name. And, thanks to his influence, the British monarchy had been reinvigorated under its queen as a democratic and moral example for a new age that had at last divorced itself from the lingering reputation of the unpopular Hanoverians.

As the Christmas holiday drew to a close and the members of the royal household dispersed and returned to their duties, the Queen and her husband settled down to watch the last hours of 1860 turn, Victoria as always confiding it all in meticulous detail to her journal:

Dearest Albert and I took leave of the old year and wished each other joy of the new, at 12, before going to bed. I felt much moved, so anxious for the future, that no War should come, and fear for the state of Europe. My precious Husband cheered me and held me in his dear arms saying we must have trust, and we must believe that God will protect us.[26]

God had indeed protected them; their children had all survived infancy, confirmation in itself, as Lady Lytton observed, of the 'numberless instances of *perfect awful*, spotless prosperity' that had blessed the royal family till now, in an age when around one in five children died in infancy.[27] Victoria and

Albert had yet to endure the anguish, at first hand, of close family bereavements. Death was still a stranger to them; it had yet to cast its shadow over the grey stone battlements of Windsor.

# PART ONE

*Albert the Good*

# CHAPTER ONE

## *'The Treadmill of Never-Ending Business'*

At the age of only eleven, the precocious Francis Charles Augustus Albert Emmanuel of Saxe-Coburg and Gotha had already planned his future. 'I intend,' he confided in his diary, 'to train myself to be a good and useful man.'[1] It was a noble, if exacting aspiration for one so young, but one that, as husband of Queen Victoria, he would more than fulfil in his years of devoted service to the British throne and its people.

He had been born three months after his cousin Princess Victoria, on 26 August 1819, and was delivered by the same German midwife—Charlotte Heidenreich von-Siebold—at the Schloss Rosenau, four miles from Coburg. The second son of Ernst, Duke of Saxe-Coburg-Saalfeld and his wife Louise (of the rather more wealthy and prestigious house of Saxe-Gotha-Altenburg), Albert was very close to his older brother Ernst.[2] Theirs was an idyllic and harmonious childhood, spent sharing a hedonistic love of nature during their summers at the Schloss Rosenau on the edge of the ancient Thuringian forest. Here they spent their time walking, hunting, shooting and fencing, as well as indulging their fascination with science and nature in a passion for collecting specimens. Both boys were trained in musical skills by their father, Albert becoming an accomplished pianist and organist as well as a fine singer and talented composer. He was always

17

at his most self-expressive when playing the organ; music, his greatest love, providing a conduit for the reflective and melancholic side of his nature. It was a refuge for the poetical streak in him, which rarely found an outlet in his public life and which in adulthood was all too soon overwhelmed by responsibility. Fearful of strangers and prone to outbursts of tears, Albert had had his young life marred by the collapse of his parents' marriage in 1824. His philandering father, who had never attempted to conceal his extramarital affairs, had abandoned Albert's young and vulnerable mother Louise to long periods of solitude while he went out shooting, hunting and womanising. When Louise later sought consolation elsewhere, he banished her from their home—and from their two sons. Albert was only five. Louise remarried, but died of cancer six years later in 1831, without ever seeing her boys again.

The loss of his mother affected Prince Albert deeply. His diffidence and insecurity manifested themselves in later life in a compulsion to be controlling over others; more significantly, his father's libidinous character and his mother's flirtations (which prompted later unproven rumours of Louise's promiscuity and Albert's illegitimacy) instilled in him a pathological horror of sexual licence and a fear of the seductive power of women.[3] The path of duty and usefulness was a far safer one and he expected life to be a 'hard school', where pleasure came second.[4] With this in mind, at the age of fourteen the young and idealistic prince established his own exacting curriculum of study: nine hours a day of ancient and modern history, theology, translation from Latin,

18

geography, English, mathematics, logic, music and drawing—all overseen by one of the most formative influences in his early life, his tutor Herr Christoph Florschütz.

As the good Herr Florschütz proceeded with kind but Teutonic vigour to educate Albert, he was guided in his task by Baron Christian Stockmar. As Private Secretary and physician to Albert's uncle, Leopold King of the Belgians, Stockmar was the Machiavellian figure who would long lurk in the shadows of Albert's life—envisioning a future role for him leading the thrones of Britain and a united Germany in the cause of constitutional monarchy. The vehicle for this would be marriage to Leopold's niece Victoria, heir to the British throne, and Albert's future life was already being mapped out for him when he was in his early teens. The subordinate, if not redundant role of consort was not the future that the Prince would have wished for himself, but as the second son of the ruler of a minor duchy the size of Lancashire and with no throne coming his way, marriage to Princess Victoria was, as Stockmar told him, a responsible task 'upon the fulfillment of which his honour and happiness depend[ed]'. Such cold logic was the stock-in-trade of the punctilious Stockmar. It would shape the austere, intellectual Albert's mind for the roles to come, so much so that he would later tell the Queen, 'To me a long closely connected train of reasoning is like a beautiful strain of music.' Stockmar's rationale lent the indelible mark of dry, Germanic formulas to Albert's abstract attitude not just to the masses and the human condition, but also to his approach to history and politics—a fact that would later put him at odds with the instinctive, empirical way in which they were conducted in Britain.[5]

After a period of intense intellectual and cultural grooming in Brussels, the University of Bonn, the Swiss Alps and the art galleries of Italy, Albert was deemed ready to take up his burden of duty. The prospect made him fearful, for despite being the most handsome student prince in Europe, he had remained supremely indifferent to the charms of the opposite sex, preferring the man's world of the intellect and philosophical debate. He had heard tell that his putative bride was 'incredibly stubborn' and, worse, frivolous, delighting in 'court ceremonies, etiquette and trivial formalities'.[6] Albert was shocked that Princess Victoria took no apparent interest in the beauties of nature, but was prone to staying up late. She didn't like getting up early either, something he would have to change. For a young man of Albert's sober mentality, marriage to the English princess had, in his opinion, 'gloomy prospects'. When Leopold and Stockmar had stage-managed the couple's first meeting in England in 1836, Albert had come away thinking Victoria 'amiable', but little more. She, for her part, had found 'dearest Albert' handsome and kind, but rather pale and sickly. Although Victoria soon came to the conclusion that her putative husband was possessed of 'every quality that could be desired to make me perfectly happy', marriage to Albert after she became Queen in 1837 was not an immediate, foregone conclusion. For the first time in her life Victoria was independent of her mother's stifling control. She was determined to enjoy her freedom and have her own way in everything, as well as relishing her sovereign power, all of which was far more attractive than matrimony and the inevitability—and dangers—of childbirth. Besides, to her mind, Albert needed to gain wider experience and improve his English in order to be the consort of a queen. As princeling-in-waiting, Albert was therefore obliged to sit it out while the impressionable and impetuous Victoria was distracted by the claims of the other candidates jostling for her hand. Leopold and Stockmar, meanwhile, began to fear their long-held dream was slipping beyond their reach.

*　　　*　　　*

An absence of three and a half years and a string of unsuitable candidates changed everything. Just as Albert was losing patience with the long wait for Victoria's final approval, he was summoned to England in October 1839. The young queen was taken aback; the shy, podgy young man of 1836 had been transformed into a storybook-handsome prince who, with his large blue eyes and his 'exquisite nose', was both 'striking' and 'fascinating'.[7] She was swept off her feet by Albert's good looks, fine figure and youthful charm. What had begun as a stage-managed dynastic union now unexpectedly burst into the full bloom of ecstatic love, certainly on Victoria's part. Five days later, using her queenly prerogative, she proposed. Albert was far less certain of his feelings at this point, playing the role of acquiescent, if not bewildered mate, happy to bask in Victoria's passionate attachment to him: 'Victoria is so good and kind to me. I am often at a loss to believe that such affection should be shown to me,' he told Stockmar.[8] Mentally prepared

21

though he may have been for the marriage to come, it was far harder for Albert to adapt in the four short months left to him to the idea of leaving his beloved Coburg for Buckingham Palace in the heart of sooty, polluted London. He contemplated his future life in England and the task of adapting to its language, the customs of its court, its chilly climate and its food with great apprehension. Marrying Victoria, and all the expectations that went with it, was a tremendous burden. He would have to leave behind everything that he loved, but he was characteristically single-minded about the sacrifice he was expected to make and the challenge that awaited him. 'With the exception of my relations towards [the Queen] my future position will have its dark sides, and the sky will not always be blue and unclouded,' he wrote resignedly to his stepmother. 'But life has its thorns in every position, and the consciousness of having used one's powers and endeavours for an object so great as that of having promoted the good of so many, will surely be sufficient to support me.'[9]

It was a terrible wrench for Albert to leave Coburg and especially the Rosenau, the 'paradise of our childhood', not to mention his brother Ernst, who had till then been his dearest and closest friend.[10] At the end of January 1840 Albert departed in floods of tears, accompanied by his faithful greyhound Eos and his Swiss valet Isaac Cart, vowing that he would 'never cease to be a true *German*, a true *Coburg & Gotha* man', and suffering violent seasickness all the way across the Channel.[11] Much as he loved Victoria, hers was the overwhelming passion. Young, introverted and inexperienced sexually, he did not know how to respond to her ardour and felt swamped by it. Never being one to express his feelings openly, he anticipated marriage more as a test of his purity of intent than as the fulfilment of any personal or emotional aspirations. Love, in his book, came second to the greater good; but for Victoria, it was absolutely everything. And even as Albert travelled, debate was raging in Britain on the thorny subject of his cost to the nation. Victoria's demand for an annual income for him of £50,000 had prompted much satirical comment on this German prince, who 'comes to take "for better or for worse" England's fat queen and England's fatter purse'.[12]

*　　*　　*

On a freezing cold 10 February 1840 Victoria and Albert were married in the Chapel Royal at St James's Palace, in a ceremony from which many of the leading members of Parliament were absent. Victoria allowed only five Tories to be invited, in retaliation for the open hostility of men in that political party to her choice of a German bridegroom: 'It is my marriage,' she declared with her characteristic stubbornness, 'and I will only have those who can sympathise with me.'[13] Critics of her beloved Albert would henceforth be given short shrift. That day, as everyone agreed, Albert had never looked more handsome, nor she more radiant as she gazed up at his beautiful face. When asked by the Archbishop of Canterbury the previous day whether she wished to promise 'to obey', Victoria had replied that she wished 'to be married as a woman and not as a Queen'.[14] Her lifelong role as Albert's votaress was born on her wedding day. After only three days' honeymoon at Windsor, punctuated by walks on the terrace and duets at the piano, she was eager to get back to business, professing herself to be the 'happiest, happiest Being that ever existed'. Albert clearly had more than fulfilled his sexual expectations; but as for the rest—he was left to shift for himself, his only perceived role being that most marginal one of royal stud; 'we should erect a statue to Prince Albert for having provided us with this additional barrier against the King of Hanover', remarked one of the royal household when the Princess Royal was born that November.[15]

Prince Albert had been only too right to anticipate the sense of alienation he would feel in England; it had been made far worse by the fact that he arrived in a country already disposed to dislike him as a German, as a 'pauper prince' and, even worse, that suspected him of being a secret Catholic. From the outset he was made fun of in the satirical press and among old-school Tories at court for his heavy German accent, his stiff and starchy manner and his outmoded style of dress. Soon after his arrival he was deeply affronted when Parliament voted to reduce his allowance to £30,000. But the worst of it was that, as a man driven by a sense of purpose, he found it very hard to deal with the idleness imposed on him by his role as husband to the monarch. He could not reconcile himself to being married to a wife who, whilst acknowledging at all times her husband's authority as head of domestic affairs, often treated him with brusque impatience and seemed intent on excluding him from any useful assistance in her official duties. In May 1840 he observed with some disgruntlement:

'In my whole life I am very happy and contented; but the difficulty in filling my place with the proper dignity is, that I am only the husband, and not the master of the house.'[16]

Albert's emasculation during these early months, as he struggled for a modicum of independence while Victoria demanded that he be at her constant beck and call on domestic matters, was frustrating and deeply humiliating. It took place against a backdrop of heated arguments between the Queen and the government over his precedence at court and his appointment as regent (should she die in childbirth). Having accepted naturalisation on his marriage to the Queen, Albert expected some official recognition of his position of pre-eminence—perhaps a peerage and, with it, a seat in the House of Lords. The Queen could not deny that she would have liked him to be accorded the status of King alongside her, but this was not to be. Albert's crippling shyness did not help matters. The artist Benjamin Haydon observed him at a ball in 1842, looking 'like a cowed and kept pet, frightened to sit, frightened to stand'.[17] Nevertheless Albert's patience paid off: he gained great influence over Victoria, subtly and by degrees, judiciously giving way in trivial things, so much so that he 'never finished a game of chess with her for the first three years'.[18] For the time being he established his influence in the only way open to him, by inculcating his own lofty ideals and interests in his impressionable wife. Victoria, whilst having natural gifts of intuition, was never his equal intellectually and accepted it. She was 'as full of love as Juliet', as Sir Robert Peel had observed, and, hungering as she did for Albert's praise and approval, submitted herself willingly, adoringly, to his greater wisdom.[19] Prince Albert became for her the much-longed-for father figure. Under his diligent tutelage, Victoria's mind was reformed: her slim grasp of the arts and science was enhanced. She eagerly accepted Albert's leadership as regards the books they read, the music they enjoyed, the paintings and sculpture they collected. She even modified her own 'bad' habits—as Albert perceived them—by ceasing to stay up late and giving over less and less of her time to dancing and idle gossip with her ladies-in-waiting.

But Albert, with his thirst for constant self-improvement, was discontented merely to sit by his wife's side, blotting her official letters as she wrote them; he sought to play an active role in the political life and culture of his adopted country. The first step came when in September 1840 a heavily pregnant Victoria made him a member of the Privy Council in order to stand in for her when she was confined; soon after she gave him a duplicate set of keys to her official boxes. From there Albert set about studying British laws and the constitution, educating Victoria, who by temperament was an autocrat, in the art of good administration and her sovereign duty. He worked hard to soften the obstinate and shamefully partisan attitude that she had displayed in the early years of her reign, weaning her away from her Whig bias towards an acceptance of the new Tory government and impressing upon her the all-essential political impartiality of the sovereign. Victoria was reluctant to relinquish any royal prerogatives, but understood the constitutional limitations placed on her, which her husband insisted she scrupulously observe. In so doing she ensured that her throne did not share the fate of those that later fell, like Louis Philippe of France's, in the revolutionary year of 1848.

In the battle to assert his supremacy over the Queen, in the autumn of 1842 Albert engineered the removal of her closest and most powerful confidante, her old governess, Baroness Lehzen. The first real opportunity to exercise his punctilious sense of order and frugality had come earlier that year when he had reorganised the royal household in a sweeping programme of cost-cutting and the rigid elimination of the 'canker' of waste, inefficiency and pilfering that had gone on for decades.[20] The money saved by this exercise would later be used to fund the building of Osborne House. By 1845, having endured the first years of his anticipated martyrdom uncomplainingly, Albert now held a position of moral and sexual power over his wife, as she slipped increasingly into the contented role of *Hausfrau*. Such was his concerted re-education of her as monarch that Victoria became convinced that her life before Albert had been worthless—entirely artificial and frivolous. The royal couple had become effectively a dual monarchy, receiving ministers together and talking of their role collectively, in terms of '*We* think, or wish, to do so and so'. They even worked side by side at adjacent desks. Officially, the only title Albert was conceded was that of 'Husband of the Queen', but the marked elevation in his role by his wife prompted the court diarist, Charles Greville, to observe that 'He is become so identified with her that they are one person.' The Queen patently disliked official business, whereas Albert relished it; as a result, Victoria's dependency on him grew as her resistance to his control waned. It was obvious to Greville 'that while she has the title he is really discharging the functions of the Sovereign. He is King to all intents and purposes.'[21] And behind the scenes Albert worked hard to repel any encroachments on the power of the Crown that he now effectively controlled.

While he was set on a determined course of slowly winning the confidence of the British government as an unofficial, self-appointed minister, as the years passed much of Albert's time was necessarily consumed by domesticity. He was to provide patient and reassuring support to his wife through her successive pregnancies and bouts of post-natal depression. Victoria's histrionic outbursts were, however, extremely hard to deal with; as a natural introvert, Prince Albert hated emotional conflicts—and those with his wife were tempestuous, to say the least. He therefore developed a habit of avoiding confrontations and writing headmasterly notes to her about her behaviour, rather than dealing with it face-to-face, a practice that infuriated the headstrong and combative queen. Albert would not be diverted from his mission to remould his petulant wife; he doggedly and repeatedly urged her to curb her temper and learn self-restraint. Duly chastised, Victoria tried hard to rise to the challenge and aspire to the levels of perfection with which her adored husband was endowed. Little by little, Albert chipped away at his wife's impetuosity, and with it, one might also say, her instinctiveness and natural vivacity. Power and control were the aphrodisiacs that drove Albert; he might never be King, but all the time his wife was his creature, and so often physically sidelined by pregnancy that he could vicariously enjoy some of the power he knew he would never officially be given.

Without doubt, Albert's domestic life with Victoria brought many pleasures, as the children arrived in quick succession, from Vicky, their firstborn, in 1840 to their ninth child, Beatrice, in 1857. As a typical patriarch, he imposed his authoritarian attitudes on the royal nursery, putting his children in characteristic Victorian awe and fear of him. He oversaw their health, diet and welfare with Teutonic precision, recommending simple food and a rigorous curriculum. Much as he loved them and enjoyed their company, the Prince was a hard taskmaster. 'Upon the good education of Princes, and especially those who are destined to govern,' he remarked to his secretary George Anson, 'the welfare of the world in these days greatly depends.'[22] With this in mind, he closely supervised the schoolroom's day-to-day running with his children's governors and governesses. One of them, Madame Hocédé—French teacher to Prince Leopold and Princesses Helena and Louise—later recalled her regular consultations with the Prince about his children's education and how he never left her 'without my feeling that he had strengthened my hands and raised the standard I was aiming at'.[23] Having a particular interest in education, Albert personally devised his children's demanding curriculum and administered corporal punishment (albeit reluctantly) when they failed to toe the line. All of the children suffered, to varying degrees, from the academic and personal pressures placed on them by both parents, as well as the constant comparisons made with their sainted

29

father by the Queen. But whereas the intellectually gifted Vicky blossomed under Albert's favouritism and tutelage, his son and heir Bertie wilted and rebelled under its rigour; the emotional scars Bertie suffered in hopeless pursuit of academic achievements beyond his grasp set the scene for future conflict between them.

*     *     *

Only a handful of people in the inner sanctum of the royal household ever came to know Prince Albert intimately; even fewer won his friendship. The majority at court and in government—whom Albert always held at arm's length—found it impossible to warm to his inhibited manner and thought him cold and egotistical, like a 'German Professor', one of several nicknames in circulation.[24] Even the Queen's jealous Hanoverian relatives, such as her uncle the Duke of Cambridge, viewed him as a 'Coburg interloper'. She might promote her husband as a paragon of virtue to anyone who would listen, but too often the Prince Consort appeared inflexible, particularly over matters of royal etiquette and protocol, and humourless too. He always seemed so decidedly superior in his detachment from court circles, and in particular in his disdain for the profligacy of the British aristocracy. They in turn could not understand why the Prince had no mistresses, or, for that matter, any apparent interest in women. It was only a matter of time, they assumed, before this would change. 'Damn it, Madam,' Lord Melbourne had remarked to the Queen when she was first married, 'you don't expect that he'll always be faithful to you, do you?!'[25] But in

30

fact Albert was. He refused to play the gallant and was notorious for being offhand with ladies at court, so much so that his secretary Anson noted that 'the Queen is proud of the Prince's utter indifference to the attractions of all the ladies'.[26]

Albert's apparent incorruptibility was infuriating, for he did not seem to be susceptible to the corrosive lifestyle of the typical courtier. He was abstemious, ate frugally and stuck to the German habit of dining early, never stopping to lounge around over the port and cigars; nor did he frequent the London clubs or cultivate any English friends. Instead, he went to bed early and walked every day with his wife and children, like any bourgeois paterfamilias. Even the way he rode to hounds was criticised: 'he did not fly his fences in true Leicestershire style,' carped the fox-hunting aristocracy who so despised him, and who hated him even more for regularly stealing the best prizes with his cattle at agricultural shows.[27] Everything about Albert was so proper; he was altogether 'too good'. The dullness and sanctimoniousness of the 'bourgeois court' over which he and Victoria ruled soon became legendary—both at home and abroad.

The prudish, antisocial streak in Albert's nature thus often made him appear more pedant than paragon, a man so formal and so circumspect that his real character was rarely divined by others. His reserve set up barriers to those who might otherwise have admired him, and people tended to respond to his personality as one of two extremes—as Queen Victoria's saintly 'Albert the Good', or as the much-disliked foreign interloper, 'Albert der King'. Steeling himself to this barrage of hostility, Albert meanwhile forged ahead with his wide-ranging interests in science, industry, education and the arts. He received a great fillip in October 1847 when—against considerable and undignified opposition—he was elected Chancellor of Cambridge University, in which capacity he would encourage a rapid and dramatic liberalising of its academic courses. In the visual arts he and Victoria collected paintings by Cranach, Dürer, Memling and Van Eyck, which would later greatly enhance the national collections; as patron of the Royal Photographic Society, Prince Albert was a passionate supporter of the genre and, with the Queen, amassed an unrivalled collection of early photographic work. In his reorganisation of the incomparable print collections at Windsor and his cataloguing of the royal collection of drawings by Raphael, Holbein and Leonardo da Vinci, the Prince left a lasting memorial to his own considerable scholarship as an art historian. In music, through his patronage of the Royal Philharmonic Society, Albert championed the work of his compatriots Wagner, Mendelssohn and Schumann.

Prince Albert's passionate interest in art and architecture had brought an invitation to join the Royal Commission of Arts, set up in 1841 to supervise the interior decorations of the new Houses of Parliament, inspiring him later to take a hand—in his spare time from all his many other pursuits—in supervising the design and construction of the royal family's new homes, at Osborne in the 1840s and Balmoral in the 1850s. As time went on he found himself increasingly in demand to give lectures on art, science, business and philanthropy, to attend exhibitions and play a high profile in the cultural life of the country. He sat on numerous humanitarian committees, such as the Society for the Extinction of the Slave Trade and the Society for the Improvement of the Condition of the Labouring Classes. Duty and yet more duty was piled on him; as a connoisseur, humanitarian and polymath, Albert found it impossible to say no. But by 1848, during the year of revolutions in Europe—when it took him all day just to get through all the French, German and English newspapers—he was complaining to his stepmother in Coburg that he could not remember being 'kept in the stocks' of work as he was now.[28] His workload intensified at an alarming rate thereafter, culminating in the drain on his energies demanded by his visionary approach to the promotion of British excellence at the Great Exhibition, which he masterminded, as chair of the Royal Society of Arts, from 1849 until its opening in 1851. Similar, smaller exhibitions had taken place before in England, in northern cities such as Leeds, Liverpool and Sheffield during the 1830s and 1840s, but Albert's plan was far more ambitious. His objective had been nothing less than 'to give us a true test and a living picture of the point of development at which the whole of mankind has arrived . . . and a new starting-point from which all nations will be able to direct their further exertions'.[29]

The Exhibition proved to be the apogee of Prince Albert's civilising and cultural aspirations for his adopted country; it was also a triumphant celebration not just of British, but of international arts and industry. Throughout the planning Albert played the role, effectively, of a government minister and refused to be deterred by the many difficulties and disappointments he had to deal with along the way. Confirmation of his achievement—despite the continued sneering and sniping of the *beau monde* who still despised him—was only too visible when 34,000 people gathered at the Crystal Palace in Hyde Park on opening day, 1 May 1851. Victoria swelled with wifely pride: it was the happiest and proudest day of her life. The exhibition was entirely 'the triumph of my beloved Albert', she had no doubt of that. And for once the press grudgingly agreed; even the unbridled antagonism of *Punch* magazine at last abated.[30]

But it was a triumph achieved at the expense of Albert's always precarious physical well-being. Shortly before the Great Exhibition, in a written exchange with the Duke of Wellington over whether or not Albert should become Commander in Chief of the Army (which he wisely declined), the Prince defined the indispensable role that he felt he was now fulfilling at the right hand of the Queen. It was a role that had required him to 'entirely sink his *own individual* existence in that of his wife' so as to:

continuously and anxiously watch every part of the public business, in order to be able to advise and assist her at any moment in any of the multifarious and difficult questions or duties brought before her, sometimes international, sometimes political, or social, or personal.

Quite clearly, Albert believed that his wife, and more importantly the monarchy, could not function smoothly without his own now-essential input.

With considerable self-satisfaction he enumerated his many roles, as 'the natural head of her family, superintendent of her household, manager of her private affairs, sole *confidential* adviser in politics, only assistant in her communications with officers of Government', besides which he was 'the husband of the Queen, the tutor of the royal children, the private secretary of the sovereign, and her permanent minister'.[31] As for Victoria, her emotional dependency on her husband was now total: 'You cannot think . . . how completely *dérouleé* I am and *feel* when he is away, or how I count the numerous children are *as nothing* to me when *he is away*!' she told her uncle, King Leopold, in 1857.[32]

During the 1850s the prince's impressive job description was further enhanced by his ambitions to break down British insularity with regard to foreign affairs. 'His foreign correspondence alone, which the public here knew nothing of,' remarked Albert's friend, the geologist Sir Charles Lyell, 'would have been thought sufficient occupation for one who had nothing else to do.' In everything, the 'quantity of work he got through, in spite of innumerable interruptions, was immense'.[33] It was during the Fifties that Albert increasingly brought his years of political study into play, as his insights deepened. He fired off endless memoranda to ministers, as well as offering advice on every possible subject to his wife, so much so that Victoria noted in her journal, 'He always lets me get the credit for his excellent ideas, which pains me.'[34] Albert's grasp of foreign policy finally found an outlet with the outbreak of war against Russia in 1854. But in time of war

Prince Albert was an all-too-obvious target for British xenophobia. Government ministers and the press resented his perceived intrusion and during the war reverted to old habits, once more whipping up hostility towards Albert as a foreigner and calling his political allegiances into question. The gutter-press spread rumours that he might be a Russian spy, and he was hissed at on his way to the state opening of Parliament with the Queen in 1854. Rumours reached an absurd level when it was suggested that the Prince was to be arrested for high treason and sent to the Tower. But Albert endured the abuse and, as the war went on, boldly called into question its mismanagement, repeatedly urging the organisation of British militia forces to be sent as reinforcements to the exhausted and beleaguered British army in the Crimea. He wrote endless memoranda on every aspect of the military campaign—a body of work amounting to fifty folio volumes of documents—yet the only publicly acknowledged contribution that he was allowed to make during this time of national crisis was the design of the newly instituted Victoria Cross. However, by the end of the war he had gained one grudging admirer. Albert's old adversary, Lord Palmerston, who had been returned to power as Prime Minister during the war in January 1855, had by its end been forced to concede the Prince's value to the nation in promoting British prestige and interests in the royal courts of Europe, as well as his beneficial effect on the Queen and her conduct of royal business.

Through it all, his loyal wife remained Prince Albert's loudest and most vocal advocate, prompting one of her most spirited responses to criticism of his influence over her. 'A woman *must* have a support and an adviser,' she insisted to Lord Aberdeen, 'and who can this properly be but her husband, whose duty it is to watch over her interests, private and public?' Were it not for Albert, Victoria was adamant that her health and strength 'would long since have sunk under the multifarious duties of her position as Queen, and the mother of a large family'.[35] By the mid-Fifties she had firmly decided that 'we women are not meant for governing' and was increasingly happy to leave the job to Albert.[36] With this in mind, she had him elevated to the title of Prince Consort by royal decree in 1857—the closest he would ever come to being named King.

\*       \*       \*

Victoria might have become more and more content to play the role of wife rather than Queen, but by the end of the Crimean War in 1856 Prince Albert's untiring service to the monarchy and Britain had begun to take an alarming toll on his health. His constant sublimation of his own needs to his wife's far more volatile emotional ones had worn him down: always putting her first, advising, reassuring, consoling, shielding her from trouble and anxiety at every turn and being the crucial stabilising force that had enabled Victoria to fulfil her duties as Queen. Had she noticed it, her husband was already showing visible signs of chronic fatigue. He had, for most of his life, been plagued by ill health. A sickly child, he had suffered attacks of croup, anaemia and nosebleeds and had always tired easily, even to the extent of falling asleep at table. He had a slow metabolism and a low pulse rate, which made him prone to attacks of fainting and dizziness; since the age of fifteen he had suffered from rheumatic pain and, intermittently, from what was loosely referred to as a 'weak digestion' that brought on visitations by what Albert called 'his old enemy'—frequent, unspecified gastric attacks accompanied by spasms of intense pain, fever and shivering.[37] Stress clearly aggravated his condition; even Victoria noticed that whenever her husband was upset or anxious it would 'affect his poor dear stomach'.[38] Albert's own response to bouts of gastric illness was rigorous: he purged himself with hot water and applied his own 'fasting cure'—'so as to rob my stomach of the shadow of a pretext for behaving ill', so he claimed.[39] What was clearly developing into a chronic condition appears never to have been subjected to any kind of rigorous examination or diagnosis by his doctors, medical science at that time defining a whole range of stomach complaints as 'gastric attacks' and having no means of differentiating between them.

As a compulsive obsessive and workaholic, the stress of the many speeches Albert had to give and the public functions he had to attend often brought on bouts of vomiting and migraines, which in turn affected his sleep. In the view of royal physician Sir James Clark, anxiety—'the great waster of life'—was dulling his senses and wearing the Prince out.[40] In addition Albert hated the damp of the English climate and succumbed with alarming regularity in the autumn to feverish chills. His wife, however, who remained rudely robust for most of her life, never made any concessions to her frailer husband's need to ward off the cold. He was left to suffer

38

in the underheated rooms in the royal palaces, permeated by gusts of cold air from the perpetually open windows that Victoria demanded, his only recourse being to enclose himself in thick long johns at night and wear a wig at breakfast to keep his balding head warm.

Yet still he laboured on, rising every morning at seven to do an hour's work in his study before breakfast; filling every day with a close reading of all the newspapers and the writing of endless letters—including a prodigious correspondence with his contemporaries on the Continent. In addition there were detailed memoranda to government ministers, as well as his extensive committee work; in every single thing he did he tried to 'do what was right by the Queen and the country'.[41] He walked fast and worked fast, often eating at speed as he did so, and rushed at 'double-quick pace' from one meeting to the next. He hated having to stop and his pace was remorseless: incessantly travelling up and down the country, making speeches, opening bridges and hospitals, laying foundation stones and appearing as patron or chair at the many scientific, cultural and academic organisations that he supported. The only respite from his self-imposed and onerous duties and so much nervous hurry came during family holidays at Balmoral and Osborne. Here Prince Albert would lose himself in his great love of the outdoors—hunting, shooting, fishing and overseeing the model farms he had created on the royal estates. But even recreation was given strict time limits and such holidays never restored his health and his spirits for very long. Work had become the all-consuming surrogate for a more normal, sociable life at court—a lifestyle he disdained and where he had never felt at ease. Prince Albert's unceasing pursuit of his many noble visions was sucking him dry. He had never got over his homesickness for Coburg, and his sense of isolation and disappointment had grown, as his mental and physical energies had dissolved. He had worked hard to make people admire him through his many services to the state, but getting them to like him in his own right (and not merely as an adjunct of the royal family) was a battle he had so far not won. He despaired at public indifference to his work and how little he was understood or appreciated in England: 'Man is a beast of burden,' he remarked gloomily in November 1856, 'and he is only happy if he has to drag his burden and if he has little free will. My experience teaches me every day to understand the truth of this, more and more.'[42]

Albert's growing sense of loneliness was exacerbated in 1849 by the sudden death of his secretary, George Anson, a loyal friend as well as servant, who had from the mid-1840s been extremely concerned at his master's punishing workload. By the late 1850s, with the departure of his adored daughter Vicky, who married the Crown Prince of Prussia in 1858, much of Albert's vital spark had irretrievably faded; he became increasingly stern and humourless, retreating into himself more and more. Without real friends or close intellectual peers, or his own entourage at court, or a supportive political faction in Parliament, his only consolation was his work. And much as he loved his wife, Albert's attachment to her was increasingly driven by the principles of reason and duty and doing the right thing. Victoria was fundamentally his *'gutes Weibchen'*—the good and loyal little wife—and mother of his children. She gave him her all, but for a man as restless as Albert it was never enough; she was not, and never could be, his soul's mistress. And for Victoria it was agony; there was nothing she could do to hold back the tide of melancholia and pessimism that was engulfing her husband. As Albert's chief acolyte, she could fulminate loud and often to their children about how their father was without equal—'so great, so good, so faultless'—but his wife's admiration and praise were no palliative for 'the dragon of his dissatisfaction' that was now starting to consume him.[43] Nor could Victoria's obsessive love disguise the growing tension between them, brought on by Albert's impossible workload, which she increasingly resented for allowing them less and less time together.

In December 1858 came the first serious warning signs of the collapse of the Prince Consort's health, when yet another regular attack of gastric illness, supposedly the result of 'over-fatigue', laid him low in the weeks before Christmas. But although he confided to his diary his growing sense of utter weariness and despondency, those about him were not aware how deep his sense of exhaustion ran. For the truth was that Albert, Prince Consort was not only being progressively 'torn to pieces with business of every kind', he was physically broken and spiritually despairing.[44]

# CHAPTER TWO

# *'The First Real Blow of Misfortune'*

By the beginning of 1859 Albert, Prince Consort—the romantic Thuringian prince of 1840—was sallow, balding and putting on weight. He was approaching forty, but already ageing fast as his reserves of strength evaporated and his virility waned. Fearful of confronting her husband's much deeper malaise, Queen Victoria put it down to overwork. Work always made Albert so irritable and 'very trying', in her view, but even she was becoming alarmed at how ill and 'fagged' he looked.[1] For now, quite apart from all his many public commitments, there were family problems preying on his mind. Ever a martyr to self-induced stress, Albert had a new and escalating anxiety, in his own and Victoria's worries about the future of the dynasty under their eldest son, Albert Edward, Prince of Wales.

'Poor Bertie', as his mother so frequently referred to him. He was a 'stupid boy' whose attention could not be fixed on anything useful, 'even at a novel'. He had grown up in the full glare of his mother's unending disappointment at his idleness and unprepossessing appearance, as well as his exacting father's constant pressure that he fulfil the impossibly high expectations they both placed on him.[2] As a child Bertie had craved parental affection and reassurance, but his naturally cheerful and ebullient nature had been cowed by the austere regime imposed by his father. Such repression had led to childish outbursts of understandable temper and frustration, a fact that caused the Queen to worry that Bertie's bad behaviour made him her 'caricature'.[3] She and Albert both dreaded that, in his laziness and egocentricity, their son and heir might grow up tainted by the blood of his disreputable Hanoverian ancestors. 'Remember, there is only my life between his and the lives of my Wicked Uncles,' Victoria retorted when later taken to task on this point.[4]

Albert's response to his son's weakness of character had been to impose a rigorous education that isolated him from his friends and would knock him into shape. A strict regime had worked for him, Albert, as a child and ought to do likewise for his dullard of a son. Bertie struggled to cope with his exacting timetable, but was endlessly chastised by his father for his poor academic performance. Albert's response to Bertie's tantrums at his workload was merely to make things even harder for him. Failure was not in Albert's lexicon. On the advice of Baron Stockmar, he demanded that Bertie study seven hours a day seven days a week, in a relentless quest for self-improvement. He personally checked his son's course-work and essays; any slight improvement in his performance was commended, but minor improvements never lasted for long. When Bertie reached seventeen he was therefore entrusted to the care of three equerries who took turns in ensuring that he behaved, as his father stipulated, like a gentleman. They were instructed to make sure he did not loll around in armchairs, or stand with his hands in his pockets. He was also to be kept from idle gossip and frivolous pursuits such as cards and billiards—

and, the ultimate anathema, smoking cigars. He should be encouraged instead to be like his father and 'to devote some of his leisure time to music, to the fine arts . . . hearing poetry, amusing books or good plays read aloud, in short, to anything that whilst it amuses may gently exercise the mind'.[5] But it did no good; the more Bertie was controlled and chastised, the more he indulged, in secret, in all the things forbidden to him.

The Queen and Prince Albert dreaded Bertie's coming-of-age in 1859, a day on which he was greeted not with warm congratulations, but by a long, pedantic letter from his parents full of exhortations about his moral duties and that 'in due, punctual and cheerful performance of them the true Christian and the true Gentleman is recognised'. It was all too much for Bertie and he burst into floods of tears.[6] By the end of that year Prince Albert had reached a state of despairing resignation over Bertie's obtuseness, informing Vicky in Berlin that although he was 'lively, quick and sharp when his mind is set on anything, which is seldom', her brother's intellect was 'of no more use than a pistol packed at the bottom of a trunk if one were attacked in the robber-infested Apennines'.[7] By April of the following year the Queen had begun seriously to wonder to Vicky what on earth would happen should she die and Bertie become King. In their shared dissatisfaction with him, she and Albert concurred that the only thing that might save him from himself would be an early marriage. But how were they to keep Bertie on the straight and narrow until a suitable bride could be found? 'We can't hold him except by moral power,' the Queen concluded.[8] For now, a stretch at a

Grenadier Guards camp at the Curragh in Ireland during the university vacation might help to make him knuckle under. It was only his father who had managed to keep Bertie out of trouble thus far. 'His only safety and the country's,' the Queen told Vicky, 'is in his implicit reliance in every thing on dearest Papa, that perfection of human beings!' But alarm bells were already sounding in Victoria's head: 'My greatest of all anxieties is that dearest Papa works too hard, wears himself quite out by all he does.' All this worry about Bertie, she was sure, was too much for her husband.[9]

With alarming predictability, in August 1859 Albert was laid low by yet another of his 'stomach attacks' and was unable to eat or drink anything but a little milk and water for days. Although he did his best to conceal from her how unwell he felt, even Victoria thought her husband looked 'fearfully ill'.[10] Whenever sickness overwhelmed him, Albert felt the additional stress of being kept from his duties. There was always so much to do. In late October he was ill again, suffering one of the severest and most obstinate attacks the Queen had ever seen, 'the more annoying as it was accompanied by violent spasms of pain', which kept him in bed for two days. 'It has been such an unusual thing to see him in bed (never except for the measles),' she observed ruefully. Whenever Albert was ill, it 'cast such a gloom over us all', the Queen remarked, for when he was not able to be out and about as usual, it turned home life 'upside down'.[11]

Albert put his latest bout of sickness down to the 'sudden incredible change of temperature of the last fortnight', and resumed his duties without taking any real time off to convalesce.[12] The royal

Physician-in-Ordinary, Sir James Clark, who had been with the Queen since her accession, but who was now in his seventies and approaching retirement, offered his own rather nebulous prognosis. It was, quite simply, all in the mind. Among the many causes of Albert's present condition, Clark reckoned that 'the worries both of body and mind to which you are daily exposed, the unusual heat of the year, and also the great strain on your strength [that] your position is constantly exposing you to' all increased the risk of him having his health 'deranged'. Clark, a physician of limited scientific understanding who had trained in an earlier, less sophisticated medical age, serving as a naval surgeon in the Napoleonic Wars, was noted for his faulty diagnoses and his timid 'watch-and-wait' policy. His presence at court, however, suited the Queen, who hated change and liked the reassurance of his familiar face. Clark, fearful always of demoralising her, kowtowed to Victoria and told her what she wanted to hear. To give him credit, Clark had at least emphasised the need for proper nursing and convalescent care, which Albert should have had whenever he was ill, but which he and his busy schedule never allowed.[13] But, for his own part, Albert placed little faith in the ageing Clark's diagnostic skills; the Prince had in the past been critical of his ineffectual management of the ailments of the royal children—most notably Clark's treatment of Vicky with asses' milk during a bout of illness in 1841.

Prince Albert was, however, only too well aware of the toll his never-ending catalogue of duties was taking on him physically and mentally. In his weekly letter to Vicky in Berlin, written on 23 May

46

1860, his sense of exhaustion was palpable. Spring in England was beautiful, he wrote: 'the most glorious air, the most fragrant odours, the merriest choirs of birds and the most luxuriant verdure', but he did not have time to enjoy any of it—not even the fresh primroses brought to his desk by his children, who knew how much Papa loved them. For Albert was totally and irrevocably chained to the 'treadmill of never-ending business'; so much so that he was 'tortured' at the prospect of his future commitments. Ahead lay two interminable public dinners at which he would be in the chair: 'the one gives me seven, the other ten toasts and speeches, appropriate to the occasion, and distracting to myself'. Later on he was to open the 'Statistical Congress of all nations'—yet more toasts and speeches—and in the interim he was faced with the prospect of:

> laying the foundation stone of the Dramatic College, etc. etc.; and this, with the sittings of my different Commissions, and Ascot races . . . and the Balls and Concerts of the season all crowded into the month of June, over and above the customary business, which a distracted state of affairs in Europe, and a stormy Parliament . . . make still more burdensome and disagreeable than usual.[14]

Later that year, during a visit to Coburg, Albert narrowly escaped serious injury in a carriage accident when the horses he had been driving took fright and bolted straight towards a railway crossing. Unable to prevent a collision with a stationary wagon, he had leapt from the carriage, anticipating oblivion. He escaped with cuts and bruises and made light of it, but the accident was yet another reminder, at a time when his spirits were already low, of his own mortality. Both Baron Stockmar and Albert's brother Ernst, who saw him before he returned to England, were dismayed by the change in him. It was not just the despondency in his eyes, it was a sense they both felt that he had no fight left in him. Something was very wrong. 'God have mercy on us!' Stockmar confided to his diary. 'If anything should ever happen to him, he will die.'[15]

Not long after his return to England, Albert once again succumbed to stomach problems, suffering 'violent sickness and shiverings' in the night, and was confined to his room. The attack was severe, but as usual he concealed from his family how ill he felt. He remained weak for several days, referring to his illness as 'the real English cholera'—he also called it 'cholerina'—a term then in use for mild, choleraic-type attacks of diarrhoea. But as usual he returned to his work before recovering sufficiently, as he hated falling behind with his correspondence. Sensing his malaise, Victoria was loath to bother him on official business, as she 'knew it would distress or irritate him, and affect his delicate stomach'.[16] But Albert's depressed state of mind received a further blow in January 1861, when his much-valued and talented new physician, Dr William Baly, was killed in a railway accident. The forty-seven-year-old Baly, a doctor at St Bartholomew's Hospital in London and a specialist in enteric disease, had been appointed Extraordinary Physician to the Queen in 1859 on the recommendation of Dr Clark, in anticipation of Clark's imminent retirement. Prince Albert had taken to him from the first; Baly's death was 'a great, great loss' for them, he told Stockmar, 'as he had gained our entire confidence, and was an excellent man'.[17] Had Baly not died, it is possible that with his greater air of authority and experience in up-to-date medical practice than the ageing Clark—who on Baly's death was called back into royal service from retirement—he would have immediately insisted on complete bed-rest for the Prince.[18]

The year 1861 started badly for Prince Albert; even the popular *Zalkiel's Almanac* for 1861 warned that 'The stationary position of Saturn in the third degree of Virgo in May, following upon this lunation, will be very evil for all persons born on or near the 26th August.' Among the sufferers, it regretted to see 'the worthy Prince Consort of these realms'. 'Let such persons pay scrupulous attention to health,' it had prophetically intoned.[19] A replacement was soon found for Baly, Dr Clark this time suggesting another rising practitioner and colleague of Baly's, Dr William Jenner, who had gained considerable attention for his work at the London Fever Hospital in identifying the differences between typhoid fever and typhus.[20] The Queen was delighted with Clark's choice, pronouncing Jenner 'extremely clever' and with a pleasing manner.[21] But the presence of another new doctor—albeit one who was the closest the royal family would have to a medical specialist—did nothing to change old habits: within days of his latest attack Albert was back at his desk struggling to keep up with his workload. In the light of his continuing poor health, on 10 February he and Victoria celebrated a rather low-key twenty-first

49

wedding anniversary marked only by the playing of some sacred music by the Queen's Band that evening. Victoria was, as ever, grateful for her beloved husband's 'tender love'; Albert was less preoccupied by the particularities of shared affection, dwelling instead on the bigger picture of a working partnership—of things achieved and yet to be done. 'How many a storm has swept over it,' he told Baron Stockmar of his marriage, 'and still it continues green and fresh, and throws out vigorous roots, from which I can, with gratitude to God, acknowledge that much good will yet be engendered for the world!'[22] But within days his grand designs were once more sublimated to physical pain, this time terrible toothache and a gumboil, which over the following two days led to inflammation of the nerves of his upper cheek.

'My sufferings are frightful and the swelling will not come to a proper head,' he wrote in his diary on 17 February. Enforced rest and restorative tonics brought some relief, but nine days of pain and two incisions of the gum by the royal dentist, Mr Saunders, in an attempt to provide some relief, 'pulled me down very much'.[23] Victoria remained entrenched in a stubborn denial of the seriousness of his condition. She grumbled to Vicky in Prussia about Albert's lack of physical stamina and hypochondria: 'dear Papa never allows he is any better or will try to get over it, but makes such a miserable face that people always think he's very ill'. In her view, it was the fault of his nervous system, which was 'easily excited and irritated'; Albert was 'so completely overpowered by everything'.[24] Nevertheless, in mid-February he resumed some of his duties, including, on the same day, a committee of the Fine Arts Commission and a visit to Trinity House (headquarters of the Lighthouse Service, of which he had been elected Master). But it was all too much and he returned exhausted. Within days his face and glands were swollen and painful.

On 21 February, once again confiding to Vicky her impatience at seeing Albert so weak and miserable, the Queen found it all 'most trying' and wearing; to her mind, it was part and parcel of the male inability to endure pain. Women, of course, were made differently. The trials of childbirth ensured that they learned to bear suffering with greater fortitude—'our nerves don't seem so racked, tortured as men's are!'[25] A day later she complained that Albert had gone against doctors' orders to keep quiet and not go out, instead 'staying up talking too long and to too many people'.[26] He was his own worst enemy. The only recourse was to drag him away from business: to Osborne on the Isle of Wight, where he went at the end of February to recuperate.

But far worse trials and tribulations awaited Prince Albert on his return to Windsor in March. The Queen's seventy-five-year-old mother, the Duchess of Kent, who had been ailing for some time, was now seriously ill. She had been suffering from a severe case of the skin infection erysipelas for the last couple of years and, more recently, a swollen right arm, which caused her such pain that it had become useless. When it was operated on, the cause, as Dr Clark had privately predicted to Prince Albert some time previously, had proved to be a malignant tumour.

On the night of 15–16 March Victoria kept

51

vigil at her dying mother's bedside at Frogmore. There, in the clutter of the Duchess's lilac-painted bedroom with its many visible mementos of her childhood, Victoria sat listening to the hours strike as the Duchess's face in its mob cap grew ever paler, the features 'longer and sharper'. From 8 a.m., as life ebbed away, Victoria knelt by her mother's bedside, holding her hand. 'It was a solemn, sacred, never-to-be-forgotten scene,' she later recalled, as her mother's breathing flickered and finally stopped at nine-thirty in the morning. It was also—in both her own and Albert's lives—their first experience, close to, of the grim ritual of the deathbed. Albert, much moved and in tears, gathered his distraught wife up in his arms and carried her into the next room—a paragon of tenderness and solicitude as Victoria dissolved into agonies of tears. The truth of her mother's condition had been kept from her and the shock was therefore intensified. How was she to endure the coming days and the thought of the 'daily, hourly blank' of life without her mother, she asked? It was all too dreadful.[27]

She felt abandoned, a helpless orphan; the whole of her miserable, repressed childhood flooded back to her, the days when she had fought her mother's control and then, on her accession, had ruthlessly replaced her, first with her governess, Baroness Lehzen, and then with Albert. It was thanks to him—for the Duchess was, after all, his aunt—that the two women had later been reconciled and had grown to love and appreciate each other. Victoria spent much time at Frogmore over the next few days sitting in her mother's room: feeling the 'awful stillness' of the house, struggling to recapture the shade of the mother she had in the past so shamefully maligned and had now lost. When she and Albert went through the painful process of sorting out the Duchess's effects—the accumulation of letters, the diaries, Victoria's own childish scribblings, and scrapbooks containing locks of her baby hair—she was shocked to find so much evidence of her mother's love and devotion. It opened the floodgates to a torrent of unresolved guilt, remorse and grief, which brought with it total nervous collapse, so much so that some feared the Queen might go mad. Only her eighteen-year-old daughter Alice (the natural care-giver of the family) seemed equipped to offer consolation. 'Go and comfort Mama,' Albert exhorted her.[28] Alice did so willingly, just as she had spent much time nursing the Duchess and playing the piano to her during her final illness. Meanwhile, withdrawing into total seclusion, as the protocols of mourning demanded—and which she followed to the letter— Queen Victoria donned her crape. Her ladies did likewise. She specified no time for the termination of mourning for her mother, setting the burghers of the Chamber of Commerce aghast at how yet another period of protracted court mourning would affect trade in the British garment industry. For mourning had become a regular feature at Court.

*     *     *

Back in 1844 when news had come from Coburg of the death of his father, Ernst I, Albert and Victoria had both descended into paroxysms of grief, the distraught Queen begging her Uncle Leopold to now 'be the father to us poor bereaved, heart-broken children'. The couple's self-indulgent display at the time had alarmed their three-year-old daughter Vicky. She could not understand why 'poor dear Papa and dear Mama cry so', nor why all the blinds were pulled down on the windows and the rooms so gloomy.[29] Overnight, death had erased the pain from Albert's memory of his father's dissolute life, his cruelty to Albert's mother and his endless sponging for money. Albert and Victoria had now viewed the deceased old reprobate as a paragon of virtue, as one, so Victoria insisted, 'who was so deservedly loved'—this of a man she hardly knew. Indeed, Albert was disappointed in the British public's lack of grief. 'Here we sit together, poor mama [the Duchess], Victoria and myself, and weep, with a great cold public around us, insensible as stone.' But what significance did this obscure German royal have for the British public? Only Albert's devoted Victoria had been able to gauge the depths of his grief and offer solace; she was, he assured Stockmar, 'the treasure on which my whole existence rests'.[30]

Ever in tune with her emotions, Victoria had taken to the performance of bereavement with aplomb. This first experience in 1844 of 'real *grief*', as she put it, made a 'lasting impression' on her, she told Uncle Leopold, so much so that she admitted, 'one loves to cling to one's grief'.[31] Years later, in a conversation with Vicky about ensuring that even young children wore mourning, she had insisted: 'you must promise me that if I should die your child or children and those around you should mourn; this really must be, for I have such strong feelings on this subject'.[32] By 1861, therefore, Victoria was already a master of the long and flamboyant mourning protocols that were in vogue, enthroning her own particular maudlin celebration of grief as a virtue to be emulated by all. She had by now been in and out of black for the best part of the last ten years, marked in particular by the grand, theatrical state ceremonials for the Duke of Wellington when he died in 1852 (the massive and ornate funeral car designed in consultation with the ever-resourceful Albert).[33] The Queen's intermittent wearing of black had continued through the deaths of various members of her extended family: her Aunt Louise, Queen of the Belgians, in 1850; her uncle, the King of Hanover, in 1851; her half-brother, Prince Charles of Leiningen, in 1856—for whom she had indulged in an excessively elaborate six-month period of mourning. Charles's death was closely followed by that of Victoria's cousin, the Duchess of Nemours, in 1857, to which she responded by holding a gloomy and 'interminable' black Drawing Room (as royal receptions were called), with only the soon-to-be-married Vicky allowed to wear white.[35] Then Victoria's brother-in-law, the Prince of Hohenlohe-Langenburg, had died in April 1860, inaugurating yet another slavish retreat into crape for three months—during which she had told Vicky how 'lovely' her darling Beatrice (just three years old) had looked 'in her black silk and crepe dress'— further fuelled by the death of Prince Albert's stepmother, Marie of Saxe-Coburg.[34] Victoria had gushed sympathy for both at a distance. Even when Tsar Nicholas I died on 2 March 1855 during the Crimean War she had insisted that the correct protocols of mourning be observed at the British court—no matter that this was for the monarch of a hostile nation. Royal blood was always thicker than water. Most recently, the death of Friedrich Wilhelm IV, the mad old King of Prussia, in January 1861 had propelled the disgruntled ladies at the British court back into crape yet again.

Friedrich Wilhelm's death had provided twenty-year-old Vicky, as wife of the Prussian Crown Prince, with her own first-hand initiation into the solemn rituals of the royal way of death—something her mother had yet to experience. Informed in the middle of the night that the end was nigh, she and Fritz had hastily dressed, to hurry on foot across the frozen streets and stand vigil at the dying king's bedside at the Sanssouci palace at Potsdam. Soon the Queen was thrilling to Vicky's 'painfully interesting details' of the scene, with nothing but the great clock ticking the hours of the night away to the accompaniment of the 'crackling of the fire and the death rattle' and then the sight of the stiffened corpse the following morning. Etiquette had required Vicky to pay her respects to the laid-out body of the King on several subsequent days and she did not spare her mother the minutiae of the fearful alteration that she observed in it before the coffin was sealed, or the 'great shudder' she had experienced when forced to kiss its face on the pillow. This time, the corpse had 'looked like death and no longer like sleep'.[36]

Mourning protocols then current in Britain demanded twelve months of black for a parent or child (with only a retreat to half-mourning in the final three months); six months for a sibling, three months for an aunt or uncle; and six weeks for a first cousin. The strictest observance of such protocols was de rigueur at the British court, though it did reduce down to a few days for very distant royal connections. But 1861 began—and ended—in black; altogether that year the Queen would issue seven declarations of official court mourning. Nothing but black silk, bombazine and crape; black gloves, black collars, black flowers, feathers, lappets and fans and festoons of jet mourning jewellery were the order of the day— except for the younger, unmarried ladies-in-waiting, who were allowed to freeze in lily-white muslin well into the winter. The Queen herself remained in mourning for much longer than the statutory time. Her withdrawal into mourning for her mother was total, obliging members of the royal household to creep around on tiptoe, conducting conversations in whispers in quiet huddles in corners, in order not to break the spell of silence that descended on Windsor. The social life of the British court was at an end. For months to come all royal family celebrations were cancelled: there were no birthday parties or outings to the theatre, and not even any music. By June everyone was complaining at the unremitting atmosphere of gloom in London. 'The Queen carries her sorrow at her mother's death to an absurd extent,' complained assistant secretary Benjamin Moran of the United States legation. 'There are no balls this season and in lieu thereof but one concert, and to this the Ministers, and their Ladies and Chief Secretaries only are to be invited.'[37]

The Duchess's funeral had been held in the strictest privacy at St George's Chapel, Windsor on 25 March. Unusually the pall-bearers had been six of her ladies, including her favourite, Lady Augusta Bruce. But neither the Queen nor her daughters had attended the ceremony, remaining,

57

in Victoria's words, 'to pray at home together, and to dwell on the happiness and peace of her who was gone'. In Victoria's absence Albert had acted as chief mourner, assisted by Bertie and ten-year-old Arthur, in a chapel festooned in black and with the great bell tolling. After the service the Duchess's crimson coffin was lowered into the gloom of the vault beneath, to be temporarily housed there until the mausoleum being constructed for it was ready. Prince Albert was visibly moved during the ceremony, his eyes filling with tears when Mr Tolley, the soloist in the chapel choir, came to the words in Martin Luther's hymn 'The trumpet sounds, the graves restore/The dead that they contained before'.[38] That evening, he took a strange pleasure in sharing in his wife's grief, reading aloud to her the letters the Duchess had written to a German friend forty-one years previously, describing the illness and death of her husband and Victoria's father, the Duke of Kent.[39] For the first three weeks after her mother's death, until 9 April, Victoria wallowed in her grief, seeing only her closest attendants and taking no comfort in her children. She did not even come down to family meals. The relentlessly sombre mood in the household at Windsor was broken only by the pert little Princess Beatrice, entertaining everyone round the dinner table with her renditions of 'Twinkle Twinkle' and 'Humpty Dumpty' and other nursery rhymes.[40] Victoria's continuing orgy of grief disturbed many at court, particularly in the levels of bathos with which she now eulogised her once-hated mother. It undoubtedly was a form of atonement for her own past sins, but the Queen's instability alarmed people such as her friend the

Earl of Clarendon, who worried about her state of 'great dejection' and her endless weeping. Her stubborn refusal to be consoled heralded what he felt was a return of the 'morbid melancholy to which her mind has often tended'. Clarendon knew it was a constant cause of anxiety to Prince Albert, who firmly begged his wife not to give way so completely and to be reconciled, remembering that 'the Blow was dealt by the Hand of the All Wise'.[41]

Not to receive this, the 'first real blow of misfortune'—a death in her immediate family—until the age of forty-one, and in an age when most couples lost more than one child in infancy, had meant that the Queen had taken her mother's death particularly hard. When Vicky arrived from Berlin, no doubt glad to see her family again, she was chastised for being in high spirits. As for Bertie, he had failed his mother's litmus test of grief too, giving 'great offence' by not bursting into tears the moment he arrived at Windsor from Cambridge University for the funeral.[42] He was also reprimanded for not using writing paper with a broad enough black border. For the royal household the Queen's hysterical grieving was an annoyance; for the egocentric Victoria, it was cathartic: 'the general sympathy for *me*, and approval of the manner in which I have shown my grief . . . is *quite wonderful and most touching*,' she told Uncle Leopold. Weeping—'which day after day is my welcome friend'—was her 'greatest relief'.[43] The more extravagant her mourning, the more she felt it demonstrated her devotion; and, as Queen, there were no limits placed on her right to indulge it. Her eldest daughter, however, was profoundly disturbed by what she saw during her visit: it was as though her mother *enjoyed* her sorrow, whilst turning a blind eye to how sick and exhausted her husband was. On her return to Berlin, Vicky discovered rumours had been circulating in the German court that her mother had lost her mind and that the mad doctors had been brought in to see her.

Absorbed in her own grief, Victoria entirely overlooked the fact that her mother's deathbed had also been Albert's first experience at close hand. Cast adrift in his own very private grief for a mother-in-law he had come to love dearly, he had little time to dwell on his own feelings; the comptroller of the Duchess's household, Sir George Couper, had also recently died suddenly, and Albert was charged—as her now sole executor—with taking on the onerous task of sorting out the Duchess's estate. He did so uncomplainingly, responding to the many letters of condolence from around the world and, more importantly, easing the mounting burden of his distraught wife's neglected dispatch boxes. Meanwhile Victoria took her mother's devoted lady-in-waiting and confidante, Lady Augusta Bruce, who had served the Duchess since 1846, to her bosom as her newly created, resident Lady of the Bedchamber. As a mournful cabal of two, they could wallow undisturbed in their shared remembrance of 'The Beloved'. Albert found himself of little use, but marshalled what remained of his emotional resources to sit with his wife reading consolatory prayers. Lady Bruce was much impressed by his tenderness and tact: 'Oh! He is one in millions,' she observed, 'well might she love him as she did!'[44]

Morning and evening Victoria persisted in

60

feeding her grief by sitting in the Duchess's rooms at Frogmore, ensuring that all was kept exactly as it had been, even down to the little canary singing in its cage. Mama 'lives much in the past and future, perhaps more than in the present,' Albert explained to Vicky, which was why it was for her 'a spiritual necessity to cling to moments that are flown and to recollections, and to form plans for the future'. He continued to listen patiently and console when the couple went to Osborne the following month, but was increasingly worried by the state of his wife's mental health. Victoria's half-sister Feodora (from the Duchess of Kent's first marriage to the Prince of Leiningen) also sent endless exhortations from her home in Baden, urging Victoria to 'look round you and feel how rich you are; how much God has given you to be thankful for'. 'I do not wish to feel better,' the Queen insisted. She was determined to hold on to her grief: 'the more distant the dreadful event becomes, and the more others recover their spirits—the more trying it becomes to me'.[45] As for the children, they were 'a disturbance' to her and she could hardly bear to be around them, or show any real concern for the increasingly fragile health of her haemophiliac youngest son Leopold.

Thus, inevitably, the burden of official duty fell entirely on Albert. He was, he admitted to Stockmar, 'well nigh overwhelmed by business', but as always he soldiered on, with Victoria steadfastly refusing to leave off her mourning.[46] Her birthday on 24 May came and went in disconsolate, sombre retreat without even any music ('That would kill me,' she told Vicky).[47] It was not until 19 June that she made her first public appearance at a Drawing Room at St James's, in deep crape mourning—'the deepest of deeps'—and with a headdress of black feathers.[48] It was crowded, hot and muggy and, after going through the barest of formalities, Victoria quickly retired. When King Leopold visited from Belgium at the end of the month he urged an end to full court mourning: he could see that Victoria's morbid state of mind was undermining Albert's health. Albert, however, would have none of it; the gloom at court was in tune with his own melancholic mood; besides, he knew that his wife would be unwilling to contemplate a transition— even to half-mourning—until six months of full mourning had passed, with her late mother's birthday on 17 August.[49]

## CHAPTER THREE

# 'Fearfully in Want of a True Friend'

Queen Victoria's fitful waves of weeping for her mother continued throughout the summer of 1861, her grief reignited on 1 August with the removal of the Duchess's coffin to a polished blue granite sarcophagus at the mausoleum at Frogmore specially constructed for it. She herself did not attend the ceremony, but visited on her mother's birthday to lay a wreath of dried flowers, consoling herself that the Duchess's 'pure, tender, loving spirit' was hovering there above them.[1] For his own part, Albert was by now more preoccupied with the very real aches and pains that plagued him, particularly continuing bouts of high temperature and agonising toothache.

His tolerance of Victoria's retreat from view was heroic; he did his duty, continuing to defer to her grief—priding himself that court mourning had not 'deviated' from her wishes in this respect by 'one hair's breadth'—and standing in for her at various levees and Drawing Rooms that year, which she would not contemplate attending.[2] Much to her annoyance, however, he insisted on returning early from their holiday at Osborne to fulfil a commitment to open the Royal Horticultural Show (the forerunner of the Chelsea Flower Show) at the beginning of June. He went there without Victoria, taking Bertie, Alice, Helena, Louise and Arthur. But the brightness of the floral displays could not dispel the dark and showery weather as the royal party trudged up the wet and muddy gravel walks to the glasshouse, where 'an endlessly long address was read and responded to' and—in the mind of Victoria's cousin, Princess Mary Adelaide—'an ill-timed prayer offered up'. Albert gritted his teeth, planted a Wellingtonia redwood tree and allowed the children to enjoy an ice cream. But the Queen's absence was noted, and many thought how pale and worn the Prince looked.[3]

Unseasonably hot weather later in the month and a stream of royal visitors further sapped Albert's energies: the bouts of feverishness and pain in his limbs persisted. It left him feeling 'very miserable', but he had to pull himself together to deal with their guests: King Leopold and his son from Brussels, Vicky and Fritz and their two small children from Berlin, Archduke Maximilian and his wife from Austria and other relatives from Hesse, Baden and Sweden, who all arrived in quick succession.[4] A trip to Ireland followed in August, primarily to see how Bertie was shaping up on his ten-week training course with the Grenadier Guards at the Curragh outside Dublin. Here he was enduring a strictly regulated regime laid down by his father, which, though it allowed for occasional dinner parties and meals in the regimental mess, endeavoured to keep him away from the corrupting influence of his more worldly fellow officers. Sadly, Bertie, while looking quite good in a uniform according to the Queen, proved to have absolutely no natural leadership skills; his disappointed parents were informed that he would not make the rapid rise through the ranks they expected of him. Indeed, his commanding officer had advised that the Prince of Wales would not even be capable of commanding a battalion by the end of his training, as he was 'too imperfect' in his drill.[5]

Whilst they were in Ireland the couple celebrated the Prince Consort's forty-second birthday on 26 August. But it was a subdued affair; Albert was in low spirits, sinking ever more into a mood of fatalism. Victoria refused to be downcast. 'God bless and ever preserve my precious Albert, my adored Husband!' she wrote in her journal. But, alas! 'So much is so different this year, nothing festive, we on a journey and separated from many of our children and my spirits bad' (only Alice, Helena and Alfred were with them). She wished her husband joy, but somewhere deep inside a germ of worry was growing: 'May God mercifully grant that we may long, very long, be spared to live together and that I may *never* survive him!'[6]

After a short stop in Killarney, where the Prince soaked up the scenery, finding the lakes 'sublime', the royal yacht took the family across the Irish Sea to Wales for the onward journey to their annual holiday at Balmoral, where they would be joined by Alice's fiancé Louis and Victoria's half-sister Feodora. When they docked at Holyhead, Albert sought some private pleasure in a day's railway excursion to nearby Snowdonia, as a prelude to the restorative peace and beauty of six weeks at Balmoral, which the family reached by special train to Aboyne station in Deeside, and thence by carriage to the castle.

\*　　　\*　　　\*

Victoria and Albert's love affair with Scotland was a passionate, visceral one. When they were first married they had enjoyed Sir Walter Scott's romantic reinvention of a heroic, feudal Scotland in his popular novels such as *Ivanhoe*, and they made their first visit together in 1842. The dry air of Balmoral, redolent with the balsamic smell of heather and pine and birch, reminded Albert of the mountains and forests of Thuringia near the Rosenau. At Balmoral he felt he had come home and it always worked its therapeutic magic on him. Even now, with his energy levels at an all-time low, it did so once again. The brief respite from his workload gave precious time in which to shake off the black dog of melancholy, as he enjoyed some excellent deer-stalking—bringing down six stags in the space of three days—and grouse-shooting and excursions taking in the grandeur of the glens and lochs of the area. He shook off the worst of his fatigue (though the staff noticed how pale and tired he seemed) and planned another 'Great Expedition' by carriage and pony like the one they had enjoyed the previous year. On 20 September he, Victoria, Alice and Louis, plus a small retinue, travelled incognito forty miles south-east of Balmoral, up through the hazy hills of Loch-na-Gar, down the wild glens of Tanar and Mark, wading on horseback across racing burns of crystal-clear, icy-cold water, to Invermark and its romantic old ruined castle half-covered in ivy. That evening, when they arrived at Fettercairn, they stayed at a local hostelry, the Ramsay Arms, under the guise of a 'wedding party from Aberdeen', taking great delight in not being recognised and enjoying a moonlit walk through the silent village before bedtime.[7]

Victoria was glad to see Albert relax, at last relinquishing his 'over-love of business' and she greedily consumed every precious moment in his company.[8] Another two-day round trip of 129 miles followed in October, in driving wind and rain for much of the time (Albert not helping his rheumatism by getting soaked through, while Victoria, who relished the invigorating cold of Scotland, had stayed cosy, wrapped in waterproofs and a plaid). With the light fading fast, they finally arrived at an inn in the village of Dalwinnie, where the cold, wet and hungry travellers were disappointed at the sight of 'two miserable starved Highland chickens, without any potatoes' for supper, and nothing but strong tea to drink. And, worse, there was 'No pudding, and no fun', recorded a disgruntled Victoria.[9]

Despite the privations, she noted that this had been 'the pleasantest and most enjoyable expedition I *ever* made'. She had 'enjoyed nothing as much, or indeed felt so much cheered by anything, since my great sorrow'.[10] With her grief temporarily receding and Albert's spirits revived, the couple made one more expedition on 16 October—a beautiful autumnal day during which they picnicked out in the open on a steep and rocky hillside overlooking the narrow valley of Cairn Lochan, where Albert left behind a note in an empty bottle of seltzer water as a memento of their visit. They returned at seven that evening as the moon was rising, 'much pleased and interested with this delightful expedition. Alas!, I fear our *last* great one!' Victoria wrote, in anticipation of their imminent departure. Six years later she would add a plaintive note in the margin: 'It was our last one!'[11]

As always, Victoria and Albert were loath to leave Balmoral. On 22 October the Queen wrote to Vicky 'My heart sinks within me at the prospect of going back to Windsor', for she knew her return would rekindle painful memories of her mother, but she did at least depart with one positive thought in mind. During this latest visit she had taken great delight in the unstinting attention shown to her by their 'invaluable Highland servant' John Brown, who combined 'the offices of groom, footman, page, and *maid*'. Victoria was impressed: Brown was '*so* handy about cloaks and shawls' and all the paraphernalia required for their expeditions.[12] She would be certain to remember him as she took one last look at the sunshine on her beloved Highlands, blue with autumn heather, and one final lungful of pure mountain air. Sure enough, the day of their departure, as Albert told Stockmar, 'the Queen's wounds were opened afresh'; 'the void' of her mother's absence once more 'struck home to her heart'.[13] Albert knew how hard it was for his wife to get a grip on the whirlwind of her feelings; it had been one of the tasks he had set her in her self-improvement plan when they were first married. Now, as Victoria once more bewailed their enforced return to a place that held terrible reminders of the loss of her mother, he felt the time had come for some firm, but straight talking. He sat down and wrote her a letter. The best advice he could offer was that she try 'to be less occupied with yourself and your own feelings', for pain was 'chiefly felt by dwelling on it and can thereby be heightened to an *unbearable extent*'. 'This is not hard philosophy,' he went on, 'but common sense supported by common and general experience. If you will take increased interest in things unconnected with personal feelings, you will find the task much lightened of governing those feelings in general which you state to be your great difficulty in life.'[14]

\*     \*     \*

On Sunday 6 October, whilst still at Balmoral, Victoria and Albert had as usual attended service at the modest little Church of Scotland kirk at nearby Crathie. The sermon that day was given by the Reverend Stewart, vicar of St Andrew's, Edinburgh, his text being 'Prepare to meet thy God, Oh Israel' from Amos 4:12. Now that she had had first-hand experience of death and had entered the inner sanctum of the initiated, Victoria felt the words of the sermon and its message so much more acutely. 'I feel now to be so acquainted with death—and to be so much nearer that unseen world,' she wrote to Vicky the following day, echoing a phrase of the Catholic cleric Cardinal Manning, whom she admired, that has long since been attributed to her.[15] The sermon had a profound impact on Albert, clearly feeding into the intimations of his own mortality that had preoccupied him since the Duchess of Kent's death, and the Queen requested that a manuscript copy of it be sent to him. She would later recall how often Albert had remarked on her own indomitable lust for life: 'I do not cling to life,' he had told her not long before his death, 'You do; but I set no store by it. If I knew that those I love were well cared for, I should be quite ready to die tomorrow.' More prophetically he had added that he was sure that 'if I had a severe illness, I should give up at once, I should not struggle for life.' It was an awful admission to make to a wife whose physical robustness was so visible, but he had, he told her, 'no tenacity in life.'[16] And yet he said these words cheerfully. They were, for him, a simple statement of belief—not a death-wish, as they have so often been interpreted. As a devout Christian, Albert was, as he had been throughout his life, ever ready to submit to God's will. 'I know of no public man in England,' remarked Sir Charles Lyell, 'who was so serious on religious matters, and so unfettered by that formalism and political churchism and conventionalism which rules in our upper classes.'[17] Such simplicity of faith had created in Albert an acceptance of what he was sure would be his own early death. His narrow escape from the carriage accident in Coburg the previous year, and his obvious distress on that visit at seeing his homeland for what he was convinced would be the last time, all fed into his increasing world weariness and spiritual detachment from the family.

The Queen remembered how strange it was

in retrospect that her husband had 'dwelt so much on death and the future state' in the six months before his death, as though he had had a presentiment of its imminence. Had she given it closer thought perhaps, it might have occurred to her that her husband's lack of 'pluck', as she would later call it, was in fact a reflection of his profound unhappiness.[18] Their shared reading at the time— chosen of course by Albert—was dominated by religious texts, including a collection by William Branks of the letters of a religious evangelical, Sarah Craven, entitled *Heaven our Home*. Indeed, the subject of the afterlife was something the couple often talked of, Albert observing that although he had no idea 'in what state we shall meet again on the other side', he was sure that he and Victoria would recognise each other 'and be together in eternity'.[19] Of that he was 'perfectly certain'. And so, most determinedly, was she; for Albert was hers for this life—and the next. Sarah Craven's letters, with their ecstatic striving for perfection on the path to eternal glory and arrival at 'those blissful shores' of heaven, endorsed the Queen and Prince Albert's own belief that heaven was a familiar and comforting home, 'with a great and happy and loving family in it'—a place indeed 'worth dying for'.[20]

The tenuousness of health and happy family life were brought home again to Victoria and Albert in early November, when new worries consumed them concerning their youngest son Leopold. Now aged eight, he had always been a thin and sickly child, prone to knocks and bangs that set up severe bouts of bleeding that laid him up for weeks. He had finally been diagnosed with haemophilia a couple of years previously, a fact that the royal family took care not to advertise at a time when the disease was little understood. By 1861 Leopold had become so frail—a 'child of anxiety', as the Queen described him—that, after yet another serious bleeding attack, the doctors had advised sending him to the French Riviera for the winter, in the care of his rather aged governor, the seventy-four-year-old General Bowater and a German physician, Dr Günther. But Bowater himself was not in the best of health and Albert worried for his son's well-being; he also grieved to see another child removed from the family nest: Vicky in Berlin, Affie away at sea, Bertie at Cambridge and now dear little Leopold gone from them on 2 November. Bertie, for all his failings, at least was not far away and came back to Windsor on 9 November for his twentieth birthday. Bells rang out across the town and—breaking her slavish observation of mourning still for her mother—Victoria allowed a military band to celebrate the occasion. She prayed to God 'to assist our efforts to make him turn out well', but found it hard not to be reminded of past, happier days. Bertie's birthday was the first family celebration spent at Windsor without the Duchess of Kent. 'I nearly broke down at dinner,' she wrote in her journal. '*The* contrast of former times—*all* in deep black . . . all was so painfully forcibly felt!' And Albert had not been well either, suffering 'a very bad headache before dinner'.[21]

Gloom and yet more gloom piled up that month; the Queen was also fretting about Vicky, newly pregnant and sick with influenza in Berlin. She talked of sending Dr Jenner out to treat her, but then news arrived by telegraph on the 10th that

71

the twenty-four-year-old Pedro, King of Portugal (to whom both Albert and Victoria were related through the Coburg line) was seriously ill with typhoid fever. His younger brother, Ferdinand, had died of the disease four days previously. Two days later Pedro too was dead. Victoria was stunned; in the habit of never taking any illnesses seriously other than her own, she had thought Pedro's complaint 'nothing but one of those frequent little feverish attacks which foreigners so continually have from not attending to their stomach and bowels'. She and Albert attended to their own digestive systems most rigorously. The royal pharmacist—Mr Peter Squire of Oxford Street—supplied them with monthly consignments of laxatives and purgatives such as tincture of rhubarb, syrup of ipecac, calomel, Rochelle salt, senna and bicarbonate of soda. But since their holiday at Balmoral, belladonna, sulphuric acid and tincture of paregoric had been added to the list to deal with Albert's continuing stomach cramps and diarrhoea.[22] Pedro's shocking and sudden death was a terrible loss for them both, but especially Albert, who had loved him as a son; more importantly, he had looked on the conscientious and hard-working Pedro as a young man in his own image, a 'model' king, whom he hoped to see uphold the integrity of the monarchy and democratise the throne of Portugal. Pedro was everything Albert had hoped to see in Bertie. These two deaths further fed into his morbid and religiose state of mind and his pathological dread of 'fever', which, in its various forms, carried so many off. The deaths of Ferdinand and Pedro were 'another proof', he told Vicky, that death might at any time come knocking

72

on the door and that 'we are never safe to refuse Nature her rights'.[23]

The Portuguese deaths had once more plunged the court into black not long after the period of mourning for the Duchess of Kent had finally ended. Victoria's spirit was greatly knocked back by these two additional deaths in the wider royal family of Europe: 'We did not need this fresh loss in this sad year, this sad winter,' she wrote in her journal, for it had already been a year 'so different to what we have ever known'.[24] Pedro's death prompted her to recall the parting words of John Brown, the day they had left Balmoral, that the family should all remain well through the winter and 'return all safe'. Above all, he had added, he hoped 'that you may have no deaths in the family'. The concurrence of the two deaths in Portugal kept returning to her mind, 'as if they had been a sort of strange presentiment'.[25] Victoria and Albert remained 'much crushed' and kept to their rooms for meals for the next few days. Sensing how 'dejected' Albert was, as she told Vicky, the Queen did her best to bear up, but there was no disguising the atmosphere of increasing gloom that the deaths provoked in him.[26] 'The sad calamity in Portugal' haunted his already-restless nights. He seemed increasingly silent and listless; in later years Princess Beatrice remarked that after the death of King Pedro she did not see her father smile again. 'It was almost as if he had had a stroke,' observed others. Prince Albert seemed to be 'half in another world'.[27]

Nothing could cheer the ailing Prince Consort— not even the hopes of a marriage soon for Bertie. For the Prince of Wales had now been dispatched

73

in obligatory pursuit of the most eligible bride that his energetic sister Vicky, enlisted by her parents, had been able to find for him: Princess Alexandra of Schleswig-Holstein-Sonderburg-Glücksburg, the sixteen-year-old daughter of Prince Christian, heir to the King of Denmark. Alexandra was pretty but poor, her father being descended from a marginal branch of the Danish royal family, and she came at the bottom of a list of other, more strategically desirable candidates who had been rejected for various reasons. Bertie travelled to Europe for a secret meeting with Alexandra in the Chapel of St Bernard at Speyer Cathedral near Baden-Baden, orchestrated by his sister. It brought no *coup de foudre*, though Bertie at least came away pleased with Alexandra's sweetness, her grace and charm. She would do well enough. Vicky was dismayed at her brother's indifference to an alluring young woman who, in her estimation, 'would make most men fire and flames'. The Princess's charms had, sadly, not produced enough of an impression on him even 'to last from Baden to England' and he remained hesitant.[28] Love was out of the question, agreed Victoria, for in her estimation Bertie was incapable of enthusiasm 'about anything in the world'.[29] She did not yet know it, but in fact his initiation into the pleasures of the flesh was well under way—and he was loath to cast them aside so soon for monogamy.

\*　　　\*　　　\*

Just before he had left his training camp at the Curragh, after a lacklustre performance, Bertie had attended a rowdy party at the Mansion House in Dublin. After it was over a group of his fellow officers arranged a farewell present for Bertie, smuggling a young 'woman of the town', Nellie Clifden, into his quarters. She was a regular favourite among the Guards and knew her way around camp in the dark, so well indeed that when Bertie staggered back to his bed that night, he found the vivacious and willing young Nellie waiting for him. Having enjoyed Nellie's welcome, he ensured her surreptitious exit via the window of his hut and arranged further assignations with her back in England—right under his parents' noses at Windsor. The gossips were quick to dub Nellie 'The Princess of Wales', for she was unable to resist the temptation to brag about her conquest around the dives and casinos of London.[30] The scandal soon hit the London clubs and appeared in the papers on the Continent. Bertie's parents remained blissfully ignorant of the fact until a letter arrived in early November from Baron Stockmar in Germany informing them of the rumours. The couple were deeply shocked, but before taking any action, Albert checked with Lord Torrington, a regular of the clubs. Confirmation that the rumours were true, Victoria later wrote, 'broke my Angel's heart'; Bertie's behaviour was painfully reminiscent of that of Albert's brother Ernst with a servant-girl in Dresden and of their father's affair with a courtesan, Pauline Panam—better known as 'La Belle Grèque'—who had later caused much royal embarrassment with a kiss-and-tell memoir.[31] But in Bertie's case there was an empire, rather than a duchy, at stake. A traditional rite of passage such as sexual initiation was par for the course in army life; but to Bertie's puritanical father, this transgression—which was almost to be expected in the mind of most Victorian fathers—was nothing short of a catastrophe. Albert's stress levels went haywire: Bertie's transgression would, he told his son, suck him irrevocably down into the vortex of sin and self-destruction.

Victoria would ever after lay at her son's door the devastating effect of Bertie's indiscretions on Albert's precarious health. For they had awakened Albert's innermost fears of the dangers of unbridled sexuality and, with it, a return by his son to the old, profligate habits of the British royalty. In his paranoia, Albert saw the spectre of vice opening the door to blackmail, scandal, pregnancy and even disease; vice had always 'depressed him, grieved him, horrified him'—and the worry of the dishonour that Bertie's encounter with a woman who was little more than a prostitute might bring on him (and the monarchy) drained his last reserves of energy.[32] A martyr now to his son's bad behaviour, he paid the price with crippling insomnia and neuralgia.

On 16 November, 'with a heavy heart', Albert sat down and wrote a long and melodramatic letter to Bertie. His behaviour had caused him 'the deepest pain, I have yet felt in this life'. His son had 'wilfully plunged into the lowest vice', and Albert berated him for his thoughtlessness, weakness and ignorance.[33] The level of Bertie's depravity, as Albert perceived it, would be sufficient, should the woman fall pregnant and drag him before the courts, to provide her with an opportunity 'to give before a greedy multitude disgusting details of your profligacy'. But, far worse, the escapade might wreck the delicate marriage negotiations with Alexandra of Denmark. Four days later Albert wrote again in response to a letter from a contrite Bertie begging his forgiveness. He softened his tone; he was 'ever still your affectionate father' and entreated Bertie to make up for his behaviour by his future actions. Having eaten of the forbidden fruit of the tree, he must now hide himself from the sight of God, for nothing could restore him to the state of innocence and purity that he had lost. 'You *must* not, you *dare* not be lost,' Albert went on. 'The consequences for this country, and for the world at large, would be too dreadful.' The past was over and done with. Bertie 'had to deal now with the future' and the only thing that could save him was his marriage to Alexandra.[34]

While Bertie threatened to break his heart, the enduring consolation for Albert was his good and clever daughter Vicky in Berlin, to whom he wrote on her birthday a few days later. 'May your life, which has begun beautifully, expand still further to the good of others and the contentment of your own mind!' He had little hope of such worthy objectives from Bertie, who seemed utterly insensitive to the quest for 'true inward happiness', which in Albert's book was 'to be sought only in the internal consciousness of effort systematically directed to good and useful ends'.[35] The pursuit of such ends had sent him, ill though he was, on frequent journeys back and forth to London since their return from the Highlands. On 22 November Albert had visited Sandhurst in Surrey to inspect new buildings constructed there for the Staff College and Royal Military Academy. It was a gloomy day of incessant rain, but he stayed for three hours splashing about in puddles, looking over plans and performing his official duties in his usual businesslike manner. He returned to Windsor cold and soaked through, unable to eat and telling the Queen he felt tired, and complaining that he was 'much of the weather'.[36] Yet the following day, despite the rain, he went out shooting with Victoria's nephew, Ernst, Prince of Leiningen, who was over on a visit with his wife. Once again he got soaked through and afterwards sat around in his wet clothes. He confided to his diary that he was full of rheumatic pains and had 'scarcely closed' his eyes at night for the last fortnight. Victoria too was worried at how 'weak and tired' her husband was from sleeplessness, which had come on 'ever since that great worry and annoyance'. It was all too 'horrid'; and it was all Bertie's fault.[37]

While Victoria might find a pat explanation for it all, Albert's physical and mental malaise now went far deeper than mere worries about his errant eldest son. The years of self-imposed overwork and exhaustion had brought an overwhelming sense of isolation. Loneliness gnawed away at him and—though he never admitted as much—this loneliness extended even to his marriage. Victoria was always there ready to adore him, to hang on his every word, his every kiss, to praise unstintingly and monopolise his time, but Albert was tiring of her relentless, cloying admiration and her never-ending emotional hunger. Her love was too inverted; she enjoyed the satisfaction it gave her, without thinking of the good it should do him. He meanwhile longed for space, for spiritual companionship and the wisdom and cool detachment of his old friend and guardian angel, Baron Stockmar. He missed their close 'interchange of thought', particularly now that his few other male allies were dead. He had wept uncontrollably at the death of Anson in 1849 and at the time had begged Stockmar to come to England to console him. The loss of former Prime Minister Sir Robert Peel in 1850 had been a real blow too, for Peel had been Albert's true friend and political amanuensis and, in the opinion of Florence Nightingale, had taught him the political skills needed to be an unofficial minister.[38] Worse still, in 1858, had been the death of Albert's loyal Swiss valet Isaac Cart, who was his last link with Coburg and had been with him since the age of seven. 'I am fearfully in want of a true friend and counsellor,' he confessed in what would be his last letter to Stockmar on 14 November; but the ageing Stockmar, an unfailing stalwart through Albert's difficult years in England, was far away in Coburg, his own life now drawing to a close.[39]

At ten-thirty on the morning of 25 November Albert somehow found the strength to take a special train to Cambridge for a man-to-man talk with Bertie, feeling 'still greatly out of sorts'.[40] They met at Madingley Hall, where Bertie had been living with his governor, General Bruce, and his wife since going up to Cambridge in January; the location four miles out of town had been chosen by Albert, who had been unwilling to trust his son to the vicissitudes of college life. Bertie was mortified by his father's distress and was duly and lengthily chastised during a long walk with him down the wet Cambridgeshire lanes. But the strain of this excursion proved too much for Albert—Bertie had seemed oblivious to his father's ill health, and his poor sense of direction had got them lost, taking them on a longer route than planned. Albert paid the price when he returned to Windsor the following day and was racked with pains in his back and legs.

Victoria found her husband's continuing irritability most trying after his return from Madingley, remarking in a classic understatement to King Leopold that 'Albert is a little rheumatic . . . which is a plague'.[41] She could not, and would not, think the unthinkable: that her husband was seriously ill. And so she convinced herself that there was nothing ominous in his symptoms. After all, it was 'very difficult not to have something or other of this kind in this season, with these rapid changes of temperature'; and, touch wood, he actually was 'much better this winter than he was the preceding year'. Albert, knowing his wife's propensity for hysteria, had determinedly kept the truth of his declining health over the last three years from her. And he would not disabuse her of the fact now, though he confided otherwise to his diary. 'Am very wretched,' he wrote, and for once he did not join the Queen on the terrace for their usual constitutional that day.[42] In contrast, the Prince's valet, Rudolf Löhlein, had by now become greatly concerned at his master's uncharacteristic listlessness and the way his mind had strangely wandered at times over the last couple of days. He was convinced that the badly drained town of Windsor (which had seen a typhoid epidemic in 1858 that had killed thirty-nine people) was a danger to him: 'Living here will kill your Royal Highness,' he had frequently repeated to him. 'You must leave Windsor and go to Germany for a time to rest and recover strength.'[43]

Talk of the notorious Windsor fever might

have alarmed Albert, but he did nothing about it. He was no better on the 27th, when, after yet another sleepless night, he had a 'great feeling of weariness and weakness'. But still he refused to take to his bed. Victoria now admitted in a letter to Vicky, 'I never saw him so low'.[44] Dr Jenner visited and stayed for the night and advised Albert not to leave the castle. Rest indoors was one thing, but all hopes of unbroken sleep for Albert were removed when news broke in the British press on 28 November of a major diplomatic incident with America, now eight months into a bitter civil war. After the eleven southern states had seceded from the Union in March, forming a Confederacy, Britain—with strong economic links to the cotton-producing South, the mainstay of the Lancashire cotton industry—had given the South its tacit support. On 8 November a British West Indies mail packet, the *Trent*, which had been conveying envoys of the Confederate forces on a diplomatic mission to Europe, was stopped by a warship of the Federal Union (the Northern states) in the Bahama Channel off the northern coast of Cuba. The ship was boarded and four Southern officials were taken off under arrest: James Murray Mason, envoy to the Court of St James in London; John Slidell, envoy to the Court of the Tuileries in Paris; and their respective secretaries. The jingoistic Lord Palmerston's government saw this as a flagrant violation of international law and of British neutrality in the war. As the diplomatic crisis deepened, the press whipped up war fever, demanding reparations. Only five years after the end of the Crimean War, the British people found themselves contemplating the unthinkable: taking up arms against the American North. The primary concern of Foreign Minister Lord John Russell was to protect British cotton interests in the South, but taking on the North, at a distance of 2,500 miles, was a tall order. Nevertheless, British warships were ordered to deploy off the American coast, munitions factories went into overtime and 8,000 troops were shipped to Canada in case of war.

News of the 'astounding outrage of the Americans' greatly alarmed the Queen, as well as Prince Albert—who was still suffering what appeared to be the continuing aches and pains of a severe chill caught at Madingley.[45] Worry over the gathering political crisis further disrupted his already fractured sleep. Nevertheless, after dragging himself from bed and taking a hot bath on the morning of 29 November, he turned out to watch a review of the 200 boys of the Rifle Corps of the Eton Volunteers who paraded for the royal family beneath the East Terrace in Windsor Home Park. He knew that his absence would be remarked upon if he did not go; 'Unhappily I must be present,' he noted in his diary, before donning his fur-lined overcoat for the twenty-minute parade.[46] The weather was mild and muggy for November, but Albert was full of aches and feeling the cold. He looked decidedly unwell and could only walk slowly, because of the pains in his legs. He seemed to be shivering all the time and later told Victoria that he had felt 'as if cold water were being poured down his back'.[47] It was the last day that he was seen in public.

Later that day Dr Jenner visited and pronounced Albert much better; 'he would be quite well in two or three days,' he reassured him, and there was no need for a doctor to stay over in the castle. 'No, I shall not recover,' Albert told him, 'but I am not taken by surprise.' He was not afraid, he assured Jenner: 'I trust I am prepared.'[48] After eating a little supper, he revived that evening, or so the Queen thought. Privately, in a letter to Vicky, Albert confided—as he often did to her about the kind of things he would never tell the Queen—that 'Much worry and great sorrow (about which I beg you not to ask questions) have robbed me of sleep during the past fortnight.' The Bertie affair was haunting him and he confessed himself to be in a 'shattered state', made worse by heavy catarrh and headache and pains in his limbs for the last four days.[49]

He awoke on 30 November after another restless night that had left him wakeful from 3 a.m. Feeling weak and chilly, he ate a little breakfast, but he was suffering stomach cramps and was too ill to go out on the terrace to take the air. Besides, he was far too preoccupied with the *Trent* crisis. The prospect of war with the North was a very stark one, of which Albert was only too well aware. It would be a disaster for British trade, and worse, with the loss of American grain imports, it could bring with it bread shortages. Letters to *The Times* were already urging moderation—an apology should be demanded for what was now seen as an 'illegal and irregular proceeding' rather than an act of aggression. An editorial in *The Times* led the way, appealing to reason and self-restraint in the hope that 'our people will not meet this provocation with an outburst of passion'.[50] Counter to his wife and Palmerston's considerably more belligerent attitude, Albert sided with *The Times* and thought the incident was not something worth going to war over. The boarding of the *Trent* must, he suggested, have taken place without the assent of President Lincoln—an assumption that, whether true or not, might provide a way out of the impasse. He was still very depressed and eating very little, as Victoria told Vicky that day, but she persisted in her own logical explanation: it was a result of all the sleepless nights, which had lowered his spirits. She refused to take any of it seriously. 'Dear Papa is in reality much better', if he would only admit it, the fault being that he was 'as usual desponding as men really only are—when unwell'.[51] She was already looking forward to their departure from Windsor for Osborne on 13 December, for a cosy family Christmas. She was 'truly thankful' that they would soon have other scenery to look at, other than 'this most tiresome—and this year to me—most distasteful place'.

That evening a draft despatch from Palmerston's government to the Americans had arrived for the Queen's approval. Its tone was aggressive and strident; Albert was greatly alarmed: 'This means war!' he told Victoria, unless the uncompromising stance of the document could be modified.[52] That night he slept in a separate room, so as not to disturb her. He rose early the following morning, Sunday 1 December, lit his favourite green desk lamp (the one he had brought with him from Coburg) and sat down, still in his scarlet padded dressing gown, to draft a more conciliatory response. This allowed for the possibility of a misunderstanding and gave the Americans room for a dignified climbdown. Later, when the Queen got up, he wearily handed the draft to her, admitting that he had been feeling so ill when

84

composing it that 'I could hardly hold my pen.'[53]

'He could eat no breakfast and looked very wretched' that morning, Victoria later recalled, but Albert managed a walk with her for half an hour on the lower terrace, though 'well wrapped up'. He also accompanied her to Sunday service in St George's Chapel, where he 'insisted on going through all the kneeling'.[54] He tried hard to make the most of a family Sunday, joining everyone for luncheon, 'but could take nothing', a fact that dismayed doctors Clark and Jenner when they visited. They were, the Queen wrote, 'much disappointed at finding Albert so very uncomfortable'. He came down to dinner that evening, but again was unable to eat, but he did his best not to show how ill he felt by chatting and telling stories and then sitting for a while listening to his eighteen-year-old daughter Alice and Marie, Princess of Leiningen, playing the piano. He went to bed at 10.30 'in hopes to sleep it off', but when the Queen joined him at half-past eleven, he was lying there, wide awake, shivering with cold and unable to sleep.[55]

Aware of the need for a prompt response to the Americans, to be sent that night by steamship, Victoria had reviewed Albert's draft memorandum on the *Trent*, made a few emendations—to what would be her husband's last act of public business—and sent it back to Whitehall in the hope that sufficient redress would be offered, along with a speedy apology.[56] It would take up to twelve days for the dispatch to reach America by sea. The British nation, with no real appetite for another war, went to church and prayed to God that a conflict could be averted. But Queen Victoria now had other far more immediate preoccupations—with her 'beloved invalid'.[57] The following morning, 2 December, after yet another night of shivering and sleeplessness, unable to eat and without even the inclination to get dressed, Prince Albert got up, sank onto a sofa and sent for Dr Jenner.

# CHAPTER FOUR

## *'Our* Most *Precious Invalid'*

With 'The American Difficulty' still preoccupying the British public and taking the lion's share of the newspaper columns, there was no inkling in the press on Monday 2 December 1861 that a very real crisis was brewing closer to home. As usual the Queen's every move over the weekend was reported in meticulous detail: on Saturday she had ridden out in the morning with Princess Alice and taken the air by carriage that afternoon, before holding a Privy Council meeting at five; the Prince Consort had accompanied her to Divine Service the following morning; the family was preparing to depart for Osborne for Christmas by the middle of December; and at the Birmingham Cattle and Poultry Show the Prince Consort's cattle had won first and second prizes in the Devon Steers class.

To the outside world all seemed well at Windsor. But for the Prince and his anxious wife it had been another 'sad night of shivering and sleeplessness', with Albert 'being awake at every hour almost'. When Dr Jenner arrived, he found him 'extremely uncomfortable and so depressed'. But he told the

Queen that 'there was no reason to be alarmed', although he did fear that the Prince's condition was 'turning into a kind of long feverish indisposition'.[1] Albert lay listlessly on the sofa in his dressing gown and from time to time sat up in an armchair as Victoria or Alice read to him, but he was still very restless and uncomfortable when Jenner visited later that day. 'He kept saying, it was very well he had no fever, as he should not recover!', Victoria lamented in her journal, but she and the doctors persisted in making light of the Prince's neuroses. Such a thing, they all told him, 'was too foolish and he must never speak of it'. He tried to eat, but even some soup with bread tasted awful, 'making him feel nauseous and his stomach uncomfortable'.[2] Albert's mood was not lifted when his emissaries, Lord Methuen and Colonel Francis Seymour, returned from Portugal—where they had been dispatched with letters of condolence—bringing accounts of the death of King Pedro. The doctors had advised that Albert should not speak to them, for fear of becoming demoralised, but he had insisted on hearing all the details of the King's illness and death, at the end of which he had asserted to Lord Methuen that his own illness also would be fatal.[3]

That night, rather than disturb Victoria, Albert got up and went to his own room, but sleep again evaded him as he lay there feeling cold.[4] The following morning he could not eat breakfast or even take any broth without being overcome by nausea. Seymour thought the Prince looked 'as if he was on the brink of a jaundice of no trifling kind', with 'severe cold, bile and rheumatic aches in his back, legs, etc.' 'There is an end to his shooting for a long time,' he remarked ruefully, seeing nothing else to be concerned about.[5]

Although the British public was still oblivious to the Prince Consort's rapidly declining health, the Prime Minister's concern was rising. At seventy-seven years of age, Lord Palmerston was far from well himself, suffering from agonising gout that caused such crippling pains in his hands and feet that he could hardly get about or even open a letter. Nevertheless he had come to Windsor for the Privy Council meeting on 30 November and had returned to the castle for a private dinner on 2 December, when he had been concerned to hear of Albert's continuing illness. He had had major problems in the past dealing with the Queen's bouts of hysteria when under pressure, and dreaded any sidelining of the Prince's role in affairs of state. Having long been sanguine about the efficiency of the royal doctors, Palmerston was extremely uneasy and requested that another medical man be called in to examine the Prince, suggesting Dr Robert Ferguson, who had attended the Queen at the births of all her children.

Queen Victoria was much put out by this. Despite her 'agony of despair' at how listless and distracted Albert was, she was 'dreadfully annoyed' by Palmerston's interference, and more so by what appeared to be his covert calling into question of the medical skills of Clark and Jenner.[6] She instructed Sir Charles Phipps, who during Albert's illness was temporarily performing the role of her Private Secretary, to respond very firmly, thanking Palmerston for his 'kind interest'. The Prince had a feverish cold of the kind that he often succumbed to in winter and she hoped it would pass off in a few days. She would therefore be 'unwilling to cause unnecessary alarm where no cause exists for it, by calling in a medical man who does not upon ordinary occasions attend at the Palace'.[7] The message was clear: Victoria and the royal doctors did not want to provoke an adverse response in the highly sensitive Albert by suggesting that his condition was in any way serious; nor, privately, did the doctors want any overattention to the Prince's worsening condition to cause the kind of hysterical outbursts that Victoria had shown over her mother.

And so a stubborn policy of cheerful optimism and illusory hope was adopted, in the face of all indications to the contrary. Victoria was already settled on a course of denial, confident there was nothing to worry about; after all, 'Good kind old Sir James' had reassured her, and that was enough in her book. 'There was no cause whatever for alarm,' Clark had told her and he felt sure that Prince Albert 'would soon be better'.[8] To reassure the Prince, Dr Jenner stayed at Windsor that night, but although Albert got some sleep between 8 p.m. and midnight, he was awake and restless for much of the remainder—wandering aimlessly from room to room, with a disconsolate Victoria trailing after him.

Was the royal doctors' decision not to take the Prince's illness with deadly seriousness at this early stage a fatal mistake? It certainly ensured that the patient was not firmly told to get into bed and stay there, in order to allow himself to be properly nursed. But the fact was that there was as yet no system of efficient nursing established in Britain to supplant the slatternly, untrained hospital nurses of Mrs Gamp fame, immortalised by Dickens in *Martin Chuzzlewit*. After her return from the Crimean War in 1856, Florence Nightingale had been given official approval to establish nurses' training at St Thomas's Hospital as a respectable profession for women, but the first Nightingale Training School had only opened in July the previous year. For now, the nursing of the sick poor was still largely carried out by nuns and similar lay orders. For the better-off, the best and often most hygienic care was that provided in their own homes by their nearest and dearest—in many cases the eldest unmarried daughter of the family.

The situation was no different at Windsor. With the Queen too emotionally unstable to cope with the stresses and strains of an increasingly irascible patient, the role of sick-nurse fell to the eighteen-year-old Princess Alice, who was assisted by the Prince's closest, but medically untrained personal attendants: his fellow Coburger, Rudolf Löhlein; his eighteen-year-old Scottish garderobier, Archie Macdonald; and his Swiss valet, Gustav Mayet.[9] For all her youth and inexperience, Princess Alice had from a young age shown a compassionate interest in the sick, visiting poor cottagers on the estate at Balmoral and, at the age of only eleven, going with her parents to see the wounded—many of them severely mutilated—of the Crimean War. Alice could see the grim reality where her mother could not, having long had an intuitive understanding of her father's state of growing weariness. From the start of this latest bout of illness Alice had had grave apprehensions. Writing to Louis in Hesse on 3 December, she openly admitted that 'poor mama' had no idea how to nurse someone, 'although she wants to help as much as she can'. (Augusta Bruce

90

thought likewise: 'The Queen's little knowledge of nursing made her rather not the best nurse in the world.')[10] Alice was steeling herself to the role expected of her—that of the sentimental archetype, the 'Angel in the House'—on whom the family relied. But it was so hard with her father not eating, not sleeping and experiencing bouts of chronic pain, and refusing to allow that he would get better. 'I have to listen to the mutual complaints of my dear parents if I am to be really helpful to them,' she wrote, 'or even carry their burden, if that were possible,' she told Louis.[11] From now on she would be an almost constant presence, hovering devotedly over her father and sleeping in the room next to him so as to be always on call.

\*       \*       \*

The first public inkling that something was amiss came in the morning papers of 4 December, which carried a small notice in the daily Court Bulletin that 'The Prince Consort has been suffering for the last three days from a feverish cold, which has confined His Royal Highness to his room.'[12] Over at Windsor the Queen had awoken after 'a very sad night' during which she had wept a great deal at seeing her husband in so much distress. After tossing and turning till 6 a.m., Albert had got up and sent for Dr Jenner, but refused to take any breakfast. Later he was persuaded to take some orange jelly and 'a little raspberry vinegar in seltzer water'.[13] Victoria pulled herself together to write a letter to Leopold in Cannes, telling him that Papa was suffering from 'a regular influenza', but when she returned from her walk on the terrace later

91

that day she was dismayed to see Albert's looks and manner 'very sad and disheartening' and, worse, how little he smiled.[14] 'It was, from the first,' she later recalled, 'as if he could not smile his own expression.'[15]

Sir James Clark arrived, and was 'grieved to see no more improvement'. But he was still not discouraged, he told the Queen. Albert rested in the bedroom for most of the day and asked to be read to. But his irritable and restless state prevailed and 'no books suited him, neither *Silas Marner* nor *The Warden*'. The Queen tried to raise his spirits with Charles Lever's *The Dodd Family Abroad*—a humorous novel about gauche British travellers on the Continent—but Albert did not like that either, so it was decided that the following day they would revert to an old favourite, a book by Sir Walter Scott.[16]

That night Albert's restlessness became even more marked; after tossing and turning in bed, he got up and once more walked distractedly from room to room in his quilted dressing gown. Dr Jenner arrived and administered a sedative, but it brought the Prince only a few hours' respite. After breakfast on the 4th the Queen found him looking 'dreadfully wretched and woe-begone', able only to take some tea, but no food.[17] Princess Alice did her best to soothe her father by reading Scott's *The Talisman*—a tale of Richard the Lionheart and the Crusades. After taking a short walk with her daughters that afternoon, the Queen found Albert no better. He was lying on the bed, but 'seemed in a very uncomfortable panting state, and saying "I am so silly" which frightened us'. Albert's persistence in taking no food roused even the usually conciliatory

Dr Jenner, who told the Queen that the Prince *must* eat, 'and that he was going to tell him so'. Yes, it was tedious to have to eat when he felt so unwell, but 'completely starving himself, as he had done, would *not* do'.[18] For once Albert's self-administered starvation cure for his 'old enemy' was not working.

Albert was once more unsmiling and distant when Victoria went in to see him the following morning. It was deeply disturbing, for he seemed 'so unlike himself and he had sometimes such a strange, wild look' in his eyes, which she could not comprehend. After being persuaded to take some broth he slept for a while, and in the evening an ever-hopeful Victoria was encouraged that he seemed 'so dear and affectionate and so quite himself'. Earlier that day she had taken her youngest daughter Beatrice in to see him. 'He quite laughed at some of her new French verses which I made her repeat.' Then Albert lay there and 'held her little hand in his for some time' while a bewildered Beatrice stood gazing at him. But he refused to undress and get into bed when Dr Jenner again suggested it, eventually settling down to sleep in his dressing room, only to change rooms restlessly two or three times in the night.[19]

Victoria was awoken at one in the morning on 6 December, 'hearing coughing and moaning'. But Albert had at least taken some tea and broth during the night from Jenner, who had sat up with him by candlelight and once more reassured the Queen that 'there was nothing alarming'.[20] Thankfully, after Victoria had been out for a drive with one of her Ladies of the Bedchamber—the Duchess of Athole—Albert's mood lifted. Clark and Jenner were pleased, for the Prince had taken some broth

93

and eaten two rusks, though he had 'vehemently remonstrated against taking any arrowroot in his broth, saying: "it is so offensive, that thick stuff"'.[21]

There were as usual urgent letters for the Queen to write, keeping her family up to date on Albert's condition. Despite her worst anxieties she confidently assured Uncle Leopold in Belgium that 'this nasty, feverish sort of influenza and deranged stomach is *on* the mend, but it will be slow and tedious'. But she had to admit how greatly alarmed she had been by 'such restlessness, such sleeplessness, and such (till to-day) *total* refusal of all food that it made one *very, very* anxious'. For four nights in succession she had got 'only two or three hours' sleep'.[22] She told a similar story to Vicky in Berlin, complaining of how irritable Albert was; she and the doctors would not of course be taking this all so seriously, were it not for the fact that 'the dear invalid' was 'the most precious and perfect of human beings'. Thankfully 'Good Alice' had been a 'very great comfort' to her; day after day, the Princess had sat reading to Albert, without ever betraying her own fears or allowing her voice to falter.[23]

That day Sir Charles Phipps wrote to the Prime Minister, having taken it upon himself to keep Lord Palmerston abreast of developments. The Prince's illness 'required much management', he warned, in order to fend off both Albert's natural depression at being ill and the Queen's extreme nervousness about it. In effect, the royal physicians were having to deal with two patients: the sick prince and his overwrought wife. As it was, a third practitioner was now also paying regular visits—Dr Henry Brown, the Windsor apothecary who, Phipps assured

Palmerston, 'knows the Prince's constitution better than anybody'. But to call in any more doctors at this stage would do more harm than good, for 'the mere suggestion the other night upset the Queen and agitated her dreadfully'.[24]

On the morning of Saturday 7 December Victoria discovered that although Albert had had 'a good deal of sleep', he had again changed rooms several times during the night before returning to his original bed. Early that morning, as he had lain awake listening to the dawn chorus, he told her he had fancied himself back again in his beloved woods at the Rosenau; such thoughts were increasingly recurring as he sat in an armchair in his sitting room, 'looking weak and exhausted, and not better, complaining of there being no improvement, and he did not know what it could come from'. Victoria once more insisted that it was all the fault of overwork. For once Albert agreed with her. 'It is too much. You must speak to the Ministers,' he told her.[25] Later Dr Jenner came to see the Queen and told her that the doctors had 'all along been watching their patient's state' and that, from their physical examination, they now feared the Prince had a 'gastric or low fever'.[26]

The suggestion that Albert was suffering from some form of 'fever' was an ominous one, for in Victorian times fever and its various synonyms—'low fever', 'slow fever', 'gastric fever' and 'bowel fever'—were catch-alls for a whole range of complaints, of which typhoid fever was the most common and the most dreaded. The word typhoid—if that is what the doctors truly believed it to be at this stage, and it had puzzlingly taken the supposed specialist Jenner a long time to reach

95

this conclusion—was never uttered in front of the Queen. The case was '*quite* clear', Jenner told her. 'He knew exactly how to treat him,' he went on, 'that it was tedious and that the fever *must* have its course—viz—a month from the beginning, which he considers to have been from the day Albert went to Sandhurst—22nd—or possibly sooner'.[27] This nebulous statement was the closest the Queen ever came to being given a diagnosis; it would also give rise to 150 years of subsequent speculation that Albert had somehow picked up a typhoid germ that day at the military academy, or possibly back home at Windsor. Thus reassured by Jenner, all the Queen had to do was wait patiently for the fever to run its course (just like scarlet fever or measles) and all would be well. It was, however, not advisable for the younger children—Louise, Beatrice and Arthur—to go in to see their father, for fear of infection, though Alice was by now indispensable and showed no fear of any perceived risk. The Prince, of course, was not to know any of this because of his 'horror of fever'; it would only bring him down in his present state.[28]

Another memorandum was sent by Phipps to Palmerston, confirming that the Prince's illness 'is to-day declared to be a gastric fever'. But he insisted there were no symptoms that gave cause for anxiety. Confidentially, however, although the Queen was presently 'perfectly composed', Phipps again reiterated to Palmerston that it required 'no little management to prevent her from breaking down altogether. The least thing would alarm her to a degree that would unfit her for the discharge of any duties.' For this reason 'as cheerful a view as possible should be taken to her of the state of the Prince'.[29] But it was already proving a struggle for Victoria; she was by now exhausted, not just with her constant attendance in and out of Albert's room, but with the task of having to deal alone with all the unfinished official business in the dispatch boxes that were piling up.

Prince Albert spent the whole of the 7th in his dressing room lying on the sofa dozing, as his wife sat by him struggling to contain her emotions. 'What trials have we not had this year?' she wrote despairingly in her journal that day. 'What an *awful* trial this is—to be deprived for so long of my guide and my support and my all!' She felt as though she was living in a 'dreadful dream', and wept at the thought of what lay in store, of 'the utter shipwreck of our plans and the dreadful *loss* this long illness would be publicly as well as privately'.[30] Needing a close friend with whom to commiserate, she sent for Lady Augusta Bruce to come and stay, as Dr Jenner and Rudolf Löhlein settled in for another disrupted night watching over Albert.

The morning of 8 December gave rise to false hopes of the Prince's recovery. He seemed very weak, but was still walking about, and although extremely irritable and impatient, the doctors thought him 'going on well'. The Prince ate a little chicken and took some tea and wine during the day. Such minor improvements were sufficient to raise Victoria's hopes. When she returned from breakfast she found Albert lying on the bed in the King's Room, a small room used mainly by the royal family at Christmas time. It provided more air and light than the couple's bedroom and Albert specifically asked to be moved there. He seemed happy—'the sun shining brightly and the

97

room fine, large and gay; 'It is so fine,' he told her; he liked this room with its eastward view, out over the garden and the orangery, and, above, the blue sky and morning sunshine. For the first time since the onset of his illness Albert asked for some music: 'I should like to hear a fine chorale played at a distance,' he said. And so a piano was brought into the next room, where Alice played several of Albert's favourite pieces: Martin Luther's hymn 'Ein Feste Burg ist Unser Gott' and the Lutheran chorales 'Wachtet Auf' and 'Nun Danket Alle Gott'. The Luther hymn, a paraphrase of Psalm 46, which reassures the faithful that 'God is our refuge and strength/A very present help in trouble', seemed to offer great comfort to the sick man: 'he listened, looking upward with such a sweet expression,' the Queen noted, but then, soon wearied, he said in German, 'That is enough.'[31]

As it was Sunday, the royal family all headed off to service at St George's Chapel, leaving the Prince in the care of Princess Alice. The Reverend Charles Kingsley preached a 'beautiful' sermon, in the view of Lady Bruce, but the Queen professed she 'heard nothing', preoccupied as she was.[32] Alone with Alice, the Prince asked to have the sofa on which he was lying pulled closer to the oriel window 'that he might see the sky, and watch the clouds sailing past'. He once more asked her to play to him and lay there reflectively as Alice 'went thro' several of his favourite hymns and chorales', including another favourite, 'To Thee, O Lord, I yield my spirit', and 'Rock of ages, cleft for me'. When she turned from the piano to look, Albert seemed very still and serene with his eyes closed, his hands 'folded, as if in prayer'; her once-strong father was now as weak and helpless as a child. She thought he was asleep, but suddenly Albert looked up and smiled at her, and told her he had been having 'such sweet happy thoughts'.[33] Perhaps they were of the home in heaven that he had already contemplated at length in his reading of William Branks's book.

The fact that her father had chosen now to settle in the King's Room—the room in which both William IV and George IV before him had died—could not have escaped Alice (though the great state bed in which the kings had died had been moved out and replaced with two smaller ones). In such precious moments together during these final days, Albert often confided thoughts and feelings to his daughter that he would never dare share with his wife, for 'she could not bear to listen, and would not see the danger he felt, and only tried to argue him out of the idea'.[34] But, as Alice recognised that Sunday, her father was already resigned to dying and was preparing himself for it. It took all her strength of character and fortitude not to betray this knowledge to her mother, whilst drawing on her own emotional reserves for what now seemed inevitable. It was only when 'she felt she could bear it no longer' that she would 'walk quite calmly to the door', and then rush into her own room to weep. Shortly afterwards she would return, 'with her deadly white face, as fixed and calm as ever, with no trace whatever of what she had gone through'.[35] But in a long letter she wrote to Louis that day, Alice admitted how 'terribly difficult' the last week had been and how unbearable it was to see 'a strong, hard man like Papa . . . lying weak and helpless like a child' and listen to his pathetic groaning.[36]

After lunch on the 8th the Queen thought the Prince looked 'less ill than we expected' and took the Prince of Leiningen in to see him. Albert was by now drifting in and out of an almost constant doze. The doctors and his valets continued to fuss round him, especially the admirable Löhlein, but Albert's weakening state was occasionally broken by moments of irritability. At one point, much to Victoria's dismay, he became so impatient 'because I tried to help in explaining something to Dr Jenner and quite slapped my hand, poor dear darling'.[37] At other more lucid times his old affection resurfaced. 'When I went to him after dinner,' Victoria recalled, 'he was so pleased to see me, stroked my face and smiled, and called me "dear little wife"'. She had spent the afternoon reading Scott's *Peveril of the Peak* and the *Memoirs* of the Prussian diplomat Varnhagen von Ense to the Prince. His tenderness later that evening, 'when he held my hand and stroked my face, touched me so much, and made me so grateful,' she recorded in her journal.[38] But Albert's occasional gentle and familiar commendations in German of Victoria as his *gutes Weibchen* and his *liebes Frauchen* were the only comfort now remaining to her.

The following morning—Monday 9 December— the British public was informed in the Court Circular of *The Times* that the Prince Consort had been confined to his apartments for the last week, 'suffering from a feverish cold, with pains in the limbs'. 'Within the last two days the feverish symptoms have rather increased, and are likely to continue for some time longer.' 'But,' the bulletin added by way of reassurance, 'there are

100

no unfavourable symptoms.'[39] Such was not the prevailing view inside Windsor Castle. In light of the Prince's continuing poor condition, Phipps and the royal doctors were grappling with the problem of how to call in additional medical advice without undermining the Prince's morale. The men they had in mind were the socialite doctor Sir Henry Holland, who had been one of the Prince's Physicians-in-Ordinary since 1840 (and because of his status could not be 'passed over'), and Dr Thomas Watson, Physician Extraordinary to the Queen since 1859. Victoria had immediately started fretting about how this might affect her dear Albert, 'and fear I distressed both Sir James and Dr Jenner'.[40] But she was persuaded to agree, on the grounds that it was 'necessary to satisfy the public to have another eminent doctor to come and see him'.[41] When Holland arrived he was confronted with a desperate Queen: 'Oh, you will save him for me, Dr Holland? You will save him for me, will you not?'; while Watson's visit was rather more subdued. It 'went off quite well', Victoria later reported. Albert had found him a 'quiet, sensible man', but had thought it 'quite absurd' that Clark had wanted to send for Holland too.[42]

Watson, who was in the first rank of his profession after a long and distinguished medical career from 1825 and a period as chair of the Principles and Practice of Medicine at King's College, University of London, took a much more serious line than Clark and Jenner. Phipps was soon writing to Palmerston to say that Dr Watson considered Prince Albert to be *very ill*. 'The malady is very grave and serious in itself,' he had told Phipps, without enlightening him as to what exactly it was. The doctors were clearly still in the dark and hedging their bets: 'the symptoms exhibited were such as might precede the more distinct characterisation of gastric or bowel fever,' Phipps went on. 'The Prince's present weakness is very great,' Watson had told him, and 'it is impossible not to be very anxious'.[43] One ominous difference had now been noted: Prince Albert had finally stopped wandering around in his dressing gown and had undressed and taken to his bed— although during the day he was transferred to a couch in the Red Room beyond.

Albert passed a reasonable night and on the morning of the 10th his pulse was good. Victoria was therefore annoyed to hear that Lord Palmerston, having been alarmed by the news from Phipps, was nevertheless insisting that Dr Watson should remain on call at the castle and was pressurising Clark to call in more specialists. The Prime Minister did not mince his words: the Prince's fate was a 'matter of the most momentous national importance, and all considerations of personal feeling and susceptibilities must absolutely give way to the public interest'.[44] Other ministers were doing likewise, writing to Phipps in deepest anxiety. Sir George Lewis recommended they consult 'Dr Tweedie, an old longbearded Scotchman', who was founder and consulting physician to the London Fever Hospital in Islington; others, like the Duke of Newcastle, worried that the Queen might have become infected from her close contact with the Prince.[45] Many now realised with escalating alarm, as did Lord Granville, leader of the Liberal Party, 'how invaluable' the Prince's life was.[46]

The Queen was, of course, oblivious to the backstage political drama that was unfolding. Later that day she went in to see Albert and 'found him wandering with the oddest fancies and suspicions', but the doctors reassured her that this was 'nothing' and quite common in such cases. Doctors Watson and Jenner in fact announced that they were both impressed with the Prince's progress over the last twenty-four hours, considering it to be 'a positive gain'.[47] Comforting herself with these small signs of progress, the Queen wrote to Vicky:

Thank God! Beloved Papa had another excellent night and is going on quite satisfactorily. There is a decided gain since yesterday and several most satisfactory symptoms. He is now in bed—and only moves on the sofa made like a bed, for some hours. He takes a great deal of nourishment—and is really very patient.[48]

Sir James Clark, meanwhile, had been called away to his own sick wife at their home at Bagshot Park, but returned as often as possible, sleeping at Windsor every other night. But there was always Alice, as well as Löhlein—'most attentive and devoted and indefatigable'—and Albert's valet, Gustav Mayet, who 'also does his best'.[49]

Victoria was able to thank and bless God for 'another reasonably good night' when she awoke on the 11th. She found her husband sitting up in bed taking his beef tea, 'which he always laments most bitterly over'. But 'his beautiful face, more beautiful than ever' had 'grown *so* thin'. A brief moment of tenderness, during which Albert lay for a while with his head on her shoulder, made her very happy. 'It

103

is very comfortable so, dear Child,' he whispered to her and her eyes filled with tears.[50] Later, when he was being wheeled along the passage to the King's Room, he had turned to 'the beautiful picture of the Madonna' that he had given Victoria as a present three years previously, 'and asked to stop and look at it, ever loving what is beautiful'. To look on such things, he told his wife, 'helps me through half the day'.[51]

A reassuring letter had arrived that morning from Uncle Leopold: Albert's illness was just another of those regular and long-familiar indispositions that he often suffered at this time of the year. Victoria should not interrupt her 'usual airings' and must be sure to take a turn outside, for to be deprived of this 'would do you harm'. In reply Victoria was happy to tell Leopold that Albert had had another good night with no worsening symptoms. It was as much as they dared hope for: '*not* losing ground is a *gain, now* of *every* day'.[52] The doctors, however, continued to be highly circumspect in what they told her, which was always hedged around with elaborately contrived positives. The symptoms were still not unfavourable, in their view, but Victoria was apprehensive. Albert now looked 'so totally unlike himself', she told Vicky; again that day he 'was very wandering at times'.[53] She sat with him that afternoon and evening, reading to him and holding his hand, and, at his request, sharing a prayer together. Albert's irritability had at last receded and he seemed anxious for Victoria to stay close by. She returned to her husband's bedside after dinner and he sent for her again later, her hungry heart filling with joy: 'I flew over, so happy that he wished to see me.'

Reluctantly she left him to rest, on Dr Brown's advice, but it was hard: 'God knows how happy I was to stay!'[54]

That evening an ominous change in the Prince was noted by Sir James Clark, who 'listened anxiously to his breathing, at his back'. But once again the Queen was fobbed off; when she asked Clark what this signified he 'said it was nothing, only a slight wheezing; of no consequence whatever'. So once more she went to her bed reassured that there was nothing to worry about, 'tho' sad to be so far' from her beloved Albert.[55] Clark was right to be worried: the wheezing suggested the onset of that dreaded complication: congestion of the lungs, or pneumonia as it is more commonly known today. Albert himself, in a lucid moment earlier that day, had recognised the danger. Princess Alice had been sitting with him at the time, when he had asked if the Queen was in the room. When Alice said no, he had told her that he knew he was dying. He wanted her to write immediately and tell Vicky in Berlin. Alice did so and when she returned he asked her what she had said in her letter. '"I have told my sister," she answered, "that you are very ill." "You have done wrong," he said to her; "You should have told her I am dying, yes I am dying."'[56]

Although Princess Alice and Albert had no illusions about his condition, the other members of the royal household were still clearly caught between a compulsion to deny what their eyes told them and confusion about the official diagnosis. Lady Ely, for example, that day told the Earl of Malmesbury that the Prince's illness was 'gastric fever and inflammation, of the mucous membrane of the stomach'.[57] Lord Palmerston, however, was now insisting to Phipps that the nation should be prepared for worse news to come—otherwise it would be 'thunderstruck and indignant' at having been kept in the dark.[58] The royal doctors were obliged to agree; the Prince's illness now presaged a national crisis. But how to convince the Queen of the danger? It was Princess Alice who took it upon herself to try and make her mother face up to reality: 'I will tell her,' she had said, and during a carriage ride that morning she had done her best, as gently as she could, to convince her mother that Albert could not recover.[59] That evening, a carefully worded bulletin was prepared: 'His Royal Highness is suffering from fever, hitherto unattended by unfavourable symptoms, but likely from its nature to continue for some time.'[60] It was signed by the four physicians: Clark, Holland, Watson and Jenner. But when the Queen asked to see it prior to it being sent out, she struck out the crucial word 'hitherto', refusing to accept even the remotest possibility of danger.[61]

Prince Albert's quickness of breath alarmed Dr Jenner the following morning, but like Clark he told the Queen there was no consequence to it, provided it did not increase. When the Prince took some broth and wine, the Queen noticed his hands were shaking; again Jenner told her not to worry; it was 'merely fever'. The Prince remained compliant and did what the doctors told him, though from time to time he seemed confused: this was yet another symptom of the fever, the doctors told her. It would work its way through Albert's system over the usual four-week course predicted in such cases. Taking them literally, Victoria recorded her false hopes in her journal: 'We rejoiced so to think tomorrow would be the 22nd day, and that in another week please God! he would be getting over it.' In anticipation of this, she 'talked with Dr Jenner of the happy convalescence, tho' always with trembling'.[62] Then she sat down and wrote a reassuring letter to Uncle Leopold stating that her husband 'maintains his ground well . . . takes plenty of nourishment, and shows surprising strength'. She was fulsome in her praise of the 'skill, attention, and devotion of Dr Jenner'. He was, after all, 'the *first fever* Doctor in Europe' and must know what he was doing.[63]

Lord Palmerston, however, remained far from impressed with the royal doctors and their persistent underrepresentation of the true seriousness of Prince Albert's condition and sent three letters to Windsor that day asking for news. Palmerston had no illusions that the Prince's illness was of a 'formidable character'. Aware that it was 'liable to take a sudden and unfavourable turn from day to day', he hoped therefore that Dr Watson, a man whose reputation he clearly respected, would stay in constant attendance at Windsor to monitor the Prince's condition, and that he 'would be allowed to have his own way as to treatment'.[64] He had no faith in Dr Clark, who in his view 'had already incurred a heavy responsibility by delaying so long to call in additional advice'. Clark had a great deal to answer for, in Palmerston's book, for not at once informing him of the graveness of the Prince's condition, 'instead of leaving me to find out by my own conclusions that it was of a much more serious nature than was represented to me by him' at Windsor the previous week. When later that day Phipps revealed the now worrying development of the Prince's impaired breathing and increasing listlessness, Palmerston was shocked. 'Your telegram and letter have come upon me like a thunderbolt,' he responded. The implications were 'too awful to contemplate'. 'One can only hope that Providence may yet spare us so overwhelming a calamity.'[65]

Refusing to contemplate the worst, the Queen was still clutching at straws that evening. The doctors were doing all they could to control Albert's rapid rate of breathing; 'another 24 or still more 48 hours without further increase of it would make one feel quite safe'.[66] But things were no better the following morning, Friday 13th. The Queen went in to see Albert in her dressing gown at 8 a.m. and noted that even the stoical Jenner 'was anxious and tired'. After a carriage drive with Lady Bruce, she returned at midday and 'found the breathing *very quick* which made me dreadfully anxious and nervous'.[67] The Prince was lying listlessly on his couch in the sitting room, only this time he had not even looked at his favourite painting of the Madonna and child as he passed it. He seemed now able only to recognise Carl Ruland, his German librarian, who came and read to him. For the most part he lay there with his hands clasped and with blank eyes gazing towards the open window, taking no notice of his surroundings and slipping in and out of consciousness, though Victoria was gratified that he did at one point take hold of her hand, calling her his *gutes Frauchen* and kissing her with affection.

At about four-thirty that afternoon, while the Queen was taking a short walk on the terrace, Dr

Jenner hurried in to Lady Bruce, telling her that 'such sinking had come on that he had feared the Prince would die in his arms'.[68] She must hurry to find the Queen and prepare her for the worst. In accordance with standard Victorian medical practice, Albert was now being dosed with brandy every half-hour in an attempt to raise his pulse.[69] By the time Victoria returned she found her husband very still and quiet. When Dr Clark arrived from attending his wife, he too was 'much perturbed' by what he saw. There could be no more prevarication: the Queen must be prepared, otherwise the shock would be too terrible.[70] Augusta Bruce and one of the children's governesses, Miss Hildyard, did their best to offer comfort to an increasingly distraught Victoria, who was now weeping in fear and dread of the worst. 'The country; oh, the country,' she kept repeating. 'I could perhaps bear my own misery, but the poor country.'[71] 'I prayed and cried as if I should go mad,' Victoria later wrote of that day. '*Oh!* That I was not then and there crazed!' Desperation was now setting in: 'My Husband won't die.' No, he could not die, he must not die, she would not accept it: 'for that would kill me'.[72]

That evening the Prince's pulse improved and he appeared to have rallied; Victoria sat in a chair at the foot of his bed with Alice at her side, sitting on the floor; Lady Bruce and Marie of Leiningen were close at hand in the next room. Albert 'was nice and warm and the skin soft', the Queen recalled. Dr Watson was gently reassuring: he had seen many infinitely worse cases recover. 'I never despair with fever,' he added—after all, as Lady Bruce observed, hundreds of people had survived 'under far more aggravated forms'.[73] But clearly the crisis had come:

it was 'a struggle of strength', the doctors told the Queen. Clark was again superficially hopeful, but the time had come, in the most roundabout way possible, to persuade the Queen that 'they must give a rather unfavourable Bulletin, which could be improved of course if our Treasure went on well'.[74] Phipps too was preparing Lord Palmerston: 'the Prince's disease has taken a very unfavourable turn,' he informed him, 'the Doctors are in the *greatest anxiety*—they have even fears for the night.' Shortly afterwards an urgent telegram followed: 'I grieve to say the Prince is much worse.'[75]

*     *     *

Over at his home at Ascot, where he was dining alone that evening, John Delane, editor of *The Times*, received a note from Lady Palmerston requesting him to come immediately to see the Prime Minister at his London home, Cambridge House on Piccadilly. 'I was both tired and sleepy but thought it right to go,' he recalled, 'and it was well I did.' Palmerston was in deep distress at the latest news from Windsor; the royal doctors were warning that Prince Albert was not expected to survive the night. Soon afterwards the Duke of Cambridge arrived with a 'despairing letter from the Queen'. 'I never saw such a party of ghosts as the few who had remained looked at the news,' Delane later told John Walter, the newspaper's proprietor. The truth, as Palmerston saw it with brutal honesty, was that at this present moment of political crisis over the *Trent* affair, 'the Queen would be a less national loss' than the Prince.[76]

Only the previous night, Thursday 12 December,

3,000 people had attended a Great Prayer Meeting of all Christian denominations at Exeter Hall in London, called by the Evangelical Alliance. But the prayers they had so fervently recited had not been for the Prince Consort, but for 'Almighty God to avert from us the calamity of war with the United States'.[77] With the political crisis still unresolved, and a wait of at least a fortnight expected before a response to Lord Russell's dispatch would arrive from America, two great iron-clad steamships, the *Persia* and the *Australasia* were preparing to sail from Liverpool loaded with field batteries and more than 2,000 troops for Canada. In the face of the very real and present danger of war, there seemed little, in comparison, to worry about with regard to the Prince Consort. The papers had made little of his illness so far. Although the Prince's name had been omitted from the Court Circular for several days, his pack of harriers had gone out hunting as usual on the Friday, with no one at the meet suspecting the worst, though his absence had been lamented at the Smithfield Club Cattle Show (where as usual his steers were picking up prizes). A few papers had, however, noted the cancellation of a shooting party planned for Windsor, and that 'in consequence of the prince's indisposition' the removal of the court to Osborne for Christmas planned for the following Friday, the 20th, had been 'deferred for the present'.[78]

If there was one other person in the country who perhaps understood the Prince's national significance at that moment it was Florence Nightingale. Commenting on his illness in a letter that she wrote on the 13th to her friend Mary Clarke Mohl from her home on South Street in

111

Mayfair, she recalled that the Prince had 'neither liked nor was liked. But what he has done for our country no one knows.' As for the Queen, Nightingale went on, she had 'really behaved like a hero. Has buckled to business at once. After all, it is a great thing to be a Queen. She is the only woman in these realms, except perhaps myself, who has a *must* in her life—who must set aside private griefs and attend to the res publica.'[79] Events were soon, however, to prove Nightingale entirely wrong in this regard.

At 5 p.m. on the evening of the 13th a subtle but significant change had come in the wording of the bulletin issued by the royal doctors for publication the following morning. 'His Royal Highness the Prince Consort passed a restless night', the public were to be told; 'the symptoms have assumed an unfavourable character during the day'.[80] It was only now that many members of the royal household, such as Prince Arthur's governor, Howard Elphinstone, began to realise how desperate the situation had become. Elphinstone first heard the grave news from one of the Prince's equerries, Charles Du Plat, and received further confirmation from Carl Ruland.[81]

It was at this point that Princess Alice made an important decision. All her gentle hints to her mother that she should prepare herself for the worst had gone unheeded. Nor had Victoria—in her total absorption in her own anxiety—given any thought to Bertie away at university in Cambridge, who had no inkling of how gravely ill his father was. The Prince of Wales should be recalled, the Queen was urged. But she refused; her husband's anguish at Bertie's recent bad behaviour was, she

112

remained convinced, still at the root of his present illness. Without her mother's knowledge, therefore, Princess Alice sent a brief telegram to Bertie that night informing him that Papa was 'not so well. Better come at once'. The telegram arrived while the Prince of Wales was hosting a farewell dinner party for Cambridge dignitaries prior to leaving for the Christmas vacation. Two hours later he boarded a special train out of Cambridge. It was 3 a.m. when he finally arrived at a silent and watchful Windsor.[82]

## CHAPTER FIVE

# *'Day Turned into Night'*

With Christmas only a fortnight away, George Augustus Sala, an ambitious young leader-writer on the *Daily Telegraph* who had already shown a talent for florid obituary-writing, was looking forward to the festive season at his lodgings at Upton Court in Slough, a few miles from Windsor. 'A yule log had been ordered; there was to be snap-dragon in the Hall, the "mummers" . . . were to come over from Slough and sing carols on Christmas Eve; and the cook had made at least a dozen plum puddings and a whole army of mince pies,' he remembered with relish. At the time Sala had been turning in two 1,500-word leaders a day for the *Telegraph* with Saturdays off, but this weekend, with friends visiting, he arranged not to go into his London office on Sunday and Monday, in order to enjoy it at home—'providing always,' he added, 'that something which the whole English nation was dreading, did not happen.'[1] For by the morning of 14 December 1861 the press knew that 'the wise and good Prince Consort' was lying desperately ill at Windsor Castle.

That day, according to the *North Wales Chronicle*, there were but three principal topics of conversation in London: 'the probability of war with America, the health of the Prince Consort, and the Smithfield Cattle Club Show'. An air of anxiety was clearly gathering with regard to how 'even the temporary loss' of the Prince Consort's services was 'a misfortune for the country'.[2] The *Birmingham Daily Post* spoke of 'much uneasiness' as to his health and the *Glasgow Herald* noted that his condition 'has not improved, and the symptoms of fever are not diminished'. What is more, 'owing to the number of inquiries at Buckingham Palace on Friday, including the French Ambassador, a bulletin will be issued there on Saturday, and a visitors' book opened'.[3] In an attempt to defuse public alarm, *The Times* hoped that 'it will be in our power shortly to announce an improvement in the state of the Royal patient'. It went on to observe that for more than twenty years now the Prince had 'been the guide and protector of the Queen, to a degree that is rarely found even in ordinary life, when the husband is both in law and in reality the guardian of the wife'; it was clear from these words that editor John Delane was preparing for the worst. Nor could public alarm be tempered by the assurances that followed that the disease would no doubt yield to the skill of the Prince's eminent physicians, or the erroneous assumption that he had on his side 'youth and strength and an unimpaired constitution'.[4] There was no denying the shock the

114

country would sustain when the news of the Prince Consort's rapid decline became widely known. Having driven to Windsor that morning and spoken to several members of the royal household, Delane was back at his offices in Printing House Square, Blackfriars, already fine-tuning the obituary for Prince Albert that he had prepared when he had first heard of his illness.[5]

Much to the surprise of the royal doctors, the Prince had in fact been able to get a better night's rest on the 13th; the Queen was brought encouraging bulletins on his progress at regular intervals during the night and, when she awoke at 5.30 a.m. that Saturday, she was greeted by Dr Brown with further good news: the Prince appeared to have rallied. 'I think he is better than he has been yet; I think there is ground to hope the crisis is over,' he told her.[6] Such was Albert's all-too-brief rally that he even 'got up & walked across the room for a purpose of nature'. Phipps dared to send word to Palmerston by telegraph: 'We are allowed again *a hope*.'[7]

At 7 a.m. the Queen went in to see her husband. 'It was a bright morning, the sun just rising and shining brightly,' she recalled. But despite what Brown had told her, there was an ominous atmosphere about the room. It had 'the sad look of night watching, the candles burnt down to their sockets—the doctors looking anxious'. That morning Albert had about him a strangely calm and beatific air: 'Never can I forget how beautiful my Darling looked lying there with his face lit up by the rising sun, his eyes unusually bright, gazing as it were on unseen objects, and not taking notice of me.'[8] It was the calm of resignation to imminent

115

death that lit up Albert's face, but Victoria would not—could not—see it. For her, Albert's tranquillity indicated hope of recovery and, much to the consternation of the royal household, she began talking as though the danger was over, hastening to telegraph the 'good' news to Vicky in Berlin. Others in the family, confused by the Queen's false optimism, 'began writing to everyone as if it were a trifling illness'.[9]

Bertie was now at his father's bedside and lucky to be one of the few he briefly recognised. At around midday the Queen asked the doctors if she might go outside for a short while to take the air. 'Yes, just close by, for half an hour,' was their response. Accompanied by Alice, she took a turn on the East Terrace, but leaving her sick husband even for a short while was more than she could bear: 'The military band was playing at a distance, and I burst out crying and came home again—my anxiety and distress were so great.'[10] Hurrying back to Albert's bedside, Victoria asked if the Prince was any better. 'We are very much frightened,' Dr Watson said to her as gently as he could, 'but don't and won't give up hope.'[11]

Princess Alice, however, knew that despite the fleeting and hopeful indications to the contrary, the turning point had come. Bertie wrote a note to Louis on her behalf: their father was 'fighting for his life. In 24 hours we will know for sure—almighty God hear our prayers.'[12] As the afternoon went on, hopes once more began to fade: the Prince's pulse dropped and his breathing became raspy and rapid as the congestion overwhelmed his lungs. By five-thirty he was perspiring heavily. The only recourse the doctors had was dosing him yet again with spoonfuls of brandy at regular intervals. 'The pulse keeps up,' they told the Queen. The Prince was not getting worse; Sir James was 'very hopeful, he had seen much worse cases'. But even Victoria could not ignore Albert's laboured breathing: 'the alarming thing—*so* rapid, I think 60 respirations in a minute, tho the brandy always made it slower when taken'. His hands felt cold and there was 'what they call a dusky hue about his dear face and hands which I knew was not good'. It was the onset of cyanosis—a loss of oxygen levels in the blood—indicating that the Prince's lungs were failing rapidly. Dr Jenner had noticed it too and could not explain it away to the Queen. Prince Albert was slipping in and out of delirium, his ramblings largely incoherent, except for the often-repeated name—of his son Bertie. He began fretfully folding his arms and then 'arranging his hair just as he used to do when well and he was dressing'. 'These were said to be bad signs,' Victoria later recalled. Anxious and bewildered, she dared not admit to herself what all this meant, but with hindsight, it was as though her husband was 'preparing for another and a greater journey'.[13]

Princess Alice was in unflagging attendance at her father's sick-bed—despite the doctors wishing to spare her the distress of it—assisted by Marie of Leiningen and Lady Bruce, who were constantly in and out of the room. Miss Hildyard also hovered solicitously, offering support to the Queen.[14] And Phipps was there too, promising to help in every way that he could though his hands shook, for he found it hard to control his own deep anxiety. Victoria would not give up, constantly soliciting Jenner for signs of improvement. Was there any hope, she kept asking him? 'Humanly speaking, it is not impossible,' he told her. There was nothing to prevent the Prince 'getting over it', and yet it seemed to Victoria now 'as though that precious Life, *the most* precious there was, was ebbing away!'[15]

*     *     *

As Saturday 14 December unravelled, it was for many an agonising time—'a horrible day of suspense waiting for further intelligences which still never came', with everyone in the royal entourage 'now hoping for the best, now again despondently fearing the worst'.[16] That morning, writing one of his regular letters to his friend and confidante the Duchess of Manchester, the Earl of Clarendon had no doubt that 'a national calamity may be close at hand'. It was not just a matter of the unique and extraordinary role that the Prince performed in ensuring the Queen's fulfilment of her public duties; it was the untold impact that his absence would have on her. 'The habit or rather necessity, together with her intense love for him, which has increased rather than become weaker with years, has so engrafted her on him that to lose him,' Clarendon warned prophetically, 'will be like parting with her heart and soul.'[17]

Phipps, meanwhile, was sending regular updates to Palmerston, lamenting that 'Alas! The hopes of the morning are fading away.' The third edition of that day's *Times* had unfortunately come out announcing the news issued by the royal doctors at 9 a.m. that there had been 'some mitigation' of the severity of the symptoms overnight.[18]

It was therefore deemed necessary to send a further bulletin, admitting that since morning the Prince had lapsed into a 'very critical state'. Not surprisingly, with the time delay in updates on the Prince's condition being published, there was a considerable degree of public confusion as to how serious things really were. The editor of the *Medical Times and Gazette*, for one, had decided that it was time for an end to prevarication. The nature of the Prince's illness, he wrote that morning, was 'pretty clear to the medical profession'. But euphemism still prevailed in the journal's commendation of Dr Jenner's integrity. It was an advantage, it said, that the Prince was in Jenner's care:

> for there is no living physician who has enjoyed a larger experience of fever in general, or to whom the profession are so much indebted for their present knowledge of its various forms, and especially of the characters which distinguish the precise form of fever under which the prince is now suffering from the dreaded typhus.[19]

But the fact was that Jenner had throughout seemed uncertain of his diagnosis and had been reluctant to admit to it.

Over in Berlin, Vicky, who was only just recovering from a bout of flu, had been extremely alarmed by the contradictory telegrams received from Windsor over the previous couple of days. Privately, Phipps had telegraphed her husband Fritz on the 13th advising him to prepare his wife for the worst, and then early the following morning they had received news of an improvement. Writing to her mother, Vicky expressed her bewilderment:

119

'The news I had been receiving every day were so reassuring and cheerful that I thought all was now going on perfectly well.' She wished she could be with her mother to 'try to comfort you and be of use', but because she was now in the early stages of her third pregnancy her doctors had refused to allow her to travel.[20]

In Windsor at least word was out: on Saturday afternoon a special service was held at St John's parish church to offer prayers for the Prince's recovery, and its congregation was large despite the short notice. The royal doctors could no longer prevaricate: at 4.30 p.m. a bulletin was issued informing the nation that the Prince was in a 'most critical state'.[21] Lady Biddulph (wife of the Master of the Queen's Household), who had been in attendance in Prince Albert's sick-room, slipped out to send the 'very, very bad news' to Earl Spencer—senior Lord of the Bedchamber and titular head of the royal household. The Prince was sinking fast, and 'the doctors say there is no hope not the slightest of His Royal Highness's life being spared,' she wrote, though 'None may say how long it may go on.'[22]

With the inner sanctum of the royal household gathering anxiously, at around 5.30 p.m. Prince Albert's bed was wheeled away from the window into the centre of the King's Room, as though to accommodate the watchers for the royal deathbed to come. The Queen, who had been resting in another room, came in and took up her place by Albert's bed:

*Gutes Frauchen*, he said, and kissed me, and then gave a sort of piteous moan, or rather sigh,

120

not of pain, but as if he felt that he was leaving me, and laid his head on my shoulder and I put my arm under his. But the feeling passed away again, and he seemed to wander and to doze, and yet to know all.[23]

She could not catch what Albert said in his delirium; occasionally words came in French, but more often it was the words of Christian comfort that meant so much to him—'Rock of ages, cleft for me'.[24] And yet, extraordinarily, when at around half-past seven that evening the doctors found it necessary to move the Prince to the other, cleanly made-up bed, in a moment of uncanny clarity, Albert insisted on rising from his bed unassisted, though he had to be helped back into it again by Löhlein and one of the pages.[25]

Ever since the previous evening, when he had heard of the Prince of Wales's recall to Windsor, Prince Arthur's governor, Howard Elphinstone, had 'felt some presentiment' of what was to come, but had done his best all day to keep the ten-year-old boy away from the gloomy atmosphere in the castle. But at about 8 p.m. that evening word was sent to Elphinstone to bring Prince Arthur down to the King's Room, where all the younger children were now gathering to say farewell to their father.[26] First Alice came, knelt and kissed her father, and he took her hand. The Queen asked if he wanted to see Bertie, who next approached the bedside, followed by the fifteen-year-old Helena, Louise aged thirteen, and then Arthur. 'One after the other the children came and took their father's hand but he did not really see or know them'—nor did he realise that three of them were absent: Affie away on naval manoeuvres in Mexico, Leopold recuperating in Cannes, and his beloved firstborn, Vicky, trapped in her gloomy palace in Berlin. Four-year-old Beatrice had been kept from her father for many days for fear of infection; Arthur had not seen him for some time either and was visibly shaken by the terrible change that had come upon him. Sobbing inconsolably, he 'lifted his father's hand to his lips and kissed it', but Albert did not seem to know him.[27] As Arthur was led away, Albert momentarily 'opened his dear eyes and asked for Sir Ch[arles] Phipps, who came in and kissed his hand, but then again his dear eyes were closed'. And he did not recognise Grey and Biddulph when they followed, or see how overcome they were. This leave-taking was, the Queen later recalled, 'a *terrible* moment, but, thank God! I was able to command myself and to be *perfectly* calm, and remained sitting by his side'. 'So it went on, *not* really worse but not better', she recalled of that terrible evening as she sat listening to her dying husband struggle for his breath, although she was not able to recall any of it in any coherent detail until more than ten years later. Dr Jenner now admitted to her that 'with such breathing it was of no avail'.[28]

After seeing Prince Arthur back to his room and to bed, Howard Elphinstone joined the other members of the royal household who were gathering in disconsolate groups in the guttering candlelight of the Grand Corridor. It was a place that was usually the scene of animated conversation among them, either before or after dinner, but which now 'presented a very dim aspect'. 'A few gloomy faces, fearing the worst, were patiently sitting, and anxiously waiting each doctor's face as they came from the Prince's room,' he recalled. But each report was different; 'hope and despair were alternately dealt out, that no one could form an idea of the truth'.[29]

Princess Alice spent the evening kneeling at Albert's bedside 'with his burning hand in mine', she later told Louis. 'I said to myself as I listened to that painful, difficult breathing, "Perhaps God will take him, and then we shall be parted from the dearest thing we have on earth—it cannot be." I expected that he would leave us, but I could not take it in.'[30] Lady Augusta Bruce had been deeply moved by Alice's conduct throughout these difficult days, dealing not just with her sick father and her anxious mother, but also with the stream of relatives who arrived at Windsor asking for news. She was, thought Bruce, quite 'wonderful'. The desperate situation had compelled the Princess, still so young herself, to 'suddenly put away childish things and to be a different creature'.[31]

As another telegram was sent to the city at 9 p.m., announcing that the Prince Consort's condition was desperate, the British public at large prepared for their beds, reassured by the third edition of the day's papers and unaware that the Prince lay dying at Windsor. 'I made up my mind that a favourable turn had been taken,' wrote Charles Pugh, a clerk in the Court of Chancery, in his diary. Like many others he was convinced 'that a sound constitution, temperate habits, and strength of manhood of the Prince would bring him through' and, with the rest of the nation, he went to bed in hopes of better news in the morning.[32]

In the King's Room at Windsor the Queen longed desperately for some sign of recognition from her husband. She leant forward and tenderly whispered in Albert's ear: *'Es ist kleines Frauchen'*—It is your little wife—and asked for *ein Kuss*, but he could barely raise his head from the pillow to do so. 'He seemed half dozing, quite calm and only wishing to be left quiet and undisturbed.'[33] And so she retired to the anteroom for a while, where she sank to the floor exhausted, her hair awry and her face buried in her hands. The Dean of Windsor, who was standing close by, spoke to her gently: 'she had a great trial to undergo and [I] prayed her to nerve herself for it'; she had governed the country once without him and she would do so again. But 'Why?' she asked him plaintively, 'Why must I suffer this? My mother? What was *that*? I thought that was grief. But that was *nothing* to this.' She and Albert were one, she sobbed; 'it is like tearing the flesh from my bones'.[34]

Within half an hour a rapid change had set in; Prince Albert was now bathed in sweat as the fever of pneumonia took hold. The only sound in the King's Room was the dying Prince's increasing struggle for breath. Alice recognised it immediately: 'That is the death rattle,' she whispered to Augusta Bruce and went to get her mother. Victoria had herself heard Albert's heavy breathing from the adjacent room. 'I'm afraid this takes away all our hope,' Alice told her.[35] Upon which, Victoria 'started up like a Lioness rushed by every one, and bounded on the bed imploring him to speak and to give one kiss to his little wife'.[36] Prince Albert opened his eyes; he seemed to know her, but was too weak to raise his head from the pillow. Even now the doctors were still, fruitlessly, trying to dose him with stimulants, this time on a sponge:

but 'he had cried out and resisted the brandy so much that they did not give it any more'. Utterly distraught, Victoria kissed Albert passionately and clung to him. His breathing became 'quite gentle'. 'Oh, this is death,' she cried out in a final agony of recognition, taking his left hand, which already felt quite cold. 'I know it. I have seen this before,' she sobbed as she knelt by his side.[37]

Outside in the Grand Corridor Elphinstone and the others, who had all been too fearful to go to bed, were still huddled anxiously when they saw a pale and drawn Dean of Windsor hurrying toward the King's Room. They knew what this signified: he had been summoned to read the prayers for the dying. Inside, Alice was kneeling on one side of the bed, with General Bruce beside her opposite her mother, and Bertie and Helena kneeling at its foot, and the Prince of Leiningen and Löhlein standing not far behind them. Beyond stood the four royal doctors—Clarke, Jenner, Holland and Watson—Sir Charles Phipps, and the Prince's closest equerries: General Bentinck, Lord Alfred Paget, Major Du Plat, Colonel Seymour and General Grey.[38] Lady Augusta Bruce and Miss Hildyard looked on from the doorway of the adjoining anteroom.

A terrible stillness had descended, broken only by the great clock in the Curfew Tower at the western end of Windsor Castle striking the third quarter after ten. It was hardly possible to say exactly when the moment came, but a few minutes later, as the Queen recalled, 'Two or three long but perfectly gentle breaths were drawn, the hand clasping mine, and . . . *all, all* was over—the heavenly Spirit fled to the World it was fit for, and free from the sorrows and trials of this World!'

Victoria threw her arms around Albert's body, covering it with fervent kisses and calling out 'in a bitter and agonizing cry "Oh! My dear Darling!"', and 'he can't be gone, he can't be gone', before dropping to her knees 'in mute, distracted despair, unable to utter a word or shed a tear!'[39] Some would later recall a far more chilling, visceral sound—one, unforgettable 'piercing shriek', that had echoed out into the Grand Corridor and beyond.[40]

For some minutes the Queen would not be torn away from Albert's corpse, until Dr Jenner said firmly to her: 'Queen, this is but the casket, you must look beyond', after which the Prince of Leiningen and Charles Phipps raised her from her knees and led her, sobbing and with such a look of despair on her face, to the anteroom, where she lay down on the sofa, with Alice cradling her head.[41] One by one the gentlemen of the royal household came in and knelt down and kissed her hand, Lord Alfred Paget weeping out loud. Alice, with her uncanny composure, managed to hold herself together as Bertie came and threw himself in his mother's arms, vowing, 'I will be all I can to you.' 'I'm sure my dear boy you will,' Victoria replied with composure, as she held him and kissed him.[42] But when Howard Elphinstone approached hesitantly to offer his condolences, she reached out and clutched at his hand 'with a violent effort', beseeching him with a frantic look: 'You will not desert me? You will all help me?'[43]

Upstairs the Duchess of Athole, one of Victoria's three ladies-in-waiting on duty that day, had been sitting with Horatia Stopford and Victoria Stuart-Wortley. None of them had seen the Queen since the previous morning and they were all deeply anxious. Finally, at around 11 p.m., the Duchess had decided to venture downstairs to enquire how the Prince was, before retiring for bed, when she was met by a footman in red livery sent in search of her. As she arrived at the door of the King's Room, the Queen came out—white with shock—to meet her: 'Oh Duchess,' she cried, 'he is dead! He is dead!' She took the Duchess inside, throwing herself with open arms on the corpse in paroxysms of weeping. Then she calmed a little and told the Duchess some of the details of Albert's final moments. They were joined by Miss Hildyard, who kissed the Prince's now-cold hands. Then Victoria dismissed her ladies, wishing to remain with Albert's body. It took some persuasion to get her to leave the room and try to rest; upon which she rushed straight up to the nursery, followed by the children, calling out as she went, 'Oh! Albert, Albert! Are you gone!'[44] One of the Queen's dressers, Annie Macdonald, recalled the awful sight: 'the Queen ran through the ante-room where I was waiting. She seemed wild. She went straight up to the nursery and took Baby Beatrice out of bed' and, 'clasping her tightly without waking her, lay her down in her own bed'. Midnight struck as the Queen, deranged by grief, still sat there 'gazing wildly and as hard as a stone' at her chambermaids Sophie Weiss, Emilie Dittweiler and Mary Andrews. Eventually she allowed them to help her undress, 'and oh, what a sight it was to gaze upon her hopeless, helpless face, and see those most appealing eyes lifted up,' wrote Augusta Bruce, as the Queen lay down next to the sleeping Beatrice, clasping Albert's nightclothes, and with his red dressing gown laid out beside her.[45] Alice settled

127

down in the small bed at the foot of the Queen's to try and rest too, but her mother could not sleep, nor could she weep, and sent for Dr Jenner, who came and sat with her for a while, and then gave her some opiates. But Victoria slept only for a short while, 'then woke and had a dreadful burst of crying, which relieved me'.[46] For the rest of the night she slept intermittently, talking and weeping with Alice between times. As soon as she awoke, little Beatrice tried to soothe her mother with her caresses. 'Don't cry,' said she, 'Papa is gone on a visit to Grandmamma.'[47]

Late that night, before he went to bed, Howard Elphinstone went in to see Prince Albert's body. His face was calm and peaceful. Elphinstone had known all along that the Prince 'had a fixed idea, that he would die of the 1st fever he got', but nevertheless he was distressed that the Prince had not tried to fight his illness. 'He had gone without a struggle, but likewise without saying a word', to the end a stranger in a foreign land, and longing still for his beloved Coburg. Returning to his room, Elphinstone found a telegram awaiting him from Cannes: Prince Leopold's ailing governor, General Edward Bowater, had just died. A long way from home, the queen's eight-year-old youngest son was having to deal alone with two deaths on the same day.[48]

*  *  *

At his home at Upton Court that evening George Augustus Sala and his friends had enjoyed a convivial meal, although he would later admit that 'my mind was from time to time perturbed', and that it had 'wandered to Windsor and the illustrious invalid there'. Nevertheless he went to bed. It was left to another newspaperman to scoop the momentous news when it came. Thomas Catling, sub-editor on a popular new penny newspaper, *Lloyds' Weekly*, had earlier that evening been instructed to head for Windsor to await developments. He had arrived at 11 p.m. on the last train and made straight for the castle, only to find the bearded soldier on sentry duty there in tears. He allowed Catling to pass on up the hill to the castle itself, where the news of the Prince's death was confirmed. Catling asked the officials on duty to telegraph the news through to his paper, but was told that the wire at the castle was 'for Court uses only'. So he headed off in the dark to hunt out the home of the local clerk of the Electric and International Telegraph Company. The clerk was reluctant to get up in the middle of the night—he had 'taken nitre in gruel and put his feet in hot water to ward off a cold', he complained—but Catling persuaded him to send a telegraph to his newspaper office, after which a friendly policeman helped him find lodgings for the night.[49] His paper would be the first with the news.

That evening the Tory politician Henry Greville, a close friend of the Queen, had been dining at the home of the French ambassador, the Comte de Flahaut, with Count Lavradio of the Portuguese legation, during which they had concurred on the extent to which the recent deaths in Portugal had played on Prince Albert's anxieties and how he had been 'constantly harping upon it' during his illness. Greville had moved on to his club when a telegram arrived late, informing him of the Prince's death. 'Every one present (and the room was full), both young and old, seemed consterned by this event, so unlooked for, and possibly pregnant with such disastrous consequences.'[50] 'I tremble for the Queen,' he wrote, as too now did Sir Charles Phipps over in his room at Windsor. He had important things to do. First, a short message was sent by electric telegraph from Windsor to the Lord Mayor of London at the Mansion House informing him of the Prince's death, and then some urgent letters: one to the Duke of Cambridge, in which he attempted to find the words to describe how he had witnessed 'the last moments of the best man that I ever met in my life'. The Queen's strength was extraordinary, Phipps told the Duke, 'Overwhelmed, beaten to the ground with grief, her self-control and good sense have been quite wonderful.' As for himself, 'my heart is broken'.[51] He also wrote a message to Lord Palmerston, hoping that he had prepared him sufficiently for the 'dreadful event' and assuring him that the Queen was 'perfectly collected', and showing a self-control that was 'quite extraordinary'. When the Duke of Cambridge brought the letter to the ageing Prime Minister at his home in Piccadilly late that night, Palmerston was so knocked back by the shock that he 'fainted away several times' in front of the Duke, who feared he would 'have a fit of apoplexy'.[52]

Palmerston's response echoed the great distress of the entire royal household that night; the Queen's eerie state of composure, they knew, was a sign of her profound state of shock. 'She has not realised her loss,' Phipps observed, and he dreaded the moment when the 'full consciousness' of it would come upon her. Like Greville, he trembled at the prospect of the 'depth of her grief'. 'What will happen,' he asked, 'where can she look for that support and assistance upon which she has leaned in the greatest and the least questions of her life?'[53] It was a question that filled everyone with dread. It would not just be a matter of coping with their own private grief at the loss of the Prince, but of dealing with its catastrophic effect on the Queen—not to mention the everyday duties of the monarchy.

Over at Slough, George Augustus Sala had been unable to sleep and had got up at daybreak. 'I hastened into the garden and gazed across Datchet Mead towards Windsor,' he later recalled. He could just dimly see the Round Tower in the distance as the early-morning mist rose from the surrounding fields. And then he saw the irrefutable proof of the disaster that had befallen the nation. The royal standard was at half-mast, floating disconsolately in a chilly dawn, greeted only by the rooks cawing in the bare trees of Windsor Great Park. Grabbing his coat, Sala hurried down to a deserted station, boarded the first train to London and headed straight to his office to write the most important leader article of his career.[54]

## CHAPTER SIX

# *'Our Great National Calamity'*

That morning, 15 December 1861, there was a terrible tolling of bells across England. It had begun just after midnight when the great bell of St Paul's Cathedral in the city of London had begun sounding a long, slow lament across the wintry streets, rousing those within earshot from their sleep. Everyone knew what it signified, for the bell was only ever tolled in times of national disaster or on the death of monarchs. It went on echoing across the streets for the next two hours as hundreds of anxious citizens rose from their beds, dressed and began assembling in the churchyard outside St Paul's, their voices hushed, their faces drawn with shock as the news was passed from one person to the next that the Prince Consort was dead.[1]

A bulletin issued at 8 a.m. by the Mansion House confirmed the dreadful event, and thence an 'electric chain' rapidly united the whole nation in grief as the telegraphic wires hummed across England, and beyond—to Scotland, Wales and Ireland.[2] All the newspapers had gone to press by the time Prince Albert had died, so there was nothing in the first edition of the Sunday papers, although a few smaller news-sheets had managed to get the story out and were being sold at a premium. 'In almost every street crowds of persons were seen surrounding the possessors of these sheets,' one eyewitness recalled, 'anxiously listening while the statements contained therein were being read aloud.'[3] Soon the news was being chalked up on walls in the back-street tenements of London. By lunchtime that Sunday special editions of papers such as the *London Gazette Extraordinary* enclosed in heavy black borders were being sold by newsboys brandishing placards and shouting, 'Death of His Royal Highness the Prince Consort'.

But the first intimation that most of the general public had—particularly those in rural areas—came with the slow tolling of bells, many of them muffled, at intervals of half a minute, which echoed across the countryside as people made their way to Sunday morning service. Others did not hear the news until they were sitting in their pews and it was whispered as the collecting box was passed round; for some, the shocking realisation came when the prayers for the royal family read out by the priest omitted the Prince's name.

The diarist Arthur Munby vividly recalled that day:

> This morning came the astounding news of Prince Albert's death: so unexpected and sad and ominous, that people are struck dumb with amaze [*sic*] and sorrow. The news-offices in the Strand were open and besieged by anxious folk; a strange gloom was upon the town; in church, the preacher spoke of it, and an awful silence there was, with something too very like sobbing, when his name was left out from the prayers.

Attending service in Whitley, Surrey, that morning, the artist James Clarke Hook remembered that the rector had heard rumours that the Prince had died, but had decided nevertheless that it 'would be all right to pray for him'. Seeking confirmation, Hook later went down to the local railway station to ask if any bad news had been received by telegraph there. 'No, sir,' the stationmaster replied, 'but I'll ring the bell to Godalming, sir, and inquire.' Shortly afterwards, letter by letter, a reply came clicking back across the wire: 'P-r-i-n-c-e-C-o-n-s-o-r-t-d-e-a-d'.[4]

Everywhere, the response to the news was the same: up at Fylingdales on the remote North

Yorkshire moors, the wife of a clergyman was preparing her usual class of farmers' daughters 'to read the Bible and settle the week's charities'. The fatal news came, she recalled, 'just as we assembled. We could not read; but we all knelt down and prayed for the Queen and wept bitterly.' News spread rapidly, even there, and 'In many parts of the wild moorland . . . the poor people have not gone to their days works without wearing some mark of mourning.'[5]

Few country vicars had time to record their reaction in their church sermons that day, but at St Paul's Cathedral a huge congregation heard Canon Champneys allude to the national bereavement and offer prayers for the Queen and the royal family in their great sorrow, before being played out at the end of the service to Handel's sonorous 'Dead March in Saul'. In Leeds, the vicar of St John's startled his congregation by reading the stark words from Samuel 3:38, 'Know ye not that there is a prince and a great man fallen this day in Israel?', without explaining its context to his bewildered flock until his sermon later on.[6] Other preachers improvised hastily revised sermons: from Bow Church in Cheapside, and the Poultry Chapel in the City, to the Lambeth Orphan Asylum and the Greek Orthodox church at London Wall, to the Roman Catholic church in Chelsea and the Scotch Church, in which the minister, Dr Cumming, deemed the Prince's best epitaph to be the text 'He doth rest from his labours and his works do follow him'. In Oxford, at St Mary's Parish Church, the Bishop of Oxford spoke 'in heart-stirring language' of 'the cloud which had that day spread over the land'. Throughout the day people everywhere instinctively turned to the Church for comfort; when Exeter Cathedral opened its great doors for afternoon service, it did so to a flood of people who filled it so quickly that many were turned away.[7]

By the time of the evening service the pulpits and lecterns of many churches were already draped in black crape. Across London the blinds of private houses had been drawn down, the brass plates on doors were surrounded with black, and mirrors and lamps indoors also covered. Omnibus drivers tied scraps of crape to their whips; in the countryside even beehives were draped in crape, as part of the age-old superstition of telling the bees of a death in the family. Many tradesmen either entirely or partially closed their businesses; steamers on the river stood idle, their flags at half-mast, as too did those of foreign vessels moored in London's docks. The royal standard was flying at half-mast everywhere across the capital, from the Victoria Tower of the Houses of Parliament to the Tower of London in the City.

But everywhere, in a spontaneous, haunting unison, it was the bells that spoke volumes for Britain's loss. Across the water meadows at Cambridge, where Prince Albert had been Chancellor of the university, the news had arrived at ten-forty that morning and spread with great rapidity, prompting the immediate announcement of the curtailment of all 'festivities incidental to the season'. The muffled peals of bells rang out all day—from Edinburgh in the north to Portsmouth in the south and across the major industrial cities of Manchester, Birmingham, Nottingham, Leeds, Huddersfield and Darlington. A similar response was recorded in Bristol, where the news had 'a most depressing effect upon all classes of citizens' as they pondered the flag at half-mast on the top of the cathedral. The burghers of Liverpool likewise spoke of a feeling of universal sorrow and regret in a town where 'his Royal Highness on several occasions endeared himself to all classes of the community by his affability and eloquence'; here, even American ships in port had lowered their flags. In Portsmouth in particular there was much grief among the army, navy and general public. On board Nelson's old flagship, the *Victory*, the royal ensign of England and that of the late Prince were hoisted at half-mast, as too 'above the town gates, the dock gate, the gun wharf, Southsea Castle . . . the fort, the ramparts, and all Government departments, as well as above the Sailors' Home'. In Southampton the 'whole of the mail packets and shipping plus various consulates and public institutions' all did likewise.[8]

Many people sat down in their homes that day confiding their thoughts to their diaries and writing letters to family and friends remarking on the mournful events at Windsor. The Prince's death would inevitably 'involve great changes', wrote the scholar Friedrich Max Müller to his mother, 'the queen can hardly bear the whole burden alone', and now she had no one who could help her in the unique way that the Prince had.[9] At Windsor, librarian Carl Ruland wrote to his family that Albert's death was 'a disaster for the entire family, for England, for the whole of Europe'. Working so closely with him, he had come to appreciate the depths of the Prince's character, for had Prince Albert not treated him 'as his own son'? Sir Moses Montefiore, a prominent leader of the Jewish community, had no doubts of its effect on them: 'we have lost a great and good prince', and also a friend, for the Prince had been 'most liberal as regards religious freedom to all'. In many cases, much as they mourned the loss of the Prince, the primary concern was its effect on the Queen; Charles Dickens predicted to his friend W. H. Wills, 'I have a misgiving that they hardly understand what the public general sympathy with the Queen will be.'[10]

The atmosphere of grief in Windsor town that grey Sunday morning was particularly acute—everywhere, even the poorest cottage, had its curtains drawn. Up at the castle 'an awful state of consternation and despair' reigned.[11] Within the royal apartments the Queen had now been joined, at her request, by her former Mistress of the Robes, the Duchess of Sutherland, who had herself been widowed earlier that year and who had driven over from her home at Cliveden to share in the Queen's grief. As the Duchess had entered the Queen's sitting room, Victoria had stretched out her arms to her. 'You know how I loved him!' she said, so plaintively, and took her in to see the Prince's body.[12] 'I feared the shock for her,' the Duchess later told her close friend, William Gladstone, for it was the first time Victoria had been back into the King's Room since the previous night when Albert had died. But she seemed extraordinarily composed, walked up to the bedside and reached out to Albert's body, which was laid out on the bed (though the doctors had forbidden her to touch it, for fear of infection). She raised her eyes, as though in a strange kind of trance, the Duchess recalled, 'and spoke every word of endearment as if

137

he had lived'. Was he not beautiful, she said to the Duchess, who herself was greatly moved by the fine, spiritual look on Albert's face. 'Never could I have believed Death's finger could be so light,' she told Gladstone. The features were as delicately wrought as marble; it was only the paleness that betrayed the mark of death.

As Victoria described the events of the previous days to the Duchess, she confided that her sole comfort was the Prince's repeated reassurance that he had had no dread of death; she fondly recalled the words of 'infinite affection' that had passed between them during those last days, but as she did so, the Duchess also noted a creeping air of desperation in the Queen's voice. 'How could it be, what was it—what was she to do?'—she who had 'spoken every thought' to her husband and had always been reassured by him so that she 'had neither anxiety or worry'.[13] He was everything to her. How was she to manage without him? The level of the Queen's grief seemed 'so *intense*, so *all-absorbing*' to the Queen's cousin, Princess Mary Adelaide of Teck, when she visited that afternoon. She recalled walking up the hundred stone steps to the castle, which, 'with all its blinds drawn looked dreary and dismal indeed'. In the Grand Corridor she had come upon the forlorn figures of Alice, Helena, Louise and Arthur, who 'all broke down in sight of me, though they strove to regain composure, and to remain as calm as possible for their widowed mother's sake'.[14]

The Queen's life would, she told Princess Mary Adelaide, 'henceforth be but a blank', though the Princess hoped that 'perhaps as months roll by the Children may in a *measure* fill it up'. But the brutal truth, as she saw it, was that the Queen's children were no substitute for their father and never would be: 'at the heart's core there must and will ever be an *aching void*'.[15] With Victoria clearly incapable of receiving consolation, yet alone giving it to her distraught children, how were they to cope with their own bereavement? 'Why did God not take me?' Louise had sobbed at her father's deathbed, sentiments echoed in a letter from her sister Vicky asking, 'Why has earth not swallowed me up?' Lord Clarendon had no doubt of the impact of his death on Albert's favourite child: 'I am afraid it will be the misery of her life not to have seen her father before he died,' he told the Duchess of Manchester.[16] As for Princess Alice, everyone marvelled at her dignity and composure: 'Could you but see that darling's face!' wrote one lady-in-waiting. 'Her great tearless eyes with their expression of resolutely subdued misery! No one knew what she was before, though I *marvelled* that they did not.'[17] Far away in Cannes, the most plaintive cry of all came from young Prince Leopold, who alone in his desolation, when told of his father's death, wept that he must go to his mother: 'My mother will bring him back again. Oh! I want my mother!' he had cried.[18]

For the moment, pending an onrush in the press the next morning, the only official words of condolence tentatively offered to the Queen were those of Lord Palmerston. Still laid up in agony with gout, and taking the Prince's death as a profound personal loss, he was unable to go to Windsor in person, but wrote that the Queen had 'sustained one of the greatest of human misfortunes'. But there was 'not one among the many millions who have the Happiness of being your Majesty's subjects, whose heart will not bleed in sympathy with Your Majesty's sorrow'. Nevertheless, as Prime Minister, there was one thing uppermost in his mind—distraught though he was—and this was the hope that the Queen's 'strength of mind and a sense of Duties' would help see her through.[19] In the meantime, from early on Sunday, members of the diplomatic corps as well as nobility and gentry had begun flocking to Buckingham Palace to enquire after Victoria's health and sign the book of condolences in a darkened and candlelit audience chamber. Emperor Louis Napoleon of France and his wife Eugénie, having already dispatched a senior emissary to London with letters of condolence, ordered three weeks of court mourning and sent frequent telegraphs from Paris, as also did the Emperor of Austria, the Duke of Saxe-Coburg and the King and Crown Prince of Prussia, where the court had immediately gone into mourning for a month. The event was announced across the Parisian newspapers 'in terms of unaffected regret' and nothing else was talked of; the flag at the Tuileries was at half-mast and British inhabitants of the city had immediately donned their black.[20] Meanwhile, in London, Charles Frances Adams, the new American ambassador, sent his condolences, recording in his diary sentiments similar to those already privately expressed by Florence Nightingale: 'The English will value him better now he is gone.'[21]

\*       \*       \*

Traumatised though Victoria was by Albert's

death, one thing was of immediate and overriding importance to her: to preserve the look and memory of him as he had been before he was taken from her for ever, down to the glass from which he had taken his last dose of medicine, which was left by his bedside.[22] Overnight, the body had been moved to the other bed in the King's Room and devotedly laid out by Albert's valet Löhlein, assisted by Macdonald. When Bertie took Princess Mary Adelaide in to take one last look 'at those handsome features', she had been touched by the wreath of white flowers at Albert's head, and single blooms placed on his breast and scattered across the coverlet; some of them sent as a gift by Prince Leopold from Cannes before he had known his father had died.[23] The room was full of people, the Princess recalled, including the artist Edward Henry Corbauld, who had come, at the Queen's request, to make a sketch of Albert on his deathbed. This would later be kept locked in a special case and circulated only within the family. The sculptor William Theed the Younger was also summoned to Windsor to take a cast of the prince's hands and a death-mask, reporting later that the Prince's face had been peaceful, bar the 'lines of suffering about the mouth'.[24] Although the Queen could not bear later to look at the mask, it was a sacred relic to be treasured. But she kept the marble hands near her bedside and would often clasp at them in the lonely moments of desperation that came during the night. The royal photographer, William Bambridge, was also called in that day to photograph Albert's private apartments as well as the King's Room, so that they could be cleaned, preserved and every object in them replaced exactly as they had been at the moment when he died—and remain so in perpetuity 'as a beautiful living Monument'.

To the Queen's mind, Albert was still very much with her in spirit, and their separation was only a physical, outward one. This emphasis on a *living* commemoration of her dead husband was fundamental to her future view of things. She resolved to fill the room with beautiful things: a bust of Albert, exquisite china, allegorical pictures—and fresh flowers. She wanted no morbid *Sterbezimmer*: the gloomy death-chamber preserved as a dusty sepulchre, so favoured by some of her German relatives, which was allowed to slowly decay and fade into dust untouched. Instead she wanted to preserve the King's Room as though her husband had just left it and would come in again at any time—his clothes and fresh linen laid out for him, hot water, towels and soap provided for his morning shave. Other, more mundane reminders were all left in their precise position too: in Albert's morning room, the reference books and directories, army lists, navy lists, clergy lists that he had regularly consulted; a small French book by the Abbé Ségur on the 'difficulties of religion'; and beyond, in his dressing room, Erskine May's book on parliamentary practice and Professor Max Müller's presentation copy to the Prince of his *Lectures on the Science of Language*.[25] But perhaps the most heartbreaking and intimate reminder of all was to be the hand-coloured copy of Bambridge's deathbed photograph of Albert, the chiselled features so fine in profile, with a small wreath of immortelles above it, which the Queen would hang above his side of their bed, in their homes at Windsor, Balmoral and Osborne.[26]

On Monday morning, 16 December, many public bodies and metropolitan vestries across the country gathered to pass resolutions expressing their profound sorrow at the Prince's death. In the City of London a Court of Common Council met at the Guildhall under the Lord Mayor to compose a loyal address of condolence, as other similar messages began to arrive at Windsor from the dignitaries of major provincial cities and towns. Along the great commercial thoroughfares of London— Cheapside, and Fleet Street in the city, the Strand, the Haymarket, Pall Mall, Piccadilly, Oxford Street in the West End, the majority of the shops 'had two or three shutters up'.[27] Theatres, concert halls and music halls all announced the cancellation of performances. The law courts, museums and art galleries were also closed, and even those places of public amusement not under the control of the Lord Chamberlain voluntarily shut their doors. Many cultural events were postponed, even those of the much-revered Charles Dickens, who was obliged, much to his annoyance, to cancel a lucrative series of six public readings in Liverpool and Chester for which thousands of tickets had been sold. Albert's death had also immediately thrown a veil of gloom over the forthcoming London Season: 'Farewell to drawing-rooms, balls, concerts, splendid soirées,' rued the exiled French politician Louis Blanc.[28] Within a day or so the stock market noted a considerable slump in trade and drops in the value of consols and railways stocks.

With so many public places closed, a distraught

stream of people hungry for news flocked to the news-stands and public reading rooms. They were not disappointed in what they found. The tone set by all of the press on Monday 16 December was uniform in its portentousness: a great calamity of biblical proportions had befallen the nation. John Delane of *The Times* gave saturation coverage in that day's edition ensuring that its circulation broke all previous records, rising to 89,000 copies. His words were stark and uncompromising: death had snatched from the nation 'the very centre of our social system, the pillar of our State' and it would be some time before the loss of the man and his services to the country could be estimated. The British people were unified in their grief, the classic adage that death was a great leveller being repeated by many papers, such as the *Morning Chronicle*, which observed that 'a bereavement such as this melts away the distinction of class'. With the country faced with such an 'incalculable affliction', the Prince Consort's death invited some of the best of contemporary obituary-writing, as well as some of the worst hyperbole: 'The eclipse of death is this day upon every home in England. More than that: a shadow has been cast over the world,' intoned the leader in the *Morning Post*. Most of the papers drew attention in particular to the destruction of the royal family as an idyllic domestic unit: 'Death has entered the highest, and what might but a few hours ago have been called the happiest, household in the land,' declared the *Scotsman*. The Prince had been 'the very stay and prop of the House which is identified with our dearest affections . . . The Home which all England recognised as the sweetest and holiest in the land is bereaved and desolate,' agreed

144

the *Morning Post*; 'the serene unbroken happiness of a long reign had now been clouded by the deepest sorrow,' echoed the *Daily News*.[29]

Outstripping them all with his characteristic purple prose came George Augustus Sala of the *Daily Telegraph*:

> It has pleased Almighty God to take unto himself the Consort of our beloved Queen. No pompous announcements in gazettes extraordinary—no sounding proclamations of his style and titles . . . no laborious enumeration of dignities telling us that he who now lies a cold corse [sic] in Windsor Tower was a Duke of Saxony and a Prince of Saxe Coburg and Gotha . . . none of the sonorous symbols of earthly state and grandeur, can abate one jot from the awful impressiveness, the ghastly puissance of those few naked words which tell us that Prince Albert is dead . . . Death has taken from us the most important man in the country.[30]

With such universality of grief and so many people automatically donning some form of mourning for the Prince, there would seem to be no need for official directives. Nevertheless, on 16 December the 'Orders for Court and General Mourning' were published in the *London Gazette Extraordinary*: 'The ladies attending Court to wear black woollen stuffs, trimmed with crape, plain linen, black shoes and gloves, and crape fans. The gentlemen attending Court to wear black cloth, plain linen, crape hatbands, and black swords and buckles.' More specific instructions followed for the Army, Royal Navy and Royal Marines. All army officers when in uniform should wear black crape 'over the ornamental part of the cap or hat, over the sword knot, and over the left arm, with black gloves, and a black crape scarf over the sash'. Military drums were to be covered with black, and black crape was 'to be hung from the head of the colour-staff of the infantry, and from the standard-staff of cavalry'. Beyond that, among the population at large, 'it is expected that all persons do forthwith put themselves into decent mourning'.[31] The middle classes needed no prompting and were already besieging the drapers and milliners' shops in order to order mourning outfits for themselves and their children; at the popular silk mercer's Lewis & Allonby on Regent Street 'people could not give their orders for crying'. But to do so was not without financial strain for many: the Chancery clerk Charles Pugh, with a wife and five daughters to support on a modest income, worried at the cost to low wage earners such as himself of putting their large families into mourning.[32]

In North Yorkshire, as in other rural areas, many of the churches and schools were 'put in regular mourning at the cost of the Inhabitants'—and everywhere the poorest of the poor found some way of demonstrating their grief, even if only by wearing black armbands.[33] But while advertisements carrying the patronage of Prince Albert were quickly amended as a sign of respect, elsewhere the world of commerce was quick to recognise the money to be made from this unexpected run on black. At the heart of the clothing industry in Leeds, the first advertisements appeared within two days, on 17 December:

146

General Mourning—Death of the Prince Consort. C. Pegler & Co., 58 Briggate, Leeds, beg to call the attention of Ladies to their present large stock of black mourning silk and black glaces [silks] from Turin, which are of a very superior make, the whole of which are now offered at greatly reduced prices.

Rising to the competition, Messrs Hyam & Co. a few doors down Briggate announced that they were 'prepared to supply mourning to any extent at five minutes' notice, or made to measure in five hours'. The Leeds Mourning Warehouse joined in, offering 'an immense stock of black alpacas, so much in demand by the French, of the best make', whilst Mrs Hartley offered her stock of mourning millinery and any other accoutrements needed, down to black ribbons, gloves, veils, handkerchiefs, collars, cuffs and artificial flowers.[34] For men, black cravats and hatbands and even black shirt studs were now in huge demand. On Monday, at the opening of trade in the City of London, crowds of buyers had besieged wholesale dealers such as Morison's, Leaf's, Boyd's and Ellis's to buy in stock.[35] But a royal death, whilst filling the coffers of the trade in funeral goods and mourning, would have a significant impact on the general textile industry. It was therefore with some concern that William Synes, President of the Chamber of Commerce, had written on 16 December to the Lord Chamberlain expressing his concern that the period of public mourning for the Prince should, unlike that previously for the Duchess of Kent, be clearly stipulated in order to 'avoid excessive injury to the trades of the country'. 'Will you excuse me by suggesting,' Synes added, 'that on the present lamentable occasion not only the commencement but the *termination* of the mourning should be stated when the order is issued.'[36]

The deepest of mourning of course prevailed at Windsor; at midday on Sunday the public had been informed that, although overwhelmed with grief, the Queen was calm—her calmness having a strange kind of childlike simplicity about it that many remarked on. Some put it down simply to her 'Christian fortitude', but other ladies thought her 'unnaturally quiet' and feared for her sanity, as she sat in dumb despair, staring vacantly around her. In response to a consolatory remark offered to her she said, 'I suppose I must not fret too much, for many poor women have to go through the same trials.'[37] But it was clear she was numb with shock and exhausted. Nevertheless, on the 17th she composed herself enough to mechanically sign some important papers brought for signature. She seemed to remember, thought Lord Clarendon, how much Prince Albert had 'disapproved and warned her against such extravagant grief as she manifested at her mother's death' and appeared to be trying hard to remain calm. 'If she can support herself in this frame of mind, it is all one can hope for,' he added. Lady Normanby echoed this: the Prince's last words to the Queen, so she had been told by Lady Ely, were that 'she must not give way to her grief, she owed it to the nation, remember that!'[38]

On Monday, Victoria had struggled to write a few anguished lines to Vicky: she was, she told her, 'crushed, bowed down'. But since that morning 'a wonderful Heavenly Peace' had come over her. 'I

148

feel I am living with him—as much as before—that He will yet guide and lead me—tho' He can't speak to me, while I can speak to Him.' She was resigned that henceforth her life would be one of sorrow, of duty, of self-abnegation and self-sacrifice. Two days later she had written again, telling Vicky that she had often prayed that she and Albert might die together or that he would survive her. All the joy had gone from her life now, all those happy times with Albert at Osborne, in the Highlands, those joyous family Christmases, their wedding anniversary—all belonged now to 'a precious past which will for ever and ever be engraven on my dreary heart'. Oh how she missed him, how she longed so 'to cling to and clasp a loving being'.[39] Close family members now began to rally round, but they were no substitute for her husband's arms. Arriving by train at Windsor from Kew, the Queen's aunt, the Duchess of Cambridge, was seen weeping bitterly on the concourse, the 'signs of her distress having a visible effect on bystanders' as she passed through. Up at the castle the strain of so much collective grief on the members of the royal household was terrible. 'We have indeed to bring all our faith and trust to bear,' wrote maid-of-honour Victoria Stuart-Wortley, for now 'this sad silent House is full of wailing and misery . . . I don't know when I shall get over it. The very fact of being *no use* is so dreadful.'[40]

\* \* \*

In the nine days from Prince Albert's death to his funeral on 23 December, a profusion of eulogies filled the newspapers, for it took time for the

149

nation to come to terms with the extent of its loss. The calamity of the Prince's death was like the 'sudden extinction of a light', wrote Delane in *The Times*, and 'an interval must elapse before we can penetrate the darkness'. This was no ordinary death, evoking 'conventional regret', but one that had brought 'real pain' to the entire nation. 'Wars and rumours of wars,' wrote the *London Review*, 'pass almost unheeded in the presence of this engrossing bereavement', for many felt as though they had lost a member of their own family. Albert's death was a personal blow that had touched everyone, and many ordinary people had been made 'dangerously ill by the shock'.[41] In the words of the *Illustrated London News*: 'Death stands within the walls of Windsor Palace—a Queen is widowed—Princes are orphans—and the Empire shrouded in mourning! Every family in the land is smitten with the awe and the sorrow which Death excites when he breaks into the domestic circle and snatches from it its chief pride and joy.'[42]

The eulogies for Prince Albert were in stark contrast to the many damning ones that had appeared on the deaths of George IV in 1830 and William IV in 1837. Previous kings, let alone prince consorts, had been nothing in comparison with him, according to the leader-writer of the *Glasgow Herald*, who described how the 'gloomy Philip of Spain', husband of Queen Mary, had been disliked, as too 'the reckless and unprincipled debauché' Lord Darnley, husband of Mary, Queen of Scots. In comparison with the 'dull-brained, wine-bibing' Prince George of Denmark, consort of Queen Anne, Albert had been a paragon.[43] The last time the nation had gone into mourning for a prince consort had been on the death of Prince George in 1708, but he had been a social and political cipher in comparison. The floodgates were now opened to a torrent of praise of Albert: as a man of genius, a wise and benevolent patron of art, science and industry with the welfare of the nation at heart, who was noted for his sagacity and eloquence, his nobility of character, his modesty, lack of ostentation and—most importantly—his domestic virtue. 'To the husband and father now lying dead at Windsor we owe the proof, new in our annals, that domestic life may be as pure, as free, as full of attachment, as pleasantly and rationally ordered, in a palace as in a country parsonage.' And yet none had really known the Prince; and many had underappreciated him and even thought ill of him; as *The Times* accentuated, Albert had been admired, certainly, but it was admiration at a distance. A distinct air of retrospective guilt about the extent to which the Prince had been underrated permeated the press. The *Guardian* emphasised how he had had to overcome the stigma of 'coming a foreigner, with foreign feelings and foreign sympathies', yet despite this 'so much good done, a most difficult part so wisely and honestly played, so many snares and stumbling-blocks escaped', adding that 'No one can say he has been an unimportant person in England.'

George Augustus Sala's uncritical hyperbole in the *Telegraph* continued to have considerable popular appeal, with its talk of 'the havoc of happiness, the blasting of prospects, the dislocation of love', and of Albert's phantom now hovering over the glistening domes of his great project, the Crystal Palace of 1851. When it came to bathos no one could touch the *Telegraph*'s leader-writer: England's queen was enduring her grief 'undaunted and indomitable, like some proud oak in Windsor Forest, from which the clinging ivy has been ruthlessly torn away, but which still stands unscathed, and defies the storm . . . She is not less the Woman, but she is more than ever the Queen!'[44]

There was, however, one other important issue already preoccupying the press—and that was Bertie. *The Times* had already given him dressing-down in its editorial on the 18th. It devolved to the Prince of Wales, Delane declared, to rise to 'all the solemnity of his position, and fit himself for the part to which he is destined'. For Bertie, the days of callow youth were over and he 'ought now to show the faculties which will make a good king'. He must 'make up his mind, if he wishes to gain the affection and esteem of the country' and choose between two paths: those of 'duty and pleasure'. But, even on his best behaviour, it was doubted that the Prince of Wales was capable of rising to the occasion. Lord Stanley thought him 'good-tempered, and apparently likely to be popular', but it was well known that he was 'not gifted with much ability', and his rebellious streak—a reaction to his repressed childhood—had left him prone to 'undignified' and immature outbreaks, 'which may be precursors of worse excesses'. He could not begin to fill the void left by his father; the writer Matthew Arnold had no doubts: there was no one with 'the Continental width of openness of mind of Prince Albert'. The worst fear was that, without Albert to guide her, the Queen would 'fall into a state of mind in which it will be difficult to do business with her, and impossible to anticipate what she will approve or disapprove'. The worst was yet to come, in the opinion of Lady Lyttleton: all the 'numberless, incessant wishes to "Ask the Prince", to "Send for the Prince", the never-failing joy, fresh every time, when he answered her call'. There was nevertheless 'such a feeling of unselfish goodwill towards Her Majesty,' wrote *The Times*, that the question of the Queen resuming public business immediately was out of the question. A degree of public forbearance would be required in the days to come, in the hope that her 'courage and independence of character' would equip her for resuming her duties. *The Times* was confident: 'we have on the throne a Sovereign whose nerves have been braced rather than paralysed by the chill of adversity'. But the newspapermen did not know the Queen as Lady Lyttleton did. Albert's death was, she had no doubt, a 'heart wound' that had torn her world apart.[45]

\*        \*        \*

It was thus in considerable distress that Victoria prepared to leave Windsor for Osborne. Much to general consternation, she was not to remain there for the Prince Consort's funeral. In fact there had never been any question of her presence at the actual ceremony, for funerals were still very much a male preserve, with women being considered far too weak to conceal their grief in public. In her traumatised state the Queen would have been incapable of enduring it; indeed, she wanted nothing said to her at all about the arrangements, leaving it all to Bertie and the Duke of Cambridge. She had, however, been extremely reluctant to leave

Windsor itself until everything was over. It was the royal doctors who prevailed on her to leave, fearful that she and the children might be infected by the supposed typhoid germ that had killed Albert. Victoria had protested: 'You are asking me to do what you would not expect from the humblest of my subjects.'[46] Alice too had remonstrated with them, but in the end Victoria had relented, having received a barrage of 'telegraphic entreaties' from her uncle, King Leopold of the Belgians, who insisted that she remove to Osborne.[47] The Queen's ladies thought this cruel in the extreme, as too did Lord Clarendon. In his opinion the Queen would have been better off staying at the White House—a small, comfortable mansion on the Beaumont estate nearby—or at Cliveden with the Duchess of Sutherland. Osborne was the worst possible place for her to retreat to, for, as Clarendon pointed out, it was a place 'where every object is so entirely associated with him'. Lady Geraldine Somerset (lady-in-waiting to the Duchess of Cambridge) agreed—going there would be agony for the Queen, but then 'every place she goes to must be a fresh *dagger*, each so *identified* with him'. Far worse, though, was the prospect of what the Queen would still have to endure: after twenty-two years of 'unparalleled happiness,' observed Lady Geraldine, 'she may live 30, 40 of as unequalled sorrow.'[48]

It had been intended that the Queen should leave for Osborne on the Wednesday, 18 December, and much of her luggage had been sent on ahead, together with the servants, but at the last minute she had not been able to tear herself away from the comforting darkness inside the castle, dreading as she did 'the sight of the glaring

154

daylight'.[49] She told General Grey that all the time 'she felt that He was still in the room near her. She could not feel that she had lost His support.'[50]

Earlier that day she made the first gesture in what would become forty years of dedicated memorialisation of her husband by choosing a site for his final resting place. She and Albert had long since agreed that they did not want to be interred in the traditional royal burial place: the dark and gloomy crypt of St George's Chapel. And so in the morning Victoria drove down to Frogmore with Alice and found a spot, close to her mother's mausoleum in the south-western end of the gardens there, where she intended to erect a much grander sepulchre for herself and her beloved Albert.

Before she left for Osborne there were other, much more personal and final farewells that she wished to make. She gave instructions that Alice, Helena, Louise and Beatrice should each cut off a lock of their hair for placing in Albert's coffin before it was sealed, probably with some of her own, along with other tokens of special significance such as photographs of the children. (Locks of Albert's hair were also taken for preservation in a variety of ways, mainly in mourning jewellery.) Most significantly, Victoria arranged for a particular photograph to be placed in her husband's hands.[51] It was a reproduction of Albert's favourite portrait of her, by Franz Winterhalter, that she had given him on his twenty-fourth birthday in 1843 and which hung in Albert's morning room—a painting so intimate and so unlike all the official ones of herself as Queen, in which she was depicted with bare shoulders, her long, partially loose hair curving over her shoulder and down across her breast. It

155

was an emphatic, parting reminder of herself as a sensual young woman: an evocation of the physical love that the Queen would now so miss about her husband, of the times 'when in those blessed arms' she had been clasped and held tight 'in the sacred hours at night'.[52] She had gone into the King's Room to see Albert twice on Sunday, but did not go again; she could not bear to, she told Vicky; she would rather keep in her mind 'the impression given of life and health' than that final vision of her husband's face so marble, and grown so very thin. Words of great affection and consolation flowed back from Vicky: 'None of us thought we could have survived this,' she comforted 'and yet we live, we love, we trust—and we hope still.'[53]

The following morning Victoria was still unable to steel herself to leave, and so at 10 a.m. Arthur and Beatrice were sent on ahead with the Leiningens.[54] Just before midday—the Duchess of Wellington would never forget the Queen's terrible sobbing—Victoria was led out to the great staircase, where she burst into 'a loud wailing cry and almost screamed "I *can't* go"'. With the greatest of effort she was assisted down the stairs and out to her carriage by Bertie and Alice on either side, whispering words of encouragement as they supported her.[55] 'It was a terrible moment,' recalled Lady Bruce, who followed close behind. 'She felt on leaving that all that could be taken from her of him, had been.'[56] In the strictest privacy and with no servants in attendance, Victoria left a deserted South-Western Railway terminus at Windsor by royal train, in the company of Alice, Helena, Louise and Prince Louis and some of her ladies, including Lady Bruce and the Duchess of Athole. At Gosport on the Hampshire coast she boarded the royal yacht, the *Fairy*, for the Isle of Wight and a cold and sadly inhospitable Osborne. For the house, with its warm Italianate architecture, had always been the family's summer home. Howard Elphinstone thought it 'so unsuited at this time of year'; all the colour was leached out of its usually vibrant gardens, which the Prince had so lovingly overseen, leaving the bare trees and flowerbeds and the empty ornamental urns on the terrace open to the bleak, cold wind from the Solent. The 'desolate look' of the frail, childlike Queen in her widow's cap was terrible: 'I felt— *what* was there that I would not do for her!' the Duchess of Athole recalled.[57] At midnight, Victoria was joined by Albert's brother, Duke Ernst, who had been brought over from Antwerp on the royal yacht and had stopped off to commiserate before proceeding to Windsor for the funeral. He came in cold, drenched and seasick, to find his unhappy sister-in-law 'bowed down with sorrow and utterly prostrate in the stillness of the night'. Soon that silence was broken by 'the loud grief which deprived us both of words'.[58]

After so many days of an icy composure that had made her entourage fearful for her sanity, arrival at Osborne finally brought home to Victoria the full force of her utter desolation, and she at last gave terrible vent to her grief. 'She cried for days,' remembered Annie Macdonald. 'It was heart-breaking to hear her.'[59] Osborne, that happy family home, had now for ever become a bitter place of mourning. All Victoria had left to cling to were the precious reminders of Albert that she kept constantly about her: his watch and chain, a golden cord with his keys and his quirky red pocket handkerchief, 'at which they had so often laughed in good old days'.[60]

Anticipating his imminent arrival, the first thing Victoria did at Osborne was to sit down and pour out her heart to Uncle Leopold, on writing paper with inch-thick black borders:

> The poor fatherless baby of nine months is now the utterly broken-hearted and crushed widow of forty-two! My *life* as a *happy* one is *ended*! The world is gone for *me*! If I *must live* on . . . it is henceforth for our poor fatherless children— for my unhappy country, which has lost *all* in losing him—and in *only* doing what I know and *feel* he would wish, for he *is* near me—his spirit will guide and inspire me.

At last anger burned through the numbness of grief, arousing Victoria's indignation. How dare God take her precious Albert from her?

> But oh! To be cut off in the prime of life—to see our pure, happy, quiet, domestic life, which *alone* enabled me to bear my *much* disliked position, cut off at forty-two—when I *had* hoped with such instinctive certainty that God never *would* part us, and would let us grow old together . . . is *too awful*, too cruel.[61]

*          *          *

On 22 December, after a week of prayer meetings up and down the country, another cold, grey Sunday dawned and the churches of Britain were packed

158

with worshippers. The solemnity of the occasion was heightened by the surfeit of black everywhere: British churches that day were festooned with a 'crapery of woe'. Worshippers sat in muted grief listening to long sermons on the death of the Prince Consort by parish priests, many of whom grasped the opportunity for issuing exhortations to their flocks to prepare for their own ends by ensuring that they live untainted, Christian lives as the Prince had done.[62]

United in a 'bond of common sorrow,' the nation now gathered its strength for the heartbreak of the funeral to come, which promised a 'grand Gothic fane . . . completely draped and carpeted with black', with dirges and anthems and dead marches, and catafalques and a hearse 'drawn by plumed and mantled steeds and hung with escutcheons of the illustrious deceased', according to Sala of the *Telegraph*, once more rising to the occasion with a lugubrious flourish.[63] Overall the tone of the Prince's obituaries that week had reflected the public wish, as Lord Clarendon saw it, 'to make a serious *amende* for the injustice too often done to him in his lifetime'.[64] It was, however, the leader-writer of the *Observer* who best summed up, in a simple sentence quoting the words of Shakespeare's Hamlet, what other obituarists had taken columns to express:

Peace to his ashes! A good husband, a good father, a wise Prince, and a safe counsellor, England will not soon 'look upon his like again'.[65]

In these final dark, sullen days of December yet

more bad news arrived: ships from America had brought discouraging dispatches. The American cabinet in Washington, whilst deliberating its course of action, still appeared to be taking a belligerent stance over the *Trent* affair. At the US legation in London, Benjamin Moran continued to fend off anxious enquiries as to the outcome of the crisis, whilst observing the protocol of ensuring that all notes to the British government were now sent on black-edged paper in black-bordered envelopes sealed with black wax. Privately he expected a speedy reconciliation, but the British public at large, as the time approached for a receipt of America's answer, seemed convinced that war was inevitable. But, if a trade-off could have been possible, to the mind of Lord Palmerston it was 'Better for England to have had a ten-years' war with America than to have lost Prince Albert'.[66]

## CHAPTER SEVEN

# *'Will They Do Him Justice Now?'*

It had been thirty-four years since the British nation had experienced a royal tragedy to match that of the death of Prince Albert. Back in 1817 the popular and vivacious Princess Charlotte of Wales, daughter of the Prince Regent, and—failing the birth of any other legitimate ones—heir to the British throne, had at the age of only twenty-one died of complications following the stillbirth of a son. For many people this sudden loss took on the dimensions of an everyday tragedy, for death in childbirth (of mother and child) was then such a common occurrence. Nevertheless, as a robust and healthy young woman, Charlotte should not have died, had she not been so unmercifully bled and starved by her misguided doctors during her pregnancy. With the Princess already fatally weakened, the failure of the royal doctors to intervene with forceps to progress her agonising two-day labour had resulted in her death from haemorrhage and shock on 6 November.[1]

Princess Charlotte's death, much like that of the Prince Consort later, was viewed as a great national disaster: 'The Catastrophe at Claremont'. It was commemorated in a torrent of sermons, discourses, dirges, elegies and epitaphs across the land, many of which were collected as 'A Cypress Wreath for the Tomb of Her Late Royal Highness the Princess of Wales'. Bonfires stacked to celebrate the impending birth were dismantled, shops closed and businesses suspended as many went into mourning. The unexpected deaths of two prospective heirs to the throne provoked much talk in the Continental press of a monarchical crisis and the looming fear—in the continuing absence of a legitimate heir of a foreign monarch yet again taking the British throne.

With perhaps the exception of the death in 1852 of the Napoleonic War hero the Duke of Wellington, the nation had 'never been afflicted by a loss at once so sudden and so overwhelming' and of such a prominent member of the royal family.[2] A great state occasion was made of the eighty-three-year-old Duke's death; an elaborate twenty-seven-foot-long funeral car, embellished with black and gold ornamentation and drawn by twelve black-plumed horses, had processed across London in front of around a million people, to St Paul's Cathedral, where the Duke was buried in the crypt alongside Admiral Lord Nelson. Prince Albert had taken a prominent role in national mourning for the Duke, and the funeral had been very much a mark of respect for a long life, well lived, that had come to its natural end. But the Duke's was the last of the great heraldic state funerals. By 1861 tastes had changed, particularly with regard to the outmoded convention of royal burial at night. This had been the norm for members of the royal family earlier in the century, including Princess Charlotte, the main reason being that the darkness reduced the need for the precise observation of the elaborate heraldic trappings traditionally required. The natural Gothic drama of such a funeral conducted in darkness was heightened by the flickering torchlight and ghostlike black weeds of the mourners. But when in 1837 the Duke of Sussex had had to endure the irreverent, overblown shambles of the funeral of William IV, he left instructions for a simple daylight funeral for himself without excessive pomp, which was observed when he died in 1843. When William IV's widow, Queen Adelaide, died in 1849, she left a similar request that her funeral be simple and conducted during the day. By then, even the royal lying-in-state had been abandoned—last seen at the funeral of Princess Sophia of Gloucester in 1844.

In his will, Prince Albert reflected the general and growing distaste among the aristocracy for pompous and protracted obsequies, stating: 'Everything I possess belongs to the Queen, my dear wife. I wish to be buried privately.'[3] The details of the will were never published, nor were any medical reports by Albert's doctors on the circumstances of his death, beyond the superficial content of the official bulletins. When King George III had died in 1830 the royal doctors had published the gruesome details of his post-mortem in *The Times*; there had been post-mortems too for Princess Charlotte and her dead baby before they had both been embalmed, but Victoria flatly refused to allow any posthumous examination of her husband's sacred corpse, a fact that aroused considerable disapproval in medical circles.[4]

It fell to the Lord Chamberlain—Viscount Sydney—as chief officer of the royal household to make the arrangements for the funeral, in consultation with Bertie and the Duke of Cambridge. With the Queen wanting no involvement in its planning, it was assumed that a repetition of the private funeral overseen earlier that year by Prince Albert for the Duchess of Kent would be the best option. The most urgent decision to be made was the actual date, which was decided on for Monday 23 December. The Lord Chamberlain and his staff were placed under considerable pressure to complete the arrangements in time, but it was seen as essential that the funeral be held before Christmas, in order to allow the nation some release from mourning over the coming festive season, even though, inevitably, it would be a very subdued one that year.

One thing at least could be relied on, and that was the discretion and efficiency of Messrs T. & W. Banting, who had conducted all royal funerals since 1811, as well as those of Nelson and the Duke of Wellington. From their fashionable premises in the West End, Banting's (like many other similar businesses of the day) combined a prosperous upholstery and cabinet-making enterprise with undertaking, contracting out the embalming and other aspects of the business. After his death Albert's corpse had been placed in the loving care of his valet Löhlein, who had laid out the Prince with the rings still on his fingers, dressed in the long dark-blue frockcoat of a field marshal, with gold cord aiguillette across one shoulder and a gold and crimson waist sash with tassels.

In accordance with royal tradition, Albert's body was placed within two coffins, similar in style and size to those used for the Duchess of Kent: the inner wooden shell lined with white satin had an outer casing of lead with massive silver-gilt ornaments and bore a Latin inscription:

*Depositum*
*Illustrissimi et Celsissimi Alberti,*
*Principis Consortis,*
*Ducis Saxoniae,*
*de Saxe-coburg et Gotha Principis,*
*Noblissimi Ordinia Perisceldis Equitis,*
*Augustissimae et Potentissimae Victoriae Reginae*
*Conjugis percarissimi,*
*Obiit die decimo quarto Decembris, MDCCCLXI,*
*Anno aetatis suae XLIII.*

['Here lies the most illustrious and exalted Albert, Prince Consort, Duke of Saxony, Prince of Saxe-Coburg and Gotha, Knight of the most noble Order of the Garter, the most beloved husband of the most august and potent Queen Victoria, who died 14 December 1861 in his 43rd year.']

On the evening of the 16th, officers of the Board of Works came and soldered the lead coffin down—Messrs Holland & Sons, undertakers of Mount Street, having placed charcoal around the corpse, again as per royal mortuary practice (in order to absorb any odours as it began to decompose).[5] Colonel Biddulph had arranged with Banting's that the entire ante-throne room be 'put in mourning to receive the body' with 'black druggett to cover floor, black cloth draperies over doors and windows'. In addition, a double-width of druggett was to be used to form an elaborate black pathway over the carpets, through two rooms, down the staircase and all the way to the entrance door of the castle, 'so as to form a mourning route for the remains', to be trod by those following the coffin.[6] When the coffin was moved down to the ante-throne room on the 22nd, it was placed inside a third, massive state coffin of mahogany covered with crimson velvet, over which a heavily embroidered black velvet pall lined with white satin was arranged, with Albert's crown and his field marshal's baton, sword and hat placed on top.

On Saturday 21 December—for one day only—and in order to satiate intense public curiosity, Banting's had put the third, ceremonial coffin made in their workshops on public display at their premises at 27 St James's Street.[7] But this is as much as the public would get to see; the ceremony itself at Windsor would be strictly private and the British people were denied any opportunity of paying their final respects at a formal lying-in-state. Even when Princess Charlotte had died, only a limited number had been allowed into a cramped

165

room at Lower Lodge, Windsor, for a few hours to take a brief glance at the coffin. This was a matter of some concern to the Mayor of Windsor, who was dismayed that no local people would be allowed to see anything of the funeral cortège. He requested a change in the route when the coffin was brought from the private apartments in the Upper Ward, suggesting that it might proceed down Castle Hill and out of the precincts briefly, before turning back to St George's Chapel. The palace and the Lord Chamberlain resisted this vigorously, insisting on absolute privacy.[8] As for the members of the press—as well as the necessary artists to illustrate the day's events—they would be allowed access, but hidden away in the organ loft above the main body of the chapel. The Mayor meanwhile persisted; there would, he argued, be 'intense disappointment' if the public were totally excluded. In the end he and a handful of people were allowed into the castle precincts, but the Comptroller would later complain that despite the tight security arrangements, a lapse by the Mayor had allowed some 'strangers' to get in; worse, the policeman on duty at the door to the organ loft had allowed the sister of the organist, Dr George Elvey, to sneak in and watch the ceremony, 'an unpardonable piece of impertinence . . . as he was perfectly well aware that no lady was to be admitted excepting by the Queen's direct order'.[9]

Preparations for the funeral in St George's Chapel went on apace. The stone flagging covering the entrance to the royal vault was removed, and a raised dais constructed over it in the centre of the chapel to take the state coffin and its huge velvet catafalque. The whole of the chapel from its west door to the entrance of the choir was carpeted in black and the doors draped with heavy black curtains. The empty oak choir stalls and canopies of the Knights of the Garter were also festooned with black, as were the steps up to the communion table. The only colour breaking the pervading gloom was that of the glittering medieval escutcheons and fringed banners high in the roof of the chapel and its stained-glass window. Otherwise there was an 'utter absence of prismatic colour'.[10]

As the days passed, one thing was all too clear, as the Duke of Argyll observed: 'The whole nation is mourning as it never mourned before.' 'During the past week,' wrote Lord Hardman, 'every shop in London has kept up mourning shutters, and nothing is seen in all drapers', milliners', tailors', and haberdashers' shops but black. Everybody is in mourning.' For Albert's death had brought 'painful reminders of the death of the Princess Charlotte and her baby' all those years before.[11] The 200 shop assistants at Jay's vast London General Mourning Warehouse on Regent Street were under siege, for, from the moment of the Prince's death, there had been an 'incalculable demand for mourning'. Sales of engravings and *cartes de visite* of the Prince Consort and the Queen had also been unprecedented, the most popular being one by John Mayall of the Prince seated, pen in hand, at his desk, which had been taken in May 1860. The *carte de visite* was a recent innovation from France that had immediately found favour with the public, with *cartes* of Mayall's photographs of the royal family selling by the 100,000. Photograph dealers were quick to capitalise on the windfall of the Prince's death and the astonishing demand for

167

images of him. Inside a week, 'no less than 70,000 *cartes de visite* had been ordered from . . . Marion & Co.', the largest photographic wholesaler in England, located on Regent Street; in Paris, a print-seller claimed to have sold 30,000 *cartes* in one day.[12] On the afternoon of 21 December, Arthur Munby had fought his way through the shoppers on Regent Street and found huge crowds outside the photograph shops, 'looking at the few portraits of the Prince which are still unsold'. He went into Meclin's to buy one: 'every one in the shop was doing the same. They had none left: would put my name down, but could not promise even then. Afterwards I succeeded in getting one—the last the seller had—of the Queen and Prince: giving four shillings for what would have cost but eighteen pence a week ago.' Munby concluded that the escalation in price was an indicator of the 'great conviction of his worth and value which the loss of him has suddenly brought to us all'.[13]

\*     \*     \*

The morning of Monday 23 December 1861 dawned cold, grey and cheerless. 'The very air felt heavy with the general gloom,' recalled Princess Mary Adelaide when she got up at eight. She could already hear the tolling of the bells and later the minute guns in St James's Park, informing London that the 'last sad ceremony' was about to take place in St George's Chapel, Windsor. Nature itself seemed to sympathise with the national feeling of despondency, for the dull, damp, leaden sky showed no sign of clearing as people ventured forth to mark the day—a day when no respectable person was seen out of doors except in the deepest of mourning.[14]

The most profound gloom of all reigned in the town of Windsor, as the correspondent of *The Times* reported: 'every shop closed, every blind drawn down; streets silent and almost deserted'. The castle's great bell chimed out its doleful sound at intervals from an early hour, joined later by the minute bells tolling from nearby St John's parish church. Early that morning Bertie, Arthur, Duke Ernst, Prince Louis, the Crown Prince of Prussia and other male mourners in the royal entourage for Albert's funeral had left Osborne and travelled by special train from Southampton to Windsor, the shutters firmly drawn down as it passed through stations en route, observed by mute and grief-stricken crowds. The entourage brought with them wreaths of moss and violets made by Alice, Helena and Louise for their father's coffin, as well as a simple, touching bouquet of violets with a white camellia in its centre from their mother.[15] These would be the only flowers in evidence, fresh flowers as such not yet being part of British funeral culture.

At eleven o'clock the principal mourners gathered in the Oak Room, wearing, as instructed by the Lord Chamberlain, plain black evening coats and white cravats. Mourning scarves and armbands, as per funeral convention, were to be provided by Banting's at the chapel. Only those with a personal connection to the Queen and Prince Albert, plus the essential Cabinet ministers and the Archbishop of Canterbury, had been invited. Much to their dismay, the Duke of Cambridge and Lord Palmerston were both too unwell to attend; the

Prince of Leiningen was also absent, having elected to remain at Osborne with the Queen. No foreign ambassadors were there either, bar the Portuguese envoy Count Lavradio, Count Brandenburg from Prussia and, on behalf of King Leopold who was yet to arrive in England, the Belgian ambassador, Sylvain Van De Weyer. Foreign royals present included the Duc de Nemours (married to Albert's cousin) and Albert and Victoria's cousins from Belgium: the Duke of Brabant and the Count of Flanders. 'Youth seemed out of place here,' remarked George Augustus Sala; the congregation for the funeral was 'a congress of old men, of patriarchs'. The only youthful exception, aside from Bertie and Arthur—and the only representative of Britain's many colonies (where the news of Albert's death was yet to arrive)—was the twenty-three-year-old former Maharaja of the Sikh Raj, Duleep Singh, now domiciled in England and a favourite of the Queen's. No women were present in the main body of the chapel, although, at Victoria's particular request, two of her closest friends—the Duchesses of Sutherland and Wellington (her former and current Mistresses of the Robes)—along with five other ladies, observed the proceedings out of sight in the Queen's Closet on the north side of the choir, specially fitted up with mourning on the Lord Chamberlain's orders. At Bertie's thoughtful request, Prince Arthur's nurse, Mrs Hull, was also at hand, in the organ loft.

As the journalists and congregation gathered in the chapel to a low sound of whispering and rustling, the faint sound of machinery could be heard as the mechanism for lowering the bier down into the vault was tested one final time. Elsewhere, workmen hurried to finish sweeping away the remaining mess from where the temporary black carpeting had been laid. Sala—whose account was published the following day across six columns of the *Daily Telegraph* surrounded in a heavy black border—had an excellent vantage point in the organ loft, from where he could see both east and west ends of the chapel. He was fascinated to note that one of the minor chapels had been converted into a temporary workshop by Banting's, where 'the busy bees of Death, the undertaker's myrmidons—plump men in raven black, rosy girls in brand new sables—[sat] stitching and tacking and folding scarves, and tying bands and sewing on rosettes, until the very last moment', these to be handed to the mourners as they arrived.

At midday the procession of fifteen mourning coaches slowly wended its way behind the hearse, under the Norman Tower and down the hill from the royal apartments in the Upper Ward. Its progress was witnessed by only a small group of spectators who were allowed to stand in front of the almshouses of the Poor Knights, immediately opposite the entrance to the south side of the chapel. As the procession drew to a halt, the minute guns were fired by members of the Horse Artillery beyond the castle walls in Long Walk, a couple of miles away. Outside the chapel Grenadier Guards, of whom the Prince had been Colonel-in-Chief, stood to attention and presented arms as the heavy black drapes at the chapel doors were pulled back to admit the coffin. From there, slowly, inexorably, it was edged forward into the chapel on a bier underneath its velvet pall (the assistants moving it, being unable to see, were guided by a narrow strip

171

of white along the floor at their feet). Following the coffin came Lord Henry Lennox, bearing the Prince's baton, sword and hat on a black velvet cushion with gold tassels, followed by Earl Spencer with the Prince's crown, which were all then placed on the coffin.

The mourners were led by Bertie and a grief-stricken Prince Arthur, his eyes red and swollen from weeping, who made the most poignant of figures in his black Highland dress. All around 'there was a dumb, cadaverous air about the chapel, swathed in its ghastly trappings'. Dukes, marquesses, earls, politicians and members of the royal household—from Albert's valets, to his farm bailiffs, his solicitor, librarian, apothecaries, doctors, and equerries—sat as one in their uniformly black and white garb, the scene relieved only by the occasional glitter of a bejewelled badge or order. As the muffled bell continued its melancholy chime a deep silence fell across those gathered. Gerald Wellesley, the Dean of Windsor, took his place to conduct the burial service, with music composed by the eighteenth-century organist and composer William Croft, which had been used at previous state funerals. A shudder of emotion went round the congregation as the choir burst into the chant 'I am the Resurrection and the Life', followed by 'I know that my Redeemer liveth'—the latter 'so touching, so inexpressibly mournful in its long, soft cadences,' as the organist Dr Elvey recalled.[16]

Of Albert's nine children, only two were present at the service: Bertie, who as eldest bore up as best he could, and little Prince Arthur, the Prince's ten-year-old youngest son, who was consumed by

172

grief throughout. When it came to the words 'So fall asleep in slumber deep,/Slumber that knows no waking'—part of a favourite chant of their father's—the two brothers hid their faces and wept. Even Dean Wellesley's voice faltered many times and was sometimes inaudible, so overcome was he. For once some of the traditional conventions of royal funerals were broken, certainly with regard to the choice of music, which was strongly oriented to Albert's own musical tastes. The service included two of his favourite German chorales: the sixteenth-century 'I shall not in the grave remain/Since Thou death's bonds hast sever'd', by the Bavarian cantor and preacher Nicolaus Decius, which was 'chanted by the choir in whispered tones that seemed to moan through the building with a plaintive solemnity'; the other a favourite hymn by Martin Luther, 'Great God, what do I see and hear?', sung by the tenor soloist Mr Tolley. These had been requested by Victoria, having been privately printed in a pamphlet—*In Memoriam*—on the death of her mother, 'which the late Prince was constantly in the habit of using'.[17] Then the Garter King of Arms stepped forward to read the proclamation in which reference was made to Queen Victoria, 'Whom God bless and preserve with long life, health, and happiness'. There was, however, one significant change; having carefully studied the details of the funeral service before leaving for Osborne, Victoria had specifically ordered that the word 'happiness' be struck out and replaced with 'honour'. For her, all worldly happiness was now, and for ever, at an end.[18]

As the ceremony drew to a close, many in the all-male congregation openly wept as the pall was removed and the gold and crimson-covered coffin suddenly flashed into view, all too briefly, in all its magnificence. In the pause that followed as the congregation gazed in awe at Albert's coffin, the wind outside gathered and 'mourned hoarsely against the casements', accompanied by the quick, sharp rattle of the troops outside as they reversed arms, to the sound of the melancholy knell from the castle spire. Then the coffin was gradually lowered quietly down through the aperture in the stone floor to the royal vault below. As it finally disappeared from view a handful of earth was thrown down 'with a sharp rattle that was heard throughout the building'. The mourners then slowly advanced to take one last look down at the coffin before departing—to the sound of Dr Elvey playing the 'Dead March from Saul'. During the hour-long service everyone had perished with the bitter cold inside the chapel and now headed into the castle to be fortified with a champagne funeral luncheon, which Lord Torrington noticed that an exhausted Sir Charles Phipps devoured with relish, no doubt relieved it was all over.[19]

In his account the following day George Augustus Sala commented on the 'splendid but ghastly toilet of the grave' that Albert's magnificent funeral ceremony had embodied, contrasting it with the last rites for ordinary people, quietly laid to rest in 'green country churchyards, where the moon shines with a soft and tender kindness on the stones above them'. In contrast, Albert's great coffin had passed 'but a few paces from the Chamber of Death to the House of Silence' and now, as the mourners dispersed, the funeral attendants prepared it for its final resting place. At the end of a stone passage, six feet wide and nine feet high—past rows of tall, black, two-armed wooden candelabra in which torches were placed to light their way— the coffin arrived at two plain, rusty, barred iron gates, which marked the entrance to the royal vault. Inside this cold and silent stone vault with its groined roof stood four tiers of marble shelves on either side, with marble slabs in the centre (the preserve of monarchs only), on which were visible the deep-purple velvet-covered coffins of George III, George IV, William IV and their wives, and to the side the crimson coffin of Princess Charlotte. Queen Victoria had had a horror of Albert's coffin being placed there, alongside 'that huge, dingy coffin' of the venal old George IV.[20] And so here, at the gates to the vault, it would rest until his mausoleum was completed a year later.

Describing that day to his friend Delane at *The Times*, Lord Torrington said he was 'inclined to think that more real sorrow was evinced at this funeral than at any that has taken place *there* for a vast number of years'. 'Brave men sobbed like children,' agreed gentleman usher Lyon Playfair, and 'even the choristers broke down when they had to sing the requiem'. All around one saw 'old, dry, political eyes, which seemed as if they had long forgotten how to weep, gradually melting and running down in large drops of sympathy,' recalled Samuel Wilberforce, the Bishop of Oxford. Arthur Stanley, one of the chaplains to Prince Albert, would himself later recall that, 'considering the magnitude of the event and of the persons present, all agitated by the same emotion, I do not think that I have ever seen, or shall see, anything so affecting'.[21]

London itself that day had been 'like a city struck by the Plague'. An unusual stillness had prevailed everywhere; it was as though normal daily life was in a state of suspended animation. Private houses were dark and 'as much closed as though each household had lost a close relative'. Shops were shuttered up, labour was suspended, money exchanges were closed, as the country 'voluntarily imposed upon itself a fine which probably cannot be estimated at less than a million sterling, in order to mark its regret for the dead and its sympathy for its survivors'.[22] At Lockinge House in Berkshire, Lord Overstone, responding to the prevailing mood, had, first thing that morning, 'invited the whole household (out of door as well as indoor servants)' to attend prayers inside the main house. 'They all attended readily I believe without a single exception,' he wrote. 'I read to them the Burial Service, with a few remarks of my own on the character of the Prince and the solemnity of the event whilst the Church Bell was tolling, almost as if it were in the very room.' All present, he recalled, were 'deeply affected; sincerely so I fully believe'.[23] No doubt many families began the day in similar manner, before heading for one of the many commemorative services held in Britain's churches, where the congregations were huge—with 3,000 crowding into St Paul's Cathedral alone. Many major towns staged large, solemn processionals ahead of the service: in Leeds not only was the parish church full to capacity, but mourners of all denominations and social classes lined the processional route all the way from the town hall. At Exeter there was again not enough room in the cathedral to take all those wishing to attend, prompting disgruntled local dignitaries to complain that hoi polloi had been allowed precedence.[24]

*    *    *

At a more modest level, among the working classes in the overcrowded East End, people were no less grief-stricken. At Bethnal Green there was 'hardly any noise in those usually noisy thoroughfares'; people gathered on street corners in subdued groups around street ballad-singers, 'whose utterances visibly moved their audiences' as they lamented the death of the Prince in song:

> Britannia, alas! is lamenting,
> And grief now is everywhere seen
> Oh think, you kind daughters of Britain,
> The Feelings of England's Queen
> What trouble and care does oppress her,
> Her loss causes her to deplore,
> The spirit of him is departed,
> And Prince Albert, alas! is no more.[25]

Philanthropists of the London City Mission noted considerable grief among the 'very poorest' of those families whom they visited at the time; one hospital visitor talked of how, when he did his round at St George's Hospital, 'not one patient spoke to him of his own wounds or ailments, while every one to whom he went up, was full of expressions of sorrow for the loss which the Country had sustained, and of tender enquiries about the Queen, in her cruel bereavement'. In rural areas Richard Monckton Milnes observed that 'The peasants in their cottages talk as if the Queen was one of themselves. It is the realest public sorrow I have ever seen—quite different from anything else.'[26]

But it was not just the Christian community that paid homage in their churches that day. Among the Jewish community, especially of London, Prince Albert was mourned in an atmosphere of profound melancholy. The Jews, who had much to thank the Prince for his impartiality on religious matters, marked the occasion with special services in synagogues, several of them draped in black. Sermons on the dead Prince were delivered at London's historic Sephardi synagogue (the Bevis Marks in the City) and the two Ashkenazi congregations (the Great and the Hambro synagogues). At the West London synagogue every seat was filled long before the service and the roads leading up to it were jammed with vehicles. Here the congregation heard a sermon by Dr Marks taking as its text the words of Jeremiah IX:19: 'A voice of lamentation is heard from Zion. How are we bereaved!' And at his own privately built synagogue on his estate in Ramsgate, the philanthropist Sir Moses Montefiore and his wife attended a special service where the reading desk was covered with black cloth, 'the only symbol of mourning we ever had in our synagogue'. All in all, as one British Jew later reported to a friend in South Africa, there had been 'not a dry eye in the synagogues'; prayers for Prince Albert had continued all day. 'The people mourned for him as much as for Hezekiah; and, indeed, he deserved it a great deal better' was his somewhat unorthodox conclusion.[27]

In all, seventy sermons preached on the Sunday and Monday would later be published in pamphlet form, their titles echoing the impact of Albert's death on the national consciousness— 'Britain's Loss and Britain's Duty', 'God's Voice from Windsor Castle', 'Death is Entered into Our Palaces', 'The Smitten Nation', 'A Nation's Lamentation over Fallen Greatness', 'A Prince's Death, A Nation's Grief'—not to mention a plethora of poetry, good, bad and awful. Even the unremittingly satirical *Punch* magazine for once took a serious tone, rising to the occasion with its own moving offering 'How Do Princes Die', in which it reflected the universal feeling:

> It was too soon to die.
> Yet, might we count his years by triumphs won,
> By wise, and bold, and Christian duties done,
> It were no brief, eventless history . . . [28]

On the day after Albert died, when she had taken the Duchess of Sutherland into the King's Room to see his body, the Queen had turned as they both looked down at Albert's dead face and asked plaintively, 'Will they do him justice now?' By day's end, 23 December 1861, there was no one in the country who could have doubted the extent to which the nation had indeed done justice to its late Prince. The day had been a great celebration, not just of the Prince, but of sober British moral values. Benjamin Disraeli had no hesitation in his own paean to the late Consort: 'With Prince Albert we have buried our sovereign,' he confided unequivocally to Count Vitzthum, Saxon envoy to the Court of St James.

'This German prince has governed England for twenty-one years with a wisdom and energy such as none of our kings have ever shown.' But as for the future: 'What to-morrow will bring forth no man can tell. To-day we are sailing in the deepest gloom, with night and darkness all around us.'[29]

Alone in Coburg, too sick and frail to travel, Albert's oldest and truest friend, Baron Christian Stockmar, was left to nurse his broken heart and the end of his life's work. 'An edifice, which for a great and noble purpose, has been reared with a devout sense of duty, by twenty years of laborious toil' had, with his protégé's death, 'been shattered to its very foundations'. He had an 'indisputable right', he wrote to Bertie, to say that 'in Him I have *lost the very best of* Sons'.[30] Stockmar would never recover from it; eighteen months later he too was dead, and the dream of a golden age of constitutional monarchy in Britain—and a united Germany—under Albert's enlightened guidance, died with him.

## CHAPTER EIGHT

# *'How Will the Queen Bear It?'*

In deep retreat on a bleak and cheerless Isle of Wight, Queen Victoria had sat watching the minutes tick by on the day of her husband's funeral, and then, as the clock struck, she had picked up her pen and written to Vicky. 'It is one o'clock and all, all is over!' Alone in Berlin, Vicky had spent the day sitting with her beloved father's photographs spread out on her knees, 'devouring them with my eyes, kissing them and feeling as if my heart would break'. She would have given anything to be there, with her family. Over at Osborne her mother had not wished to have any reminders of that day's solemnities. She made certain that she would not have to suffer within her earshot the agonising and very audible sound of the minute guns being fired by ships and batteries across the Solent. She therefore instructed Sir Charles Phipps to ask the Duke of Cambridge, as C-in-C of the Army, to see to it; 'nor should any guns for practice or other duties be fired at Portsmouth, or within reach of being heard at Osborne'. She had, she said, already found the constant practice-firing from Portsmouth on the morning of 20 December greatly distressing and shuddered at the thought of being further reminded.[1]

Sir Charles Phipps, who had remained with the Queen at Osborne until leaving for the funeral early on the Monday morning, had dreaded how she would react that day, but, he told Lord Sydney, was convinced that 'the coming here has been a *very good* measure'. Informing the Duke of Cambridge of the Queen's instructions, he hoped her deep grief would 'resume the same quiet, unexcited character' once the funeral was over.[2] Thin she might be, and still suffering from disrupted sleep, but the initial fears they had had when the Queen's pulse had dropped alarmingly had been unfounded and she was otherwise in good health. Her continuing state of calm, despite bouts of weeping, impressed everyone, as did her acceptance— Victoria claiming that she did not feel the same bitterness as she had when her mother had died. 'I was so rebellious then,' she admitted, 'but now I see the mercy and love that are mixed with my misery.'[3]

When he arrived by royal yacht from Prussia en route to the funeral, her son-in-law Fritz remarked on Victoria's composure and her 'greatness of spirit in such terrible times of grief'. They spent much time in quiet conversation, during which she told him how she had already plucked up the courage to go into Albert's rooms at Osborne. Fritz thought this highly therapeutic, urging her to 'seek out all the places they shared in times of happiness at the first sign of pain' in order to get herself 'used to the loneliness'.[4] On her arrival at Osborne, Victoria had sent for the gardener who had worked so closely with Prince Albert and had asked him to walk round the garden every morning with her, as Albert had done, and never to be afraid of speaking to her of his late master, 'as it was a solace to her to hear him spoken of.' She took a turn in the gardens too with Fritz, and went over to the Swiss chalet that Albert had commissioned in 1854 as a playhouse for the children. Victoria longed so much to have Vicky there, for she, of all her children, 'had her father's mind' and so would be able to 'help me in all my great plans for a mausoleum . . . for statues, monuments, etc.'[5]

But at least from 18 December Victoria's devoted relatives had begun arriving to offer moral support, ferried over from the Continent by a succession of royal yachts, most importantly her widowed half-sister Feodora from Baden. One person, though, was still absent and much missed— Victoria's uncle, King Leopold of the Belgians. Back in 1817 Prince Leopold of Saxe-Coburg, as he then was, had witnessed the dying agonies of his first wife, Princess Charlotte, and had taken centre stage during the days of public grief and mourning that had followed her tragic death. But now, faced with a horrifying repetition of events of forty-four years ago, as well as having lost a second wife (to tuberculosis) in 1850, he proved unequal to the task of supporting his widowed niece and did not arrive at Osborne until 27 December. (Others would claim that Leopold's motives were entirely selfish and that he had not wanted to go to Windsor for fear of infection.)

With her mother clearly unable to resume official business, Princess Alice had found the strength to take on the necessary day-to-day management of the household and deal with ministers and urgent letter-writing—all of it conducted on inch-thick black-bordered paper, with the help of Victoria's private secretaries, Phipps and Grey. But her heart, she told Louis, was 'quite broken' and her grief 'almost more than I can bear'. With so much attention directed towards the Queen, some had failed to notice how shockingly frail Alice had become. When he arrived in England for the funeral, Louis had been disturbed to see her so changed—thin, pale, exhausted and overwrought. Fritz thought likewise: Alice was hardly sleeping, he wrote to Vicky on the 20th, she spent most nights in her mother's room. 'We're working to make sure that she doesn't do this too often, otherwise she will annihilate herself by her love of self-sacrifice.' Nevertheless Alice was consumed by a sense of duty to her mother and that she should remain with her to fill the gap left by Albert. She could not be persuaded even to take a break outside in the fresh air, noted Fritz, 'so much so that she, with strict

183

admonishment, needs to be reminded not to overdo it'. Burdened by all her additional responsibilities, Alice admitted the great change in herself to Bertie: 'I feel years older since that dreadful time.'[6] Her wedding to Louis would, of course, have to be postponed.

One of Alice's most important tasks as the year drew to a close had been to send a message via Phipps to the Poet Laureate, Alfred Tennyson, requesting that he write something in memory of her father. Tennyson, who had met Prince Albert in May 1856, hated being asked to write to order, but the royal couple were among his most dedicated admirers and he could not refuse. Being unwell at the time, he protested that he did not at present feel able to do Albert justice and hoped, in due course, to be 'enabled to speak of him as he himself would have wished to be spoken of'. He therefore suggested that, rather than come up with something completely new, he should write a prefatory dedication to the Prince Consort, to be added to the new edition of his epic Arthurian romance in verse *The Idylls of the King*, which was due out the following year.[7] It was a work that Victoria and Albert had both been 'in raptures about' when they had first read it. For the time being, the Queen would continue to take comfort in his *In Memoriam*, which she and Albert had also greatly loved, a copy of which Tennyson had signed for Albert in May 1860. She felt 'much soothed' by it: 'only those who have suffered as I do, can understand these beautiful poems'.[8]

In the midst of her crippling grief the Queen was, meanwhile, very clear about one thing: she was determined to retain absolute control of matters of state. ('She has the *habit* of power and once taken it is hardly possible to live without it,' as Queen Sophie of the Netherlands shrewdly remarked to one of the ladies at court.)[9] With this in mind, Victoria told Fritz that she had made it known that all enquiries should be directed to her 'which would normally have gone to papa', and that nothing should be addressed to Bertie. 'Oh that boy,' she complained to Vicky, 'much as I pity I never can or shall look at him without a shudder'.[10] Others, in private, agreed that Bertie was a lost cause. There was, for writer and journalist Harriet Martineau, 'no hope in that wretched boy!' His 'natural goodness and docility' had given way to 'impenetrable levity'; Bertie had been fatally corrupted at the Curragh and at Cambridge, and 'there is nothing more to hope'. Even Lord Stanley gossiped that among Bertie's own entourage he was thought immature and childish and that they seldom addressed him 'when serious subjects were discussed'.[11]

The failings of her errant oldest son were uppermost in Victoria's mind when she wrote to Uncle Leopold on Christmas Eve, her sharp, angular hand scratching at and underlining the paper in an intensity of feeling that made plain her intentions for the future—intentions that would brook no interference, even from benevolent uncles:

I am also anxious to repeat one thing, and *that one* is *my firm* resolve, my *irrevocable decision*, viz. that *his* wishes—*his* plans—about everything, *his* views about *every* thing are to be *my* law! And *no human power* will make me swerve from what he decided and wished . . . I live *on* with him, for him; in fact, *I* am only *outwardly* separated from him, and *only* for a *time*.[12]

Albert died in the belief, above all others, that he had trained his wife to do her duty. And in the dazed and disjointed days of grief that followed, Victoria kept repeating it like a mantra: yes, 'they need not be afraid, I will do my duty'. But she had yet to prove that she could, or would, do so, and meanwhile life for the royal household was in a state of stasis: 'the utter consternation of everyone—the standstill everything has come to—the spring and centre of each being gone, is more apparent every moment,' maid-of-honour Mary Bulteel admitted in a letter to her mother. 'I cannot *conceive* what she will do, for if her will were ever so strong, she cannot have the power or capacity to do his work.'[13]

\*     \*     \*

As Christmas Eve 1861 drew in, everyone at Osborne, as well as in the royal family at large, was in a depressed state. 'We have not the heart to keep Christmas in the usual manner,' wrote Princess Mary Adelaide. 'The tree is at all events for the present to be dispensed with.'[14] For Victoria the festive season that had once been such a joy was irrevocably changed: 'Think of Christmas Eve and all!!!' she wrote to Vicky. 'It shall never be spent at Windsor again—for he left us in those rooms.' That same day, Vicky in Berlin also turned her thoughts to happier times:

186

This is Xmas Eve! I should not know it sitting *all alone*—with none but my own sad thoughts for companions, but the noise in the streets, the merry bustle, forces the dismal contrast upon me . . . the bells are ringing—to me they seem tolling for the dear departed one! All the world is sad and dark and empty—mourning is the only thing that gives me satisfaction.

Christmas, Vicky concluded, *'never will* be *happy* again'.[15]

Osborne that year was, inevitably, a 'house of mourning'. Everyone was looking thin and wan and exhausted, and even Christmas presents took on a very different character: the household all received tokens of remembrance of Albert—black-bordered photographs for the men, and for the ladies lockets with Albert's portrait. Fritz had already been sent back to Berlin with locks of Albert's hair and other mementoes for Vicky. Casting his mind back to the happy Christmas he had witnessed at Windsor the previous year, Lord Torrington could not help but make comparisons in a letter to Delane. 'I need hardly say we are very dull here,' he began, though personally he was not downhearted. 'All things considered it is not so bad as I expected. People must eat & drink & in spite of grief, we sometimes laugh.' But for the exhausted Phipps, Christmas dawned no brighter. 'What a Christmas Day we have to pass here!' he told the diplomat Lord Cowley. 'You can hardly form an idea of the desolation of this house.'[16]

Back on the mainland, the British nation at large was doing its best to overcome its still-profound grief at the Prince Consort's death, but the prevalence of people in mourning on all the streets and in all the shops continued to cast its gloom. In Manchester 'No one wishes each other "a *merry* Xmas" this year,' observed the writer Elizabeth Gaskell, whilst at the American legation in London, Benjamin Moran was resigned that 'Xmas bids fair to be as funereal as the grave'.[17] A despondent press reiterated what was in everyone's minds. 'What a sad and solemn Christmas falls so unexpectedly upon us! What a dismal close of the year!' ran the editorial in the *Morning Post*. 'These few sad days of Christmas must be consecrated to grief,' lamented the *Daily Telegraph*. Everywhere families were gathering around their hearths, where they would normally have raised a Christmas glass to the Queen, 'with an affectionate thought of her Consort, her children, our Princess in Prussia, our Prince coming of age, the young sailor, the sisters to be married, and the rest of the cherished family'. But now, 'The home which all England recognised as the sweetest and holiest in the land is bereaved and desolate,' observed the press, prompting many to remember 'those who are absent from the family gathering, and to forecast the further severing of family ties, which fate may have in store for us'. Recalling past Christmases at the close of this difficult year, George Augustus Sala in the *Telegraph* thought that 1861 would 'always to be associated with its numerals. When the hale among us are gray, and the gray are in their peaceful graves, it will be said: "At that Christmas the people buried the noble Consort of the Queen, and waited over their festal cheer to know if America would be at war with them or peace!"'[18]

Yet despite the continuing political crisis, war,

mercifully, had not come. The American Civil War raged on—and with it the blockade of the southern ports, which was bringing short-time to the Lancashire cotton mills and an impending economic crisis at home. But life had to go on. And so, after the necessary respectful pause for the obsequies for Prince Albert, newspapers published the lists of theatrical entertainments on offer, as once again the pantomime season came around. Families could forget the mournful atmosphere at large with a trip to 'Little Miss Muffet and Little Boy Blue' or 'Whittington and his Cat', or take the train to the Crystal Palace at Sydenham and thrill to the heart-in-mouth spectacle of the French tightrope-walker Monsieur Blondin. Churches that had been festooned in mourning for Albert's funeral removed it—for Christmas at least—and brought in the holly and the ivy to try and cheer things up. In parishes everywhere, church dignitaries and charities handed out coal, food, warm clothing and other comforts to deserving families. Continuing a tradition started by the late Duchess of Kent, the poor in Kensington were given gifts of bread, meat, coals and blankets, and 'a good Christmas dinner' was provided by the Duke and Duchess of Cambridge to poor families in Kew. Appeals to Christian charity were also made to ensure that in Britain's 490 workhouses more than 14,000 inmates enjoyed a decent Christmas dinner of roast beef, potatoes, plum pudding and a pint of porter.[19]

\*       \*       \*

Across the Atlantic, news of the Prince Consort's

death had arrived in New York and Washington on Christmas Eve. *The Times* correspondent William Howard Russell, who had pioneered war reporting during the Crimean War and was now covering the American Civil War, remembered how the telegram when it came had 'cast the deepest gloom over all our little English circle. Prince Albert dead! At first no one believed it.' Their Christmas too would be a subdued one: 'the preparations which we had made for a little festivity to welcome in Christmas morning were chilled by the news, and the eve was not of the joyous character which Englishmen delight to give it, for the sorrow which fell on all hearts in England had spanned the Atlantic, and bade us mourn in common with the country at home.'[20]

In New York harbour the premier vessel of the Cunard line, the *Persia*, as well as other English steamers had lowered their flags to half-mast. The British Vice-Consul, Sir Edward Archibald, immediately convened a meeting of British residents in order to arrange a commemorative event, as too did residents in Nova Scotia and elsewhere in Canada. The *New York Times*, whilst of the opinion that the death of Prince Albert was 'without political significance', published the apprehensions of its London correspondent about its effect on Britain's 'nation of shopkeepers'. 'Christmas is just at hand, and the shops were hoping to make a little money for the first time this year. But now the death of the Prince, coming as it does, in the midst of the American difficulty, has reduced them to despair,' it reported, adding that 'The proprietors of the mourning establishments may be happy behind their bales of crape, but everyone else will lament.' Yet even here, in

America, in the midst of a political crisis, the protocols of mourning were observed, with one Union lady complaining that at an official dinner in Washington the 'affectation of court mourning' for the Queen's loss was utterly absurd. 'It is too sad to see such extravagance and folly in the White House,' she wrote, 'with the country bankrupt and a civil war raging!'[21]

The state of agonising suspense over the 'American Difficulty' lasted to the very end of the year, as ships, guns and troops continued to sail for Canada from British docks. In Washington, Russell noted a rampantly bellicose attitude all around; 'press people, soldiers, sailors, ministers, senators, Congress-men, people in the street' were all agreed about the two arrested Southern commissioners: '"Give them up? Never! We'll die first."' The following day, therefore, he was greatly surprised to hear that Secretary of State William Seward—Abraham Lincoln's adviser on foreign policy—had capitulated to compromise. He had agreed to release the two men, after the President had argued during a heated cabinet meeting on Christmas Day that the North must at all costs pursue a policy of 'one war at a time'.[22] A climbdown by Seward in response to the British note drafted by Prince Albert was contrived that would not alienate American public opinion and was presented to the British minister to the United States, Lord Lyons, that day. News was telegraphed to Palmerston in England that Mason and Slidell were to be released, but the Prime Minister decided to suppress its announcement until after he knew for certain that this had indeed happened. The two men eventually sailed for Southampton on 14

January 1862. There would therefore be no crumb of comfort for the British nation that Christmas.[23]

But as one international crisis came to an end, another and very different domestic one loomed. With the Queen determined that her life was at an end 'in a worldly point of view', Sir Charles Phipps by now had very clear intimations of a catastrophe to come. The royal household was cast adrift, affairs of state abandoned, the Queen beyond consolation. He initiated a flurry of memos to government ministers about the ongoing and now even more crucial role of Private Secretary to the Queen—a role that Albert had long unofficially fulfilled. 'It must be evident to the world that there are many things which the Queen may, & indeed *must*, do through others,' Grey told Lord Glanville, as a clear rivalry developed between himself—as Albert's Private Secretary of twelve years—and Sir Charles Phipps.[24] It was essential that the Queen had someone confidential to take custody of her papers. Gossiping away to Delane, as was his wont, Torrington confided that Phipps and Grey 'although they keep up appearances *are at war*'. There was no unanimity of advice being offered the Queen and he expected that 'there will be trouble before long'. Everywhere people were whispering in corners, giving their own personal view of how and by whom the Prince's former roles should be taken over; 'but there is *no head* in the palace,' continued Torrington and he heard a different story from everyone.[25]

The true extent of the Queen's voracious, unquenchable mourning, as everyone now could see, was only just beginning to unravel. 'They cannot tell what I have lost,' she kept insisting, levelling the barrage of her grief at her devoted and uncomplaining half-sister Feodora, Princess Alice and Lady Bruce—four women in black, who sat silently over meals together, day in, day out, all words of consolation long since exhausted. It was clear to Phipps that the Queen was incapable of thinking straight about anything: 'Her grief *gnaws* to the *very* core of her heart into the *very depth* of *her soul!*' True, Victoria did what she was asked by her doctors in order to sustain her health, but she was obsessed with one thought: to die, to 'join what was the *sun shine* of her *existence*, the light of *her life*'.[26] At the end of the year she gave instructions to the Lord Chamberlain that the public mourning for the Prince Consort should be 'for the longest term in modern times'; members of the royal household would not be allowed to appear in public out of mourning for a year.[27] Royal watchers in the press were becoming apprehensive, with the London correspondent of the *New York Times* already predicting that the Queen's seclusion would be 'as absolute as is possible'. 'My own belief,' he added, 'is that the glory of her reign is departed.' 'I have no hope that *she* will keep up her reputation now,' echoed Harriet Martineau—a regular, anonymous correspondent of the *Daily News*—'Her temper is *not* cured; & of course we all fear for her brain . . . those who know what *his* trials were must have more depressing fears.'[28]

On New Year's Eve, looking out over the River Thames as the clocks struck midnight, the diarist Arthur Munby recalled events of the past two weeks. The whole nation had seemed 'sublimed by a noble sorrow and a noble anxiety, into a purity and oneness that I never remember to have seen before . . . England, knit together as one man by grief and indignation, has poured out its heart . . . in a passion of sympathy and love and veneration for the Queen, for which mere loyalty is a cold name indeed.' But for how long would that loyalty last, with a queen now in the deepest retreat from her public?

For Victoria, the days of her life at Osborne passed as one, in utter darkness and stark despair. And it was only now, as people gathered to lament the year that mercifully was over and raise a hopeful glass to a better one to come, that the full horror of the Queen's solitude began to sink in. For, despite being surrounded by loyal family and retainers, Queen Victoria had in reality 'none to cast herself upon and weep out her Soul'. Recalling a story he had once heard about the islanders of Honolulu, the country parson Robert Hawker noted in his diary that in the Pacific they called a king 'by a word which signified The Lonely One'. This was because 'their lofty place is shared by none and they are therefore solitary above their people'. Sympathy, he added, 'can only be complete among those who are equal', and who was the Queen's equal now that Albert had gone?[29] 'Oh! Who is so lonely as she,' echoed the *Daily News*, as one thought gained currency over and above all the many expressions of shock and grief and apprehension that had filled the press for the sixteen days since Albert's death. It lingered in every heart and on everyone's lips. In the days to come, they all asked, 'How will the Queen bear it?'[30]

# PART TWO

*The Broken-Hearted Widow*

# CHAPTER NINE

## *'All Alone!'*

'What a sad new Year, what a cloud more impenetrable than ever has settled upon it,' wrote Lady Augusta Bruce to her family on 8 January 1862 as she contemplated the cheerless landscape at Osborne with the winter sea roaring in the distance. 'I can not tell you what it is to be here, to watch day by day the progress of this agony, and to see rising up one by one all the trials and difficulties that such a terrible visitation brings with it.' Osborne was still full of relatives who had arrived for Albert's funeral, yet for all of them New Year's Day had been, according to Lady Bruce, an intensely bleak one: 'The whole house seems like Pompeii, the life suddenly extinguished.'

For Queen Victoria, the New Year—like Christmas—brought only aching memories of what had gone before. 'This day last year found us so perfectly happy and now!!! Last year music woke us, little gifts, new year's wishes, brought in by [my] maid, and then given to dearest Albert. The children waiting with their gifts in the next room.'[1] All was so terribly, irrevocably changed; the clock of Victoria's happy life had stopped on 14 December 1861. Like Dickens's Miss Havisham, she had no desire to move forward but only to remain in stasis, locked into that terrible moment of loss, in perpetuity. She confidently expected to die soon, and made her will and arranged guardians for her children. Meanwhile, in anticipation of that

197

longed-for day, she sank into a state of lethargy and gloom, enshrouding herself in the veil of widowhood as the sunshine of her marriage faded into the interminable monochrome of her new 'sad and solitary life'.[2] Day after day the great, inconsolable bouts of Victoria's weeping could be heard along the corridors of Osborne.

She had, at first, resolved differently: she would not give way to despair. Shortly after Albert had died, she had gathered her children round her and told them, 'Your father never blamed me but once and that was for my grief about my mother—that it was selfish . . . I will not do so now,' she promised them, 'I will have affliction, but not gloom.'[3] She had tried hard to remember those words of advice that Albert had given her after they left Balmoral the previous October—to be less occupied with herself and her own feelings. She had copied his letter carefully into the 'Album Consolativum' that she now kept as a compendium of personal consolation. Here Albert's wise counsel was joined by copious extracts from Tennyson's *In Memoriam*—its content so closely mirroring her own feelings on loss:

> Far off thou art, but ever nigh;
> I have thee still, and I rejoice;
> I prosper, circled with thy voice;
> I shall not lose thee tho' I die.
> (Canto CXXX)[4]

There were verses too by Goethe and Schiller, extracts from letters, and sermons and hymns— even by notable Roman Catholics such as John Henry Newman and Cardinal Manning. All

198

were carefully copied mainly by her daughters or ladies-in-waiting in the neatest of handwriting, interspersed with a few in Victoria's own inimitable scrawl with significant words heavily underlined. The small gold-tooled, morocco-leather album with its gilt clasp went everywhere with her; by June it had already been filled.[5]

The courage needed to face up to her lonely task as monarch had, meanwhile, totally deserted her; her relationship with Albert had been crucial to her own sense of self and the way she lived her life, and without him she was rudderless. Indeed, her whole life had been one long pattern of reliance on others: during her childhood she had become used to incessant surveillance, imposed by her mother. She had never had to stand and act alone until the first months of her reign, after which she had quickly let go of her early promise as an active queen, to accept the guidance of a powerful man—her Prime Minister, Lord Melbourne. Then Albert had come along and, as she was sidelined by pregnancy after pregnancy, he had assumed many of the onerous responsibilities of state on her behalf. However, it went against the grain for Victoria not to fulfil her role conscientiously, as he had so assiduously trained her, but alone as she now was, she was so mistrustful of her own judgement that it was much easier simply to give way to grief and do nothing. Every act, every decision seemed so daunting without Albert. All she could do was filter things through the prism of what he would have said, or done, or wanted. Carl Ruland noted the dramatic change in the once-wilful queen: 'she used to say "I never will do it," and now it is "How shall I be able to do it?"'[6] Having lived her life in a unique position of power as a woman—enacting, initiating, granting permission and, when she chose, withholding it—Victoria was presented by Albert's death for the first time with something totally outside her control. She felt angry, worthless, inadequate and guilty too: that perhaps in her own self-obsession she had omitted to take her husband's failing health seriously enough and might even, somehow, have done something to prevent it. Unending grief was therefore not just an escape from responsibilities she did not wish to shoulder alone, but also a necessary form of harsh self-punishment.

'There is no one to call me Victoria now,' she had wept, though this is the popularly quoted version of a far more wrenching form of the loss of intimacy, as she expressed it to her German-speaking relatives: 'I have no one now in the world to call me "du",' she had told Princess Mary Adelaide.[7] The terrifying loneliness of her position was brought home to her even more at night when she missed Albert's presence the most. She was still young (only forty-three), still a sexual being full of longing: 'What a dreadful going to bed! *What* a contrast to that tender lover's love. *All alone*!'[8] The great waves of debilitating grief were relentless; how she envied her daughter Vicky, who had a husband 'on whose bosom you can pillow your head when all seems dark'.[9]

For the rest, Victoria remained calm and quiet and largely uncomplaining. No exhortations to find comfort in her children moved her. 'The children of lovers are orphans,' observed the writer Robert Louis Stevenson, and in Victoria's case it was only too apparent that her love for Albert had transcended her love for all her children,

200

who remained the 'poor half' of her life.[10] Albert had thought it 'a pity', he told her in 1856, that she found no consolation in their company, and Victoria did not deny it. She was quite candid when Lord Hertford arrived for a private visit: 'she had never taken pleasure in the society of her children as most mothers did,' she admitted to him, 'but always preferred being alone with him [Albert].' It was Albert who 'gave all the gaiety and life to the house'. It made her so angry to hear people talk of '*her* management of the children, of *her* attention to business, and *her* doing this and doing that when they ought to have known it was all *him*, that he was the life and soul of the family and indeed of all her counsels'.[11]

Feeling as she did, Victoria made it much harder for her children to come to terms, in their own way, with the loss of their father. Rather than comforting them in their grief, she punished them, expecting them to share in the levels of her own conspicuous, unrelenting mourning. In so doing she cast a blight over their lives for many years to come. No one— in the family or entourage—was to be allowed any respite: she sent out an 'injunction' making clear the impossibility of her ever again joining in the 'frivolities of court'.[12] Personal pleasure, light-heartedness and laughter in her presence were absolutely frowned on, as too was all but the most necessary social contact. Anything more frayed her nerves. She who had so loved dancing as a young woman would never again attend a ball or give one. The private theatricals and fancy-dress parties that the children had so enjoyed during their father's lifetime were forbidden, and none of the family would be allowed to appear at the opening ceremony of the 1862 Great London Exhibition, despite their father's close involvement in its planning. The only exception made was for four-year-old Beatrice, whose disarming candour and innocent good humour were impossible to repress. 'Cousin Mary, am I too merry,' the little girl whispered guiltily to Princess Mary Adelaide when she visited in January. Poor Beatrice, 'prattling' amidst all 'the sad grave faces' as Mary noted, had heard her siblings wishing they could die and go to be with Papa. 'I don't wish to die,' Beatrice told her, 'I want to live, and want Mama to take care of me.'[13] 'I always hope her little innocent cheerfulness may be one of the first things to rouse the poor Queen,' wrote the Duchess of Wellington, but far from it: with time, even the irrepressible Beatrice succumbed to the overwhelming atmosphere of gloom at home, becoming strangely solemn and introverted.[14]

Weak and exhausted she may have been, but in a perverse way Victoria's thin, pale appearance made her look younger, more vulnerable, as though recovering from a severe illness. Indeed, she rather liked it when people told her how thin she had grown—it was comforting confirmation of the visible depths of her grief and her feminine frailty. Her sister Feodora and Princess Alice tried repeatedly to persuade her to engage in the gentlest of occupational therapy, some light reading or perhaps browsing the newspapers; she might even like to dictate her reminiscences. But nothing could rouse Victoria from her lethargy. She was suffering what no doubt today would be diagnosed as clinical depression. It left her incapable of doing anything more than reading the odd letter, taking short walks in the garden and talking—endlessly, obsessively—of Albert, as though by constant mention of his name she was keeping him alive, maintaining a seamless continuity between his death and her life, the only difference being that he was now invisible and she had yet to reach the end of her own mortal journey.[15] Soon there would be no avoiding a return to Windsor and to affairs of state and she dreaded the pressures already being put on her: 'The things of this life are of no interest to the Queen,' she told Lord Russell wanly, but the excuse—for all the ready sympathy offered her—would not wash with ministers anxious for her to resume her official duties.[16]

For most of those first weeks of grinding melancholy at Osborne the Queen kept almost totally to the company of Alice, Feodora, her most trusted lady-in-waiting Augusta Bruce and her head-dresser, Marianne Skerrett. Lady Bruce's growing power as right-hand woman did not go unnoticed, and was not without occasional jealous comment. When Vicky arrived in February she noted that Lady Bruce had more influence over her mother than anyone else, 'simply because she said "Yes, Ma'am" to everything and that if she said "No, Ma'am" a few times the Queen would cease to think her the paragon of cleverness she now did'.[17] Augusta Bruce had been a lady-in-waiting for fifteen years; after Albert died she was offered a highly privileged, permanent place with the Queen (as opposed to the normal three-month periods on and off duty). Many of the Queen's other (unmarried) ladies during that first year never saw her from one day to the next and found their imposed idleness enervating. For, aside from

Bruce and Skerrett, Victoria now demonstrated a decided preference for the company of widows such as the Duchess of Sutherland, Lady Ely and Lady Barrington, and, when she visited from Germany, her devoted friend Countess Blücher.[18]

But it was not just the well-born ladies-in-waiting and of the bedchamber who became the Queen's confidantes, for her dresser Marianne Skerrett played a key role. She was a tiny, thin creature, shorter even than the Queen (under five feet) and 'comically plain', but a good linguist and fiercely intelligent. Appointed in 1837 when Victoria came to the throne, Skerrett, a woman 'of the greatest discretion and straightforwardness', became one of Victoria's most intimate and protective friends and played an increasingly important role, performing various personal and administrative tasks for her, as well as reading to her.[19] When Skerrett retired, Annie Macdonald (the widow of a footman), who had been Prince Albert's general cleaner, was promoted to wardrobe-maid and largely took over Skerrett's role. All of these women would increasingly be called upon—often unreasonably so—to fill the void of the Queen's loneliness, kowtowing to her often bullying demands during the first difficult ten years of her retreat. They formed a human barrier, used by Victoria to protect herself from what she saw as the unkind onslaughts of demanding ministers, and carried messages back and forth to male members of her entourage when she did not feel up to dealing with them.[20] Lady Ely rather enjoyed showing off her trusted position of important go-between—often on highly sensitive political matters—and delighted in whispering confidences in the Queen's ear in front of the other ladies. In general, though, self-effacement was an unwritten prerequisite of the job, as too was all thought of personal aspirations such as marriage. None of the ladies-in-waiting were supposed to keep diaries when on duty, but of course several did; with life at court so deadening and restricted, it was one of the few pursuits left to them.[21] The Duchess of Athole, with her vigorous common sense, was perhaps the most resilient and least awestruck of the Queen's ladies, understanding the utter folly of trying to contradict Victoria's wishes and learning how to cleverly manage her intractability. The Queen *would* have her way and they had all better spare themselves the pain of trying to contradict it. Victoria in return recognised the Duchess's unique value and refused to allow her to retire.[22]

While the well-rehearsed commiserations of her ladies were all too readily available, Victoria found greater comfort in the honest words of ordinary people, who had sent endless 'expressions of universal admiration and appreciation of beloved Albert' since the day he died. 'Even the poor people in small villages, who don't know me, are shedding tears for me, as if it were their own private sorrow,' she noted in her journal.[23] When, in mid-January, there was a terrible disaster at the Hartley Colliery in Northumberland, in which 205 men and boys trapped below ground had suffocated and died, a distraught Victoria was quick to share in the sorrow of their wives and mothers, sending £200 to the disaster fund with her 'tenderest sympathies' and telling them that 'her own misery only makes her feel the more for them'.[24] On 11 January the Home Secretary, Sir George Grey, presented her with some of the many hundreds of addresses of condolence received from municipalities and other bodies across the country. There were in addition dozens of letters received at Windsor from heads of state—from the Emperor of Mexico to the Sultan of Turkey—all with their stereotypical expressions of grief and consolation, inscribed in immaculate copperplate handwriting. But none of them had the directness and honesty of the letter from the American President, received from Washington in February. 'The offer of condolence in such cases is a customary ceremony, which has its good uses,' he wrote, 'though it is conventional and may sometimes be even insincere.' Despite the recent political crisis, the bond of friendship between Britain and the USA ran deep and the American people deplored the Prince's death, sympathising in the Queen's 'irreparable bereavement with an unaffected sorrow'. Certain that 'the Divine Hand that has wounded, is the only one that can heal', he therefore commended Victoria and her family to God's mercies, concluding, with utter sincerity, 'I remain Your Good Friend, Abraham Lincoln'.[25]

It was the end of January before news reached South Africa via the paddle steamer *Jin Kie*, en route to China from Plymouth. It 'created great consternation here', wrote Lady Duff Gordon. Flags in the harbour were immediately lowered to half-mast and forty-two minute guns at the British fortress at Cape Town were fired as a mark of respect that evening. General mourning for the Prince in the Cape was called for the 1 February, and Lady Gordon noted that deep mourning was 'more general than in an average village of the same size at home' in England.[26] She also noted in particular the response of many Malays in the Cape, who 'hope the people will take much care of her, now she is alone', their feelings being 'all about her'—the Queen—rather than the dead man. In Penang in the Straits Settlement, British official Orfeur Cavenagh remembered the Prince's death casting 'a great gloom across the station'; all the residents of standing met to prepare a joint message of condolence to the Queen, reiterating their 'loyal attachment and sincere affection' for her in her affliction. On the island of Madagascar, which had come under British influence, King Radama ordered his court to go into mourning for Prince Albert for twenty-one days, as well as the firing of twenty-one cannons at Antananarivo and Tamtave.[27]

With the electrical telegraph in its infancy, it took some weeks before responses started trickling in from the Antipodes. The *Star of India*, an emigrant ship from Liverpool, brought the news to Australia and from there it was passed to New Zealand. A poignant response from Maori chiefs eventually wended its way back to London via the Governor of New Zealand. 'O Victoria, our Mother!' it lamented:

We, your Maori children, are now sighing in sorrow together with you . . . who hast nourished us, your ignorant children of this island, even to this day! We have just heard the crash of the huge-headed forest tree, which has untimely fallen, ere it had attained its full growth of greatness . . . Yes, thou the pillar that didst support my palace has been borne to the skies. Oh, my beloved! You used to stand in the very prow of the war canoe, inciting all others to noble deeds. Where, oh physicians, was the power of your remedies? What, oh priests, availed your prayers? For I have lost my love, no more can he revisit this world.[28]

But it was one of Albert's own children, Prince Alfred, who was the last to be given the news of his father's death, which finally reached him at sea off the coast of Mexico in early January, relayed to his governor, Major John Cowell, by a Spanish steamship, the *Ceballor*. But Affie did not arrive back in England until 16 February 1862.

\*  \*  \*

From the moment Prince Albert's death was announced, British manufacturing went into mass production of every conceivable kind of commemorative item: plaques and busts, plates, handkerchiefs, pot lids, jugs, book marks, even special mourning teasets, all feeding into the middle-class fashion for extravagant mourning. But this was nothing compared with the ambitious plans nursed by Victoria for 'numberless' memorials to her dear departed.[29] The process had already begun with the preservation of Prince Albert's rooms at Windsor, Osborne and Balmoral, as well as the King's Room in which he had died. Nothing connected to Albert and his memory and their life together was to be overlooked, even down to the first bouquet he had ever given Victoria, and her bridal wreath, which—like Miss Havisham's—was now slowly, inexorably turning to dust.[30] The cost of maintaining this meticulous status quo, and

Victoria's insistence on keeping on all of Albert's personal retinue (albeit in reassigned roles), was placing additional strain on her overstretched finances. But Lady Bruce understood precisely the impetus behind it: 'It was idolatry, but I am sure that God allowed and pardons it.'[31] And the idols to Albert were many: in the months that followed, the Queen commissioned numerous busts and statuettes of him—in marble and in bronze—to be placed in her various homes as well as presented as gifts to her family and members of the household. A marble bust of Albert by William Theed, and garlanded with wreaths of immortelles, became the centrepiece of a series of photographs Victoria commissioned from William Bambridge of herself and her children taken at Windsor; several even more poignant ones of his mother and Alice were taken by the young Prince Alfred when he arrived home from sea.[32] With what some considered undue haste—given Victoria's absolute retirement from society—mourning photographs of the Queen and her children were being marketed as *cartes de visite* for public consumption as early as March, providing an almost voyeuristic glimpse into her private grief. The *London Review* decried these perversely distasteful, intimate images and the role of the camera in spying on such 'sacred feelings . . . to commercial account'.[33] But in fact Victoria *wanted* people to know how grief-stricken she was; she wanted them to understand the great gaping chasm in her life. By allowing the nation to see her grief she was keeping Albert alive in their memories too. Many of these photographs, showing even little Beatrice decked out in baby black mourning, were beautifully framed and distributed

209

by Victoria to friends, family and politicians alike. Other photographs were set as miniatures into pieces of gold and enamelled jewellery, such as lockets, bracelets, rings and stick pins, by Garrard's, the royal jewellers, for the Queen, her children and other favoured recipients.[34] A locket with Albert's hair was sent to Leopold in Cannes with the instructions to wear it 'attached to a string or chain round your neck'; Victoria also enclosed one of Papa's pocket handkerchiefs, which he was instructed to 'keep constantly with you'.[35]

As early as 4 January, Queen Victoria had a conversation with General Grey about her plans for a statue for Balmoral, and soon afterwards began looking at sketches by William Theed of Albert in highland dress.[36] In so doing she was immediately contravening one of her husband's most explicit wishes, expressed in the wake of the excessive memorialisation of the Duke of Wellington in 1852: 'If I should die before you, do not, I beg, raise even a single marble image to my name.' He had resisted all suggestion that a statue of himself be placed in Hyde Park to celebrate the success of the Great Exhibition of 1851. 'I would rather not be made the prominent feature of such a monument,' he told Lord Granville, 'as it would both disturb my quiet rides in Rotten Row to see my own face staring at me, and if (as is very likely) it became an artistic monstrosity, like most of our monuments, it would upset my equanimity to be permanently ridiculed and laughed at in effigy.'[37] Having professed that she would fulfil her husband's wishes to the letter, Victoria nevertheless immediately set about spearheading a concerted nationwide memorialisation that would have appalled him.

Lord Palmerston gave his full support for a statue of the Prince 'of heroic size' to be erected on a suitable site in London, and persuaded Parliament to agree to £50,000 towards the fund; anything less seemed paltry in Victoria's eyes, for she herself envisioned a great obelisk. Vicky, whose own ideas closely mirrored those of her father, objected, finding the idea lacking in artistic taste. As too did Lord Clarendon; the Queen, he remarked wearily, 'has no more notion of what is right and pure in art than she has of the Chinese grammar'.[38] Nevertheless the Duke of Argyll offered a 120-foot-long red granite stone weighing 600 tons from his Ross of Mull quarries. But the Lord Mayor, William Cubitt, doubted 'whether the roads would not fall in under such a weight or whether wheels could be made strong enough' to transport it.

Another plan, according to Lord Torrington, who was put in charge of inviting subscriptions to the fund, was melting down old cannons and 'making a column 400 feet high'.[39] It was also suggested that Cleopatra's Needle (languishing in Alexandria since being presented to the British in 1819 by Mohammad Ali, in gratitude for Nelson's victory on the Nile) should be brought to England for this purpose. This idea too was rapidly abandoned, as a Prince Consort National Memorial Fund Committee was established under Cubitt and the triumvirate of Sir Charles Eastlake (President of the Royal Academy) and a reluctant Lord Clarendon and Lord Derby, both of whom felt ill equipped for the task to which they had been co-opted. The committee's role would be to choose a design and fund-raise, through a network of sub-committees across Britain, for a lasting memorial to Albert, 'commemorative of his many virtues, and expressive of the gratitude of the people'. The obvious location for such a monument was Hyde Park, somewhere near the site of the Great Exhibition and just up from the Victoria and Albert Museum in South Kensington. Henry Cole, with whom the Prince had worked closely on the development of the museum and the planning of the Great Exhibition, suggested a more ambitious project to be located in the area: a whole range of institutions covering science, art and literature—an Albert University, which would serve as 'a palace of all learning, over whose gate his name should be written'.[40]

The Albert Memorial project was dogged by controversy from the outset, with the *Morning Post* firing a broadside at the committee, accusing them of favouritism over and above the wishes of the government. Lord Clarendon buckled at the onerous task foisted on him:

> we shall be inundated with designs of the late Consort in the robes of The Garter upon some furious and non-descript animal that will be called a horse, and Albert Baths and Washhouses, and the good Prince inaugurating some drinking pump with the Q[ueen] and the royal children round him looking thirsty: etc. etc.[41]

With the same thought in mind, Charles Dickens had refused point-blank when invited by Henry Cole to join the committee. Despite his loyalty to the Queen, he professed himself 'much shocked

212

by the rampant toadyism that has been given to the four winds on that subject'. He had no faith in such a memorial, he admitted: 'With this heresy in my heart, how can I represent myself as one of the Orthodox?'[42]

Many local municipal bodies up and down the country also broke rank and ignored the national appeal, determined to make their own mark locally. Lord Torrington feared that the impact of the national memorial would therefore be dissipated, resulting in every town in England having 'some miserable work of art, the production of a relation of the then mayor—aided possibly by some of the Corporation who are bricklayers, painters, and what not'. Such 'local acts of folly', in his view, would ruin the objectives of a grand and unifying national work, but nevertheless local authorities went ahead with their 'little town jobs' and raised statues to the Prince, not to mention renaming a plethora of streets, pubs, tenement buildings, bridges, parks and wharves in Albert's memory.[43]

Meanwhile Victoria had already initiated her own personal architectural project: the royal mausoleum at Frogmore. In accordance with Albert's wishes, she settled on a Romanesque design inspired by the mausoleum erected in Coburg for his father, Ernst I. It was to be built by the architect Albert Jenkins Humbert from a design by the German Ludwig Grüner, the two men having worked together on the Duchess of Kent's mausoleum. It featured an octagonal copper dome over a cruciform base, and would be constructed in British granite and Portland stone with an interior decorated in the style of Albert's favourite Renaissance painter, Raphael. From Berlin, Vicky

213

liaised closely on the design and execution of the project, wishing 'to contribute in some measure to beautifying it'.[44] A favourite sculptor of the Queen and Prince Albert, Baron Carlo Marochetti, came to Osborne in January to work on a model of Albert's head from the Theed death-mask, which would form the basis of a marble effigy of the Prince wearing his robes of the Order of the Garter, to be placed in the mausoleum in due course (Victoria's effigy was made simultaneously, so that she would not look older than the eternally beautiful Albert when her own time came).

Excavation of the site began on 27 January, and Victoria began pumping the first of £200,000 of her own money into the project, having seen off one of its more unlikely opponents in Gerald Wellesley, the Dean of Windsor. The Dean, along with other churchmen, had feared that the loss of Albert's coffin from St George's Chapel would undermine its traditional associations with royalty. There was more than enough room: he wanted the side-chapel (now the Albert Chapel) to serve not just as Albert's memorial, but also as his mausoleum, and even sounded out the architect Gilbert Scott on ways of providing a private covered walkway to and from the chapel for the Queen. However, Victoria resisted, for nothing would deter her from erecting a purpose-built mausoleum for herself and Albert and, in order to spare her from criticism about its undesirability and 'foreignness', it was decided to release no details of the Frogmore project until it was completed.[45] Lord Clarendon was appalled that she had set upon such an insignificant location as 'that morass at Frogmore which is constantly flooded', and later heard that it would be necessary

214

to heat the mausoleum all year round 'to keep off decay'; Bertie had already announced that he had no intention of being buried in such a place.[46]

*     *     *

From early January 1862 the Queen began receiving private visits at Osborne from individual politicians such as Lord Clarendon, who despite being out of office was her most trusted friend in Parliament, 'the *only* person who had quite understood her feelings and put himself in imagination exactly in her situation'.[47] Clarendon spent an exhausting day at the receiving end of her outpourings of grief, closely followed by those of Dr Clark, Princess Alice, King Leopold, Sir Charles Phipps and Bertie. For the time being, however, Victoria could only tolerate infrequent meetings with selected members of the Privy Council.[48] On 6 January she was nursed through her first such meeting by Arthur Helps, clerk of the Privy Council, whom she had already enlisted to edit a collection of Albert's speeches. Sitting in a darkened room swathed in black, she conducted the meeting through an open connecting door. Her ministers in the next room were obliged to shout, for fear the Queen could not hear. The official business was quickly wrapped up in a couple of paragraphs, with Helps even reading out the word 'approved' on Victoria's behalf.

She had been greatly relieved to be informed by Palmerston on 9 January that the Trent Affair had finally been resolved and that her husband's eleventh-hour intervention had contributed to a peaceful settlement of the dispute. Her ministers were by now extremely anxious that she should take

215

up her dispatch boxes once more and return to the long-standing protocol on which she and Albert had insisted—of reviewing and commenting on every official document before it was sent out. For the time being Phipps marked the important passages for her, and that was all she would read. But she felt utterly unequal to the task; her 'reason', she feared, would not hold up to it. Nor would it hold up to the prospect of a change of government that was in the air: '*that* would be what she could not stand'; it could well induce her to 'throw everything up', she warned Clarendon. The quickest way of killing her—'and most *thankful* to them she would be for that result'—would be for Lord Derby, leader of the Opposition, to push for a general election. Nevertheless, it was the end of January before Victoria saw her Prime Minister, Lord Palmerston, for the first time since Albert's death. The old man was quite overwhelmed when he arrived at Osborne and could hardly speak for his tears, a fact that Victoria found unnerving when she thought of how she and Albert had so despised him in the past. But she also took comfort in it, for she liked to see others as grief-stricken as she was. 'I would hardly have given Lord Palmerston credit for entering so entirely into my anxieties,' she remarked, which is probably why she forgave him for overlooking the correct protocols of full mourning—by turning up in a brown overcoat, light-grey trousers, green gloves and blue shirt-studs.[49] Palmerston's genuinely expressed concern, his solicitousness over her health and whether she was eating enough went some way to easing the inevitable meetings with her other ministers, as too did Benjamin Disraeli's panegyric to the Prince when Parliament reconvened on 6 February. It prompted a grateful response from Victoria, struggling to come to terms with 'the afflicting dispensation of Providence which bows me to the earth'.[50] By now she had been obliged to resume the minimum of official business, but felt totally overwhelmed: 'so much to do, so many boxes, letters'; never before had she had to deal with so many responsibilities on a regular, daily basis.[51]

On 14 February, Victoria was greatly cheered by the arrival of the pregnant Vicky from Prussia. Yet despite her eldest daughter's presence, she was reluctant, even then, to allow an exhausted Alice out of her sight. In the end she was prevailed on to agree that Alice should go and rest with close friends, the Belgian consul Sylvain Van De Weyer and his wife, at their home near Windsor for ten days. Confronted with her mother's deep desolation and the helplessness of her siblings, Vicky thought they all seemed 'like sheep without a shepherd'. Her mother was as much in love with Papa 'as though she had married him yesterday', she told Fritz in Berlin. Vicky struggled hard with her grief; her mother's alone was more than she could contend with: 'there is always the empty room, the empty bed, she always sleeps with Papa's coat over her and his dear red dressing-gown beside her and some of his clothes in the bed'. As for Osborne, a home of which Vicky had till now had happy memories: 'It is nothing but a great vault; everything is so different, the old life, the old customs have gone'.[52] Like everyone else, she was greatly alarmed at how difficult it was to manage her mother or contradict her in the slightest degree; but even more alarming was Victoria's continuing, undisguised dislike for Bertie.

During his stay at Osborne, Uncle Leopold had done his best to try and reconcile mother and son, to no avail. Indeed, Victoria had openly admitted to Lord Hertford when he visited that she could never forget that her eldest son 'had been the chief cause of his father's illness'; she never could see Bertie 'without a shudder', she told Vicky. As soon as Bertie entered the room, Victoria became visibly agitated; his presence irritated her and from now on he would effectively be banished except for brief holidays. Such intransigence was 'a positive monomania with her', in the view of Lord Clarendon.[53] Lord Hertford begged Victoria to take her son into her confidence and 'give him something to do besides shooting and hunting— something that would make him feel himself of use to her and would improve his character'.[54] But Victoria would have none of it; there was no question of Bertie taking the place of his sainted father as her adviser, or of her giving him any useful employment in preparation for his own role one day as monarch. Palmerston presciently confided to Clarendon that he saw her 'unconquerable aversion' to her son and heir as a major problem 'looming in the distance'.[55] She had already resolved to go ahead with Albert's plans—shelved on his death—to send Bertie on a tour of Egypt and the Holy Land. He sailed from Osborne on 6 February; in his absence his mother would continue planning her son's road to salvation: marriage to Alexandra of Denmark. She and Vicky vetted the Danish royal family, gossiping about the Princess's various undesirable relatives and the financial embarrassment of her parents, Prince and

Princess Christian, who had only a paltry £800 a year to live on. Nevertheless, as far as Victoria was concerned, Bertie was lucky to have Alexandra, though the prospect of a necessary meeting with the in-laws later in the year at Laeken in Belgium filled her with dread. Worse, though, was the prospect that Bertie, who still seemed utterly indifferent to his future bride, might change his mind. In this event, Victoria had a contingency plan: 'Affie would be ready to take her at once', for she was already sizing up possible other candidates for her second son too.[56] The complexities of royal marriage-brokering were one diversion from which even grief did not keep her.

For the time being, however, Victoria found no joy even in the approach of spring. Referring to herself in the third person, as was her wont, she lamented to Lord Derby that: 'She sees the trees budding, the days lengthening, the primroses coming out, but she thinks herself *still* in the month of December.'[57] The Duchess of Sutherland, who had joined Victoria's household on her accession in 1837, could see the potentially detrimental impact on the monarchy of the Queen's retreat. Whilst being sensitive, as a fellow widow, to Victoria's grief, the Duchess took advantage of her position of trust in these early months to try and persuade Victoria to return to her public duties. The Duchess's friend William Gladstone had written to her in alarm, 'we cannot afford to create an intense degree of pity for the woman at the cost of her character as a Queen, in which above all things balance and measure are required'. Whilst agreeing with Gladstone, Sutherland perceptively pointed out a necessary shift in how the public viewed the Queen—from active monarch to a revered national symbol of grieving; 'It is *The* Widow speaking to Her children,' she argued.[58] Several of Victoria's ladies-in-waiting already shared the Duchess's apprehensions about the Queen's insatiable commemoration of Albert. It seemed an 'unhealthy state of mind'; and one of them, when coming off her three-month period of duty, informed Charles Dickens that the Queen insisted on 'striking out the word "late" from all formal mention of him in documents that come before her'. This state of denial extended to the visitors' book at royal residences, where Albert's book was still maintained alongside that of Victoria and visitors were required to sign their names in it just as before, like 'calling on a dead man', as Disraeli noted.[59]

In March, when the mournful processional of the black-garbed royal household arrived back at the 'living grave' of Windsor, Victoria kept a close watch on the careful positioning of every last possession of her husband's in its correct place: his hat and gloves laid out, the handkerchief he last used lying on the sofa, 'the blotting book open with a pen upon it, his watch going, fresh flowers in a glass'. Without fail she daily cast freshly cut white flowers and cypress over the bed in which he had died—an act of display more Catholic than Protestant, as Clarendon noted—as well as stooping down to kiss the pillow whenever she entered. The last thing she did at night before retiring to bed was to kneel and pray by Albert's bed in the Blue Room, her communion with his spirit constant and all-consuming.[60]

Work on the mausoleum, meanwhile, had

progressed sufficiently by 15 March (the anniversary of the death of the Duchess of Kent) for the Queen to lay the foundation stone, containing coins and photographs of the Prince, herself and the royal children. The project had raised her spirits: 'She is better, stronger, calmer, more resigned, more courageous and determined to walk in the path of duty,' thought Lady Bruce.[61] On the given day, in front of 100 members of the royal household and workmen involved in the construction, a dignified Victoria fulfilled her task, 'laying the mortar and knocking the stone three times with the mallet just as any man would' and without shedding a tear. She later recorded her 'trembling steps' as she performed the ceremony, but her subjective view of her 'weakness' was not shared by those who watched; Lord Torrington thought she looked 'like a *young girl* and showed great nerve'.[62]

In addition to the mausoleum, Victoria now had a precious literary commemoration of her husband to cling to. In early January, Tennyson had sent the draft of his promised Dedication to the *Idylls of the King* for approval. The Duchess of Sutherland commended his 'beautiful verses' as 'worthy of the great and tragic subject', recommending one or two minor amendments, after which it was sent to Princess Alice on 13 January. In his verses the Poet Laureate expressed his profound admiration for the Prince as his own 'ideal knight':

Who reverenced his conscience as his king;
Whose glory was, redressing human wrongs;
Who spake no slander, no, nor listen'd to it;
Who lov'd one only and who clave to her . . .

Dear to thy land and ours, a Prince indeed,
Beyond all titles, and a household name,
Hereafter, through all times, Albert the
    Good.[63]

The seductive image of Albert as the perfect, gentle knight of old, a heroic figure who wore 'the white flower of a blameless life', put into words Victoria's own long-held romantic fantasies about her husband. The verses, she said, 'soothed her aching, bleeding heart'.[64] Tennyson's idealised vision of Albert would be captured by Edward Henry Corbould in the Queen's favourite posthumous painting of him—as medieval knight in armour sheathing his sword, with the German inscription 'I have fought a good fight; I have finished the struggle; therefore a crown of rectitude is awaiting me' written below. Based on an 1844 portrait of Albert in armour by Robert Thorburn, this watercolour was set into the door of the Blue Room in 1863.[65] Tennyson's Dedication was rapidly taken to their hearts by the British public, setting its stamp on a century's hagiography of the Prince and forming the cornerstone of the cult of the Prince Consort of which Victoria would be the chief votary.

In April 1862, ten years after appointing him Poet Laureate, Victoria finally met her hero Tennyson when he visited her from his home at Farringford, not far from Osborne. Tennyson admitted to the Duke of Argyll to being a 'shy beast' who liked to 'keep to [his] burrow' and he was extremely apprehensive about what seemed an ordeal to come. The Duke reassured him: the Queen liked nothing more than 'natural signs of devotion and sympathy'. He should be guided by his feelings: 'what is *natural* is right—with Her'. He should talk to the Queen 'as you would to a poor Woman in affliction—that is what she likes best.' When the moment finally came, the Queen completely disarmed Tennyson. 'I am like your Mariana now', she told him, in an allusion to one of his poems about a widow who longed to be reunited with her dead husband in a much-repeated lament: 'I am aweary, aweary,/I would that I were dead!'[66] Despite her obvious state of deep melancholy, Tennyson found her sweet and kind; there was an extraordinary stateliness about her that set her apart from other women. He was so overcome by the emotion of the occasion that he could recall little of it later on. For her own part, Victoria had found the poet strange but arresting—'tall, dark, with a fine head, long black flowing hair and a beard'. He may have been 'oddly dressed', but she had found him totally lacking in pretension.[67] Aware of Tennyson's strong mystical streak, she had had no inhibitions about discussing their shared experience of sudden death: he of his closest friend Arthur Hallam in 1833 and she of Albert. She recognised the poet as a kindred spirit who knew only too well that terrible feeling: the breaking of each 'blank day'.[68] *In Memoriam* had provided her with an emotional literary capsule that mirrored her own torrent of fluctuating feeling, ranging from resignation, to morbidity, to hope, to anger, to a final overwhelming desire for reunion with the dead, until which time she—like Tennyson of Hallam—sought Albert's spirit reflected in everything around her. Tennyson's portrait of Hallam reminded her greatly of Albert,

223

she told him—even down to the same blue eyes. 'He would have made a great King,' Tennyson told her, to which she replied, 'He always said it did not signify whether he did the right thing or did not, so long as the right thing was done.'[69] Tennyson came away profoundly impressed with Victoria's strength of character. A year later he was invited back with his wife and two sons, on which occasion Emily Tennyson found the Queen 'small and childlike, full of intelligence and ineffably sweet and of a sad sympathy'. She too was captivated; Victoria talked 'of all things in heaven and earth . . . laughed heartily at many things that were said', but 'shades of pain and sadness' often passed over her face. 'The Queen,' she concluded, 'is a woman to live and die for.'[70]

# CHAPTER TEN

## *'The Luxury of Woe'*

The year 1862 was a very good one for Messrs W. C. Jay's London General Mourning Warehouse. At its prime site on the south-east corner of Oxford Circus it was enjoying a boom in trade as never before in its twenty years of business. Although general public mourning had officially ended on 10 February, there was no let-up in what had become an 'almost incalculable demand' for mourning goods. Victoria herself had already sent out a memorandum explicitly stating that 'The Queen intends to wear her weeds (if she lives) at least till the beginning of 1864.'[1] Her intention to remain in full mourning—

224

of the deepest, dullest crape—for the maximum two years was in itself not exceptional, but merely emphasised an already existing code of mourning observed by many pious widows. But such was the level of public sympathy for her at this time that many of the middle classes decided to follow suit and remain in mourning for longer—not just for the Prince, but, following Victoria's example, for their own deceased relatives.

Victoria soon changed her mind about leaving off mourning after two years, determining that although she might make the transition from the gloomy crape that was favoured in the first stage of mourning, she would remain in black for the rest of her life. She also demanded that her closest ladies-in-waiting remained in black with her when on duty. After the statutory two years, the rest of her female entourage and daughters would be allowed to wear half-mourning of grey, white or the newer shades of lilac, violet and mauve, which had become popular with the introduction of aniline dyes in the mid-1850s. The lugubrious drapes of crape—a matt gauze of silk and cotton tightly crimped like the crêpe paper named after it—were left off by most widows after the first, traditional stage of retreat of a year and a day, and replaced by lighter, shinier black fabrics such as satin and silk thereafter. But for now and throughout 1862 Victoria's children and the entire royal household, down to the footmen, remained in full mourning, and none of them was allowed to appear in public or receive anyone at home unless so dressed. Extra money was made available to less well-off members of her household, such as Marianne Skerrett and the Queen's two dressers and her wardrobe-maids, to buy additional clothes for this extended period of mourning.[2]

Mourning for Prince Albert predictably cast its pall over the London season of 1862, which was, as the theatrical newspaper the *Era* observed, 'at one blow strangled in its birth'. In anticipation, many of the aristocracy stayed put on their country estates that year or went abroad—to the detriment of the London trades that serviced their needs, as well as the theatres and concert halls. That year the mourning houses were the only businesses making money. The Victorian textile trade was in overdrive, offering a vast range of fabrics for mourning: 'black silks, crapes, paramattas, French merinos, Reps, Queen's Cords, Lustres, Barathea, Coburgs, French de Laines', and there was a huge demand too for the dye to make them black.[3]

Thanks to the unprecedented demand for its 'Noir Impériale' black silks and its best patent crape, Jay's had had to substantially enlarge both its 1862 catalogue and its premises on Regent Street.[4] The company's substantial intake of cheap imports, rushed in from the recession-hit trade in France 'under peculiarly advantageous circumstances', meant they could offer them at knock-down prices. French black silk was flying off the shelves at 2s. and 6d. (15p) per yard, and Jay's boasted that its stock of family mourning was now the largest in Europe.[5] By importing cheaply from France, Jay's and other mourning warehouses challenged the monopoly of the powerful Courtaulds, an Essex firm established by Huguenot refugees, which had since the early nineteenth century dominated crape manufacture and was even now developing a cheap substitute—the opportunistically named 'Albert

226

Crape'—to cater to growing demand.[6]

Currently on offer at Jay's for the bottom end of the market was a 'complete suit of domestic mourning' at two and a half guineas, suitable for household servants. But for those seeking to indulge in the full 'luxury of woe', Jay's prided itself on ensuring that its morning and dinner dresses, capes and mantles, whilst scrupulously tailored to the distinct stages of bereavement, should follow the latest fashions. 'In the present day our ashes must be properly selected, our garments must be rent to pattern, our sack cloth must be of the finest quality,' observed social commentator Henry Mayhew sardonically after a visit to Jay's; grief, like everything else, counted for nothing if it was not fashionable.[7] With this in mind, Jay's brought out elegant outfits 'in accordance with the strictest Parisian taste and fashion' direct from top fashion houses such as Charles Worth of the rue de la Paix. The protocols were complex: the first year of deep mourning was followed by secondary mourning less dominated by crape; then three months of ordinary mourning (black of livelier fabrics, with ribbon and ornamentation); and finally six months of half-mourning, for which Jay's offered the best French silks in black, white, grey and suitable 'neutral tints'. The company's staff were the souls of discretion and calm within its harmonious, softly carpeted walls.

But Jay's was now facing stiff competition from Peter Robinson's Family Mourning Warehouse across the road in Regent Street, which kept a brougham ready to be dispatched, at a moment's notice, with two black-garbed fitters to the homes of distressed lady clients. Jay's too promised a similar rapid response on the fulfilment of orders, and delivery anywhere in the country. Its seamstresses were provided with hot dinners in Jay's own canteen, but such was the overload that for a time Jay's had to resort to laying on sandwiches and sherry in an adjoining room, so that the overworked seamstresses could 'run in and get a mouthful when they can'. But while Jay's employees enjoyed reasonably good working conditions, excessive workloads took their toll on the eyesight of the beleaguered armies of poor seamstresses working fourteen-hour days in ill-lit back rooms on black fabrics with black thread, which were particularly deleterious to the eyesight.[8]

In the rush to remain fashionable whilst in mourning for Prince Albert, publications such as the *Lady's Magazine* had been quick to feature do-it-yourself patterns for suitable black lace and beaded trimmings, for gowns, or handkerchiefs without their usual lace trimmings, but instead embroidered with mournful symbols such as black and white tears. Even Victoria had one of these, but otherwise she paid little attention to fashion in her own choice of mourning clothes; she was no longer dressing to please anyone. As a result, the Queen's spending on dress decreased noticeably, and with the years the corsets were increasingly left off as her waistline spread, and the same dreary gowns were made up in duplicate by her dressmakers Sarah Ann Unitt and Elizabeth Gieve with fabric from the local draper, Caley's opposite Windsor Castle.[9] The only additional trapping she wore was her widow's 'sad cap', as Beatrice called it, indented at the top in the style of Mary Stuart.[10] Framing her face in a heart shape of crisp white tulle, with a veil of black crape falling away behind, the cap enhanced Victoria's look of resigned, nunlike widowhood and accentuated the image of vulnerability that she sought to cultivate. Beneath her skirts, her white lingerie was threaded with black rather than coloured silk ribbon; black dyes were not yet stable enough to be used on fabrics worn next to the skin without discolouring it. As for jewellery, the Queen's strict rules on black applied equally here. Jet ornaments were de rigueur and dominated at court for the next thirty years or so, though diamonds, amethysts and pearls would be allowed during half-mourning. The Queen also favoured the morbid fashion for lockets and brooches made out of the deceased person's hair.[11] Her strict directives on appropriate jewellery would prompt Sir John Bennett, royal watchmaker and jeweller, who often attended court at Windsor with a selection of his wares, to complain that 'the Queen's deep mourning has utterly spoilt my market. If it were not for the honour of coming to Windsor, I should give it up.'[12]

As the trade in jet mourning jewellery expanded, so did the fortunes of a small fishing village, formerly a whaling port, on the north-east Yorkshire coast, which was the primary source of the best-quality jet. Layers of shale in the sea coast around Whitby had long been a rich source of fossils and petrified coniferous wood, of which jet—from a prehistoric tree similar to the monkey puzzle—had been the most prized, once cut and polished. Much of this jet was washed up on the Whitby coast, and was sought out by armies of beachcombers; as demand escalated, it was also mined inland at Bilsdale and Kildale and other locations on the North Yorkshire Moors. Jet from the area had been fashioned into jewellery for centuries (by ancient Britons and the Romans) and long prized as a kind of 'black amber'. With the coming of the railways and the influx of seaside visitors to Whitby, decorative household items made of jet—beaded lampshades, Bible and prayer-book covers, vases, seals, card trays, ink stands, paper knives, board games of all kinds, even doll's house furniture—had been produced as souvenirs and rapidly took their place in Victorian homes.

But it was the jewellery trade that catapulted local Whitby craftsmen and their wares unexpectedly into the limelight. It took considerable skill to work the brittle material without fracturing it, but jet jewellery manufacture rapidly extended to cover every aspect of Victorian mourning accessories, including beading for bodices, hair combs and headdresses, as well as jet birds, insects and clasps for hats and bonnets. In the 1830s the Whitby jet trade had employed around twenty-five people, but by the mid-1850s jet-working had become the principal occupation in the town, with 200 workshops accounting for an annual turnover of around £20,000. Jet ornaments became ever more popular and were shown at the Great Exhibition in 1851, and the trade received a further boost with the elaborate mourning for the Duke of Wellington a year later. In 1855, on a state visit to France, Victoria presented the French empress Eugénie with four bracelets of Whitby jet, setting a fashion soon followed by the French aristocracy.

But it was Prince Albert's death that sparked

230

the meteoric rise of the industry, not just with jet jewellery, but also many commemorative mementoes of Albert: medallions, miniatures and even small busts. Lightweight jet was perfect for producing the kind of large and bulky jet jewellery needed to complement the full-skirted mourning dresses of the day, although during the first year widows did not wear the highly polished version of jet, and those with less money favoured the cheaper vulcanite, or bog oak—from semi-fossilized peat. Onyx and black enamel were also used, and cut-steel and Berlin ironwork were introduced later, but nothing had quite the cachet of the best-quality jet. The income of the Whitby trade rose rapidly to £50,000 in 1862 and reached its peak in the 1870s at £90,000, when it employed more than 1,000 local men and boys as jet-finders, carvers and polishers.[13] The highly paid workers even had their own pub, the Jet Men's Arms on Church Street, and the popularity of jet was further fostered at court by the Marchioness of Normanby on whose husband's estates much of the jet was found.[14]

\*      \*      \*

The fact that the Queen had, inadvertently, set a fashion trend at the most unlikely and tragic time in her life was of little comfort at court. 'The dreary *painful* effect of all this *mass* of black all round one,' wrote Lady Geraldine Somerset, was 'altogether too inexpressibly sad and dreadful'.[15] They all now dreaded the Queen's return to Balmoral for the first time since Albert's death, which came on 30 April 1862, earlier in the year than her usual visits.

231

Victoria wanted to be as far away as possible from London when the Great London Exposition of 1862 opened on 1 May, because of all its painful reminders of Albert; her son-in-law Fritz came over from Berlin to act as her surrogate. But the pain she felt on entering her Highland home for the first time since her beloved husband's death was acute. The 'agonising sobs' as she was assisted by Alice and Affie past the many everyday objects that reminded her of Albert: 'The stags heads—the rooms—blessed, darling Papa's room—then his coats—his caps—kilts—all, convulsed my poor shattered frame.'[16] Most of her time in Scotland was taken up with revisiting the places associated with her happy marriage and finding comfort in the homely sympathies of an old, recently widowed cottager on the estate. Victoria poured out pages of woe to Palmerston: her nerves were 'more shaken even than before,' she told him—he had only to look at her handwriting. No one knew or understood her bitter anguish and suffering. Her existence was pure 'torture'.[17] As the months of her intense, deranged state of grief wore on, with Victoria pausing to remember every significant date, object, memory connected with Albert, to the exclusion of everything else, those unaffected by such profound levels of grief found it harder and harder to sympathise.

But how could the vast majority of Victoria's staff and ministers begin to show sympathy for the turmoil, the sheer disorientation of her very personal sense of loss? She was after all the Queen and head of state; and in a court grounded in formality and protocol, they could hardly give her a hug or hold her hand, or offer the kind of intimate consoling gestures seen in normal families. Queen Victoria's regal authority, in all its terrifying loneliness, precluded that. It was therefore hard to commiserate, and all the Queen's entourage could do was carefully watch what they said, as the Duke of Argyll noted when he visited: 'one may easily say things which go against her, even when one least suspects it'. Holding a conversation with the Queen required considerable tact—and patience—for there was only ever one topic of conversation that interested her: Albert. The Duke tried hard to steer Victoria in conversation towards the 'hills, birds, and waterfalls' that he had seen at Balmoral. Such a change of tack would work for a few minutes, he later recalled, and even provoke a watery smile, but inevitably Victoria would turn the topic back to Albert: 'the birds *he* had liked, the roads he had made, his speeches, etc., but all as if he were still with her'.[18] Meanwhile, her forty-third birthday came and went in May in 'utter *loneliness* and *desolation*'. There was only one consolation—'dear Baby' (Beatrice)—who was 'the bright spot in this dead home'.[19]

For all her stubborn insistence, others did not agree with Victoria's perception of her own physical frailty. When Lord Derby visited her on 16 June he thought she looked much better. Victoria was extremely put out to hear people say this; she had been 'much annoyed at a paragraph to that effect which appeared in *The Times*' and had, reported Derby, 'ordered it to be contradicted'.[20] She did not want to look or feel better and was convinced that she ate nothing and never slept; Lord Clarendon noted that she was even 'anxious that all her hair should be grey', as though by becoming so

233

it would define her unending grief. Victoria had very good reason not to wish to recover, for when this happened she would be expected once more to take up her onerous ceremonial responsibilities as monarch—only this time alone, a thing she dreaded. This was not what she was used to: she wanted everyone else to shoulder her burden for her, to take care of *her*, as Albert had done. Her mind was set, as Phipps confided to Gladstone: 'I hope and believe that Her Majesty's health is not in that precarious state in which her Grief makes her almost wish it to be.'[21] For all her protestations and hypochondria, there were signs that Victoria's exceptionally resilient constitution—the 'vein of iron' that Lady Lyttleton back in 1844 had observed as the hallmark of her tenacious character[22]—was fighting back, but on 20 June she resolutely refused to acknowledge her Silver Jubilee. 'Beloved Albert had wished Fetes to take place in honour of it', but no, it had 'passed in complete silence'.[23] Her prolonged state of grief was making her unreasonable, irrational, impossible, in the view of those on the outside looking in. But Victoria was unable to help herself. She could not, however, ignore her daughter Alice's impending marriage at Osborne in July. It would be a wretched business and she wished it were 'years off', she told Vicky. She already expected it to be a 'dreadful, awful day' for her, with her broken heart and shattered nerves. Matters were made worse when Louis's aunt, Mathilde, Grand Duchess of Hesse, died shortly beforehand: 'The Angel of Death still follows us,' wrote Victoria, 'so now Alice's marriage will be even more gloomy.'[24]

Louis of Hesse was not the best, top-drawer royal bridegroom Victoria and Albert had hoped for; like Bertie's fiancée Alexandra, he was the product of a rather impoverished princely house that wasn't quite up to scratch—and, of course, not a patch on beloved Fritz, Crown Prince of Prussia. A couple of weeks before the wedding Victoria went to inspect Alice's trousseau. It was 'nothing but black gowns'.[25] In her present 'reduced state' she would not have allowed the marriage for another year, had not Albert already planned it, and had done so on the understanding that Alice would spend half the year with her, making over to her daughter and Louis the use of Clarence House for the purpose. (Victoria was soon to be disappointed in her anticipation of having a married daughter to hand and a useful son-in-law around the house, for Louis's modest income would not stretch to the expense of living in London.)

As for Alice herself, just turned nineteen and still far from recovered from the stress of her father's death and the ceaseless demands made on her by her mother, she had been close to breaking point. Lord Clarendon admired her tenacity: 'there is not such another girl in a 1000,' he told the Duchess of Manchester. Despite being 'boxed up in a gilt cage all her life', Alice, for all her youth, had 'such sound principles, so great judgement and such knowledge of the world'; his only regret was that 'she is going with a dull boy to a dull family in a dull country'. He had a presentiment that she would not be happy.[26] But Alice could at least look forward to seeing her dear brother Bertie, back from his tour of the Holy

Land in time for the ceremony. Bertie's return was not, however, a source of joy for Victoria. Before he arrived she sent a missive to Bertie's governor, General Bruce, telling him to warn the Prince that on his return he should be careful not to indulge in his mother's presence in 'worldly, frivolous, gossiping kind of conversation'. The Prince must be prepared to face 'in a proper spirit, the cureless melancholy of his poor home'.[27]

The morning of 1 July 1862 broke dull and windy; Alice had spent the previous night sharing her mother's room, listening to her toss and turn, not in anticipation of her daughter's happiness, but of her own ordeal to come. The modestly sized dining room at Osborne had been specially rearranged for the ceremony and filled with flowers, with a temporary altar covered in purple velvet and gold and surrounded by a gilt railing. This had been placed under one of Winterhalter's large canvases of the royal family in happier days, in which Albert took centre stage; there would be no avoiding his ghost at the wedding. Queen Victoria's ladies were hugely relieved to be allowed two days' respite from black—for 1 and 2 July— and wore half-mourning of grey or lilac for the ceremony; Alice too was allowed to get married in white. She looked delicate but lovely in her wedding dress, with its deep flounce of Honiton guipure lace and veil, both carrying a motif of rose, orange blossoms and myrtle, and the bottom of her skirt trimmed in artificial flowers of the same. On her head she wore an unostentatious wreath of orange blossom and wax flowers, much as her mother had worn at her own wedding in 1840. Eight bridesmaids had originally been planned for, but in the circumstances were reduced to four: Alice's sisters Helena, Louise and Beatrice and Louis's sister Anna. That morning Victoria had pressed her own special gift into Alice's hand—a prayer book similar to the one given to her by her mother on her wedding day.

Only a small gathering of hand-picked guests attended the wedding and were obliged to stand throughout: Louis's best man, Prince Henry of Hesse; the Cambridges; Louis's parents, Prince and Princess Charles of Hesse; Duke Ernst of Saxe-Coburg, who gave Alice away; Feodora; and a few other French and—in the eyes of Victoria's ladies—badly dressed Hessian relatives. The service was conducted by the Archbishop of York, standing in for an indisposed Archbishop of Canterbury. It was 'a *sad* moment, to see her come in leaning on her uncle's arm, instead of on *His*!' thought Lady Geraldine Somerset, as the service began just after 1 p.m. Alice's voice faltered during the ceremony, but she did not break down; it was the good Archbishop, himself recently widowed, who found it hard to hold back the tears. Victoria too retained the 'most wonderful command over herself' as she watched from the sidelines, seated in an armchair and protectively obscured from view by her four sons. The whole occasion had seemed to Lady Geraldine 'inexpressibly mournful'.[28] Despite being proud of Alice's 'wonderful bearing' throughout, the Queen had found it 'more like a funeral than a wedding'.[29]

Although a children's party was held in nearby Ryde to celebrate Alice's wedding that day, the local population saw no signs of the subdued celebrations going on at Osborne, and news

237

reporters who headed there in search of a story came back empty-handed. The area had been as quiet as the grave; 'it certainly was a strange and solemn sight for the few of the public who flitted about the Osborne Road,' wrote the correspondent of the *Daily News*, for the surrounding park was deserted 'beyond a few servants, in the deepest mourning, passing almost stealthily up and down the avenue'.[30] Most of the papers covered this disappointing news story in brief; only the republican-minded *Reynolds's Newspaper* was bold enough to complain about the Queen's 'virtual abdication' and her continuing 'snug seclusion' at Osborne and Balmoral and its impact on trade, especially in the West End of London. For the milliners, tailors, dressmakers, perfumers and jewellers of the West End, who profited from catering to court dinners, balls and presentations, were now suffering a severe reduction in trade. Instead, the country had yet another royal to support, Louis of Hesse-Darmstadt, newly promoted by Victoria to His Royal Highness. Once more the nation was obliged to submit to 'those bleedings for the benefit of starveling Germans', while the Queen did nothing to revive severely depressed trade, with cotton famine—in the wake of the continuing war in America—now raging in Lancashire.[31]

Queen Victoria did not join her guests for the wedding breakfast held in a pavilion specially erected on the lawn at Osborne, but lunched in private with the newly weds in the Horn Room, surrounded by furniture made from stags' antlers purchased by Prince Albert. At 5 p.m. Alice left, complete with her black trousseau, for three days' honeymoon not far away at St Clair, the home of General Harcourt near Ryde. On 8 July she sailed on the royal yacht for Antwerp and her new home in Darmstadt, with a long memorandum provided by Dr Clark at her concerned mother's request, on how she should safeguard her frail health with lots of fresh air and cold baths. Victoria hoped her still-delicate daughter would not start a family too soon, but within the month Alice was pregnant.

At the end of July the Queen was only too anxious to escape once more to the quiet and stillness of Balmoral. A chink of respite for the younger children was allowed, when the artist William Leighton was asked to come and give them painting lessons, but he was shocked by the many great changes since his first visit:

> the joyous bustle in the morning when the Prince went out; the highland ponies and the dogs; the ghillies and the pipers. Then the coming home—the Queen and her ladies going out to meet them, and the merry time afterwards; the torch-light sword-dances on the green and the servants ball closing the day. Now all is gone with him who was the life and soul of it all.[32]

It was such a huge void to fill, and Victoria's every waking thought whilst in the Highlands was of Albert and his continuing memorialisation. At 11 a. m. on a bright, sunny 21 August, with the air soft with summer and the surrounding hills pink with heather, Victoria followed by her 'six orphans' was taken by pony carriage—led by her ghillie, John Brown—up the rugged hillside to the top of Craig Lowrigan, where a thirty-five-foot-high pyramid of granite dedicated to Albert was under construction.[33] Here the family placed stones in the forty-foot-wide foundations, which would have their initials carved on them alongside a plaque: 'To the beloved memory of Albert the great and good Prince Consort. Raised by his broken-hearted Widow, Victoria R., 21 August, 1862.'[34] Four days later, on Albert's birthday, the whole family once more toiled up to the Craig for another mournful ceremony. Unable to join them, Alice wrote from her new home in Darmstadt, offering loving words of consolation and encouragement to her mother:

Try and gather in the few bright things you have remaining, and cherish them: for though faint, yet they are types of that infinite joy still to come. I am sure, dear mamma, the more you try to appreciate and to find the good in that which God in His love has *left* you, the more worthy you will daily become of that which is in store. That earthly happiness you had is, indeed, gone for ever, but you must not think that every ray of it has left you.[35]

But it *had* left her. Could they not all see that it had? Like all the other words of comfort offered that year, Alice's did little to dent her mother's crippling, all-consuming grief. In September came yet another 'terribly trying ordeal' to be got through: the dreaded journey to Laeken, Uncle Leopold's palace near Brussels, where Victoria was to negotiate Bertie's formal engagement to Princess Alexandra with her parents. When she arrived, her nerves once again failed her and she declined to join the official luncheon, finally steeling herself to meet the party later that afternoon in an excruciatingly awkward and subdued exchange of pleasantries. Bertie, who was not present at the meeting, later formally proposed to Alexandra, though no public announcement was made till his twenty-first birthday on 9 November. Much to her surprise, Victoria was greatly taken by the gentle and unaffected Alexandra, to whom she touchingly presented a sprig of white heather sent from Balmoral by Bertie, but she made no bones about what lay in store for her: Alexandra would be welcomed, on her imminent visit to England (for initiation by Victoria into her duties as a member of the family), into a 'home of Sorrow'.[36] Back in London, Lord Clarendon sent the Queen his congratulations, though found it 'rather difficult to steer clear of the idea that the marriage could be any alleviation of her grief', for the Queen would countenance no such suggestions.[37] True to form, a few days later she was writing to Palmerston insisting that 'To the poor Queen this event can no longer cause pleasure, for pleasure is for ever gone from her heart!'[38] But at least she would, with this wedding, be acquiring a daughter-in-law, rather than losing a daughter; she only hoped that Bertie would be worthy of his lovely wife.

Whilst on the Continent, Victoria had travelled to Baden to see her half-sister, spending much of her time trying to persuade Feodora to live half the year with her in England as a glorified lady companion. But much as she loved her sister, Feodora politely declined, declaring that she did not wish to give up her independence at her advanced age. Privately she found Victoria's inexhaustible grief burdensome. They visited Albert's childhood home at Coburg together, where, amidst the expected anguish, Victoria also wallowed in recollections of happier times. Hearing Albert's native tongue and being in a place where the 'very air seems to breathe of her precious one' was a great comfort, she told Howard Elphinstone. Both were 'soothing and sweet in their very sadness to her bruised spirit and her aching, bleeding heart'.[39]

Back at Windsor she took almost daily walks to the mausoleum to inspect the building works. The dome was already in place and work on the interior had begun. She had already seen and approved Baron Marochetti's effigy of Albert, pronouncing it 'full . . . of peace, blessedness and beauty'.[40] Her thoughts increasingly dwelt on the anniversary to come, but meanwhile she had the diversion of Princess Alexandra's visit in November. 'This jewel!' she declared, was 'one of those sweet creatures who seem to come from the skies to help and bless poor mortals and lighten for a time their path!' Everyone could see how 'quite devotedly in love' Alix (as they all called her) was with Bertie, thought Augusta Bruce. She was being 'unutterably sweet' with the Queen, winning her over with her piety, gentleness and sympathy.[41] Her 'bright joyous presence has done much to rouse the poor dear Queen, who seems doatingly fond of her, and has her a great deal with her,' remarked a relieved Princess Mary Adelaide. The Queen was 'able to smile and even laugh cheerfully at times, and talks readily and with interest on every subject'. Well, for a little while at least; soon enough Victoria's conversation would revert to 'the sad, sad past'.[42]

It was far too soon to hope for a fair-weather change to her deeply depressed state. As time moved remorselessly towards that first 'dreadful anniversary', Victoria went several times a day into the Blue Room (as the King's Room was now called, for the colour of its decoration) to pray, reiterating to Vicky that her misery was now a 'necessity'. She could not exist without it: 'yes, I long for my suffering almost—as it is blinded with him!' She would never adjust to 'that dreadful, weary, chilling, unnatural life of a widow'.[43] Fearful that the strain might provoke another mental and physical collapse, the pregnant Alice travelled over from Hesse to be with her, but once again Vicky could not join them.

At ten o'clock on 14 December 1862 the royal family gathered in the Blue Room for a special service conducted by Dr Stanley, comprised of the Burial Service, hymns and prayers, and readings from Chapters 14 and 16 of St John on resurrection and reunion in the hereafter: 'A little while, and ye shall not see Me; and again, a little while, and ye shall see me, because I go to the Father.' Victoria knelt by Albert's bed, gazing at his white marble bust, with its fine profile and naked shoulders surrounded by flowers and palm leaves, which had been laid down there reverentially, replacing the living man a year since consigned to his coffin. But it was not a gloomy event. 'The room was full of flowers, and the sun shining in so brightly,' Victoria recalled. She told Dr Stanley that 'it seemed like a birthday', to which he answered reassuringly, 'It *is* a birthday in a new world.'[44] Two more services were conducted that day—at midday and 9.30 p.m.—inaugurating a sacred annual ritual that, like all others connected with Albert's life and death, would be followed to the letter till the day Victoria herself died.

Three days later the family made their way in the pouring rain down to Frogmore for the consecration of the mausoleum conducted by Samuel Wilberforce, Bishop of Oxford. The choir of St George's Chapel in their white surplices stood lining the steps as they entered. The sight, the Bishop recalled, was 'one of the most touching scenes I ever saw, to see our Queen and the file of fatherless children walk in and kneel down in those solemn prayers'.[45] Inside, a temporary wooden sarcophagus had been erected: it would be another six years before Marochetti's splendid double sarcophagus, to take both Albert's and eventually the Queen's coffins, was constructed from a single, enormous, flawless slab of Scottish granite. Meanwhile Albert's marble effigy had been placed in position and, one by one, the members of the royal family and household placed wreaths around it. During the service, verses from St John (19:41) were read: 'There was a garden, and in the garden a sepulchre', which everyone found most 'wonderfully appropriate' and moving. The process of investing Albert and his tomb with Christlike significance was completed the following morning at 7 a.m., when his coffin was quietly transferred from the crypt of St George's Chapel. Victoria did not attend, but was comforted that the sacred ritual of the 'translation' of Albert's remains was complete.[46] Henceforth he would always be near her, in their own private sepulchre in the garden. Later that day she was much comforted by the presentation of a sumptuously bound Lausanne

Bible from 'loyal English Widows', the cost of which had been raised by a subscription set up by the Duchess of Sutherland. Eighty women who had lost their husbands in the Hartley Colliery disaster in January generously donated to it. Victoria was deeply touched and, in a personal letter of thanks for the loyalty and devotion of her 'kind sister widows' and the nation in general, talked of how her one consolation was 'the constant sense of his unseen presence and the Blessed thought of that Eternal Union hereafter which will make the bitter anguish of the present appear as nought'.[47] Her heartfelt communion with other widows and her perception, by them, as a role model was an important saving grace during these dark years of retreat.

As December drew to a close, Victoria was relieved that 'One dreary, lonely year has been passed, which I had hoped never to live to the end of.' But now, 'with a weakened, shattered frame I have to begin the weary work again'.[48] The widows of England might grieve with her, but elsewhere in her kingdom sympathy for the Queen's unending grief was beginning to wane. 'Another year of royal mourning, another year of Queenly wo!' commented the leader in the *Era* for 28 December. 'A year and a week have come and gone, and we are sorry to learn that our prospects are not brightening, as we had trusted they would. We learn with sincere regret that her majesty will remain in mourning for another year.' Whilst the entire royal household and government might be tiptoeing around the Queen's extreme sensitivity on this point, the editor of the *Era* reminded his monarch that, for the good of the country, it was important

245

she now resume her public life as sovereign and the 'mother of her people'. There were strong practical reasons for this: 'the manufacturers and artisans of England claim a public duty from her, as Sovereign, in return for the discharge of theirs, as taxpayers'. The Queen's retreat, and its effect on trade, was causing economic hardship to 'many, many thousands of struggling, hard working men'. The Prince of Wales was soon to be married, and Parliament would be asked to rubber-stamp an annual income of £100,000 a year to support himself, his wife and their household. Her Majesty therefore had 'an excellent opportunity to come into the sunshine again, brighten the gloom of the past, and inaugurate a brilliant series of London seasons!'

The *Era*—like *Reynolds's Newspaper* earlier in the year—was as yet a rare voice of dissent; speaking for the rest of a still largely sympathetic nation, the *Belfast News-letter*, without realising it, more accurately captured the Queen's present state of mind. Hers was 'a grief which cannot forget itself, and what is more, no longer desires to do so'.[49] All hopes of the Queen returning once more to the bosom of her people were still a very long way off.

# CHAPTER ELEVEN

## *'A Married Daughter I Must Have Living with Me'*

In the spring of 1863 the British public resolutely shook off its gloom and enjoyed a few days of unprecedented national rejoicing. Its monarch might still be in self-imposed retirement, but a new and enchanting personality was about to shine a ray of light on the beleaguered royal family. On Thursday 7 March Princess Alexandra of Denmark arrived at Gravesend. Bertie was there to meet her and together they made their way across Kent by train, past cheering crowds and flags flying from every haystack and cowshed. Enormous numbers gathered in London for a glimpse of the Princess and something of the royal pageantry of old. The Corporation of London had spared no expense in anticipation of this precious respite from continuing royal despondency: £40,000 had been allotted for massed bands, decorated triumphal arches of evergreens and orange blossom, bunting and illuminations along the route. The windows and balconies of private houses too were festooned with flags, and some residents rented out their windows and balconies for large sums of money. The press took a vigorous interest in the story, whipping up public excitement at the prospect of seeing Bertie and his beautiful fiancée's royal progress. This ensured that their journey across London was witnessed by huge crowds, strung out across seven miles of streets, from the rather prosaic rail terminus on the Old Kent Road to Paddington, via London Bridge, Pall Mall, Piccadilly and Hyde Park. The crush was appalling, the journey interminably slow, the carriages laid on for the procession somewhat shoddy and, in the opinion of John Delane of *The Times*, 'unworthy of the occasion'.[1] But through it all Alexandra smiled warmly and bowed graciously 'as all those thousands of souls rose at her, as it were, in one blaze of triumphant irrepressible enthusiasm; surging round the carriage, waving hats and kerchiefs, leaping up here and there and again to catch sight of her; and crying Hurrah'.[2] Darkness had fallen by the time the couple arrived at Windsor station, where they were again enthusiastically greeted by patient crowds frozen from standing for long hours in the driving rain.

Victoria's greeting inside the castle had been warm and affectionate, but her self-absorption was such that she could not disguise how low and depressed she felt at what was to come, and she did not join the couple for dinner. Indeed, with undisguised bitterness she expressed her 'surprise' that the public had given such a warm ovation to the future wife of the Prince of Wales, 'when none was offered to the husband of the Queen' in his lifetime.[3] She had wanted the Prince of Wales's wedding to take place on her own wedding day of 15 February, but everyone had feared a repetition of Alice's funereal ceremony and she had been persuaded to postpone it to March. She overrode objections to it taking place in Lent, as she was determined to be rid of all her guests before Alice gave birth to her first baby—at Windsor, as she, Victoria, had ordained. Much to general disappointment, the Queen had resisted any suggestion of a grand state ceremony at Westminster Abbey, thus depriving the majority of her people of any glimpse of the proceedings. The wedding would take place under strict control at St George's Chapel, Windsor, where *her* privacy would be paramount and where she could not be made the object of unseemly curiosity.

In the fifteen months since Albert's death time had at least mellowed Victoria's attitude to her wayward son. She had to admit that there had been a distinct improvement in Bertie's looks and manner since his engagement to Alexandra, although he would always suffer by comparison with his absent married sisters Vicky and Alice. Bertie, for his part, was trying hard to be affectionate and 'do what is right', but Victoria still found his idleness and inattentiveness 'trying', as too his *joie de vivre*; his noisiness gave her bad headaches. She had been particularly anxious that he should be suitably 'Germanised' in time for his marriage, for she had been alarmed to discover that he wrote to his fiancée in English rather than his sainted father's native tongue: 'the German element is the one I wish to be cherished and kept up in our beloved home,' she told Vicky. To lose it would be a betrayal of Albert; it never occurred to her that to keep it would feed into already hostile feelings about the excessive favouritism of things German by the British monarchy.[4]

Before his death, and in anticipation of Bertie's marriage, Prince Albert had secured a 7,000-acre country estate for him at Sandringham in Norfolk for £220,000, paid for by the profits from the Duchy of Cornwall that Albert had so carefully managed during Bertie's minority. When in London, Bertie and Alexandra would reside at Marlborough House, but despite the couple's anticipated high profile, Victoria continued to veto any suggestions that Bertie take a greater role in public life, such as involvement in the learned and scientific societies that Albert had taken up, or attending the House of Lords. The problem, as Victoria well knew, was that Bertie was an incorrigible gossip and his indiscretion meant he could not be trusted with sensitive state papers. Ever mistrustful of him, she gave instructions for a close watch to be kept on the comings and goings at Marlborough House and on the calibre of people being invited there.

Having been instrumental in finding Bertie a wife, his sister Vicky was hugely excited at the wedding to come, which she would be attending with Fritz and their eldest son Wilhelm. Victoria was only too glad to delegate to her eldest daughter the task of receiving the many guests at the necessary official Drawing Rooms prior to the wedding, but nevertheless chided her: 'Dear child! Your ecstasy at the whole thing is to me sometimes very incomprehensible.' Neither Vicky nor anyone else would believe her when she insisted that she had to have quiet: 'I must constantly dine alone, and any merriment or discussion are quite unbearable.'[5] Besides, she already had enough to deal with, worrying about Alice's imminent confinement; and about Affie, who had committed a sexual transgression while away in Malta, prompting fears that he would turn out as much of a reprobate as his brother. It was all such a burden for her, not just as Queen, but as a lone woman with 'no near male relation of sufficient age and experience' to whom she could turn for advice.

Who was there, Victoria asked General Peel, to 'help her with her sons' and 'keep them in the path of duty'?[6]

For the wedding on 10 March the Queen allowed one major concession: the guests could wear colours, although her own ladies, like her children, should be in the half-mourning colours of grey, lilac or mauve. She was choosy about who she invited—certainly not the immoral Frederick VII of Denmark or most of Alix's mother's questionable Danish relatives; nor too most of her own Hanoverian cousins. But even with such exclusions, the guest list was large, with 900 people in their best finery crammed into St George's Chapel. Many of the male VIPs were obliged to leave their wives at home, and others fought jealously for invitations to be there. It was a spectacular gathering: diplomats and distinguished Cabinet ministers, Knights of the Garter in their sumptuous robes, tiers of 'gorgeous Duchesses' in their bright colours and flashing tiaras, not to mention the glorious sight of 'beefeaters and gold-encrusted trumpeters and heralds in their tabards'. Ladies of fashion grasped this rare opportunity to vie with each other over the splendour of their jewels, Lady Westmorland's diamonds having the edge over Lady Abercorn's sapphires, in the view of Henry Greville, though he thought the beautiful young Lady Spencer, wearing Marie Antoinette's lace, was way and above the best dressed that day.[7]

Yet it was not the fashionable ladies, but their absent monarch, whom everyone really wanted to see. In her stiff, heavy crape and wearing Albert's badge and star of the Garter on its blue ribbon and a diamond brooch with his miniature, Victoria

251

made her way to the chapel away from prying eyes via a covered walkway. She took her place in Catherine of Aragon's closet, specially draped with heavy purple velvet and gold, high up in the south-eastern corner near the organ loft, with Lady Churchill, Lady Lyttleton and the Duchess of Sutherland hovering in the background. All attempts to defuse morbid curiosity failed, as everyone craned their necks trying as discreetly as possible to catch a glimpse of this great figure of imperial grief. When Benjamin Disraeli raised his eyeglass to take a closer look, he was greeted with an icy stare.

Princess Alexandra, however, could not be eclipsed: her radiant beauty that day was breathtaking, as she entered pale and childlike in her dress of Spitalfields satin, covered with a skirt of Honiton lace garlanded with leaves and orange blossoms. Eight bridesmaids in lace and tulle decorated with rosebuds followed, carrying her long silver-moiré train. Bertie too looked the picture of nobility in his scarlet and gold of a general in the Guards, over which he wore the dark-blue robes of the Garter; Princess Mary Adelaide thought he demonstrated 'more depth of manner than ever before' that day, and his sisters Alice and Vicky wept with pride at the sight of him. The whole event had been a 'fine affair', in Disraeli's estimation: 'A perfect pageant with that sufficient foundation of sentiment, which elevates a mere show.'[8]

But it was Victoria's haunted black figure watching the gathered guests from on high that everyone talked about afterwards. Whether by accident or design, the wedding had inevitably drawn attention to the widow as much as the bride, reigniting public sympathy for the bereaved Queen alone on her glorious pinnacle of solitude. Victoria had expected to find it all a 'fearful ordeal' and at times quivered with anxiety.[9] She had, however, borne up very well for most of the time, though certain key moments had brought back painful memories: the flourish of the trumpets reminded her of her own wedding day, and when she heard the glorious voice of the Swedish opera star Jenny Lind singing a chorale written by Albert she cast her eyes up to heaven. 'See, she is worshipping him in spirit!' remarked one of the deans of the Chapel Royal. Her face, to all those who caught sight of it that day, 'spoke all that was within'.[10]

Immediately after she had witnessed the signing of the register and embraced Bertie and Alix, Victoria fled, avoiding the assembled thirty-eight royals at the private wedding reception, or the crush of the general guests in St George's Hall, but dining alone with Beatrice.[11] There was only one place she wanted to be: at the mausoleum, communing with Albert. She kept the keys to it about her at all times, so that she could go down and let herself in to what had by now become an essential extension of home. The night before the wedding she had taken Bertie and Alix there to pray and receive Albert's blessing, and immediately after lunch on the 10th she returned once more. That evening she poured out her anguish in her journal. The wedding had been a day of pure 'suffering' for her without Albert, and she had only got through it 'by a violent effort'. She had consented to sit for her photograph with the happy couple, but resolutely refused to look to camera, instead gazing up in adoration at Albert's marble bust. After all was over, a despondency once more descended, made worse by an uncontrollable envy of her children's happiness: 'Here I sit lonely and desolate, who so need love and tenderness, while our two daughters have each their loving husbands and Bertie has taken his lovely, pure, sweet bride to Osborne.'[12]

As the overdressed members of the aristocracy engaged in an undignified scrum to find places on the special train back out of Windsor, a range of celebrations and parties took place that evening across London and elsewhere in Britain. At long last the nation was out enjoying itself: two and a half million people flooded the streets of London, 'dense enough to hide every stone of the streets from one who had seen it above'.[13] The night was cold and raw, and the crowds jamming central London to see the wedding illuminations at London Bridge, Nelson's Monument and the fountains in Trafalgar Square were 'frightful'; the monumental traffic jam of wagons, vans and omnibuses blocked the streets for hours. Privy Council member Frederick Pollock found himself trapped on Pall Mall, where he was jammed up against the lamp post in the middle of the road, unable to move. At Northumberland House near Charing Cross he witnessed 'a surging vortex of struggling humanity' unlike anything he had seen since the Queen's wedding day.[14] On Bedford Street the Archbishop of York's wife had her crinoline set on fire when their carriage became caught in the crush and some boys tossed a firework inside. All this mayhem, just to see 'a few gas stars and Prince's feathers', grumbled Henry Greville.[15] 'It wasn't worth the hours of jam and wedge,' agreed maid-of-honour

254

Lady Lucy Cavendish. But it was proof, if ever it were needed, of how much the British people hungered for a renewal of the ceremonial of old. On the 11th sales of *The Times* containing an account of the wedding rocketed from its usual 65,000 to 112,000. Crowds turned out again in June for the public unveiling of the memorial to the Great Exhibition, featuring Albert's statue, at the Horticultural Society's Gardens. But it was the Princess of Wales who took centre stage. The monarch was nowhere to be seen.

\*     \*     \*

On Easter Sunday, 5 April 1863, Alice's daughter Victoria was born 'at poor, sad, old Windsor' in the same bed in which Victoria herself had given birth to all her children and wearing the same shift her mother had worn. Victoria had sat up all night with Alice during her labour, even now at forty-three wishing it could have been her giving one last child to Albert. The arrival of another grandchild and an improvement in her state of mind made her feel that she had at last made 'great progress' through all her burden of sorrow.[16] But the worm of jealousy kept gnawing at her—jealousy that her children one by one were entering into their own separate lives and she was no longer the centre of attention. With Alice now a mother, Victoria felt that only Baby (Beatrice) and Lenchen (Helena) still loved her 'the most of any thing'. She knew that this was the natural progression of things, but nevertheless it was a bitter pill to swallow: she who had been 'the dearest object of two beings [Albert and her mother] for so many years, is now daily learning to feel that she is only No. 3 or 4 in the real tender love of others'. She had to admit that she was sadly *de trop* in her married children's lives and that she did not belong to anyone any more. Soon Alice would be returning to Hesse and Victoria dreaded it. It was no good; her querulous self-centeredness once more rose to the surface. 'A married daughter I *must* have living with me, and must *not* be left constantly to look about for help,' she insisted to Uncle Leopold. The daughter designated to fill Alice's shoes and be sacrificed on the altar of her mother's neediness was the docile and dowdy Lenchen. A husband would have to be found for her who would agree to the couple spending the greater part of the year with Victoria in England; she could not give up another of her girls to a foreign country 'without *sinking* under the *weight* of my desolation'.[17] Nor was she willing for Helena to give her heart to one whom she, Victoria, deemed beneath her. After Albert's death Helena had developed a crush on his German librarian, Carl Ruland, and on discovering this Victoria had sent the loyal Ruland packing, even though she had begged him on Albert's deathbed: 'do not leave me and my children'.[18] Lucy Cavendish thought Helena already had that sad look—as had Alice before her—of 'one who has thought and done too much for her age and been a comforter'. She was 'cruelly overworked', the Queen having no notion of how her daughter's mind and body were strained by her onerous duties and her mother's endless dissatisfaction.[19]

Within months of their wedding, Bertie and Alix too fell under Victoria's critical eye: he for reverting to his old bad manners and hedonistic lifestyle, and she for looking thin and sallow and losing her *'fraîcheur'*—probably from too many late nights out socialising, in Victoria's view. Bertie should take better care of his wife, yet again he was no equal to his father, whose 'wise, motherly care' of her, when he was 'not yet 21', had 'exceeded everything'. Had Vicky noticed what a curiously small head Alix had? She had inherited her mother's deafness, too. Victoria dreaded the physiological outcome: combined with Bertie's 'small empty brain', their children, when they had them, might well prove 'unintellectual'.[20] Affie was a continuing worry as well; now home from sea, having survived a bad bout of typhoid fever, he was spending too much time at Marlborough House. Victoria feared that under his brother's influence he might once more 'fall into sin from weakness'. Time therefore to 'fix his affections securely' and see him married off as well. Once more a succession of German princesses—of Altenburg, Oldenburg and Wied—was put under the microscope, as Victoria discussed their relative merits with Vicky in Prussia.[21]

Although she continued to complain of feeling tired and overworked, the Queen had, throughout 1863, slowly begun to recover some of her equilibrium. But then, in July, a new death had knocked her back again—that of her 'dearest, wisest, best and oldest friend', Baron Stockmar.[22] That he was gone to 'brighter regions' where he would be in the company of Albert was at least a comfort and, like Albert, he must be commemorated. Did Vicky have 'plenty of the beloved Baron's photographs and also some of his precious hair?' she enquired. If not, she could send some.[23] Births, marriages, deaths and memorials were now increasingly the focus and pattern of Victoria's shrinking world and the morbid romanticism at the heart of her very existence. Even *The Times* noted that the Queen's unceasing grief had become 'a sort of religion' with her.[24] After her fleeting appearance at Bertie's wedding, the gentlemen of the press once more found their reporting on the Queen reduced to a daily catalogue of her brief walks and carriage drives. Her stay at Balmoral that autumn was particularly bleak in the face of the loss of Stockmar; as usual, the loyalty of the Scottish locals saved her from despair. 'There is nothing like the Highlanders— no, nothing,' she told Vicky.[25] But the loneliness of Balmoral was dreadful. She tried, and failed, to persuade a succession of relatives to come and keep her company, but they all made their excuses, leaving her with only Lady Augusta and Lady Jane Churchill for company, until the family gathered for the unveiling of a new memorial to Prince Albert.

On 13 October 1863 the Queen travelled from Balmoral to Aberdeen to unveil a statue of Albert by Baron Marochetti. It would be her first public appearance since her husband's death (the wedding in March having been by private invitation). But there were no bands or street decorations on this occasion and the public, who stood patiently waiting for two hours in the rain, were given strict instructions that there should be no cheering. Victoria was visibly agitated, but at least all her adult children had joined her—even Vicky was over from Prussia. But the day was filled with melancholy as she drove along the densely crowded, but respectfully silent streets, the dark, leaden sky unforgiving and the only bright point the profusion of flags on the ships docked along the quay, though even these hung limp and sodden in the drenching rain.[26] Victoria was anxious for it all to be over as quickly as possible and was clearly annoyed when—with the rain falling fast as she huddled under an umbrella held by Vicky—she had to endure a ten-minute-long prayer by the Principal of Aberdeen University prior to the unveiling. Even the spectators became restive, thinking the delay intolerable for their widowed Queen: 'Cut it short,' came a voice from the crowd. 'Ay man, gie us the rest on the neest Sabbath,' shouted another.[27]

As 1863 drew to a close, members of the royal household were on the constant lookout for hopeful signs of a return to normal. December would mark the end of the traditional two-year period of mourning and everyone hoped that her appearance at Aberdeen might mark the beginning of the Queen's return to public life. 'Two years it must be said, are a long period to be consumed in unavailing regrets and in dwelling upon days which cannot be healed,' observed *The Times*.[28] But for Victoria nothing had changed; her reaction to being on public display at Aberdeen had been no different from her other brief forays into the outside world: psychosomatic headaches, insomnia and stress preceded and followed every minor exertion and she continued to protest bitterly at being put upon. In response, Doctors Jenner and Clark stuck to the traditional line of petting her and pandering to her protestations, fearing her total mental collapse; thoughts of hereditary madness—she was, after all, the granddaughter of King George III—still lingered, in the absence of any real medical understanding of the Queen's psychological state. Victoria herself put it down to 'her *hard*, slavelike labour *for* the Country'. She felt persecuted, 'like a poor hunted hare, like a child that has lost its mother'.[29] Any disruption to her familiar daily routine was an extreme provocation for her, and she was beside herself with rage and disappointment in November when her most loyal lady committed an unforgivable act of betrayal: 'My dear Lady Augusta, at 41 . . . has most unnecessarily, decided to *marry*!!' she wrote to Uncle Leopold in high dudgeon. 'I thought she *never* would leave *me*!'[30] Victoria's own life might be in stasis, but the lives of others were not, and Lady Augusta, having long steeled herself, had finally plucked up the courage to grasp the happiness of marriage with Dr Arthur Stanley, Dean of Westminster. Victoria grudgingly gave her blessing, with the proviso that Lady Augusta would nevertheless be 'a great deal with me afterwards'; but for now Ladies Ely and Churchill would be the main butt of her increasingly volcanic personality.

The Queen's frequent explosions of temper and determined opinion prompted William Gladstone to think that he had detected signs of recovery and 'the old voice of business in the Queen' of late, and many of the newspapers were openly suggesting that she might even open Parliament the following year. 'There is strong pressure from without from almost the highest in the land down to the smallest boy in the streets of London to get the Queen once more to come to London,' Lord Torrington told General Grey:

The public accept *no one* as a substitute and the

danger is considerable if once that public cease to care or take an interest in seeing the Queen moving amongst them. It will not do for people to be accustomed to Her Majesty's absence. Do away with the outward and visible sign and the *ignorant mass* believe Royalty is of no value. There is not a tradesman in London who does not believe he is damaged by the Queen not coming to London.[31]

The suggestion that Victoria should open Parliament in 1864, however, received a brisk refusal. Her health simply was not up to it; it was all she could do just to keep up with the mountains of paperwork on her desk. How could she perform any of these public duties, 'trembling and *alone* at Courts, and Parties and State occasions, without her Sole Guardian and *Protector*'?[32] Sir Charles Phipps and General Grey (with whom Phipps shared the still-unofficial role of Private Secretary to the Queen) were both beginning to detect worrying signs of avoidance in their reluctant monarch, and one of their closest supporters in this view was the Queen's own daughter, Princess Alice. She had seen her mother that autumn on a private visit to Coburg, and had thought her very well. Victoria had got through a formal luncheon with the Emperor of Austria and eighteen other guests, talking animatedly and even running to the window to see him off. In a private moment Victoria had even admitted to Alice that she was 'afraid of getting too well—as if it was a crime and that she *feared* to begin to like riding on her Scotch pony, etc.' Behind the scenes, the royal entourage agreed that something must be done: 'after the next anniversary, we must all try, *gently*, to get her to resume her old habits'.[33]

Ironically, it was one of the most complex political crises of the 1860s that galvanised Victoria into a flurry of activity—be it only by letter and memorandum—for although she continued adamantly to refuse to take part in public ceremonial, she had by no means abandoned her vigorous interest in foreign affairs. It was an interest she had shared with Albert; this and her defence of her prerogatives as monarch had never dimmed. Indeed, when she had travelled to Coburg in August she had specifically instructed Gladstone that, in her absence, 'no step is taken in foreign affairs without her previous sanction being obtained'.[34] For the Queen was well aware that a political crisis of long standing was coming to a head. It broke in November 1863 with the death of King Frederick VII of Denmark and the accession of Alix's father, Christian IX. This had prompted renewed calls for the independence of the Danish duchies of Schleswig and Holstein, with the former being incorporated into Denmark and the latter retaining separate status under Danish suzerainty. Rival claims to the territories by the Duke of Augustenburg were disputed by the Prussian Prime Minister, Bismarck, who, supported by the Austrians, sought the ceding of both territories to Prussia.

The crisis forced a split in the deeply conflicted loyalties of Queen Victoria's European family and feelings became very heated, so much so that she forbade all political discussion at table. Like Albert, Vicky and Fritz, she was pro-Prussian; Bertie and his wife, naturally enough, supported the Danes;

and Victoria's half-sister Feodora was firmly in the Augustenburg camp. Most of the British public sympathised with the underdog Denmark, abhorring Prussia, the aggressor. Ever the sabre-rattler Palmerston, now approaching eighty and fading fast, contemplated sending in British troops in defence of a beleaguered Denmark, but Britain had no stomach for war now, any more than it had in December 1861. Without the military support of France or Russia, it would have been madness to take on the Prussians.

Victoria was appalled at the prospect of conflict, but also wished to protect her own family interests. 'I have, since he left me, the courage of a lioness if I see danger,' she told Vicky, 'and I shall never mind giving my people my decided opinion and more than that!'[35] But she had to fight hard against her innermost prejudices: her 'heart and sympathies were all German', but she did not want to sanction 'the infliction upon her subjects of all the horrors of war'; or, on the other hand, see any help given by her government to the Danes. Publicly, she knew she had to do as Albert had so carefully taught her—be seen to be impartial, sticking to an insistence on British neutrality, as he had so honourably done over the American crisis. But oh, how she rued the inconvenient fact that her daughter-in-law Alix had not been 'a good German'.[36]

Such a shameful thought was soon forgotten when, as the crisis deepened, a pregnant Alix went into premature labour—giving birth two months early to a sickly son, Albert Victor, on 8 January 1864. In February Prussian and Austrian troops invaded Schleswig, prompting Victoria to

263

seek comfort and courage from Albert's spirit by praying frequently in the Blue Room and at the mausoleum. She was pained by hostile comments in the press about her pro-German sympathies and was enraged when Lord Ellenborough criticised her in Parliament. Such accusations, she told Palmerston, 'ought to be put into the fire'.[37] She also had to ask Lord Clarendon to caution Bertie on his 'violent abuse of Prussia'; it was 'fearfully dangerous for the Heir to her throne to take up one side violently'. The British public, however, were on Bertie's side—anti-German feeling in Britain was 'quite ungovernable'. But it made no difference: in June the Danes were defeated, and in October Holstein and the German-speaking territories of Schleswig were ceded to joint Prussian and Austrian control.[38]

Victoria marked the end of the Schleswig-Holstein crisis by showing herself briefly to her public, taking a drive through Windsor Great Park in an open carriage, but only as far as the nearby railway station—a matter of a mile or so. Convinced that the newspaper criticism of her seclusion was unrepresentational of the view of the nation at large, she felt that this excursion and a couple of fleeting appearances at court that summer had 'pleased people more than anything'. 'If done occasionally in this way', she was sure such appearances would 'go farther to satisfy them than anything else'.[39] She was sadly deluded, for public sympathy was now clearly on the wane. The Queen's continuing absence from central London prompted some practical jokers to tie large placards to the palace gateposts, announcing: 'These commanding premises to be let or sold,

(*Left*) The East Terrace, Windsor Castle, location of the royal apartments. Victoria never liked the castle very much and after Albert's death avoided spending much time here.

(*Left*) Design for the interior decorations of the Royal Mausoleum at Frogmore, inspired by Albert's favourite painter, Raphael. His marble effigy was not placed in position on top of the granite sarcophagus there until November 1868; the interior was completed in August 1871.

(*Left*) The one time Windsor Castle came into its own was for happy family Christmases during Albert's lifetime, such as this one c. 1850, promoting the public image of a happy, domestic royal family.

(*Below*) A popular, but inaccurate Victorian scrap book cut-out of Prince Albert's deathbed, depicting Victoria, Alice, Bertie and Arthur. In fact, Arthur had not been present at the death, having said farewell to his father earlier that afternoon. Two of Albert's other sons were abroad at the time: Alfie at sea and Leopold in Cannes.

(*Left*) Bertie, Prince of Wales. Kind, sociable and well-meaning but academically underachieving, he failed to live up to the high expectations of both his parents.

(*Below*) Princess Alice, Victoria and Albert's second daughter, who took upon herself the devoted nursing of her father during his final illness and was the butt of her mother's agonising grief in the first six months after it.

(*Above*) Princess Louise, wearing jet, the only jewellery that the Queen would allow her daughters and her ladies to wear at court for more than twenty years after her husband's death.

Commemorative items produced after the death of Prince Albert. (*Above*) A pot lid based on one of the last photographs of him; (*above right*) a popular postcard of the widowed queen and her children; (*right*) a typical memorial card recording the Prince's death.

*Sacred to the Memory of*
**H. R. H. PRINCE ALBERT,**
Consort of Her Majesty, Queen Victoria,
Who died at Windsor, December the 14th, 1861,
IN HIS 43rd YEAR.

(*Below*) A Whitby jet workshop photographed during the heyday of the industry, which boomed after Albert's death.

(*Above*) Albert's brainchild, The Royal Albert Hall, constructed between 1867 and 1871 as an exhibition centre and concert hall for the promotion of British arts, industry and culture.

(*Left*) This equestrian statue of Prince Albert was the first public monument to be unveiled by Queen Victoria herself, in Wolverhampton in November 1866.

(*Right*) The gilded statue of Prince Albert at the newly restored Albert Memorial in Hyde Park. Completed with the statue in position in 1875, the memorial was never popular and came close to being demolished. It was saved and restored during the 1990s, thanks to a concerted campaign by the Victorian Society.

(*Below*) Bertie and Queen Victoria riding in an open landau to the Thanksgiving Service held at St Paul's Cathedral on 27 February 1872 for his recovery from typhoid fever. Note the presence on the box of the ubiquitous John Brown.

in consequence of the late occupant's declining business.' The placards were immediately torn down and police duty outside the palace doubled, only for them to be posted again a few days later.[40] Some put it down to 'Republican propaganda', but gossip was further fuelled by an April Fool's joke published mischievously by Delane in *The Times* on 1 April, intended once more to draw Victoria out. 'Her Majesty's loyal subjects will be very well pleased to hear,' the paper announced, 'that their Sovereign is about to break her protracted seclusion by holding courts for the diplomatic corps at Buckingham Palace.' At long last the monarchy was about to 'recover from its suspended animation'. An aggrieved Victoria, who read her press cuttings avidly, immediately wrote her own anonymous rebuttal, which was published in *The Times* on 6 April:

An erroneous idea seems generally to prevail, and has latterly found frequent expression in the newspapers, that the Queen is about to resume the place in society which she occupied before her great affliction; that is, that she is about again to hold levees and drawing-rooms in person, and to appear as before at Court balls, concerts etc. This idea cannot be too explicitly contradicted.

She would, she said, do her very best to fulfil her duty in matters of national interest, and give the support to society and trade that was needed, but would not be put upon for the sake of expediency. At the core of Victoria's objections was her continuing and consuming sense of being overwhelmed—not just with work, but at the prospect of once more taking up those public duties 'of mere representation' and spectacle, which she had never enjoyed, even when Albert was alive. Her ceremonial functions, she insisted, could be 'equally well performed' by other members of the family. 'More the Queen cannot do; and more the kindness and good feeling of her people will surely not extract from her.' The British people had indeed been most forbearing for three years now, but it was precisely in the realm of theatre and ceremonial—as Bertie's wedding had all too clearly demonstrated—that the Queen was most missed and most needed. Her growing unpopularity was beginning to endanger the very fabric of constitutional monarchy, as Lord Cecil pointed out in the *Saturday Review*: 'Seclusion is one of the few luxuries in which Royal personages may not indulge. The power which is derived from affection or from loyalty needs a life of uninterrupted publicity to sustain it.'[41]

'The country knows nothing of the Queen's peculiar desolation,' sympathised Lucy Cavendish; it were better they prayed for her than goaded her. Within the safe four walls of her study Victoria felt she was as hard-working and conscientious as she had ever been, but the problem was that the public could not see this; her labours were 'as secret and invisible as those of the queen-bee in the central darkness of the hive'.[42] As a palliative, the Lord Chamberlain's office announced that three Drawing Rooms hosted by Princess Alexandra would be held during the London Season and three levees by the Prince of Wales. In addition, two state concerts and two state balls would be held at Buckingham Palace and, after a three-year lapse,

Victoria ordered that her forty-fifth birthday—24 May—be celebrated that year 'with trooping of the colours and general festivities, which had been suspended since the death of the Prince Consort'.[43]

But as spring turned to summer, discontent rumbled on and rumours continued to circulate: the Queen was ill, or mad; she would never live in London again, and—according to all the French papers—was about to abdicate, an event that had been anticipated on the Continent almost from the day of Victoria's widowing. Lord Howden agreed, confiding to Lord Clarendon that 'for her own interest, happiness and *reputation*', the Queen should have abdicated on Bertie's coming-of-age. 'She would then have left a great name and great regret.'[44] Instead, there was now much dissatisfaction among London tradesmen, as well as 'among that class to whom an invitation to a palace ball is a mark of their social position'.[45] Victoria was mortified by the gossip, but it did nothing to undermine her resolve or diminish her consuming self-absorption. Indeed, she appeared 'less inclined to appear than ever and more inclined to have her own way', according to Lord Torrington. The contradictions were boundless; claiming with one breath to have the business of the country at heart, time and time again Victoria forbade a topic of conversation which was 'precisely that on which it is most important that she should be informed'.[46] The problem, as Torrington explained to Delane, was that 'Every one appears more or less afraid to speak or advise the Queen', so much so that she now had a habit of sending word prior to any meeting with ministers on what she would and would not discuss, 'lest it should make her nervous'. If those about her had a little more courage, 'things might mend'.[47] But no one did.

The continuing failure of anyone to face up to the Queen's intractable personality was also creating diplomatic problems. She flatly refused to entertain visiting royalty or reciprocate hospitality given to her family abroad. The King of Sweden was obliged to stay at the Swedish legation on a recent visit to London, and during that of Prince Humbert of Italy in September 1864 the aged Lord Palmerston had had to traipse up from his home, Brockett Hall in Hertfordshire, 'to give him a dinner'. Later, when Prince Humbert visited Windsor, he had to be entertained with a modest lunch at the White Hart Inn rather than at the castle. Even when Alix's parents arrived for their daughter's wedding in March, they had been accommodated not at Windsor Castle, as would have been expected, but at the local Palace Hotel. Despite their conspicuous impoverishment they had, however, entertained Bertie and Alix lavishly when they visited Denmark later that year.

The Queen's neglect was verging on the rude as well as the mean, and was even more shameful when the Civil List could more than afford it.[48] Delane agreed, and published another pointed reminder in *The Times* of 2 November: the monarch's 'melancholy bereavement' might excuse her absence to visiting foreign dignitaries, 'but the presence of the Sovereign, although the highest ornament and the most attractive part of the nation's hospitality, is not absolutely indispensable to its exercise'. The Prince and Princess of Wales should, he argued, be given the task of entertaining foreign dignitaries in the Queen's continuing absence. They had already proved to be an enormous success at the heart of the London Season and, with her grace and beauty, Alexandra was becoming a trendsetter in fashion, providing the best boost to trade in the absence of her mother-in-law. At a Drawing Room in May she had turned even the wearing of black into high fashion, appearing in full mourning for her maternal grandmother who had recently died, resplendent in a black silk train and skirt elaborately trimmed with jet beading, as well as a headdress and tiara of jet and black feathers. Going on this description, wrote the *Whitby Gazette*, 'the manufacturers of our town need not despair of the jet trade'.[49]

Before 1864 was out, as the country faced yet another year of the Queen's retreat, John Delane renewed his attack in *The Times*. 'In all bereavements there is a time when the days of mourning should be looked upon as past', he began:

> It is impossible for a recluse to occupy the British Throne without a gradual weakening of that authority which the Sovereign has been accustomed to exert. The regulation of a household may be in the power of such a ruler, but the real sway of an Empire will be impossible.
> For the sake of the Crown as well as of the public we would, therefore, beseech Her Majesty to return to the personal exercise of her exalted functions . . . and not postpone them longer to the indulgence of an unavailing grief.[50]

Inevitably Delane's editorial, measured though it

was, provoked much controversy, with papers such as the monarchist *Morning Post* accusing *The Times* of disloyalty and rising to the monarch's defence: 'In seclusion or in society, Queen Victoria will reign in the hearts of her subjects.'[51] The *Observer* on the 18th agreed that the attack was unwarranted: only the sufferer could best judge when the time has come to give up mourning. Victoria thought *The Times* article 'vulgar and heartless'. Finding herself cornered, she resorted to her most effective and provocative weapon—emotional blackmail. Overwork had killed Albert; did they want it to kill her too? She was worn out with 'constant proposals as to what she is to do and not to do'. Privately, however, even her cousin the Duke of Cambridge had written to her begging her to come out of retirement and 'save her country'.[52]

The case for the Queen's continued seclusion was becoming increasingly difficult to argue, for her appearance now contradicted her repeated protestations of physical weakness. The logic shared by many was that she looked well and was therefore up to the job. Torrington 'never saw her in better health, spirits or looks' that summer. Yet such had been the rising levels of Victoria's perceived tetchiness that by the end of the year Jenner and Clark suggested a new form of therapy that might soothe the Queen's nerves and revive her interest in the outside world. If she were to go out for pony rides at Osborne, as she did at Balmoral, rather than just sitting in her carriage, it might do her a world of good. With the connivance of Phipps, and Princess Alice, who was eager to see her mother resume her public life, it was recommended that Victoria's Scottish ghillie, John

Brown—so indefatigable in his attention and care of her, in Victoria's own view—should be brought down from Balmoral with her favourite pony, Lochnagar, for the winter. The monarchy in Britain was approaching crisis: 'Two years and a half have sufficed to destroy the popularity which Albert took twenty years to build up,' observed Lord Derby.[53] In that short space of time the Queen had disregarded every single lesson that her husband had taught her about her essential state duties in preserving the integrity of the throne.

## CHAPTER TWELVE

# 'God Knows How I Want So Much to be Taken Care Of'

In January 1865, three years on from Prince Albert's death, the only visible evidence the nation had of its widowed queen's existence was vicariously, through the continuing memorialisation of her dead husband across the country—a process inherently more about Victoria's obsessive grief than her husband's increasingly elusive memory. For some, like Charles Dickens, the continuing cult of the Prince Consort was oppressive. 'If you should meet with an inaccessible cave anywhere to which a hermit could retire from the memory of Prince Albert and testimonials to the same,' he told his friend John Leech, 'pray let me know of it. We have nothing solitary and deep enough in this part of England.'[1]

The relentless dead march of Albert continued

to echo across Britain throughout the 1860s, as the public, in deference to their grieving queen, loyally raised statue after statue on the urban landscape. After Victoria had unveiled the seated monument at Aberdeen, a succession of standing figures of the Prince, usually in his Garter robes or military dress, were unveiled in Perth, Dublin, Tenby, Birmingham, Edinburgh, Salford, Oxford (an uncharacteristic pose in informal dress for the Natural History Museum) and at Madingley—with Albert in his robes as Chancellor of Cambridge University. Although the consensus was to present the late prince as a man of learning, a few equestrian statues also appeared: at Liverpool, Glasgow and Holborn Circus in London.

Elsewhere in Britain, Prince Albert's name was being commemorated in the form of clock towers—at Hastings, Manchester and Belfast—while new buildings in his memory sprang up everywhere: the Albert Memorial College in Suffolk, the Royal Albert Memorial Museum at Exeter and the Albert Institute in Dundee. In central Manchester a large square named after the Prince was several years under construction on a derelict site that had been specially cleared for the purpose, its focus to be a seated statue under a medieval-style canopy similar to the one of Albert already commissioned in London, but finished long before it, in 1865. Plans in London were also under way, under the architect Captain Francis Fowke, to build a concert hall, an idea that the Prince had first mooted with Henry Cole at the time of the Great Exhibition, but which, after Albert's death, had been sidelined in favour of work on the national memorial in Hyde Park. The latter project was proving extremely protracted and

272

costly. In 1864, after seven leading architects had been invited to submit designs, Gilbert Scott had been awarded the commission. His Gothic design was not favoured by the artistic establishment, who saw it as rather a safe and unchallenging variation on the traditional Eleanor Cross, and snobbery abounded in the professional press. 'Mr Scott's design is scarcely worthy of his reputation, and we should deem its adoption a discredit to the present state of knowledge of the principles of Gothic architecture,' sneered the *Civil Engineer and Architect's Journal*.[2] Queen Victoria, however, had executive power over the final decision; Albert had been a great supporter of Scott's work and the Gothic Revival, and what Albert liked the country got.

Work began on the Albert Memorial in the spring of 1864, when the site in Hyde Park was fenced off. But the money required was considerable—estimated at £110,000—with £60,000 already raised by public subscription. In 1863 Disraeli and Palmerston persuaded a reluctant Parliament to come up with the balance. Grateful that in Disraeli she had found a soulmate who would endlessly gratify her adoration of Albert's 'spotless and unequalled character', Victoria sent her effusive thanks for his support together with a signed copy of Albert's collected speeches bound in white morocco.[3] Once the Queen had set her seal on Scott's design (though her critical powers stretched only so far as to deem it 'handsome') there was no toleration of further argument. By 1866 the *Art Journal* was agreeing with Disraeli that the memorial was 'worthy of its object' and that it resembled the character of the Prince Consort 'in the beauty and the harmony of its proportion'. It was, the editor concluded, 'the type of a sublime life, the testimony of a grateful people'. The satirical press disagreed, pointing out—presciently as it turned out—that such an ornate monument would soon succumb to the dirt and pollution of the London atmosphere and need 'periodical pumpings with a fire engine' to keep it clean.[4]

Scott's design was based on the style of ornate, canopied shrines found on the Continent in cities such as medieval Nuremberg and Renaissance Milan, taking inspiration too from the monument to Sir Walter Scott in Edinburgh and Scott's own design for the Martyrs' Memorial in Oxford's St Giles—both erected in the 1840s. The centrepiece was to be a gilded fifteen-foot seated figure of the Prince, wearing his robes of the Garter and holding the catalogue of the 1851 Great Exhibition, the objective being to promote the Prince as a patron of the arts, science and industry. Carlo Marochetti was commissioned to execute the statue in bronze, which would be placed under the canopy on a raised platform thirty feet above the ground. The canopy itself was to be decorated with mosaics and raised on granite marble columns, surrounded by carved angels. Below this central podium, and enclosing it on four sides, would be a frieze of sculptures in white Sicilian marble, with statues at each corner representing agriculture, manufactures, commerce and engineering. At ground level, at the foot of a series of marble steps, four further statuary groups would be placed at each outer corner, representing the continents of the British Empire: Europe, Asia, Africa and America. Marochetti's initial plaster model of the statue was, however, twice rejected by Scott, and when Marochetti died suddenly in Paris in December 1867 before completing his third version, the commission for the statue was passed to another favourite royal sculptor, John Foley. This, and other delays, as well as logistical problems and fierce arguments over escalating costs, meant that the whole project would take more than a decade to be completed.

In the meantime, in the summer of 1865, the entire royal family and more than a dozen near-relatives gathered in Coburg for the unveiling of a statue to Albert that was, of all of the many representations of him, perhaps the most personal, erected as it was so near to his birthplace and unveiled on Albert's birthday, 26 August. Victoria complained of having to endure the full glare of publicity during what was a particularly theatrical ceremony, and ensured that she arrived back in England unobserved, avoiding the public reception being prepared for her at Woolwich when she landed. Tickets had already been issued when she sent instructions that she wished for 'the greatest privacy'—a fact that rankled with the many dockyard workers and officials denied any sight of her. Her 'dismal debarkation' back home in England on 8 September was thus in marked contrast to all the pomp and ceremony indulged in at Coburg, where everyone agreed that she had, surprisingly, looked the picture of good health.[5]

To compensate her public for this disappointment, Victoria agreed to a rare public appearance the following year to unveil a statue of Albert on horseback at Wolverhampton, in the heart of the Black Country; 100,000 people

275

turned out to see her, but the Queen's very name sounded 'strange and odd' to a mining community so far from the capital and whose denizens slaved for the most part in the darkness amidst its black slag-heaps. Victoria remained for the short time she was there a distant figure huddled in black, almost lost in the bleak industrial landscape.[6] As she drove back along a three-mile route through the poorest part of the town she was gratified to see flags and decorations celebrating her visit on even 'the most wretched-looking slums'. The people were half-starved and in tatters, she noted, but how comforting was the warmth with which they greeted 'their poor widowed Queen'. In reporting the visit, the normally uncontroversial *Ladies' Companion* could not contain its sense of cynicism: the good people of Wolverhampton had been 'mad with pleasure' at the all-too-rare sight of Her Majesty '*in propria persona*', but what was the point, it asked, of 'yet another statue to Albert the Good'? A better example had been set by the widow of the explorer Sir John Franklin—lost at sea while charting the North-West Passage in the Canadian Arctic. The bold and intrepid Lady Jane had 'not allowed her bereavement to drive her into retirement but rather to mix with humankind to her own benefit and theirs'.[7] Far away on the Indian subcontinent the press was stirring, with the Calcutta-based newspaper the *Friend of India* remarking of the Queen's tedious inauguration of endless statues to Albert that her grief was 'overdone' and that, as sovereign, she had 'higher duties to perform': if Albert were alive, the paper had no doubt that 'he would have been among the foremost to discourage the redundancy of such displays'.[8]

In the meantime, all attempts at coaxing the Queen out of retirement other than to commemorate Albert (and no matter how subtle) were still being met with total obduracy. Nothing could supplant him as her first and greatest preoccupation: not her religious faith, not her children, not even her duty to her country. Duty had been the motivating force in Albert's life, but with Victoria it was different. She wanted more; she wanted love. Without it—without Albert—all she had to cling to was her great and enduring grief. But as her family and court watched in dismay, the damage of such pathological mourning to her normal functioning as monarch was becoming ever more apparent. Her recovery was not, as one might normally expect, contingent on the passage of time, as a simple matter of 'getting over it'. What was needed was a crucial and necessary shift in dependency, from her dead husband to a living substitute: a strong and protective male, who would look after her as Albert had done. This role now fell to the most unlikely of candidates—the blunt and down-to-earth John Brown, who after his arrival at Windsor at the end of 1864 had slowly begun to break down the incapacitating pattern of the Queen's grief at a time when every other option had failed.

*　　　*　　　*

The second of nine sons in a family of eleven children, the blond-haired, blue-eyed Brown had been an ostler at Balmoral when it was leased by Sir Robert Gordon prior to the estate being purchased by Victoria and Albert. It was Prince

Albert who first spotted Brown's usefulness, and promoted him to the role of ghillie to the royal family in the autumn of 1849. In 1851 Brown found favour with the Queen when he began leading her out on her pony during her annual holiday at Balmoral. By 1858 Prince Albert had appointed him the Queen's 'particular ghillie' in Scotland, as one of several favoured Highland attendants, from which position he rapidly gained the ascendant by proving himself indispensable when accompanying Victoria and Albert on their incognito 'expeditions' in and around the Highlands during 1860 and 1861. Brown's roles were several: groom, ostler, footman, page, and even maid—for the terms of his employment included cleaning Victoria's boots and brushing her skirts and cloaks. He also performed the role of self-appointed bodyguard whenever the Queen drove out. In the autumn of 1863, returning as darkness fell from an excursion to Altnagiuthasach, Victoria, Helena and Alice had narrowly escaped serious injury when their carriage, thanks to the ineptitude of its aged and drunken coachman, had overturned on the road. Brown, who was thrown in the fall and clearly hurt, had immediately insisted on attending to them, wrapping them in blankets in the shelter of the overturned carriage and standing guard till help arrived. Such manly protectiveness went straight to Victoria's needy heart.

Within a couple of months of Brown's arrival at Windsor, the Queen's mood rapidly lifted, much of it down to the effect of his physical presence: she felt safe when he was around. Here was a strong arm on which she could depend, and whose every waking thought was concerned with her sole comfort, for, as she told Vicky, 'God knows how I want so much to be taken care of.' She poured out her admiration for Brown in a letter to Uncle Leopold, informing him that she had appointed the thirty-eight-year-old 'to attend me always'. She accorded him the title of 'The Queen's Highland Servant' on a generous salary of £120 per annum, making Brown second in rank only to Rudolf Löhlein, Albert's former valet, who on his master's death had been promoted by the Queen to Principal Personal Servant.[9] She was now riding daily, with Brown always at her side, and gave him sole responsibility for the organisation of her horses and carriages, as well as taking charge of her many dogs and even deciding which members of her household were allowed to ride which of her 'dear little Highland ponies' up at Balmoral.[10] Under Brown's influence, Victoria's adulation of all things Scottish—so far removed from the 'mere miserable frivolities and worldinesses of this wicked world'—swelled into panegyric. Highlanders, in her opinion, were 'high bred' and full of poetry, simplicity and truth, and 'might be trusted with all the secrets of the universe'.[11] She revered Brown's feral masculinity and brooked no criticism of him; he was 'superior in feeling, sense and judgment' to all her other servants, even her maids. She fretted when he got cold and wet out leading her pony in all weathers, bare-legged in his kilt and with no protective clothing. She was concerned that he never took proper care of himself and refused to take holidays, which is no doubt why she turned a blind eye to the essential whisky flask that accompanied him everywhere; in fact she issued a general order that all royal coaches should carry a

279

bottle of whisky under the coachman's seat, in case of emergencies. Victoria herself had long enjoyed her favourite brands of Auld Kirk and Lochnagar whisky (the latter brewed on her own estates). She had been in the habit of taking whisky in a glass or two of burgundy at dinner and of adding it to her tea; in later years she increasingly enjoyed the medicinal benefits of whisky with Apollinaris mineral water, supposedly on her doctors' orders (whisky being considered beneficial in countering rheumatism). The comforts of whisky appear to have grown rather than diminished during her widowhood, no doubt easing the pain of her bereavement, but also conceivably triggering some of her more irascible and unreasonable behaviour.[12]

But Brown's meteoric rise to the position of favourite inevitably caused problems in the royal household. Her children remained stubbornly immune to his wholesome Scottish charms and were uneasy at his increasing influence over their mother. They were shocked to learn that she tolerated him—a mere servant—calling her 'wumman' with almost marital familiarity, and that she allowed him unprecedented access to her apartments. Soon Brown was gaining a say in everyday, domestic affairs, which alienated the other servants, who hated his gruff and autocratic manner. The Queen's entourage also bridled at his brusqueness and his crude political and religious views, in the main dismissing him out of hand as ill-mannered, coarse and dictatorial. In so doing they failed to understand the value of John Brown's essentially honest personality—which was so like the Queen's—and his absolute fidelity to her, as head of the clan. None seemed able to comprehend the power of his natural magnetism (as the epitome of the Noble Savage), any more than those at the Russian court would understand the similar influence Rasputin had over Victoria's granddaughter, the Tsaritsa Alexandra. The Queen's equerry Henry Ponsonby (who came to know the Queen very well later on as her Private Secretary) was perhaps the most tolerant and came closest to understanding Brown's charisma as a 'child of nature', but others, seeking to debunk him and his hold over the Queen, put it down to some kind of sinister mystic power—of supposed second sight—with Brown acting as the spirit medium through whom the Queen communicated with Albert on the other side.[13]

\*       \*       \*

Persistent and unsubstantiated rumour that the Queen sought the help of spiritualists and mediums during her widowhood first reared its head in the 1860s and has never entirely gone away.[14] Much was made of Victoria and (prior to his death) Albert's passing interest in spiritism, mesmerism and magnetism, all of which had become fashionable when the cult of spirit-rapping and table-turning first arrived from the USA at the end of the 1840s. Since childhood Victoria had had a fascination for ghosts and hauntings, coupled with a tendency to be superstitious, and the enormous popularity of spiritualism fed into her natural curiosity. She and Albert had tried out table-turning, almost as a party game, when it had been all the rage, and they were said to have attended demonstrations by the sought-after medium David Dunglass Home, who was patronised by their friends Napoleon III and Empress Eugénie of France. But their interest in these and other such phenomena had been more as performance art—or, in Albert's case, as pseudo-science—rather than out of religious conviction. Many Victorian notables, from Gladstone to Harriet Martineau to Elizabeth Barrett Browning, Tennyson and Dante Gabriel Rossetti, had all, at one time or another, been drawn to psychic phenomena; as too were several ladies at court, such as the Queen's close friend Madame Van de Weyer, who was fanatically devoted to spiritualism.[15] But Prince Albert was too great an admirer of science and the rational, and Victoria too practical, too grounded in basic common sense, to be taken in by a spiritualist movement that was rapidly becoming tainted by fraudulence and deception.

The religious faith that Victoria and Albert had shared, and had openly discussed at length during their marriage, was based on a profound Christian belief in the spirit's survival after the death of the body. From the moment of his death Victoria had had a strong sense of Albert's continuing presence, both at home and especially in the mausoleum. In her widowhood she found her own very personal way of communing with him—often by sitting in front of his bust or holding some memento of him in her hand, such as the ivory miniature bust that she always carried in an oval case in her pocket. Before she signed any official documents Victoria was often seen to look up at Albert's marble bust and ask him whether he approved. Sometimes, when she was out driving in Scotland, she would open a small brooch that she wore with Albert's likeness in it and 'show' him an interesting view. She often talked out loud to him on a problem, or concentrated her thoughts on what he had said on a particular subject in a letter or memorandum in order to find inspiration.[16] With the reassuring presence of Brown close at hand (a man in whom Albert himself had invested great trust), she felt more connected to her dead husband and their former happy life together. Scotland— as represented by Brown—was the powerful, symbiotic link that bound her to Albert. She had no need, as the gossip alleged, of Brown's supposed psychic power (or anyone else's) to conjure Albert's spirit for her; her husband was there with her at all times, as a life presence.

John Brown's therapeutic effect on the Queen was in fact a quite simple one: like Albert before him, he took no nonsense from her and spoke his mind, treating her with the kind of male machismo that she admired. His presence gave her a new grip on life and, thanks to him, her depression had lifted and her terrible sense of yearning was, at last, abating, so much so that after visiting the mausoleum one day in June 1865 she confided to her journal: 'thank god! I feel more and more that my beloved one is *everywhere* not only there.'[17] Brown understood her loss; observing her at the mausoleum on Albert's anniversary that December, he told Victoria how sorry he felt that there was 'no more pleasure' for her, with her husband now in the tomb. 'I feel for ye but what can I do though for ye?' he had asked, adding, 'I could die for ye.' He promised her she would 'never have an honester servant', and she knew it, which is why any connivance at Brown's displacement failed dismally.[18]

John Brown was Queen Victoria's lifeline. Sensing the mounting resentment towards him in her household, she went to great pains to defend his position, even hiring a genealogist to trace his pedigree. An ancestral link with the Farquharsons of Inverey was discovered, which entitled Brown to carry a coat of arms and brought promotion and a role indoors, as well as out; soon afterwards Victoria further endorsed Brown's position of favour by commissioning a bust of him by the sculptor Joseph Edgar Boehm. Gradually a new, lighter tenor emerged in her journal and her letters to her family. Eulogies to Albert still played their part, as too did the constant insistence on her state of desolation without him, but there was room too for reiterations of her deepening romantic admiration for John Brown and his fine, upstanding qualities: his simplicity, kindness, disinterest, devotion, faithfulness, attention, care, intelligence, discretion and common sense. The Queen's comments were full of her usual, disarming truthfulness and innocence, yet there were already gossips on the lookout for something more sinister—if not sexually compromising.

*　　*　　*

On a rare outing in April 1866 to visit the army barracks at Aldershot, the press first noted the presence of the 'stalwart form and picturesque dress' of the Queen's ghillie John Brown 'seated in the rumble of her majesty's carriage'. 'Gillie Brown', it was noted, was to be seen in regular 'respectful attendance' on her; indeed, he seemed to already enjoy the unique position at court previously held by men such as 'Rustan, the Mameluke slave who had loyally served Napoleon the Great'.[19] Brown was now always at the Queen's side during her carriage drives or pony rides, morning and afternoon, whatever the weather. At Balmoral it was Brown, rather than her secretary, who brought Victoria each day's mail and remained alone in her study with her, ready to fold and seal her responses. He became extremely protective, defending her from anyone whom he felt to be a time-waster. Increasingly the royal household found themselves held at arm's length from the Queen, whilst Brown enjoyed unprecedented access to her behind closed doors. When she worked on official business in her sitting room at Windsor, Brown would stand outside, barring the way in and 'fending off even the highest in the land'.[20] He would often be the one chosen to pass on orders and even reprimands from the Queen to members of her household, a fact that particularly rankled with her secretary, General Grey. Such unconscionable familiarity with the Queen, combined with Brown's peremptory, tactless behaviour, provoked bitter complaints from the Queen's children, especially Bertie, who detested him. It also inspired jealousy in the household and sometimes led to outright quarrels in which Brown always got the upper hand. The gentlemen at court were greatly annoyed to discover that while the Queen disapproved of their drinking and smoking—notably that of her own sons—with characteristic inconsistency she indulged Brown's addiction to whisky and turned a blind eye to his regular bouts of inebriation and his stinking pipe, which she even allowed him to light in her presence.

As Victoria's friendship with Brown blossomed, the years 1865–6 were tempered by a succession of deaths. In October 1865 the loss of Lord Palmerston—who had doddered on in Parliament, dying in harness at the age of eighty-one—was a great sorrow, and another link with Victoria's safer 'happy past' gone for ever.[21] The death of her ailing Uncle Leopold was another blow when it followed on 10 December, with Victoria feeling even more the loneliness of her position as head now of the Saxe-Coburg family. In her widowhood she became accomplished at the art of heartfelt womanly condolence, writing with great kindness always to the widows of those who had served her, and in turn remembering those, when they died, who had commiserated with her own earlier distress. She was quick to pick up her pen and write to Mary Lincoln when the US President was assassinated in April 1865, offering her own 'deep and heartfelt sympathy', while taking advantage of yet another opportunity to reiterate how 'utterly broken hearted' she remained at the loss of her own husband.[22] She likewise consoled the widow of Sir Charles Phipps when he succumbed to bronchitis at the age of sixty-five in February 1865, prematurely worn out in loyal and unstinting service to her. Victoria insisted on paying her respects to his laid-out corpse. She did the same for John Turnbull, Clerk of the Works at Windsor, whom both she and Albert had regarded highly, when he died in April. 'I saw him lifeless in his coffin, looking like a fine old knight,' she told Vicky, adding rather proudly, 'It is the fifth lifeless form I have stood by within five months.'[23]

The rituals of death and mourning were so much

part and parcel of her life now that she found their celebration consoling. She liked to be told the deathbed details of those she knew, went to see them laid out and, when she could not, requested photographs of them in their coffins to be sent to her. Even the tragic death of Vicky's two-year-old son Sigismund from meningitis that summer elicited requests for every last detail, which Vicky in her agony felt unable to write down. They discussed the power of sympathy and a comforting presence in their letters, but such was Victoria's solipsism that even this exercise in condolence was more about her own than her daughter's loss. 'There is one person whose sympathy has done me—and does me—more good than almost anyone's,' she told Vicky, 'and that is good, honest Brown.' His positive presence in her life was, however, also provoking a crisis of conscience: her grief, she had to admit to Vicky, was 'less poignant, less intensely violent' and was giving way to a 'settled mournful resignation', for now at last she had someone to fill the void of her 'dreadful loneliness'.[24]

\*       \*       \*

In the autumn of 1865 Queen Victoria came to a decision about the future of her third daughter, Helena. After considering the limited choice of candidates, she had plumped for the rather unprepossessing Prince Christian of Schleswig-Holstein. He was about the best husband she could hope to find for her daughter, who at twenty-four was not blessed with good looks and was rapidly getting past a decent marriageable age. The Prince was already looking old for his thirty-five years; he had been rendered stateless as a result of the recent war, and was penniless to boot. With Christian having little to offer, as well as an unwholesome addiction to tobacco, Victoria was sure that he would not mind the fact that poor Lenchen had 'great difficulties with her figure'. She just wished he 'looked a little younger'; he needed to get out and exercise more, and stop coddling himself and eating so much.[25] The engagement was a relief, but brought with it an unavoidable duty that filled Victoria with terror. In order to obtain government approval for a £30,000 dowry for Helena—as well as a £15,000 annual income for Affie, who came of age that year—she would have to make a major concession and open Parliament in February 1866. It would be the first time since Albert's death that she would undertake a major state appearance. The cup of Victoria's anguish and resentment overflowed in a letter to the Prime Minister Lord Russell, in which she compared the ordeal to come as an 'execution'. The public had a right to want to see her, she could not deny that, but it was unfeeling to insist on witnessing 'the spectacle of a poor, broken-hearted widow, nervous and shrinking, dragged in deep mourning, alone in State as a Show, where she used to go supported by her husband'. The thought of being 'gazed at, without delicacy of feeling' filled her with horror. [26]

In retaliation, Victoria made the occasion as difficult as she could for everyone involved; she changed the date of the ceremony because it did not fit in with her settled plans for travelling between Osborne and Windsor. She refused to travel in the usual, gilded state coach, but went in the dress-carriage instead, accompanied by

Helena and Louise—though she did allow a brief glimpse of herself through its open windows en route to Westminster, despite the cold wind. She gave a small bow to the enthusiastic crowds when she got out of the coach on arrival. Arthur Munby thought his monarch looked 'very stout, very red in the face' and, although she was well received, her reception was not as warm at that for the Princess of Wales, who followed in the next carriage.[27] Victoria entered, dressed in her habitual crape with white lace cap and veil, though on this occasion there was a surprising addition—the cap was edged at the front with diamonds, and topped with a small diamond and sapphire coronet. Even thus subdued, she had an inescapable aura of queenliness, enhanced by the famous Koh-i-noor diamond, which she also wore, set as a brooch. But she refused to wear her ermine robe of state, which was instead draped across her chair; as she sat in it, Louise and Helena arranged it around her. Seeing Albert's robe lying on the vacant seat beside her, she paused and touched it, 'as a Catholic might a relic'.[28]

Victoria sat there motionless as she waited for the members of the Commons to be admitted; 'they came with a tremendous rush and noise and scrambling', in contrast to the members of the Lords in their robes already assembled.[29] Never, since Victoria opened Parliament in 1837, had 'so many peeresses applied for tickets for admission', wrote one commentator, all of them eager to see 'how the Royal widow would bear the sudden blaze of publicity'. To many, her presence that day seemed a long-awaited 'resurrection of royalty'.[30] Here was a scene of pageantry on a far grander scale than Bertie's wedding, of ladies in their finest jewels and court dress, the chamber 'billowy with necks and shoulders'; and there was the Queen, 'the only homely woman in the house', whose drab appearance was accentuated all the more by the presence of the superbly dressed Princess of Wales.[31]

Victoria's face remained stony and expressionless as her speech was read for her by the Lord Chancellor. She sat there stiff and erect, 'as though carved on the throne'.[32] 'Not a nerve in her face moved . . . but her nostrils quivered and widened . . . Tears gathered on the fringe of the drooping eyelids. A few rolled down the cheeks.'[33] After it was over, she made a slight bow, then bent and kissed a respectful and dignified Bertie, who escorted her out via the back door to her coach and thence, post-haste, to the privacy of Osborne. The following day she was, she claimed, in a state of physical collapse: 'shaken', 'exhausted' and still reeling from the 'violent nervous shock' of it all.[34] But like it or not, during 1866 she was coaxed out into public again: to London Zoo, the South Kensington Museum, the Union Workhouse at Windsor and even a visit to the women's wing at Parkhurst Prison on the Isle of Wight, where she was shocked to see the number of women incarcerated for murdering their illegitimate babies. During her stay at Balmoral she attended the Braemar Gathering for the first time in five years, and opened the sluice of the new waterworks at Aberdeen. But none of it—even her social appearances at a Drawing Room, two garden parties at Buckingham Palace and the weddings of Helena and Princess Mary Adelaide—changed

290

her determination to 'lead a private life'.[35] She still felt hard done by, that she was being treated 'as an unfeeling *machine*' rather than the 'poor weak woman shattered by grief' that she really was.[36] The public had a rather different view of things: 'What do we pay her for if she will not work?' . . . 'She had better abdicate if she is incompetent to do her duty' were the kind of accusations now going round, according to Lady Amberley. Would it not be a good thing, pondered the *Pall Mall Gazette*, if the Queen could 'find in the capital itself her Balmoral? . . . If she needs comfort and consolation, let her know them among the denizens of her metropolitan city. The gratitude of a million hearts is worth a good many miles of Highland scenery.'[37]

The *Pall Mall Gazette* had good reason to carp: the Queen's clear preference for the company of John Brown and Scotland was beginning to cost her public image dear. Rumour and salacious gossip were circulating about the nature of their relationship and his seemingly insidious control over her. Some suspected it of harbouring a familiarity that went way beyond the bounds of decency, and the rumours in Britain and on the Continent prompted much satirical comment. *Punch,* in a parody of the dreary and uneventful Court Circular so typical of the Queen's sojourns at Balmoral, described a day in the life of Mr John Brown, who 'walked on the slopes . . . partook of a haggis' and in the evening 'was pleased to listen to a bag-pipe'. The local Scottish press took delight in spreading stories about 'The Great Court Favourite' and his fondness for whisky.[38] With the Queen now being widely referred to as 'Mrs

Brown', it was insinuated that Brown was not only the power behind the throne, but that he had also found his way into the royal bed. Other papers, seeking to undermine his position, spread a story that Brown was about to leave to get married.[39]

Criticism of the Queen took a new turn in the summer of 1867 when a rival publication to *Punch,* the *Tomahawk,* launched a much more combative line on the Queen's favouritism of Brown and her continuing abdication of her duty. A major controversy had broken in May, when Sir Edwin Landseer had exhibited a painting at the Royal Academy's Spring Exhibition. Entitled 'Her Majesty at Osborne, 1866', this had depicted Queen Victoria sitting side-saddle in her widow's weeds on her pony Flora and reading a letter, with Brown standing at its head holding the reins. Such an informal painting of the Queen in close proximity with a servant provoked much sniggering by onlookers, as well as disapproval in the press for its 'imprudence'. 'A more lugubrious, disagreeable, and vulgar production we seldom remember to have seen,' remarked one reviewer.[40]

Rising to the occasion, the *Tomahawk*—which was subtitled *A Saturday Journal of Satire* and featured cartoons in the tradition of the Regency satirist Gillray—responded with a caricature of the Landseer painting, entitled 'All is black which is not Brown!'[41] The joke was picked up by *Punch* soon afterwards, but it was the *Tomahawk* that continued to lead the fray in ever bolder, more scurrilous challenges to the Queen, running a front-page leader entitled 'Where is Britannia' and a cartoon of the same title in its issue of 8 June; it followed on 10 August with a double-page

292

pull-out cartoon, 'A Brown Study?', highlighting the Queen's symbolic abdication by showing a vacant throne with the discarded robes of state lying on it, the disused crown under a bell jar, and a nonchalant Brown, leaning against the throne, pipe in hand. The issue sent *Tomahawk*'s sales rocketing to a massive 50,000 copies. Yet another *Tomahawk* cartoon followed soon after, entitled 'The Mystery of the Season', with Brown again leaning against an empty throne, accompanied by an article calling for a regency of the Prince of Wales: the Queen should retreat permanently 'to an honourable retirement' while she still had the affection of her people. She could then revel in the 'congenial solitudes of Osborne and Balmoral without any reproach'. With the *Tomahawk* putting the Queen's behaviour down to her 'deplorable mental health', the old rumours about madness once again surfaced, fanning the flames of gossip.[42] Some, like Harriet Martineau, rose to her defence: 'If the widowed grandmother of a dozen children is not safe from London tongues, the less we say about English morals and manners the better.'[43] But this was as nothing compared to the innuendo circulated on the Continent by the *Gazette de Lausanne*. The Swiss newspaper not only alleged a secret morganatic marriage between the Queen and Brown, but suggested that she was in an 'interesting condition'. This, in the view of the British consul in Berne, so seriously impugned the Queen's reputation that he lodged an informal complaint, but was forced to withdraw it by the Foreign Office because it had not been submitted through the proper channels. The British press respectfully declined to comment, though the republican-minded *Reynolds's Newspaper* could not resist the teasing remark, 'We do not care to reproduce in our columns the many extraordinary causes that are assigned for the Queen's seclusion in the pages of our foreign contemporaries.'[44]

Queen Victoria was kept in ignorance of this latest scandal on the Continent; as for the rest, she was adamant on the issue of Brown's incorruptibility. None of the gossip, or the publication of scurrilous penny pamphlets such as 'John Brown, or, The Fortunes of a Gillie', deterred her from her continuing preference for Brown's close attendance on her at all times. 'He is only a servant and nothing more', attested Henry Ponsonby. In his opinion, what had begun as a joke had been 'perverted into a libel'; the Queen understood only too well her unique position as monarch, and Brown's as her social inferior.[45] Nevertheless, yet another crisis involving Brown soon followed. In May 1867 he had been much talked about when he had appeared in the procession behind the Queen when she laid the foundation stone for the Royal Albert Hall of Arts and Sciences. Shortly afterwards Victoria announced that he would accompany her on the box of her open carriage to a Military Review in Hyde Park. Her Prime Minister, Lord Derby, and the Duke of Cambridge, as C-in-C of the Army, objected most forcefully, seeing such an appearance as seriously compromising to the integrity of the throne, in the light of so much unfavourable recent gossip. But all attempts to dissuade the Queen from taking her 'faithful Brown' with her that day failed—even warnings of anti-Brown demonstrations. Victoria professed herself 'astonished and shocked' at being 'plagued by the interference of others' and refused to go without him.[46] The monarchy was, however, spared a major public embarrassment when shortly afterwards Victoria's Hapsburg relative, Emperor Maximilian of Mexico, was executed by rebels during an uprising. An immediate—and in this case merciful—retreat into court mourning saved Victoria's face. But she made her feelings clear in no uncertain terms: 'The Queen will not be dictated to, or *made* to *alter* what she has found to answer for her comfort.' She put the whole affair down to 'ill-natured gossip in the higher classes, caused by the dissatisfaction at *not forcing* the Queen *out*'.[47] The more pressure was put upon her, and the more lies circulated about her 'poor good Brown', the more her hackles rose. Digging in her heels, she continued to punish them all for hounding her, and locked herself away at Balmoral.

The Queen's stubbornness about spending five months of the year at her Scottish home—600 miles and a twenty-four-hour train journey away—involved her ministers in long and tedious journeys to Scotland in order to conduct essential business with her and was creating serious administrative problems. In the summer of 1866 political crisis in London had broken over the stormy passage of the 2nd Reform Bill to extend the voting franchise. Victoria had failed to remain in the capital to exercise her constitutional role as figurehead during the debates, instead decamping to Balmoral on 13 June in order to avoid the ugly experience of 'that stupid reform agitation'.[48] Lord Russell's Liberal government fell on 20 June when they lost the vote by a narrow margin of eleven votes.

Greatly inconvenienced by this turn of events and not wishing to leave Balmoral, Victoria insisted that, because the division had been so close, Lord Russell should for the present remain in office. The Cabinet, however, pressed for him to do the right thing and resign. Constitutionally the Queen was obliged to return to accept her retiring ministers' seals of office, but she refused to budge until she was ready. Such a wilful reversion to the kind of old-style absolutism that she had first displayed as an inexperienced young queen in the late 1830s, and which Albert had worked so hard against, sent her household into despair. The Queen had been 'forgetting her duties in the pleasant breezes of Scotland', commented Henry Ponsonby. Lucy Cavendish, normally so loyal and defensive of her mistress, was shocked at 'the poor Queen's terrible fault in remaining (or indeed being) at Balmoral', for it had 'given rise to universal complaint, and much foul-mouthed gossip'.[49] This was not an action that would 'gratify the spirit' of her late husband, argued the *Tomahawk,* 'any more than it is consonant with the spirit of your people'. The Queen's behaviour was 'unbusinesslike' and 'childish', railed *The Economist.* The popular explanation was simpler: 'John Brown would not let her come.'[50]

At a public meeting in support of electoral reform held at St James's Hall in London, the Liberal MP Acton Smee Ayrton condemned the Queen's continuing retirement, only to be chastised by the Quaker John Bright, who like many in the middle classes was still prepared to defend her womanly grieving 'for the lost object of her life and affection'.[51] Bright's response rallied the crowd that night to loyal choruses of 'God Save the Queen', but dissent did not die down. Abandoned by its monarch, the capital seethed and buzzed with republican talk, as hopes of reform collapsed and the country was left in limbo until Victoria finally returned on 26 June. General Grey was no longer able to conceal from her the very strong feeling among the public that, in her retirement from view, the 'tone of society is much deteriorated'. The situation had been further exacerbated by the continuing absence of state ceremonial; already that year Victoria had adamantly refused to entertain Tsar Alexander II and the Khedive of Egypt when they were in London; and now she was doing her damnedest to avoid the Sultan of Turkey, who was due on a visit. Faced with this latest and most unwanted of duties, Victoria called on good Dr Jenner to produce a royal sick-note. He could always be relied upon to extricate her from duties that she did not wish to undertake, and obliged in the most lurid tones. The Queen's health simply was not up to it. 'Any excitement produces the most severe bilious derangement, which induces vomiting to an incredible extent,' Jenner told Grey. Just to be doubly certain, he waved the madness flag that always silenced Victoria's critics: any further undermining of the Queen's health might precipitate complete mental breakdown. At Victoria's request, Jenner also inserted an announcement about her indisposition in *The Lancet*.[52] In the end the Queen did not entirely wriggle out of entertaining the Sultan. The bulk of her duties were offloaded onto Bertie and Alix, but despite it being 'extremely inconvenient and disadvantageous' for her well-being, she grudgingly agreed to meet the Sultan on board the royal yacht at a naval review off Spithead, during which, despite all her protestations of ill health, her own sea legs proved a great deal stronger than his.[53]

*　　　*　　　*

By the end of 1867 it was clear that anti-monarchical, if not outright republican sentiment was mounting in Britain. Victoria had been hissed and booed en route to the state opening of Parliament, which she had once more deigned to undertake that year. She saw at last the ugly faces of anger in the crowd, and even admitted to Grey that she felt 'something unpleasant' might happen 'with the existing agitation about Reform, and the numbers of people out of employment'. Yet still she failed to connect the pattern of overt public disapproval with her own stubborn behaviour; still she clung to power and her royal prerogatives, while increasingly lauding the homely Scots as being infinitely superior to the English people who clamoured for her presence in London.[54] She remained wilfully oblivious to the everyday realities of hunger and urban poverty at a time when cholera was once more rife; of political unrest and increasing class divisions. 'The Queen is teaching the people to think too little of her office,' observed the *Daily News*. In the House of Commons, Viscount Cranbourne went further, stating that in Britain 'the monarchy was practically dead'.[55] By no means, responded *Reynolds's Newspaper*: the monarchy 'lives, eats, drinks, and breeds as vigorously as ever'. In all, the royal family plus 'the shoal of German and English parasites' connected to it accounted for one million pounds of public spending per annum.

General Grey had no doubt that unless something was done, the situation would get worse and 'very serious consequences may be the result'. The Queen was the only person, he told her, who had the power to stem the growing tide of her own public disfavour, 'by resuming the place which none but Your Majesty can fill'. But he knew that putting pressure on her would only undo what little power he had to do any good.[56] Before Sir Charles Phipps's death, Grey had concurred with him that 'The Queen is *perfectly* aware of what her subjects wish, nor can she be ignorant of what her position requires.' But so far none in government had had any sway over the vagaries of her volatile temperament and her stubborn self-interest. Only Prince Albert had known how to handle what Dr Clark had called the Queen's propensity to 'mental irritation'. Albert himself had said as much to Lord Clarendon. 'It is my business,' he had told him, 'to watch that mind every hour and minute—to watch as a cat watches at a mousehole.'[57] John Brown might be able to boil potatoes and cups of tea by the roadside in Scotland, and bully the Queen into wrapping up warm when out in her carriage, but only Prince Albert had had the moral power to induce her to fulfil her much more important constitutional duties when she least wished to.

Victoria meanwhile remained breathtakingly impervious to the criticism, confident as ever in the unassailability of her position. She thought the country 'never more loyal or sound'. 'I would throw myself amongst my English and dear Scotch subjects alone . . . and I should be as safe as in my room,' she told Vicky, shrugging off a recent Fenian plot to kidnap her that had been uncovered by the Home Office. 'There has been a great deal of nonsense and foolish panic, and numberless stories which had proved sheer inventions!' she continued, knowing full well that the hysteria generated by her household at the lack of security at her country residences was just another ploy, along with all the criticism of Brown, to get her to spend more time in London. With public disfavour mounting, she continued vigorously to fight off her critics, without the slightest inkling that help was about to come from the most unexpected of sources: the publication the following January of her 'poor little Highland book'.[58]

## CHAPTER THIRTEEN

# 'The Queen Is Invisible'

From the moment Prince Albert died it had always been Queen Victoria's intention to commemorate his life, not just in visible monuments to him, but also in words. The process had begun soon afterwards, with her request to Alfred Tennyson to write a tribute in verse. This had been followed by a collection of *The Principal Speeches and Addresses of HRH The Prince Consort*, edited by Arthur Helps, which had been released for public consumption in 1863 after a private printing for the royal family the previous year. The speeches had rapidly sold thousands of copies, but Victoria was keen to establish a fuller written legacy of her beloved Albert and had herself embarked on a project to

'put down an exact account of our happy life'—
again for family use.[1]

With this in mind, she started sorting through her
mass of personal papers, but soon felt overwhelmed
by the task and passed the commission over to
General Grey, whose post as her Private Secretary
had finally been officially ratified in 1866. Having
already written a biography of his father, Grey
was the obvious choice to write the first account
of the Prince's life, although *The Early Years of the
Prince Consort* would only cover the story up to
the birth of Vicky in 1840. Grey's name might be
on the title page, but in fact the book was written
under Victoria's close instruction and supervision,
using translations from the German of Albert's
journals and letters provided by herself and
Princess Helena. During the process Grey had had
to tolerate the Queen's constant interference, to
the extent that the bulk of the work—even down to
the footnotes—was largely hers, with Grey fulfilling
little more than the role of dutiful compiler, adding
the Queen's personal interpolations in many
places.[2] Having so much sensitive material put at
his disposal, Grey worried that some of the book's
candour, even for private circulation within the
family, should be modified. As a former military
man—bluff, stolid and formal, with a strong sense
of his own independence—he found the experience
of working on the book with the Queen a trial that
had tested his patience to the limit.

Nevertheless *The Early Years of the Prince
Consort* was an overnight success when Victoria
agreed to its publication for general consumption;
so much so that within two days of it going on sale
in July 1867 not a copy of Smith & Elder's original

301

print run of 5,000 was to be had in Printers' Row, home then to the British publishing industry. A second edition of 7,000 was immediately ordered, and a third shortly afterwards. An American edition and numerous translations followed, and soon it was announced that future volumes covering the rest of the Prince's life would be undertaken not by Grey, who was too overburdened by work, but by the Scottish scholar and German translator, Theodore Martin.

Predictably, the level of sycophantic review of *The Early Years* matched the hagiography of the original. Copious quotations from the book appeared across the press; *The Early Years*, it was asserted, provided the nation with a 'picture of purity, of self devotion to the claims of duty, of chivalric endurance of obloquy—in a word, of thorough high mindedness in every sense'.[3] The *Quarterly Review* went to extravagant excess in bolstering the inviolability of Albert's 'imperishable reputation'. Spanning twenty-three pages, its exhaustive and adulatory review commended Grey for his discretion as the Queen's amanuensis in 'thread[ing] together the pearls intrusted to him', adding that 'though the threading is his, the pearls are the gift to us of a higher hand'. In short, the book was an example of 'the Sovereign casting herself in her speechless grief upon the sympathy of her people'. Such emotive language of course drew the expected loyal response.[4] Elsewhere, the reviewer of the *Medical Times and Gazette*, while lauding 'the overwhelming affection of the wife' as demonstrated in the book, took this opportunity to suggest that it 'explains her Majesty's present position—a nervous system thoroughly out of gear'—the nearest any published observation on the Queen's state of mind had come to an overt assertion of mental depression. It also provided a typical Victorian circumlocution on her female frailties: 'If we have a queen, we must be content to bear the peculiarities of her sex, even though some of its distinctive virtues may be felt to have become, by excess, somewhat of defects.'[5]

Victoria's intention of producing edifying memorials to Albert for the benefit of her family did not stop with *The Early Years*. At the end of 1867, at a time when she was anxious to defend her favouritism for John Brown and all things Scottish, she was prevailed on by the Dean of Windsor and others to actually publish something of her own: the journals of her life at Balmoral. The Dean had thought their 'simplicity' and 'kindly feelings' might do 'so much good' to Victoria's flagging reputation, but having allowed their private circulation in the family already, she had had no intention of them being published.[6] The success of Grey's biography, plus a desire to circumvent extracts from the Balmoral journals appearing in garbled and pirated form, persuaded her to agree. At a time of gathering crisis, they proved to be the perfect palliative. If the Queen would not make herself visible to her public, then she could at least lift something of the veil hiding her from view, vicariously, through her Highland journals. It was an unprecedented royal act, the only previous sovereign to have published his own opinions in any shape or form having been King James I with his treatises on monarchy, and his famous and idiosyncratic swipe at smoking, 'A Counterblaste to Tobacco' of 1604.

303

From the outset Queen Victoria was under no illusions about her creative gifts, modestly protesting that the journals were mere 'homely' descriptions of her outings in and around Balmoral—which indeed they were. That did not deter her, however, from sending a copy to Charles Dickens, 'from the humblest of writers to one of the greatest'.[7] In Victoria's case it was precisely the book's intrinsic qualities of simple sentiment and mundanity that proved to be pure marketing gold. Arthur Helps was once more recruited as editor and did his tactful best, as unobtrusively as possible, to eradicate some of the Queen's lapses in grammar, her repetition and use of colloquialisms and slang, as well as expunging some of her more excessive underlining. The published edition that appeared early in January 1868 was handsome to look at, bound in moss-green leather with gold tooling; a large quarto edition that followed a year later was illustrated, in addition to the original engravings, with some of Victoria's own charming watercolours of Scotland. Entitled *Leaves from the Journal of Our Life in the Highlands, from* 1848 *to* 1861, the book was dedicated, of course, 'to the dear memory of him who made the life of the writer bright and happy', its every page bearing the stamp of the husband who had inspired it and of his wife's inexhaustible love for him, in entries such as that for 13 October 1856:

Every year my heart becomes more fixed in this dear paradise, and so much more so now, that all has become my dearest Albert's own creation, own work, own building, own laying out, as at Osborne; and his great taste, and the impress of his dear hand, has been stamped everywhere.[8]

But while the book celebrated Albert as archetypal Highland laird, out shooting, fishing, riding and walking, it was the book's innate simplicity and warm-heartedness, and its projection of Victoria as an ordinary, private individual rather than as Queen, which immediately endeared it to the public and reviewers and restored something of her lost reputation. The British press in the main was disarmed by the lack of pretension of this 'woman's book'; to criticise its patently honest intentions would have been churlish, for here was something, in the estimation of *The Times*, that appealed 'directly to the common heart'.[9] Like *The Early Years*, it was heaped with excessive, if not outlandish praise, with the reviewer of the *Morning Post* commending it as being one of the best things ever written.

Victoria was delighted with her reviews, which came thick and fast. 'Newspapers shower in,' she told Vicky on 22 January.[10] She had even indulged in a little manipulation in the process; having liked the review of *The Early Years* by the Scottish writer and literary critic Margaret Oliphant, and expecting her to be likewise favourably disposed to her own modest offering, Victoria specifically requested that Oliphant review *Leaves*. Oliphant was extremely reluctant to be sycophantic to order; 'the queen's book,' she told a friend, 'looks mighty like a little girl's diary of travel and is innocent to the last

305

degree. Would that it was consistent with loyalty to make fun of it.'[11] But she could not do so, for she was shrewd enough to know the value of the royal seal of approval and so she agreed, 'on condition that I am not asked to tackle the holy Albert again'. Privately Oliphant had scant regard for Victoria's amateurish literary endeavour and warned of the danger of her conceiving literary ambitions above her most limited ability. But she knew what the Queen could do for her, and so in her review in *Blackwood's Magazine* in February 1868 she admired the book's artlessness, spontaneity and simplicity, ensuring a generous fee of £100 and the award soon after of a Civil List pension, while keeping to herself her judgement on its literary merits.[12]

Other reviewers, however, could not restrain their excessive panegyrics to 'the queen's book'. 'She has claimed her place in that great freemasonry which is open to all ranks and races—the freemasonry of those who believe still in love, chivalry, romance,' proclaimed *Fraser's Magazine*. It was 'a homely book, made up of human nature's daily food,' extolled the *North British Review*.[13] The *Daily Telegraph* voiced the hope of many that in its very personal tone the book might in some way fill the void of the Queen's absence from view, by drawing her public 'nearer to the every-day life of a living queen than any persons not courtiers ever came before'; and indeed, the archetype of virtuous family life celebrated within the book was set in stark contrast to the artificiality of court life. 'Thank god there are many thousand English homes like this,' it went on, for the Queen had 'no Royal monopoly of that pure light of household love which shines by so many English hearths'.[14] Only the *Tomahawk* dared to poke fun at the book's crippling ordinariness: 'the bubble about the queen walking about her royal parks in her coronation robes has long since been exploded,' it remarked. *Leaves* had little to tell Victoria's public, for 'we all know that Her Majesty wears a bonnet in private life'.[15]

Some papers, such as the *Chronicle*, derided the endless references to Victoria's humbler servants, particularly John Brown and the Queen's detailing of 'what he said of the Prince, how he got into the way of changing plates, how he brushed the queen's boots, and wore the royal plaid, how fast he walks and how loudly he cheers, and how much rather she would trust him than the Duke of Athole at an awkward ford'. Such mundanities did not fit the public profile of a sovereign, but, the *Chronicle* added, it 'would not have been made public if the public had not provoked it'.[16] *Reynolds's Newspaper* as usual pulled no punches:

If this book were issued to the world as the work of Mrs Smith, instead of Victoria, Queen of England, it would not sell a dozen copies. People would wonder at how it came to pass that any sane individual could possibly be induced to publish so many pages of sheer and unmitigated twaddle. Readers would weary of the incessant laudation of her husband by the authoress, and, after throwing the book on one side, pronounce her an amiable monomaniac.[17]

But *Reynolds's* could not hold back the tide of enthusiasm for *Leaves from the Journal.* Respectable middle England fell upon it, attracted by the engaging spontaneity of the Queen's thought. With its warm depiction of the lower classes as embodied in her Scottish servants, *Leaves* was seen as an exemplary lesson in Christian goodness and social tolerance. Victoria knew that the book had no great literary pretensions, but felt that its popularity was a vindication of her own and Albert's deeply held values; 'the kind and proper feeling towards the poor and the servants will I hope do good, for it is very much needed in England among the higher classes'.[18] It was certainly a timely lesson in the virtues of the respectable lower middle classes, who admired the book and had been newly enfranchised with the passing of the 2nd Reform Bill. The aristocracy could not afford to be complacent about the voice of the common man, which was now demanding ever more to be heard, and Victoria was gratified that the public had appreciated how her book had got to the heart of 'what is simple and right'. A Mrs Everett Green, writing on behalf of English wives and mothers everywhere, agreed, telling Arthur Helps that the book provided 'a pattern for every home in the country'; after all, 'a royal example is more potent than a volume of sermons'.[19] In assessing its impact, the diarist Alfred Munby made the shrewd observation that *Leaves* 'may turn out to have been, by its very artlessness, a masterstroke of art', and he was right. Arthur Helps felt the same; the book provided a 'new bond of union' between the Queen and her people at a time when it was sorely needed.[20] Victoria was thrilled with the critical response, but determined not to let it go to her head. She was, she told Theodore Martin, 'much moved—deeply so—but not uplifted or "puffed up" by so much kindness, so much praise'.[21]

Not everyone, however, approved of the openness with which the Queen described her life at Balmoral; Lord Shaftesbury thought it entirely inappropriate that the monarch should reveal 'all that she thinks and does in the innermost recesses of her heart and home'.[22] The reaction in high society was one of horror; the Queen's otherwise devoted former ladies, Lady Augusta Stanley and Lady Lyttleton, had both been less than impressed with her uncritical admiration for all things Scottish, and Henry Ponsonby's bluestocking wife Mary sniggered at the Queen's rather amusing 'literary line'.[23] While Stanley admitted that the journal was 'nice' and 'very interesting', and that it evoked many happy memories of her own years in the Queen's service, she was also highly critical. Arthur Helps's 'apologetic introduction' had made her 'blood boil'; the frenzy of overpraise for this rather guileless book was excessive—as well as politically unfortunate. If the Queen had plumped for Ireland instead of Scotland as the object of her affections, Lady Augusta remarked, 'the ecstasies and interests that would have grown up would have been just as great—and fenianism would never have existed'.[24] Stanley's criticism like that of others in the royal household focused precisely on the element that had won it popular acclaim: the details of the lives of the lowliest of household servants at Balmoral, which gave the impression that the Queen considered them on the same footing as the aristocracy. An entire entry for 16 September 1850, accompanied by an engraving of him, sang the praises of John Brown as having 'all

309

the independence and elevated feelings peculiar to the Highland race'.[25] And the Queen's children, who thought their mother's book in poor taste, winced at her revelations of what, in their opinion, were far too many personal details. Ministers also worried that, with the decision having been made to exclude all comments relating to issues of public or political importance, it painted a false picture of the Queen's life. With its endless descriptions of picnics, drives, expeditions and pony treks, as well as Albert's voracious stag-hunting, it seemed to suggest that she and her consort had spent most of their time on holiday and at their leisure.

Nevertheless, the book was a huge critical and financial success and quickly became a best-seller, selling 80,000 during the first three months; by the end of the year it had sold 103,000 copies.[26] It was so in demand that 'the circulating libraries ordered it by the ton'.[27] On 14 March the Queen wrote excitedly to Vicky that her book 'had had such an extraordinary effect on the people' that a cheap, 2s. 6d. edition was coming out to deal with pre-orders of 20,000, and another 10,000 were to be printed.[28] In all, it is estimated that the royalties on *Leaves* totalled around £30,000 and most of the profits were given to charity, in the form of educational bursaries for pupils of parish schools, including the local one at Crathie near Balmoral. The book turned out to be an even greater publishing success in the USA; a German translation appeared within a couple of months, as too did one into Gaelic; and many others followed, including Hindustani, and—at the Shah's specific request—Persian.

The enormous success of *Leaves from the Journal*

*of Our Life in the Highlands* was, as a bemused Dean of Windsor observed, 'a most curious turn of the wheel of fortune', for the Queen's book (in addition to General Grey's *Early Years*) had given the monarchy a much-needed boost when its popularity was hitting an all-time low.[29] Victoria felt vindicated by the popular success of her idyllic portrait of family life with Albert and was convinced of 'the good it will do the Throne'.[30] She was hugely relieved, for back in January she had had an anxious conversation with Theodore Martin in which she had urged him to find some way of letting the public know the truth about her withdrawal from public life. It was not her sorrow, great though it still was, she told him, that kept her secluded, but the 'overwhelming amount of work and responsibility':

> From the hour she gets out of bed till she gets into it again there is work, work, work—letter-boxes, questions, etc., which are dreadfully exhausting—and if she had not comparative rest and quiet in the evening, she would most likely not be alive. Her brain is constantly overtaxed. Could this truth not be openly put before people?[31]

Martin himself had seen the piles of dispatch boxes requiring the Queen's attention, but had advised against making any public statement on her workload, telling Victoria that her people 'had entire trust in her doing what was best, and that she would appear in public whenever the necessity for doing so arose'.[32] Mercifully, the enthusiastic reception given to her book confirmed this. Scores

311

of 'beautiful and touching' letters had poured in to the Queen, thanking her and 'saying how much more than ever I shall be loved, now that I am known and understood'. Having opened a window on to her private life with Albert, she hoped the book would act as a surrogate for her lack of personal appearances, and that that would be an end to criticism.[33] Slipping back into a dangerous complacency, Victoria felt her confidence further boosted by the attentions of a new and adoring Prime Minister—Benjamin Disraeli.

\*     \*     \*

In February 1868 the seventy-five-year-old Lord Derby had been forced to retire, to be replaced by Disraeli, who had first entered government as Chancellor of the Exchequer under Derby in 1852. Victoria's first impression of him had been somewhat guarded; he seemed to her 'most singular', with his strongly Semitic looks and his shiny black ringlets. He 'had a very bland manner' and she thought his language 'very flowery', but after Albert died, Disraeli's gift for soothing flattery had worked its magic on Victoria with his eulogies to the late Prince as a sovereign manqué and his tributes to Albert's rich and cultivated mind.[34] In March 1863 Victoria, by now entirely won over, had deliberately passed over leading members of the aristocracy to grant seats to Disraeli and his wife at Bertie and Alix's wedding. 'The present man will do well,' she now told Vicky with confidence, for her new Prime Minister seemed 'particularly loyal and anxious to please me in every way'. But Vicky had heard differently; wasn't Mr Disraeli 'vain and

312

ambitious', she asked? That might be so, but all that mattered to Victoria was that he had always treated *her* well and had 'all the right feelings for a Minister towards the Sovereign'; also to his credit was the fact that he had argued vigorously for additional government money for the Albert Memorial.[35] Disraeli's first fawning meetings with the Queen in the spring of 1868 demonstrated to her that he was 'full of poetry, romance and chivalry'—the emotional touchstones on which she thrived. His devotion, his penchant for kissing her hand and his saccharine praise of her authorial gifts, with remarks such as 'We authors ma'am' (he himself being the author of fifteen novels), clearly struck a chord.[36] After being sent a copy of *Leaves* hot off the press, he had lauded its 'essential charms'. 'There is a freshness and fragrance like the heather amidst which it was written,' he told Arthur Helps, words that no doubt found their way straight to the eager ears of the Queen.[37] In response she sent him primroses hand-picked by her at Osborne.

The narcissistic Disraeli had never easily won the admiration of other men, who had resolutely refused to take him seriously; there was just 'too much tinsel' about him, according to Lady Nevill, too much of the poser and dandy.[38] But he did have an extraordinary gift for winning the lifelong devotion of women, and soon proved to have a unique and winning way with his Queen, knowing full well that, in her case, the personal touch was all-important. Thanks to his charms and the warm public reception given to her book, Victoria's mood that year greatly improved. In March she attended her first Drawing Room in London since her widowhood, followed by another in

April; she reviewed the troops at Aldershot and in Windsor Home Park, attended the Royal Academy exhibition and a 'breakfast' at Buckingham Palace. As an admirer of Florence Nightingale, she agreed to lay the foundation stone for the new St Thomas's Hospital, where Lucy Cavendish noted how she 'went thro' the ceremony with all her old grace and wonderful dignity, ending with several deep curtseys to the audience'. It was a 'sight to see', she wrote, confirming how well and cheerful the Queen now seemed: 'really our little Queen in her deep black was not outshone even by the lovely, radiant Princess of Wales'.[39]

However, Victoria continued to place very firm restrictions on more onerous public appearances, declining to open Parliament and continuing to resist being in London for more than a few days a year. She constantly complained of how exhausting and noisy she found it there—not to mention the terrible, dense yellow fog. But her spirits were clearly reviving: she started playing the piano again and sketching. She felt she was making a real effort, so she bridled at what she saw as the 'shameless' articles about her that continued to appear in some of the press, such as that in the *Globe* in May, which took her to task for preparing to disappear off to Balmoral while Parliament was in the midst of a crisis and Disraeli's government seemed about to fall.[40] For no sooner had she begun to bask in the warm glow of her new Prime Minister's flattery than in May the Conservative government lost the vote over Opposition leader William Gladstone's resolution to disestablish the Irish Protestant Church. Disraeli offered to resign; loath to lose him, Victoria sought to dissolve Parliament instead, hoping that by going to the country the Tories would be returned in a general election later in the year. Disraeli, after all, was already showing 'more consideration for my comfort than any of the preceding Prime Ministers since Sir Robert Peel and Lord Aberdeen'.[41] She fiercely resisted the pressures to shorten her visit to Balmoral, telling Disraeli that she would return to Windsor only if anything 'very serious should render it necessary', but that she was completely 'done up' by fatigue and worry.[42] Was not the whole week she had spent in London already that year enough to satisfy people?, she asked Theodore Martin, in a letter she sent enlisting his support and that of Arthur Helps in ensuring that no further swipes at her should follow in *The Times* and *Telegraph*.

It all seemed a case of the lady doth protest too much, for Victoria knew full well that later that summer she was planning to go on holiday yet again—this time abroad, to Switzerland—and that further criticism was bound to follow. But nothing for now would induce her to change her plans; on 18 May she departed for Balmoral. It was a highly provocative act: two days later Delane of *The Times* rightly objected to the fact that during this most difficult time 'the first person in the State, to whom recourse must be had in every momentous juncture, was hurrying at full speed from the neighbourhood of the capital to a remote Highland district, six hundred miles from her Ministry and Parliament'. The Queen, he pointed out, would be virtually incommunicado, and it was 'an act of culpable neglect' on the part of Mr Disraeli not to advise her against it.[43] The following day Denis Rearden, the MP for Athlone, submitted a question in the

Commons for the Prime Minister as to whether, if the Queen's health 'appears to be so weak that she cannot live in England', she might not best be advised to abdicate or establish a regency under the Prince of Wales.[44] A month previously a seditious placard had been put up in Pall Mall to the same effect. Constitutionally, only the government could put pressure on the Queen, but Disraeli had little power over her at this stage. Victoria was enraged and responded from Balmoral two days later, making the ultimate threat in a letter to Disraeli. She had no doubt that she might look well, but people had no idea how much she really suffered: '*if* the public will *not* take her—as she is—she must *give all up*—and give it up to the Prince of Wales'.[45] She felt totally justified in taking her two scheduled visits to Balmoral that year, which she did with Dr Jenner's full encouragement. Jenner himself saw the Home Secretary soon afterwards and assured him of the Queen's present state of agitation. Without rest he was convinced she would break down completely. Victoria was clearly most determined to have that holiday in Switzerland.

The idea of going there had sprung from accounts Albert had sent her of his travels in Switzerland in 1837 before they married. She had long planned it, in secret, but was determined to go somewhere completely secluded, where 'she can refuse *all* visitors and have *complete* quiet'. In the event, the compliant Disraeli made no objections and the Queen left England on 4 August 1868, 'entirely on the recommendation of her physicians', so the press were told.[46] She travelled under the rather transparent pseudonym of the Countess of Kent, with her three youngest children and a reduced entourage that included Dr Jenner and her favourite lady-in-waiting, Jane Churchill. Bringing up the rear came a disgruntled John Brown—who hated going abroad—following in a carriage full of all the Queen's picnicking equipment and a few bottles of best Scottish malt. For the next month Victoria made her home at the Pension Wallace overlooking Lake Lucerne. Never since Albert's death had she been so cheerful as during this holiday: talking animatedly and laughing at dinner and, despite the difficulty of her increasing weight and the terrible heat, taking sedate walks, drives and excursions to enjoy the view of mountains and glaciers. In Switzerland she was, for once, relieved of endless mournful reminders of Albert.

Back in England on 11 September, she barely made her presence felt at Windsor before, three days later, heading straight for Balmoral. She was dismayed at the prospect of the imminent general election and the possible loss of Disraeli, who paid her a ten-day visit there; after which she turned her attention resolutely away from politics to disappear off to a new holiday retreat that she had had built at Glassalt Shiel at the northern end of Loch Muick. She and Albert had in the past enjoyed the use of a small cottage three miles away at the other end of the loch, at Altnagiuthasach, but the memories were too painful for Victoria ever to return there. And so she had built this small hunting lodge, nestled in a wild spot at the base of the bare, snow-covered screes up at the northern end, as her 'first widow's house'. With its ten rooms, including her own with its single bed, it was modest by royal standards, but it was her own special refuge, 'not built by him or hallowed by his memory'. In

October she held a house-warming there to which her servants were invited. Reels were danced and everyone drank 'whisky-toddy' toasts to the Queen's health and happiness.[47]

After almost two months at Balmoral, Queen Victoria finally arrived back at Windsor in time to regretfully say goodbye to the congenial Disraeli, whose government had been ousted by the Liberals in the general election. She was now obliged to welcome the dour Mr Gladstone as Prime Minister, a man who venerated her as Queen, but who, unlike Disraeli, had none of his gifts of flattery. Knowing this, the Dean of Windsor had advised Gladstone that he must treat his monarch with kid gloves: 'you cannot show too much regard, gentleness, I might even say tenderness towards her,' he had said, but when it came to it, Gladstone was a clodhopper in comparison with the swooning Disraeli.[48] Victoria was of course greatly inconvenienced by this changeover, but tried hard to like Gladstone at first. He seemed cordial and kind, but she soon came to dislike his heavy-handed manner and, worse, he talked too much. After thirty-one years on the throne she did not appreciate being lectured to by him. She missed Disraeli's gossipy informality and charm; nor was she protected any longer by an apologist for her entrenched behaviour. As another year turned, there was no doubt in the mind of Lord Clarendon that the Queen was perfectly up to the job. 'Eliza is roaring well and can do everything she likes and nothing she doesn't,' he told the Duchess of Manchester, using an irreverent nickname current in the royal household.[49] General Grey was in despair; his situation had become 'intolerable', he had told Disraeli; he had been on the brink of resigning and it was only Disraeli who had persuaded him to stay. [50] He shared his apprehensions with Gladstone; it was clear to them both that the Queen had got it into her head that she was far less capable of fulfilling her duties than she really was, that she was playing the feminine-frailty card far too often. What had become of the young queen who had been so anxious to fulfil her duties, when first married, that she allowed herself only three days of honeymoon, insisting to Albert that 'business can stop and wait for nothing'?[51] Seven years on from her husband's death, business had stopped and waited for far too long.

Grey had no doubts that they were dealing with a 'royal malingerer', but that *nothing* will have any effect but a strong—even a peremptory tone' with the Queen. Having convinced herself that she could not cope, she had become entrenched in a 'long unchecked habit of self-indulgence that now makes it impossible for her, without some degree of nervous agitation, to give up, even for ten minutes, the gratification of a single inclination, or even *whim*'.[52] Her children, particularly the twenty-year-old Princess Louise—who had assumed the role of resident daughter-on-duty after Helena's marriage in 1866—were very worried about her continuing seclusion. In Louise's view, neither her mother's health nor her strength was 'wanting', as Victoria continued to insist. Grey found a new ally in Louise, who told him that she was '*very* decided as to the ability of the Queen to meet any fatigue, and is most indignant with Jenner for encouraging the Queen's fancies about her health'.[53] As for her constant protestations about her volume of work, for all her claims to Theodore Martin, Grey

319

of all people knew the true extent of the Queen's workload. It was as follows: 'In *very* short notes; in shorter interview, Her Majesty gives me her orders to "write fully" on this or that subject.' Beyond reading the letters or dispatches that Grey placed in front of her, the Queen, in his view, had little else to do, other than 'to approve of the draft which I submit to her'. The put-upon Grey felt that he was the unacknowledged one doing all the donkey work; the Queen only 'exercised her brain or her pen' on matters that affected 'her own comfort' and was happy to delegate the rest to him. 'Pray dismiss from your mind any idea of there being any "weight of work" upon the Queen,' he told Gladstone, adding, 'and this, Princess Louise, emphatically repeats'. Her sister, Princess Helena, had by now come to the conclusion that the only way to get their mother to cooperate was to 'put it plainly upon her duty as head of affairs, and above all, not use the "People say" argument', which 'exasperates Mama'.[54]

Grey anticipated a fight to come as Gladstone weighed in with attempts to persuade Victoria to leave Balmoral early in the autumn of 1869 in order to fulfil an important public engagement—a visit to the city for the first time in eighteen years, to open first the newly built Blackfriars Bridge and then the Holborn Viaduct constructed over the old Fleet Valley, connecting Holborn Hill with Newgate Street. Victoria agreed, on condition that the whole thing would be dependent on the state of her fragile health on the day in question. *The Times* feared that the many loyal Londoners eagerly looking forward to seeing her might be disappointed. A pavilion and stands to take 4,000 people were erected on the bridge, but what were 4,000 tickets compared to the half a million or so that *The Times* anticipated would assemble out of a 'natural yearning' to see their monarch?[55] High winds and heavy rain the night before spoiled the street decorations and dampened spirits, but Saturday 6 November dawned fine as special trains brought thousands of people into the city for the occasion. Many more flocked to Paddington Station to see the Queen arrive by train at 11.30 a.m. before processing by carriage with an escort of Life Guards (carrying loaded revolvers in case of trouble from Fenians) across London, past Buckingham Palace and over Westminster Bridge to the Surrey side of the river. After Victoria had speedily declared Blackfriars Bridge open, the royal carriage crossed over to the City and on up to the viaduct above Farringdon Street where even greater crowds awaited her. Here John Delane was waiting to see events for himself, having been apprehensive of demonstrations in the wake of a string of recent Fenian outrages and arrests. 'The cold intense, the show poor, but the loyalty great,' he recorded of the event in his diary.[56] Victoria thought the day had gone well, and the enthusiasm had been 'very great', though as usual it had been 'a hard trial' for her.[57] But not everyone that day came to admire, and hissing had been heard from the crowd when her carriage had passed along the Strand.

Victoria did not stay for the banquet given by the Lord Mayor at the Mansion House that evening, where her reply to the loyal address was read for her. Without being unduly overtaxed, she had left London on the royal train for Windsor by 1 p.m. Nevertheless, the *Morning Post* waxed lyrical on the magnanimous gesture she had that day bestowed on her adoring subjects. Her Majesty, it said, had 'broken through the habits of her ordinary life' to 'come up from that Highland Home in which she finds so much tranquil pleasure and consolation, to make evident to her subjects practically the interest which she takes in every occurrence that contributes to their welfare or adds to their enjoyment'.[58]

An hour and a half of the Queen's time in the capital had, however, been a paltry gesture and did nothing to prevent the spectre of unpopularity from rising once more. Victoria as usual remained oblivious to it. 'Nothing could be more successful than the progress and ceremony of Saturday,' she told Theodore Martin. 'The greatest enthusiasm prevailed, and the reception by countless thousands of all classes, especially in the City, was most loyal and gratifying—not a word, not a cry, that could offend any one.' There would therefore, in her estimation, be no need for any public statement on the reasons for her continuing seclusion; the story she would eventually tell in Martin's forthcoming life of Albert 'should fully open the eyes of her people to the truth'.[59]

Unfortunately, the first volume of *The Life of the Prince Consort* would not be published until 1874; meanwhile, early in 1870 the royal family was once more plunged into controversy, when Bertie, his reputation already plummeting thanks to his addiction to racing, gambling and clubbing, was called to give evidence in a scandalous divorce hearing. The petitioner, one of Bertie's acquaintances, Sir Charles Mordaunt, had threatened to cite him as co-respondent along

322

with two others, but in the end had petitioned for a divorce on the grounds that his wife was insane. Nevertheless Bertie, who had written some innocent letters to Lady Mordaunt, was subpoenaed as a witness by her counsel. In the witness box he denied all accusations of misconduct. The whole scandal was, for Victoria, 'a painful, lowering thing'. She did not doubt Bertie's innocence, but she despaired at his imprudence in his choice of friends and his repeated social indiscretions. As his mother, she closed ranks to protect him, but not without lecturing him on abandoning his frivolous lifestyle. 'Thank goodness beloved Papa was not here to see it,' she told Vicky; he would have 'suffered dreadfully' with the worry of it all.[60] The case had come at a time when the press were once more on the attack, and a broadside entitled 'The coming K—', parodying Bertie's pleasure-seeking private life in the style of Tennyson's *Idylls of the King*, was doing the rounds. Echoes of the past dissolute behaviour of Bertie's Georgian ancestors reverberated across the accounts of the trial, with talk once more of the cost of the royal family to the nation when they did little in return to earn it.

\*　　　\*　　　\*

Radical opinion in Britain, which had been on the rise since the agitation for the 2nd Reform Bill of 1866–7, had received a major boost in the summer of 1870 with the outbreak of the Franco-Prussian War, a conflict that had once again divided Victoria's loyalties—between her friend, the French emperor Louis Napoleon, and her Prussian relatives. The war had ended in the defeat of the French at Sedan in September and the flight of the Emperor into exile. The establishment of the Third Republic in France after the romantic heroics of the Paris Commune had prompted a surge in the political left in Britain, as middle-class radicals, trade unionists and socialist-minded politicians gathered at a series of meetings at which calls were made for Queen Victoria to be deposed. Having let go of virtually all her ceremonial duties, she was accused of accruing large amounts from the Civil List for her own private use, while the Prince of Wales had been busy doing little but amass a pile of debts. The radical *National Reformer* argued that it 'seems proved by the experience of the last nine or ten years that the country can do quite well without a monarchy'.[61] *The Republican*—the organ of the Land and Labour League—equalled it, calling for social justice and an end to an oppressive government that cared nothing for the poor.[62] Republican clubs were springing up in major cities across the country: Aberdeen, Birmingham, Cambridge, Cardiff, London, Norwich and Plymouth, and with them came the increasing urgency, in Gladstone's mind, of addressing 'The Royalty Question' once and for all.[63] The fund of public goodwill for the monarchy was drying up and he did not see 'from whence it is to be replenished as matters go now'. 'To speak in rude and general terms,' he told Lord Granville in early December 1870, 'The Queen is invisible, and the Prince of Wales is not respected.'[64] If Victoria could not be coaxed out, then all he could do was campaign for better ways of showing the royal family 'in the visible discharge of public duty'. He therefore argued for a greater and more responsible role for the Prince of Wales, urging the Queen that Bertie be based in Ireland for half the year, as permanent Viceroy. Victoria was ruthlessly dismissive of the suggestion: the weather was awful, the damp climate would be bad for Bertie's health and the expenditure of money on royal public duties in Ireland would be a waste of time and money. As far as she was concerned, 'Scotland and England deserved it much more.'[65]

Ensconced at Windsor, Queen Victoria remained deaf to the warnings not far away in the heart of London. On 18 December a demonstration was called by the International Democratic Association in Trafalgar Square, at which up to 3,000 men and boys converged, carrying banners decorated with French republican mottoes and devices as well as the chillingly familiar red cap of liberty, 'to acknowledge the struggle of the people of France against despotism' and offer their full support for the new Republic, which the British government had yet to recognise. The aggression of Victoria's Prussian relatives in the recent war against France had further fuelled popular support for the republican spirit in France. *Reynolds's Newspaper* took advantage in its reporting to see the rally in Trafalgar Square as a sign of the stirring of allegiance among the working classes to 'the republican form of government'; it gave the lie to the supposedly monarchical loyalties of the British people that Victoria had for so long been cushioned by in her retreat from public view. 'Dynastic considerations are paralyzing the best energies of England, and rendering us the laughing stock of the whole world,' it warned. 'Englishmen are not the servile, grovelling idolaters of royalties and aristocracies our contemporaries delight in depicting them.'[66]

On a mild, calm afternoon in October 1870 diarist Arthur Munby had been out taking a stroll in Kensington Gardens. 'Close by was the gilded pinnacle of the Prince Consort's Monument, now all but finished,' he noted, but he was sanguine about its future, concluding that 'a hundred years hence' it would be looked upon as a 'tawdry yet interesting memento of an extinct monarchy'.[67] Earlier that summer, voicing the gathering anxieties of all his siblings, Bertie had tried to encourage his mother to show herself more to her people: 'If you sometimes came to London from Windsor and then drove for an hour in the Park (where there is no noise), the people would be overjoyed,' he had urged her, adding a sobering warning. 'We live in radical times, and the more *People see the Sovereign* the better it is for the *People* and the *Country*.'[68] In this view Bertie had the backing of Victoria's new Private Secretary, Henry Ponsonby, the exhausted and demoralised General Grey having collapsed and died on 26 March. The Prince of Wales would soon be thirty, but still had no useful ceremonial role; his mother, as she aged, was becoming increasingly intractable. With republicanism in Britain on the rise, a renewed and far more serious assault on the Queen's continuing seclusion was about to be launched.

# CHAPTER FOURTEEN

## *'Heaven Has Sent Us This Dispensation to Save Us'*

After less than a year in his new post as Private Secretary to the Queen, Henry Ponsonby was still very much feeling his way when, in 1871, the monarchy was confronted with its most serious crisis yet. The Queen's invisibility was not just a frustration to her public and her ministers; it extended to her staff and created many difficulties for Ponsonby in his job. Queen Victoria did not volunteer him much of her personal time, frequently sending scribbled notes rather than issuing verbal instructions, and not even calling for him when she dealt with her official dispatch boxes. The expectation of at least being solicited for advice had rapidly faded, and Ponsonby's role was often reduced to the farcical sending of the same papers back and forth, via footmen, to the Queen a few rooms away. He already had the distinct impression that his monarch did not work as hard as she claimed, despite the sycophantic protection of Dr Jenner. The perception of some, like Disraeli, that she worked tirelessly on Foreign and Colonial Office dispatches in the seclusion of her rooms was a fiction, in his view. And how could she do the work of government properly at Balmoral in isolation from her ministers? Ever more entrenched in going nowhere and seeing only the few people she liked, Victoria did not even enjoy having her children around her. If there was a choice between staying at Balmoral for one of the riotous ghillies' balls arranged by Brown or returning to London when the political situation demanded her presence, she always chose the former.[1]

The subtle and self-effacing Ponsonby had arrived at a time when the Queen most needed him. Unlike his predecessor—his uncle-in-law General Grey—Ponsonby was able to temper his exasperation at Victoria's most provocative bad qualities with a deeply felt affection and loyalty, where Grey had simply been worn down by them and, ultimately, alienated. Ponsonby demonstrated great skill in fielding Victoria's often irrational outbursts about the pressures placed on her with a discreet irreverence behind the scenes for their unreasonableness. But while his sardonic wit was his great saving grace, it required all his considerable resources of patience, tact and tolerance to carry out his duties in the face of the Queen's now-legendary intransigence. He was under no illusions as to the precariousness of the situation that year: 'If . . . she is neither the head of the Executive nor the fountain of honour, nor the centre of display, the royal dignity will sink to nothing at all,' he warned.[2] The Liberal minister Lord Halifax agreed: 'the mass of the people expect a King or a Queen to look and play the part. They want to see a Crown and a Sceptre and all that sort of thing. They want the gilding for their money.'[3]

Early in 1871, faced with the prospect of another daughter to marry—this time one of her least popular ones, Louise—Victoria for once showed no reluctance in doing her queenly duty by opening Parliament. It was a repetition of the situation she had faced in 1866 with Helena and Affie; she needed to secure a £30,000 dowry for Louise, followed shortly afterwards by an annuity of £15,000 for Prince Arthur when he came of age. But these further demands on the privy purse prompted renewed criticism of her failure visibly to earn her income, fuelled by publication of a pseudonymous pamphlet asking 'What Does She Do With It?', which accused her of secreting up to £200,000 a year of her Civil List monies, tax-free, for her own private purposes.[4] The immensely wealthy Argyll family into which Louise was marrying—and for once the groom was a British commoner rather than an impoverished foreign prince—hardly needed the money, and there was widespread public objection to the demand. Animosity was whipped up once more: it was time the Queen stepped down or the monarchy was done away with altogether. Charles Bradlaugh, President of the London Republican Club, argued that 'the experience of the last nine years proves that the country can do quite well without a monarch', urging not violent overthrow, but a peaceful transition. After so many years of only nominal monarchy, the Act of Settlement that had established the House of Brunswick on the British throne in 1701 should be revoked on the Queen's decease.[5]

Gladstone loyally defended the Queen throughout the controversy and threw his full political weight behind her requests, but was not helped by gossip about Bertie's huge gambling losses in the casinos of Homburg; the Prince's popularity was plummeting in tandem with the Queen's. Eventually Parliament agreed to both sums, though fifty-four members supported a call for Prince Arthur's annuity to be reduced to £10,000. Continuing demands for the Queen's greater visibility met with a tepid response from Victoria, who agreed to a couple of Drawing Rooms held consecutively at Buckingham Palace (so that she only had to tolerate one overnight stay there), a review of the troops in Bushey Park and a brief showing of herself in an open carriage on 21 March, when she drove with Princess Louise on her wedding day the short distance down the hill from the Upper Ward of Windsor Castle to St George's Chapel. But the ceremony itself, at which the Queen played a more prominent role giving Louise away, was witnessed only by the select few and the date, during Lent, was chosen entirely to suit the Queen's holiday schedule and not that of her churchgoing public, many of whom protested at its inappropriateness.

Eight days later Victoria re-emerged for the official opening of Prince Albert's brainchild, the Royal Albert Hall, which had been under construction for four years as a centre for the celebration of British culture. It was a key moment in the memorialisation of her dead husband, and the Queen faced this gathering of 8,000—the biggest function she had attended since Albert was alive—with considerable trepidation. Her public were to be disappointed by her lack of visible engagement; during the brief ceremony, despite looking well and smiling and impressing everyone with her compelling regal dignity, Victoria could barely muster more than a brief sentence, in which she expressed her 'admiration of this beautiful hall' and her good wishes for its success.[6] Was she playing to the gallery, one wonders? When it came to the moment of declaring the hall open, she appeared totally overwhelmed and Bertie was obliged to say the words for her. Beyond this, she remained obdurate in her resistance to any other demands on her for the performance of ceremony. Gladstone, for all his loyalty to the throne, privately found her waywardness increasingly difficult— if not repellent in its self-servitude. But try as he might, his inducements to the Queen to increase her official duties brought only peremptory, if not hysterical lists of objections.

By the late summer of 1871, with the press warning that 'England might virtually be left without a Sovereign for half a century' if Victoria lived to a ripe old age, conspiracy was brewing even at Windsor.[7] The Queen's children were seriously alarmed that their mother was prejudicing the future of the throne. Her conspicuous habit of grief had now become a habit of avoidance, made worse by Jenner's constant pandering to Victoria's neuroses, which they all felt had to be confronted once and for all. During a family gathering at Balmoral, and under the guidance of Vicky and a gloomily pessimistic Princess Alice, who were both visiting from Germany, they composed a letter to their mother in which they tried as respectfully and affectionately as they could to make her see the truth of her position. Signed by them all, the letter assured the Queen that they had '*each* of *us* individually wished to say this to you', and that they had done so from the conviction that had come upon them all 'that some danger is in the air, that something must be done . . . to avert a frightful calamity':

No one has prompted us to write . . . No one knows except we ourselves . . . It is we your children, whose position in the world had been made so good by the wisdom and forethought, and the untiring care of yourself and dear Papa, who now feel how utterly changed things are, and who would humbly entreat you to enquire into the state of public feeling, which appears to us so very alarming.[8]

Just as the children were collectively gathering their resolve to hand the letter over to their mother, however, events overtook them. For Victoria fell ill—and seriously so—for once allaying any accusations of malingering. In early August what seemed like a bout of her usual insomnia and headaches was accompanied by a sore throat and complicated soon afterwards by the development of a painful swelling under her arm.[9] Her sufferings all the more justified Victoria's professed intention to decamp as swiftly as possible to the sanctuary of Balmoral. Gladstone objected, asking her to postpone her departure until after the Privy Council meeting to be held when Parliament had been prorogued—thus sparing her ministers the arduous journey north. Victoria was incensed by his 'interference with the Queen's personal acts and movements'; it was 'really abominable'.[10] She railed at the wicked persecution to which she was being subjected. Feeling ill as she now did, she had no intention of being further inconvenienced or made to stay in London to gratify what she saw as Gladstone's political ends, and once again she resorted to the bottom line: 'unless the Ministers *support* her . . . she *cannot* go on and must give her heavy burden up to younger hands'.[11]

With the Queen having protested endlessly for the last ten years about the precarious state of her health, no one believed her at first; but on 14 August her sore throat rapidly got worse, affecting her ability to eat and speak. Unaware of the true extent of her illness, Gladstone found her continuing protests 'sickening', confiding in Henry Ponsonby (who also felt she should stay until the prorogation) that 'Smaller and meaner cause for the decay of thrones cannot be conceived . . . it is like the worm which bores the bark of a noble oak tree and so breaks the channel of its life.'[12] Victoria was by now too ill to care; on 17 December she summoned all her strength to undertake the long train ride to Balmoral. Once there, she was soon bedridden. Although the agonising pain in her throat finally gave way on the 20th, she was in increasing discomfort from the swelling under her arm, which had developed into a large abscess; her appetite vanished and she rapidly lost weight.

With no sign of the abscess breaking, Dr Jenner was worried that it might lead to septicaemia. Although the public had had no inkling of it, nor too Victoria's ministers, Jenner even feared for her life. He dared not summon her children, knowing that their presence would only alarm Victoria and make matters worse; in any event, at such times she preferred the solicitous presence of Brown and her close personal servants Löhlein, Annie Macdonald and her dresser Emilie Dittweiler.[13] Unwilling to explain the true nature of her illness and uncertain as to what had provoked it, Jenner nevertheless felt compelled to defend the Queen against criticism from her ministers that she was once again crying wolf. From such a distance they could hardly be blamed, for they did not know the true facts. In an anonymous piece in *The Lancet* on 19 August he therefore catalogued her precarious physical state, her inability to tolerate crowded and overheated rooms and the continuing severe headaches, insomnia and loss of appetite that she was suffering. He also argued long and forcefully with Ponsonby about the necessity for her to spend any time in London. Ponsonby was dismayed by Jenner's action—he felt it played straight into the hands of those claiming the Queen was no longer fit to rule and should abdicate: 'Why should we wait any longer,' they would say, 'she promises not to do more, but positively to do less.'[14]

With complaints gathering in the English press, the Scottish papers loyally rebutted criticism of the Queen, praising her for not kowtowing to the trifling gestures of London life or suggestions that she allow Bertie to take over Buckingham Palace. Jenner weighed into the political arguments too: it wasn't the Queen's fault; all this criticism directed at her was symptomatic of the 'advancing democracy of the age'. 'It is absurd to think that it will be checked by her driving about London and giving balls for the frivolous classes of Society,' he told Ponsonby. Jenner felt beleaguered; in the end he could only warn, as he had done since the death of Albert, of the dark prospect of the Queen suffering a breakdown if pushed too hard: 'these nerves are a form of madness, and against them it is hopeless to contend'.[15]

Queen Victoria was little better by early September; she had not felt this ill, she said, since her bout of typhoid fever in 1835. It was therefore decided to call in a surgeon, Dr Joseph Lister, from Edinburgh. On the 4th he lanced the abscess, which had now reached six inches in diameter and was very deep-seated, first freezing it with ether. Lister was a pioneer of antisepsis and, in order to minimise the risk of infection, used his own carbolic-acid spraying machine—the 'donkey engine' as he called it—during the procedure. Jenner was enlisted to work the bellows of the spray, inadvertently choking the Queen in a cloud of pungent phenol.[16] When the wound still did not drain properly, Lister applied a rubber drainage tube, the first time this procedure had been used. It was, Victoria declared, 'a most disagreeable duty most pleasantly performed'.[17] Within a week she was showing clear signs of recovery. Thin and pale, she was wheeled around in a bath chair for days—everyone who saw her was shocked at her frailty. It was only now that news of the Queen's serious illness was released to the nation, prompting a mass stirring of public sympathy and anxiety, if not expressions of guilt for having accused her of malingering. The royal children, agreeing that any shock tactics with their mother might now backfire, quietly put their letter away, agreeing not to present it to her till early the following year—'if at all'.[18] The illness had now played into Victoria's hands, and Princess Alice thought that nothing could be done to remedy her mother's infuriating complacency: 'She thinks the Monarchy will last her time and that it is no use thinking of what will come after . . . so she lets the torrent come on.'[19] Victoria was satisfyingly vindicated by the remorse of newspapers such as the *Daily News*, which on

15 September published a toadying apology. The people 'may have caught from a discontented Court a complaining spirit', it observed ingenuously:

> They may have been induced to feel that the Queen was hardly giving proper splendour to her Queenly position and was showing some slackness in her Queenly duties; but today all such complaints are hushed, the nation is ashamed of them and rebukes itself for uttering them, and feels nothing but an affectionate solicitude for her speedy recovery.

Three months on from the onset of her illness Victoria was still weak and in a lot of pain. Despite recovering from the abscess, she had been further disabled by a severe attack of rheumatic gout in many of her joints, and her hands and feet were badly swollen and bandaged; her nights were restless and she was dosing heavily on chloral. She felt utterly helpless, unable to feed herself or write her journal, which for weeks now she had been dictating to fourteen-year-old Beatrice. John Brown was constantly in attendance, carrying her to and from her bed, and her couch and up and down stairs. It was November before she could manage the stairs again. To be so incapacitated had been 'a bitter trial', and just as she was finally recovering her strength, a renewed attack on her was launched by the rising young Liberal MP for Chelsea, Sir Charles Dilke.[20] In a speech at Newcastle on 6 November 1871 he criticised the cost to the nation of the Civil List, particularly when the Queen rarely held court in London. He accused her of hoarding a private, untaxed fortune, as well as draining the royal coffers through the maintenance of an excessive number of obsolete sinecures—did Her Majesty really need a Hereditary Grand Falconer or a Master of the Buckhounds? Or, for that matter, did she require a collection of twenty-one assorted physicians, dentists, oculists and apothecaries to safeguard the health of the royal family? 'If you can show me a fair chance that a republic here will be free from the political corruption that hangs about the monarch, I say, for my part—and I believe the middle classes in general will say—let it come.'[21]

'Sir Charles Dilke has given the Queen notice to quit,' proclaimed the *Pall Mall Gazette*; and indeed his rhetoric was highly provocative.[22] But, when it came down to it, Dilke proved to be a man of words rather than action, prone to wild and unsubstantiated claims about Victoria's supposed squirelling-away of money from the privy purse. His stance was symptomatic of a groundswell of opinion that was inherently anti-monarchist rather than truly republican. But it lacked any real political—let alone genuinely socialist—backbone. *The Times* was quick to retaliate. On 9 November its editorial accused Dilke of 'recklessness bordering on criminality'. Victoria was incensed; press criticism of her had been cruel and heartless. Behind Gladstone's back, and oblivious to the extent to which her Prime Minister had doggedly defended her, she complained that he had not done enough to protect her against Dilke's treasonable onslaught, ungraciously telling Vicky that he was 'so wonderfully unsympathetic'. Yet at heart Gladstone held his Queen in awe. His instinct was to ignore Dilke (the loyalist reaction to the Queen's illness would take care of that) while voicing to his colleagues his continuing fears for the monarchy and his deep-seated distaste for the 'vehemence and tenacity' with which the Queen resisted the fulfilment of her sovereign duties.[23]

Dilke's attack was, in any event, rapidly laid aside when the Queen received a telegram at Balmoral on 21 November informing her that Bertie had fallen ill with typhoid fever at Sandringham. He had probably picked up the infection from contaminated drinking water during a recent pheasant-shoot at the estate of Lord Londesborough at Scarborough, where the lodge house in which he stayed was overcrowded and its drainage primitive.[24] The prognosis was enough to send shock waves of apprehension through the entire royal household. Victoria immediately dispatched Dr Jenner to Sandringham, and on the 24th the public were informed of the prince's illness, with the reassuring proviso that 'There are no unfavourable symptoms'. But they had all heard that line before—when Prince Albert had fallen ill exactly ten years previously.

Princess Alice was on a visit to Sandringham at the time Bertie fell ill and immediately did her best to take over the role of sick-nurse. Having nursed Louis through a mild attack of the disease in 1870, as well as organising field hospitals in Hesse during the Austro-Prussian War of 1866, she felt qualified to monopolise things, much to the annoyance of Alix, who had already proved herself more than competent at the task. Alice was ably assisted by two professional nurses, as well as Bertie's valet and a new and rising practitioner, Dr William Gull, who was Bertie's personal physician. Victoria arrived on 29 November to be met by Alix, 'looking thin and anxious with tears in her eyes'. When the Queen entered the sick-room the reminders of 1861 were many and vivid, and even more ominous when Jenner told her that 'it was a far more violent attack than my beloved Husband's'.[25] The following day Bertie's temperature was 105 degrees and his lungs were congested (bronchitis was setting in). But on the 1 December he rallied, enough for Victoria to feel it was safe to return to Windsor, after which she headed straight for Albert's mausoleum to pray. But hopes were not raised for long. On the 7th Bertie suffered a relapse and on the morning of the 8th Victoria received a telegram from Jenner: 'The Prince passed a very unquiet night. Not so well. Temperature risen to 104. Respirations more rapid. Dr Gull and I are both very anxious.' She hurried back to Sandringham with Louise, arriving late in the icy chill and snow, looking 'small and miserable' according to Lady Stanley.[26] The press too were by now flocking to nearby Wolferton station, and from there to Sandringham on every gig and fly that could be hired, to camp out at the gates. Royal illness—particularly when knocking at death's door—was a great circulation-booster, as they all knew. Very soon word was out that the Prince had succumbed to the full force of the fever and had sunk into a terrifying, raging delirium.

No sooner had she arrived than Victoria took control of the household from under the nose of its mistress Alix and commandeered what little space remained for herself, her entourage and the rest of Bertie's siblings as they arrived. Alice and Alix's young children were all packed off to Windsor for their own safety. The atmosphere inside the newly built but overcrowded house, with its windows shut fast against the cold and snow outside, rapidly became noisy and quarrelsome as the various members of the family vied for space; others tiptoed round in sheer terror at being in such close proximity to the Queen, as 'dread and gloom' prevailed.[27] The Duke of Cambridge in particular was dubious about the sanitary arrangements, fearing the spread of typhoid germs among them, and went round the house inspecting it for bad smells.

Hour after hour Victoria watched over her son in the dark and claustrophobic room. 'It was too dreadful to see the poor Queen sitting in the bedroom behind a screen listening to his ravings,' recalled Prince Leopold later. 'I can't tell you what a deep impression it made on me.'[28] For once she was completely taken out of herself; mindful only of Bertie. The Queen's innate good qualities—her 'best self', as Lady Augusta Stanley called them—rose to the surface as, against the odds of her own recent debilitating illness, she drew on the great store of physical and emotional strength that she always had in reserve, when she chose to enlist it.[29] She was far from optimistic about the outcome, yet remained a paragon of calmness, patience and solicitude, listening to Bertie's stentorian breathing as he tossed and turned and raved. His outbursts of singing, whistling and talking—in several languages—were sometimes so embarrassing and compromising that his wife had to be kept out of the room.

Sunday 10 December was designated a day of national prayer, as the family and household gathered round, anticipating with dread the unthinkable: a repetition of the deathbed of Prince

Albert ten years previously. Bulletins were being issued twice a day and posted at public places like the Mansion House and Charing Cross for all to see. Across Britain's places of worship the nation was once more united in a 'common anxiety'. On Monday the 11th the doctors called Victoria from her bed at 5.30 a.m. The patient had had a severe spasm, closely followed by another. Jenner warned her that 'at any moment dear Bertie might go off'.[30] She hurried to his bedside as the rest of the household congregated outside the door in their dressing gowns. 'The awfulness of this morning, I shall never, never forget as long as I live,' wrote the Duke of Cambridge in his diary. Even outside the door everyone could hear Bertie's loud and incessant delirious ramblings. 'All looked bewildered and overcome with grief,' the Duke recalled, 'but the doctors behaved nobly, no flinching, no loss of courage, only intense anxiety.'[31] All day an exhausted Victoria, Alice and Alix kept vigil, as Bertie's life hung by a thread; by 7 p.m. that evening the doctors were not expecting him to survive the night.

Letters and telegrams meanwhile poured into Sandringham, many from the public with recommendations for homespun remedies for typhoid, some 'of the most mad kind'.[32] Words of comfort and support also came from ministers, including a heavy-hearted Gladstone, who found it difficult to find words adequate enough that would not 'mock the sorrow of this moment'. Even the chastened members of London's republican clubs sent a joint message expressing their sorrow at the Prince's illness and their hope that his life might be spared.[33] Reporter Henry James Jennings of the

341

*Birmingham Mail* remembered how he sat huddled in his cold and draughty office for three or four days on end: 'we were there, editor, compositors and machine men, from eight in the morning until twelve or one at night, ready to bring out at short notice an edition recording any important change'.[34] On the morning of the 12th, as he went to his work at the Ecclesiastical Commissioners' Office, Arthur Munby noticed how everyone felt as 'one family' at this time of crisis:

> Another day of public anxiety—shown more strongly in London than I ever remember. People asking for telegrams, listening for the passing bell; chance words heard in the street or elsewhere, showing that most men were thinking of the Prince. Home Office telegrams posted in our hall, as usual; at the Cheshire Cheese, the latest news written up in the dining parlour, in the Strand and Fleet Street, little details from the sickroom hastily brushed in with ink on large flysheets, which were stuck on shutters of newspaper offices; and crowds pressing to read them.[35]

Victoria was greatly comforted: 'The feeling shown by the whole nation is quite marvellous and most touching and striking,' she noted in her journal; it proved to her 'how really sound and truly loyal the people are'. For thirty-six hours the delirium consumed Bertie. On the 13th 'the worst day of all' as Victoria recalled, she was allowed to dispense with the screen and sit on the sofa within sight of her son as he battled for life. 'Alice and I said to one another in tears, "There can be no hope"'; all she could do as his temperature rose and he tossed and turned, clutching at the bedclothes and gasping between each incoherent word, was hold Bertie's hand and stroke his arm. In a brief moment of clarity he suddenly noticed her sitting there. 'It is so kind of you to come,' he whispered.[36]

Beyond the wintry flatlands of Sandringham the nation was gripped by 'an epidemic of typhoid loyalty' as *Reynolds's Newspaper* later described it, berating the fashionable journals for the 'mean, toadying, craven spirit of so-called loyalty' that covered their pages. Typhoid fever, as it rightly pointed out, was an endemic disease of the poor that brought grief and suffering wherever it struck: 'The Life of John Smith in Whitechapel, or of John Jones in the "Black Country", is exactly the same to a family as the life of the Prince of Wales.'[37] But nothing could dispel the collective sense of foreboding as the nation contemplated the significance of the date—14 December—to come and the prospect of another funereal Christmas. The leader-writers were sharpening their pens and finalising their obituaries. George Augustus Sala at the *Daily Telegraph* geared himself up for a repeat performance of his 1861 panegyrics: 'All England may be said to have gathered at the little Norfolk cottage,' he gushed, 'in a thousand nameless households . . . hearts close together, and hands linked with hands . . . against the dreaded approach of death.'[38] Jay's were on standby for the stampede, having judiciously inserted an advertisement in *The Times* on the 13th announcing that its staff were at the ready to serve anyone, anywhere, 'in the event of immediate mourning being required'; over at St Paul's the bell-ringers were primed for action.

343

With a longer run-in for its weekly deadline, *Punch* instructed illustrator John Tenniel to prepare two alternative cartoons: one entitled 'Suspense', depicting Britannia standing vigil outside Bertie's door; the other, 'In Memoriam', with her weeping in despair.[39]

Alone among newspapermen Wemyss Reid, editor of the *Leeds Mercury*, having received no telegram announcing the Prince's death by midnight, decided to go to press the following morning, the 14th, with an article assuming he would still be alive: 'in every other newspaper office the conviction that he was at the very point of death was so strong that no preparation had been made for his possible survival'.[40] His paper and *The Times* were the only ones to do so that day, most of the others having had to stall on printing the black-bordered obituaries they had prepared. As the 'dreadful anniversary' of Albert's death approached, a strange kind of fatalism gripped the royal family as they sat and watched through the evening, everyone filled with a superstitious dread that history might repeat itself. Mercifully, things improved late that evening. 'Instead of this date dawning upon another deathbed, which I had felt almost certain of, it brought cheering news,' recalled Victoria. Overnight Bertie's temperature began to drop; he slept quietly for several hours and his breathing eased. With all the royal family gathered at Sandringham, for once—and only once—there would be no commemoration that day of Albert's death in the Blue Room and the mausoleum at Windsor.[41]

Having issued six bulletins on the Prince's condition during the 13th, the doctors were very cautious about any immediate announcement of recovery. But with crowds huddled all day in the cold outside the newspaper offices and Marlborough House waiting for news, a bulletin was finally released at 1 a.m. on the 14th announcing that the prince was 'less restless'. Bertie's recovery from here on would be a slow and difficult one, with a worrying relapse on 27 December, but eventually he was on the mend. It was nothing short of a gift from providence to a beleaguered monarchy in a time of desperate need. 'What a sell for Dilke this illness has been!' wrote Lord Henry Lennox to Disraeli. 'The Republicans say their chances are up,' a relieved Duke of Cambridge told his mother. 'Heaven has sent us this dispensation to save us.'[42] Predictably the papers gushed with a tide of sentimental rhetoric honouring God's mercy in sparing Bertie and praising the fortitude of his mother and the devoted nursing of his virtuous sister Alice. Victoria, whose relationship with Alice was always difficult, was rather put out: 'beloved Alix I can never praise enough . . . so true, so discreet, so kind to all'; in Victoria's estimation, for all her frail constitution her daughter-in-law had more than equalled Alice in her sick-bed devotion.[43]

Despite Bertie's recovery, Christmas that year was a subdued one for the royal family. Victoria returned to Windsor on the 19th and spent the holiday there instead of at Osborne—for the first time since that last Christmas with Albert in 1860. But there was no tree and few festivities. 'It was, if not a sad, yet at any rate a very serious Christmas to us all,' she told the Duke of Cambridge, 'from the recent week of terrible anxiety and also for the consciousness that dear Bertie is still in an anxious state. His recovery is so slow, and there are such fluctuations from day to day, that I must own I do not feel easy about him.'[44] She professed herself humbled by the experience: 'It was a great lesson to us all—to see the highest surrounded by every luxury which human mortal can wish for—lying low and as helpless and miserable as the poorest peasant.'[45] On 26 December *The Times* published her letter of thanks to the nation:

> The universal feeling shown by her people during those painful, terrible days, and the sympathy evinced by them with herself and her beloved daughter, the Princess of Wales, as well as the general joy at the improvement of the Prince of Wales's state, have made a deep and lasting impression on her heart, which can never be effaced. It was indeed nothing new to her, for the Queen had met with the same sympathy, when just ten years ago, a similar illness removed from her side the mainstay of her life, the best, wisest and kindest of husbands.

Over in republican France, where the worst excesses of the Paris Commune had raised the ugly spectre of 1789 and soured the successful overturn of the monarchy, the response to the political turnaround in Britain was one of incredulity. England had supposedly been on the brink of becoming a republic, yet the last few days of the Prince's illness had been a lesson to all. As one Parisian journal observed, instead of mocking their royal family, the people had prayed, showing that they 'have the courage, the good sense not to disown either their history, their Government, or their God'. The British were still a free people and the French had much to learn from them about the 'powerful bonds of union' that a country relies upon in times of trouble. 'When shall *we* learn to pray altogether for anyone?' it asked.[46]

Gladstone had no doubt that Bertie's six-week near-fatal illness had provided the monarchy with a 'last opportunity' to capitalise on a renewal of public loyalty. 'We have arrived at a great crisis of Royalty,' he said, and he was determined to overcome it. The Queen had 'laid up in early years an immense fund of loyalty, but she is now living on her capital,' he told Ponsonby, who agreed that 'royal matters' had become stuck in a 'deep and nasty rut'.[47] Word meanwhile had come from Sandringham that some kind of service of thanksgiving might be in order, and Gladstone gave it his full support. Such a ceremony would set the seal on the important strengthening of the bonds between monarch and people that had occurred during the Prince's illness, as well as putting a hopefully reformed Bertie back on track . . . For the Prince of Wales had confided to his nurse when he first fell ill that 'if he got better he should lead a very different life to what he had hitherto done'.[48]

\*       \*       \*

Plans were put in place early in 1872 for a royal progress across London, followed by a service at St Paul's Cathedral, with Gladstone providing the Queen with supporting ammunition—a list of precedents, including the celebrations there for the recovery from illness of George III in 1789. Victoria immediately shrank at the prospect of being the centre of a display of 'ostentatious pomp'.[49] She objected to St Paul's as a venue: 'a most dreary, dingy, melancholy and undevotional church'; Westminster Abbey was smaller and a lot nearer to Buckingham Palace.[50] Uppermost in her mind was of course the physical strain on herself, not to mention Bertie, of a long and fatiguing service, but in the end Alix persuaded her. While the Princess of Wales agreed that her husband's illness had been a very personal experience and that she, like the Queen, did not want what was fundamentally a religious act being made a vehicle for a grand public show, the nation—having taken such a *public* share in our anxiety'—had shown such solidarity 'that it may perhaps feel that it has a kind of *claim* to join with us now in a public and universal thanksgiving'.[51]

Victoria had to concede, but her old, familiar obstructiveness ensured that nothing went smoothly. Fraught discussions with Gladstone followed over her various 'peculiar fancies', as he saw them: the length of the service (which she wanted shortened to half an hour); the carriages to be used (she vetoed a full state procession); the route (which was lengthened to appease public demand); and the number of tickets to be issued for the ceremony (under pressure from *The Times* this was increased from 8,000 to just under 12,000). When it came to the question of who was to pay for it all, Gladstone knew that the government must foot the bill or Victoria would pounce on this as a reason to resist.[52] In the end a series of compromises were made to ensure Victoria's participation, with the Queen refusing to kowtow to the list of precedents presented to her, but agreeing only out of personal recognition that some kind of 'show' was required as a thank-you to the nation.[53] 'I have no doubt that he is "gauche",' thought Lady Augusta Stanley on hearing the news that Gladstone had prevailed, 'but I must say I honor him for pressing her duty on her—And Oh! That she should at this moment resent it!'[54] And there were compensations for Victoria for this act of veiled capitulation: in return she was able to duck out of opening Parliament the same month.

The Service of National Thanksgiving held at St Paul's Cathedral on 27 February 1872 proved to be the long-wished-for public celebration of nationhood and monarchy. The whole of London was on the move from before dawn, on a day punctuated with bursts of chilly rain followed by sunshine.[55] Victoria and Bertie—he still very weak and haggard and walking with a limp (the result of a severe attack of gout)—traversed streets festooned with flags and bunting, floral wreaths and triumphal arches, with military bands playing 'God Save the Queen' and 'God Save the Prince of Wales'. Despite the cold, Victoria had specified an open landau so that the people could clearly see them in the convoy of nine carriages accompanied by a guard of honour. It took its route along Pall Mall, Trafalgar Square, the Strand and up Fleet Street, past tiers of specially constructed seating to Temple Bar, all to 'one mighty multitude and one continued acclamation'.[56] As on the occasion of Princess Alexandra's progress across London in 1863, the best vantage points were sold at a premium, from ten shillings, to forty guineas for a balcony view on Fleet Street. But this royal occasion saw crowds larger even than the 'Coronation, Exhibition, and

Wellington mobs' of 1838, 1851 and 1852. A major lack of provision for viewing the procession led to chaos: many who climbed trees in St James's Park for a better view ended up in hospital with broken limbs, as did others who fell from windows and scaffolding; spectators were kicked by horses or knocked down by carriages; women and children fainted in the crush on Ludgate Hill and had to be hauled by ropes from the crowd.[57]

Victoria was still in deep mourning, though she had at least left off her crape in favour of black silk, her jacket and skirt trimmed with a deep border of ermine and her bonnet decorated with white flowers. She seemed happier than she had been in the last ten years, waving and at one point raising Bertie's hand and kissing it. He repeatedly lifted his hat in acknowledgement of the crowds; their deafening cheers as they passed were a 'wonderful demonstration of loyalty and affection, from the very highest to the lowest'.[58] The congregation at St Paul's had been awaiting them for several hours, but only fifty of these seats were set aside for 'working men', the rest having been fought over by the Upper Ten Thousand, as *Reynolds's Newspaper* noted. Why had there been no provision, it asked, for the 'people who labour', who instead were left outside, 'hustled, crushed and driven to and fro for the accommodation of "the quality"?'[59] French diplomat Charles Gavard and his entourage had gone to the cathedral wearing full ceremonial uniform—'It would tickle the Republic to see us pass,' he quipped. 'What a human flood as we drew near the City, as foul too as the waters of the Thames,' he recalled. 'No mob is like an English mob; the signs of misery are so unmistakable.

They are both violent and humble under the blows dealt by the police; and the ragbag reigns among them.' Gavard had taken up his place in the tiers of specially constructed benches at 11 a.m., 'in a draught of cold air that douched us till two o'clock'.[60] Arthur Munby had been in the cathedral even longer—since 8 a.m. to be sure of a good view.

At last the bells boomed out 'like a volley of artillery' as the Queen and Prince of Wales entered through the main doors, over which hung the inscription from Psalm 122: 'I was glad when they said unto me, I will go into the House of the Lord.' Victoria leaned heavily on Bertie's arm as they processed up the nave to the raised scarlet gangway lined with Beefeaters. There they took their special pew in the centre of the aisle, amidst a congregation of army and navy officers, peers, MPs and ministers, judges, Kings of Arms and royal heralds. The whole congregation, as they did so, was gripped by a 'royal silence that the sacredness of the place and the majesty of her office demanded—a real silence.' Gavard had not been particularly impressed with the sight of the Queen: 'fat and short . . . with a discontented-looking face'; but that silence—not the natural silence of the void, as he recalled, but 'the silence of thousands of people holding their breath at the presence of the monarch finally among them'—was quite extraordinary.[61] It was a 'thrilling moment', Munby recalled, when the organ sounded out, just as the sun broke through the clouds outside and 'sent beams of slanting light down through the misty vault of the dome, upon the gold and scarlet and purple crowds below'. As the 250-strong choir burst into the words of the *Te Deum*, Lucy Cavendish, like many others, felt a shudder of recognition: 'Never before had I realised what a Psalm of Thanksgiving it is, and most beautiful and moving were the words specially dwelt upon by the music: . . . "When Thou hadst overcome *the sharpness of death*".'[62]

After an hour-long service—'cold and too long', as far as Victoria was concerned—the royal carriages returned to Buckingham Palace by a different route, taking an hour and a half to make their way the seven miles across the crowded streets.[63] Gratified by what had been 'a most affecting day', the Queen appeared shortly afterwards on the balcony to loud cheers, with Beatrice, Leopold, Arthur and Alfred.[64] As night fell the crowds were still out, as they had been in March 1863, linking arms, singing and dancing as they enjoyed the fireworks and gaslit illuminations across London. The dome of St Paul's was encircled with coloured lights, 'like St Peter's in Rome on Easter day', recalled Wemyss Reid; Fleet Street 'looked quite medieval again', thought Munby, 'its gabled houses bright as day with lights and colour—flags on the houses, flags festooned across the street, and legends, such as the Te Deum, stretching all down the way on either side, white letters on a scarlet ground nailed to the windows.'[65]

Inevitably criticisms were raised afterwards that the semi-state ceremony had not been sufficiently grand to match the significance of the occasion; *Reynolds's* took the opposite line. Under the banner 'Pinchbeck Loyalty: The Thanksgiving Tomfoolery', it damned the whole thing as 'a sickening display of hypocrisy, sycophancy, idolatry, idiocy and buffoonery'.[66] But such criticism was isolated; it had been, as Victoria herself noted, a 'day of triumph' during which both she and Bertie had been greatly moved and had found it hard to suppress their tears.[67] The common humanity displayed on the streets of London captured everyone's imagination; Thanksgiving Day had in the end been as much about the Queen reappearing to 'perform a function of Royalty in the Metropolis of her Empire' as it had been about Bertie's recovery.[68] In so doing she had prompted a resurgence of deep-rooted sentimentalism towards the monarchy that had not been witnessed since the early days of her reign. The real spectacle, though, as Gavard observed and the press echoed, was not that of monarchy on show, but of 'the people, the never exhausted masses which covered all the pavements, filled all the windows and balconies and stands from street to housetop and spread themselves even over the roofs'. All of them demonstrated 'the wisdom, the moderation, and the sound heart' that had merited their recent wider enfranchisement.[69] This great and potent human spectacle had not just been one for the monarchy to take note of; it had also underlined the collective power of the nation at large to ensure the throne's very survival.

Two days after the Thanksgiving Service a further and even more emphatic death-blow was dealt to the republican cause. In response to the enormous public affection shown to her at St Paul's, Victoria had driven out in Regent's Park late on the afternoon of 29 February in an open landau with Arthur and Leopold to show herself once more to her people. She had returned as usual via the Garden Gate, where a dense crowd awaited her as the carriage entered the palace grounds. Just as Brown dismounted to help Victoria's lady-in-waiting down from the carriage, a gaunt and shabby young man pushed forward, thrusting a pistol close to the Queen's face. As Victoria screamed out 'Save me!', Brown 'with a wonderful presence of mind' seized the man, even as Prince Arthur jumped out to do likewise.[70]

The author of this supposed 'assassination' attempt—the fifth that Victoria had faced since 1840—was a seventeen-year-old Irishman named Arthur O'Connor, a great-nephew of the Chartist leader Feargus O'Connor. In the mêlée at the gates he had managed to climb unnoticed over the ten-foot-high railings into the courtyard beyond, in order to get close to the Queen. His flintlock pistol, bought for four shillings a few days previously in a pawn shop, was faulty and unloaded—filled with scraps of leather and blue paper. His intention had not been to kill, but rather to frighten the Queen into signing the petition he carried for the release of Fenian prisoners. He had wanted to press the petition on her during the service at St Paul's, but when he had been found lurking inside the cathedral the night before he had been ejected.[71] Soon after the attempt newsboys were, so Lucy Cavendish heard, running round the streets shouting, 'Assassination of the Queen'. 'If anything was wanted to send loyalty up to boiling-point, this attempt had done it!' she remarked. A couple of days later, when Victoria drove out in Hyde Park once again in an open carriage 'with no extra precautions', the crowds 'cheered famously'. Londoners once more returned to the gates of Buckingham Palace to stand and stare. When O'Connor's case was tried at the Old Bailey,

Victoria was offended that he did not receive a stiff penalty, for she took the whole thing as a serious attempt on her life. *The Times* disagreed, viewing it as absurdly overhyped: 'Anything wilder or more irrational cannot well be conceived than this shop-boy's plan of over-awing the crown.'[72] Claims that O'Connor was deranged were dismissed and he was sentenced to twelve months' hard labour and twenty strokes of the birch. Victoria was relieved to hear later that he had accepted the option of a one-way ticket to Australia, but O'Connor returned a couple of years later and, after being caught loitering near the palace again, was locked up in a lunatic asylum.

Further outpourings of gratitude—this time for the Queen's safe deliverance from mortal harm—again boosted public sympathy for the monarchy in the wave of renewed loyalty that continued to spread across Britain. Back on the campaign trail in the provinces, Charles Dilke found that his republican speeches encountered an increasingly hostile response. At Bristol, Leeds and Birmingham his words were often drowned out by loud singing of the national anthem. His appearance at Bolton provoked a riot and numerous casualties. On 19 March, when he introduced a motion in Parliament calling for a full public inquiry into the Queen's personal expenditure, he was shouted down and defeated in the vote by 276 to two. Lady Lucy Cavendish had no doubts: these two recent, dramatic events had 'melt[ed] all hearts' and finally put paid to 'grumbling Republicanism'. 'What would seem like the one disloyal hand among three millions, and the fresh rush of loving feeling caused by it and by her courage', had finally brought an end to Dilke's cause. It had also raised the status and integrity of John Brown to new and unassailable heights. Certain that she owed her safety to him and him alone, Victoria rewarded her good Highland servant with a gold Devoted Service Medal, promoted him to the ancient title of Esquire and gave him an annuity of £25. The 'trusty, respectable yeoman' John Brown, so long despised by the royal household, was now a hero to the working classes.[73]

## CHAPTER FIFTEEN

# *Albertopolis*

The events of winter 1871–2 and the National Thanksgiving that followed proved to be a significant turning point for the British monarchy. By the end of 1872, with the return of economic prosperity and an easing of public disgruntlement, Charles Dilke and many of his supporters had retreated, realising that the future lay with increased representation of the people and the maintenance, however flawed, of the political status quo. When it came down to it, the Queen was a stabilising force, if only for her longevity, and they shifted their attention instead to the abuses of privilege among the aristocracy in the House of Lords. Working-class republicanism might stumble on for a year or two more, but it lacked political focus. The 'fearful storm of loyalty' that had marked the Prince of Wales's recovery had, declared the *National Reformer*, proved 'how little at present republicanism had permeated the general population', confirming that a deep-seated loyalty to the throne and a veneration of Victoria as monarch still largely prevailed.[1] The moral example of the throne, dormant for ten years since Albert's death, had found its renaissance in adversity.

Victoria's worries about her son and heir did not, however, abate for long; hopes that Bertie's near-death experience might reform his character faded as he slid back into old habits, confirming his mother's long-standing mistrust of him. By June 1872 she was once more bewailing the shortcomings of her thirty-one-year-old son: 'If only our dear Bertie was fit to replace me!'[2] Had Albert lived, she told Vicky, he would never have coped with the shame not just of Bertie, but also of his brother Affie's immoral behaviour: 'he would have suffered from many inevitable things which have taken place and which he never would have approved'. She was glad he had been spared this, for 'he could not have borne it'.[3] It was better to shoulder the burden alone. She would never relinquish any power to her son all the time there was breath in her body; nor did she feel the need for his advice on matters of state. Albert had set the template on that score, and to that she rigidly adhered. Since Bertie's illness she was more forgiving, learning to live with his inadequacies and appreciating better his innate kindness and affection. But for the rest of his mother's reign the Prince of Wales had to pay the price of a life of imposed idleness—frittering away his useful years in the shallow pursuit of women, horses and gambling in the watering holes of Europe and country houses of England.

As for a resumption of Victoria's public duties, the events of 1871–2, while doing much to turn the tide of her unpopularity, did little immediately to alter the deeply ingrained habits of the previous decade. The insularity and self-absorption of those lost years had seen a hardening of her least-attractive image as the dour, prudish, humourless and repressive Widow at Windsor—an erroneous view that has come down through history, and which has marginalised the Queen's many good attributes. These worst excesses of stubborn self-interest had indeed seen her become at times 'maddening, cruel, hateful, pitiful, impossible'.[4] But out of so much darkness and negativity there finally emerged the monarch whose great virtues—lack of vanity, human sympathy, an absolute honesty and sound common sense—finally gained the ascendant in her later years. True, Victoria still stuck to her favoured routine of long periods out of sight at Balmoral and Windsor, and avoided Buckingham Palace at all costs. But her resistance softened after 1872, for she now better understood how crucial her public popularity was and that she could no longer remain totally invisible. Her increased appearances were never enough to silence her critics entirely; complaints about her seclusion persisted, with pamphlets such as 'Worthy a Crown?' and 'The Vacant Throne' raising the issue again in 1876 and 1877; but in general, by the end of the 1870s, public antipathy had waned and the level of complaint had died down. Much of Victoria's emergence from the cocoon of mourning at this time came thanks to the return to power of her adored Disraeli in 1874, when under his persuasive guidance she gradually became more visible at the head of the kind of informal, accessible monarchy initiated by Prince Albert before his death. Her elevation to Empress of India under the Royal Titles Act of 1876, at her own request, did much to swell national pride as well as Victoria's ego. The triumph of her Golden and Diamond Jubilees in 1887 and 1897 respectively incontrovertibly set the seal on the Queen as the figurehead of an ideology linking monarch and people with burgeoning colonial expansion, imperial greatness and national pride.[5]

While the Queen's grief for Prince Albert inevitably mellowed as the years passed, it was clear to all that the ageing monarch would never give up her widow's weeds. It suited her needs: Victoria might at last be reconciled to life without her husband, but to leave off her black, apart from being a betrayal of his sacred memory, would be to give notice of a return to normality—the one thing she wished to avoid. Her widow's weeds had become her shield and protector, and she clung steadfastly to them as she continued to battle with her irrational feelings of being overwhelmed and unable to cope. It was, to a certain extent, a very warped self-image; Victoria's perception of herself as the poor, weak, broken-hearted widow with shattered nerves had trapped her in a contradiction of what time and again she had demonstrated so clearly to others: her natural intelligence, the force of her indomitable personality and her great powers of endurance.[6]

Inevitably the ostentatious mourning rituals that she indulged in became outmoded, as social mores changed and the discussion of death increasingly became a taboo subject, but by now they had become the signifiers of Victoria's personal style as monarch, remaining very real, very visceral and absolutely central to who she was. Victoria's ladies-in-waiting, meanwhile, would continue to sigh about the cross they had to bear of wearing only lavender, white and grey for the remainder of her reign, for they were never allowed out of half-mourning when on duty; and time and again they were sent back into black as Victoria's friends and relatives died. If anything, the Queen's meticulous observation of the minutiae of bereavement deepened with the years, extending to her drawing-up of a detailed code of etiquette for the arrangement of all royal layings-out and funerals, which included specific instructions on the different types of shroud to be used for male and female, married and unmarried. With a series of deaths in the family and her entourage, she was kept indefinitely preoccupied, turning the performance of grief into her own very personal art form. There were many deaths for her to mourn, and in quick succession. In the 1870s she lost Lord Clarendon, Sir James Clark, General Grey, the former head of the royal nursery Lady Lyttleton, her favourite Scottish minister Reverend Macleod, her dear friend Countess Blücher, her old governess Baroness Lehzen, the devoted Lady Augusta Stanley, her literary hero Charles Dickens and her old friend Napoleon III—to name but a few. Dwelling on such losses was consoling for her; the constancy of the loyal mourner carrying the flame for the departed 'till all my widowed race be run' was a virtue she had long cultivated.[7] None was more mourned than her dear half-sister Feodora, when she died of cancer in September 1872. Victoria saw it as a turning point, one of the last links with her past. 'God's will be done,' she wrote in her journal, 'I stand so alone now, no near and dear one near my own age, or older, to whom I could look up to, left. All, all gone! She was my last near relative on an equality with me, the last link with my childhood and youth.'[8]

For Victoria, the death of her half-sister was 'the third great sorrow of her life'—along with the loss of Albert and her mother.[9] Reminders of Feodora took their place amidst the busts, statues, mourning jewellery, photographs, memorial cards and all the other *memento mori* that Queen Victoria gathered round her in one great mausoleum at Windsor dedicated to her many dear and departed. The security offered by all the paraphernalia of this 'obsolescent world' was infinitely preferable, always, to the 'anxiety of reality'.[10] For her the celebration of death was a kind of 'melancholy entertainment'—a piece of theatre that other pious widows aspired to emulate—and the more mournful, the better. If a ceremony was a tad cheerful the Queen 'always treated [it] with the utmost indifference', recalled lady-in-waiting Marie Mallet.[11] Many felt, as Mallet did, that Victoria's excessively lugubrious manner was perhaps a reflection of 'the dim shade of inherited melancholy from George III'.[12] She certainly made a great deal later in her reign of the funerary rites for her devoted John Brown in 1883, her haemophiliac son Leopold when he died in 1884, her grandson Eddy, Duke of Clarence in 1892, and Beatrice's husband, Prince Henry of Battenberg, in 1896. But she took a close interest too in the far more modest obsequies for lesser members of her household. In 1891, when one of the servants who had accompanied her on her holiday to Grasse in the south of France died, she gave instructions on the laying-out of the corpse, which were followed to the letter.

361

Marie Mallet found it very curious 'to see how the Queen takes the keenest interest in death and all its horrors'. 'Our whole talk,' she wrote home, 'has been of coffins and winding sheets.'[13] Nor did Victoria's interest in the rituals of death stop at human beings; she went to equal lengths when her favourite dogs died, ensuring they were buried with great ceremony and that monuments were erected over their graves.[14]

Queen Victoria's long intimacy with death at least had one transformative effect: it opened up her naturally consoling heart and made of her, in her old age, a great 'arbiter of grief'.[15] Always, and at every turn, she drew strength and comfort from commiserating with others in their bereavement, and many very personal and touching letters of condolence flowed from her pen. She of course continued to mourn the terrible void in her life left after Albert's death; forty years on from it she still missed his 'sheltering arm and wise help'.[16] Tennyson's great poem *In Memoriam* remained her touchstone, lines such as 'Ah dear, but come thou back to me' immortalising the longings of so many other widows and joining Victoria with them in 'one great rhythmic sigh of hopeless love'.[17]

With time and the deaths of so many she loved, public sympathy grew for the ageing queen. The British people respected her capacity for unending sorrow; there was something majestic, almost mystical about it. Victoria celebrated the mythic power of death like a pagan queen in tune with rituals beyond the understanding of ordinary mortals. And there were concessions in return: the remorseless black of her official image by degrees softened in its severity as the Queen took to relieving its monotony for official functions with white lace and diamonds, pearls and even her small diamond coronet rather than her widow's bonnet. Eventually her long-familiar image in black had come to represent not just the monarchy and, by association, the age, but also Victoria's most-admired qualities of solidity, respectability and dignity as benevolent, matriarchal widow. By the end of her reign she had become an inspiration to middle-class women everywhere; women such as writer H. G. Wells's mother, who for forty years had followed 'her acts and utterances, her goings forth and her lyings in, her great sorrow and her other bereavements with a passionate loyalty'. For ordinary women such as her, Queen Victoria was their 'compensatory personality'—an 'imaginative consolation for all the restrictions and hardships that her sex, her diminutive size, her motherhood and all the endless difficulties of life, imposed upon her'.[18]

In a triumphant subversion of the traditional image of the monarch in splendid robes of state at the heart of great ceremonial set-pieces, by the century's end Queen Victoria dominated the national consciousness as its antithesis—in all her bourgeois ordinariness—as revered widow and 'Mother of the People', and (on an international scale) as Grandmama of Europe. It was an extraordinary alchemy, unique to Queen Victoria as monarch. For by the end of her reign there was no one to rival her in her wisdom, her years of experience and her grasp of statesmanship and international affairs. 'She was the grandmother of us all,' as one Eton schoolboy fondly remembered her:

She was our fond old lady, guiding the land, the nation, the world almost, with her venerable influence, but also sharing and living in our lives and fortunes, those of the simpler sort especially, and all without pomp or display, though with a dignity so massive, till the glitter of other courts, the brilliance of other times appeared meretricious and tawdry beside the homeliness that she loved . . . She belonged to us all, and none in the world beside ourselves had a queen and a grandmother to compare with her.[19]

The role of grandmother to her extended European family in Scandinavia, Germany and Russia had brought Queen Victoria many preoccupations as she spent her old age planning, negotiating and frequently meddling in her family's dynastic marriages, in the process maintaining a prodigious, opinionated and lively correspondence with them all. Although never particularly fond of children she was in the end greatly consoled by her grandchildren, particularly the children of Beatrice and her husband Prince Henry of Battenberg, who lived with her for much of the time. The proliferation of photographs, paintings and magazine articles about them all—with the comings and goings of their many christenings, weddings and funerals—satisfied public demand and kept the royal family in the public eye even when the monarch herself was still out of sight.

\*     \*     \*

Queen Victoria had always viewed her bereavement as an inviolate 'sacred sorrow' and admitted to Vicky that 'those paroxysms of despair and yearning and longing and of daily, nightly longing to die . . . for the first three years never left me'.[20] But as she recovered from her debilitating grief—the grief 'that saps the mind', as Tennyson had called it—nothing would dim her determination to continue the public commemoration of Albert's memory and her own personal financial investment in it.[21] For the remainder of the century Albert's legacy proliferated in many more statues: some twenty-five in all, the one in Dublin narrowly missing destruction in a Fenian attempt to blow it up. Innumerable posthumous portraits, often based on *cartes de visite* of Albert, were commissioned for official bodies such as the Royal Society of Arts and municipal buildings across the United Kingdom, many of them paid for through public subscription. Stained-glass windows in churches were particularly popular, inspired by the one in St George's Chapel, Windsor, which had been constructed just in time for Bertie's wedding in 1863. Close by, the smaller Albert Memorial Chapel was remodelled by Gilbert Scott on the shell of the disused Wolsey Chapel and financed by Victoria, well in excess of the original estimate of £15,000. It opened to the public in December 1875, featuring yet another elaborate, Gothic cenotaph with a medieval-style recumbent effigy of Prince Albert in armour by the sculptor Henri de Triqueti.

By August 1871 the interior decorations of the Royal Mausoleum at Frogmore had been completed, using marble from Belgium and Portugal for the walls, altar and inlaid floor. But the beauty of the interior was only seen by the royal family and their entourage, and has been opened to general view only on a very occasional basis.[22] Its most frequent visitor for the forty years until her death was Victoria herself. Having her own set of keys, she would often go there to think and pray and contemplate Albert's effigy in times of trouble, national emergency and even moments of gratitude, such as Bertie's recovery from typhoid. In summer she often took picnics outside under the shade of a cedar tree. There was nothing morbid about it; it was her way of feeling close, of never forgetting. Above the entrance to the mausoleum she had had inscribed the words 'Farewell best beloved, here at last I shall rest with thee, with thee in Christ I shall rise again', but it was not until 4 February 1901 that she finally joined Albert there.

In the meantime, she had enough years and will left in her to oversee the expansion of the enduring national focus of Prince Albert's life and contribution to British art, architecture, science and culture. This was the complex of educational buildings popularly known as Albertopolis that sprang up in South Kensington in the last third of the century. The term had first been coined around the time of the Great Exhibition to refer to the land purchased with its profits—a site stretching from the northern to southern ends of what is now Exhibition Road. At one point Victoria had nursed ambitions to have all the great national collections of art and science collected here from across London, in one defining Albertian repository dominating the architectural landscape of late-Victorian London.[23] By 1866 the word 'Albertopolis' was in regular (though often irreverent) use; but it was many years before the entire complex was finished. The Victoria and Albert Museum was extended piecemeal until the mid-1880s, but the main frontage—for which Victoria laid the foundation stone in 1899—was not completed till 1909. Albertopolis reached its full incarnation with the addition of the Natural History Museum, the Science Museum, the Royal Albert Hall, the Royal College of Art, the Royal College of Music and the Imperial College of Science, Technology and Medicine. But the emotive focal point would always be the Albert Memorial in Hyde Park, which gave a sense of unity and identity to this ambitious Victorian exercise in Wagnerian grandeur.[24] With her popularity still on a high after the assassination attempt of February, on 1 July 1872 Victoria travelled to Hyde Park to inspect the completed memorial prior to it being opened to the public, after years of being surrounded by hoarding. However, only the outer shrine was complete—the central statue of Albert by Foley had been delayed by the sculptor's long illness and then death in 1874. It was not put in place until November 1875 and finally unveiled, after it had been gilded, on 8 March 1876.

The architect—the newly knighted Sir Gilbert Scott—had designed the Albert Memorial, he said, *'con amore'*, though the process had been 'long and painful'. He was proud of the 'exquisite phantasy' of its shrine-like character, but knew that he would have to bear the brunt of criticism of a work 'of a character peculiar, as I fancy, to this country'.[25] French diplomat Charles Gavard thought that the late Prince (a man who was very much *'comme il faut'*) would have been 'greatly

367

embarrassed' by this 'temple, kiosque, pagoda' being erected to his memory. 'It is enough to make Wellington jealous—he has only two statues,' he quipped.[26] On a visit to London in 1872 the American writer Mark Twain took a drive round Hyde Park and was struck by what he recalled as 'the brightest, freshest, loveliest bit of gigantic jewelry in all this battered and blackened old city'; Napoleon Bonaparte's tomb at Les Invalides in Paris paled in comparison. Twain had nothing but praise for the memorial's attention to detail and its artistry; but, having no idea at the time to whom the monument was dedicated (the statue of Albert not yet being in place), he assumed it was a memorial to Shakespeare. But no, it turned out to be a tribute 'to a most excellent foreign gentleman who was a happy type of the Good & the Kind, the Well-Meaning, the Mediochre, the Commonplace'. But who was Prince Albert now to the nation? A man who 'did no more for his country than five hundred tradesmen did in his own time, whose works are forgotten'. The monument was magnificent, but Twain was discomforted by the fact that it did not celebrate someone of the status of Shakespeare—but 'maybe he does not need it as much as the other'.[27]

By the time the memorial was fully open, fifteen years after Albert's death, its emotional impact had dissipated; for all its imposing magnificence, the Albert Memorial never won popular public approval. Viewed as a 'hideous Germanised eyesore', it fell into such neglect in the late twentieth century that there was talk of demolishing it. Several eccentric schemes were mooted for protecting it from further decay,

(*Right*) One of the last official photographs taken of Prince Albert during a sitting conducted by the French photographer Camille Silvy on 3 July 1861.

(*Left*) This engraving, probably based on one of the photographs taken by Silvy, emphasises how exhausted and puffy-faced Albert looked in the last months of his life.

(*Right*) Queen Victoria made a major concession for Bertie's Thanksgiving Service at St Paul's Cathedral on 27 February 1872 by adding a deep border of ermine to the unrelenting black of her costume.

(*Right*) The Queen's youngest daughter, four-year old Beatrice, prettily decked out in baby black mourning, much to her mother's considerable pride.

(*Above*) A grief-stricken Bertie, Prince of Wales and his ten-year-old brother Arthur, in Highland costume, were the only two of Albert's nine children to attend his funeral.

(*Top and above*) Popular engravings such as these from the *Illustrated London News*, show the solemnity of the funeral held at St George's Chapel Windsor on 23 December 1861.

(*Left*) Lady Augusta Bruce (later Stanley) the Queen's most trusted lady-in-waiting who with Princess Alice was her major carer in the first months after Albert's death.

(*Above*) William Jenner, the Queen's physician-extraordinary; (*Above right*) Henry Ponsonby, her long-suffering private secretary; (*Below*) the Queen's favourite physician, Sir James Clark;

(*Below*) Alfred Tennyson, her adored Poet Laureate.

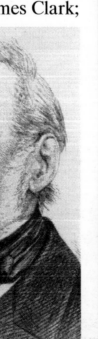

(*Left*) John Brown, Queen Victoria's Highland Servant, filled much of the void left by Albert, after he was transferred from Balmoral to Windsor in December 1864. He loyally served the Queen until his death in 1883.

(*Right*) This popular cartoon, 'John Brown Exercising the Queen', highlighted the growing indispensability of Brown, a fact which disturbed many at court and laid the Queen open to ridicule.

(*Above*) This cartoon from the satirical journal *The Tomahawk* of 16 November 1867 entitled 'God Save the Queen – The Past and the Future' encapsulated popular disquiet about the Queen's continuing absence from public duties.

JAY'S
LONDON GENERAL MOURNING WAREHOUSE,
247, 249, 251, REGENT STREET.

(*Left*) Jay's London General Mourning Warehouse at the corner of Regent's Street and Oxford Circus was one of several funeral outfitters that did a roaring trade after Prince Albert's death.

N° 4 ANNA        N° 5 KILLARNEY        N° 6 EDGAR

(*Above*) This fashion plate from Jay's catalogue of 1862 typifies the stylish mourning dresses that were available.

(*Above*) Anxious crowds gather outside the Mansion House in the City of London to read the latest bulletins on the Prince of Wales's serious illness, December 1871.

(*Left*) In November 1869 Queen Victoria was coaxed into a rare public appearance, to open London's newly constructed Blackfriars Bridge.

(*Above*) Benjamin Disraeli and (*below*) William Gladstone, the prime ministers who made concerted efforts during the 1870s to coax Queen Victoria out of retirement.

including enclosing it in a massive glass box. Fortunately the Victorian Society came to its rescue in 1987 and launched a concerted campaign that finally, after numerous crises over funding, saw it restored to all its magnificence (to the tune of £11 million) and reopened in time for the millennium in October 2000, to a firework display spelling out 'Albert Saved'.[28]

The written legacy of Prince Albert's life and work also continued, in tandem with the architectural one, at the Queen's behest and against the odds of fading public interest. At the end of 1874 the first volume of Theodore Martin's epic *Life of the Prince Consort* was published, but it would not be completed till volume five in 1880, by which time it already seemed passé in subject, sentiment and content. The dogged Martin was knighted for his labours that year, but, despite its heroic attention to detail, his *Life* was not a work of independent thought, but—much like Grey's *Early Life* before it—set in stone the Queen's prescribed view of her husband as plaster saint. It presented a portrait, wrote Lytton Strachey, of an 'impeccable waxwork' rather than a more rounded one of the real man. Nor did it go down well with some reviewers, due to the extent to which it revealed Victoria and Albert's close involvement in foreign affairs, to the point of interference. The real Prince Albert, whom Martin's book and all the other written memorials to him in their slavish hagiography had failed ever to capture—'the real creature, so full of energy and stress and torment, so mysterious and so unhappy, and so fallible, and so very human'—had completely disappeared.[29] By the 1880s public resistance was growing to any further representations of a prince who had been dead for more than twenty years and whom few had ever seen, let alone understood in his lifetime. People wanted their living queen among them, not interminable marble and bronze memorials to her dead, and increasingly remote, consort.

\*       \*       \*

It took many difficult years of crucifying self-doubt for Queen Victoria to overcome the sense of sexual inferiority that had become ingrained during her marriage to Prince Albert. Her grief had been deeply disempowering for the best part of ten years, but the supreme irony is that Albert's death was, perversely, the making of her as Queen, releasing her in the end from the perception of her own shortcomings as the dutiful 'little wife'. Despite all Albert's reassurances, Victoria had never been quite reconciled to what she considered the unseemliness of being a female monarch—consumed by official business at the expense of domestic and wifely duty. Albert, along with Melbourne and Peel, had taught her her trade as monarch and, had he lived, she would gladly, willingly, have given up her throne to him. Left without him, however, she had never for one moment—despite all her hysterical threats to abdicate—wanted to give up her sovereign power. That was the one thing she had always relished. Together, she and Albert had summoned an inglorious British monarchy from the dead during the years of their marriage, revolutionising the old Regency order and setting new moral standards. But had Albert lived, history would have been quite different; Victoria would have retreated further and

370

further into the background, ceding much of the day-to-day control of affairs of state to her husband. It was Albert's voice that had rung out ever louder across the pages of her official memoranda during the 1850s as he increased his power base, seeking to aggrandise the prerogatives of the Crown over the position of the Cabinet.[30] Albert's burgeoning power had created apprehension even then among Victoria's ladies-in-waiting Lady Ely and Lady Churchill, both of whom felt that his virtual control of government business as uncrowned king would have led to political and constitutional difficulties resulting in 'direct conflict between the Throne and the People'.[31]

In the end, boosted by the assumption of her new title of Empress of India and her unrivalled supremacy over her royal relatives in Europe as 'the *doyenne* of sovereigns', Queen Victoria grew into the familiar, imposing image that has come down to us of *'Victoria Regina et Imperatrix'*.[32] The British monarchy retained its firm hold upon the affections of the middle classes, who could relate to Victoria and her 'comfortable' motherliness and, through her, 'felt related in some degree to something that [was] socially great'—their very own royal family. It is a sentiment that has survived into the reign of her great-great-granddaughter, Elizabeth II, a monarch whose unerring sense of duty bears all the hallmarks of the tradition set by Prince Albert. But whether it will survive beyond her is doubtful.[33]

In retrospect, the years 1840–61 of Queen Victoria's marriage to Prince Albert might be more accurately described as Albertian in tone, a fact of which, in deference to her late husband, Victoria wholly approved.[34] For during the second half of the

1870s there came a sea change; people finally began referring to themselves as 'Victorians', endorsing what Victoria had herself said, after Albert's death in 1861, that it was 'the beginning of a new reign'.[35] By the 1880s Prince Albert's memory had so rapidly faded in rural areas, with no visible reminders of him, that villagers only knew that 'he had been the Queen's husband, though, oddly enough not the King, and that he had been so good that nobody had liked him in his lifetime, excepting the Queen, who "fairly doted"'.[36] The real man—so elusive to the British public in his lifetime, yet elevated by his grieving widow as a mythical, Arthurian figure— had by then been reduced to a cipher, languishing in the imposing shadow of his resurgent widow. Yes, hers had been a magnificent obsession and Victoria had stayed true to it, exhaustively commemorating her late husband in the way *she* saw fit. But the true Victorian age—of pageantry, pride and empire—was never his. It was entirely Victoria's. And it was yet to come.

# EPILOGUE

## *Christmas 1878*

For much of the 1870s Queen Victoria and her second daughter Princess Alice had been increasingly alienated from each other. Much of the breakdown in their relationship had to do with Alice's disapproval of her mother's retreat from duty and, by the same token, Victoria's dislike of her daughter's criticism and interference. Alice, in her view, could be tactless and unkind; she had become 'sharp and grand and wanting to have everything her own way'.[1] She was also rather too forward-thinking for Victoria's liking, affronted as she was by Alice's 'indelicate' interest in women's gynaecological matters and her passion for nursing. The truth of it was that so much enforced intimacy with her mother during Albert's last illness, and the six terrible months of grief she spent with Victoria until her marriage the following year, had left Princess Alice with a much deeper critical understanding of their mother than any of her other siblings, except perhaps Louise.

As a young girl Princess Alice had been shy, sweet-natured and compliant. She had shared many personality traits with her father, having the same thoughtful, studious nature. Prince Albert had always considered her to be the most beautiful of his children, although the severe features and sharp nose suggest a rather ethereal, mournful beauty and the last photographs of her convey a lingering sense of disappointment with life. She

373

always seemed physically frail, particularly after an attack of scarlet fever in 1855, and her health (like her father's) began to deteriorate at an early age. Once married and removed from her mother's domineering presence, Alice rapidly proved to be less compliant than she had been of old, and more than capable of standing up to Victoria's endless demands that the members of her family should subordinate themselves to what suited *her*. On visits to England Alice began to question Victoria's dictatorial manner and, at times, resist it.

Her marriage to Louis had begun happily enough in 1862, but a perennial shortage of money had imposed considerable constraints on the way Princess Alice ran her household and she was constantly having to make economies (as well as regularly appealing to her mother for financial help). Darmstadt, situated in the hills of the Odenwald near the River Rhine, was something of a social and cultural backwater. Alice was a devoted wife and mother and unquestioningly loyal, but she was not content to be consigned to a life that consisted solely of having babies to populate the minor principalities of Europe. Like her father, she wished to be of service to her adopted people and, also like him, set herself high standards of duty. At times she would appear overwhelmed by her sense of *noblesse oblige*, of the onerous responsibilities of her supposed position of privilege. 'Life was made for work and not pleasure,' she once remarked, and stoicism—if not an unhealthy propensity to martyrdom—became her enduring quality.[2] As time passed there was no disguising her increasing disappointment in her husband's emotional and intellectual shortcomings, which heightened her sense of loneliness and isolation. Louis, a born soldier, never shared Alice's passionate interests in the arts, nor did he comprehend her wide-reaching social concerns. She loved him as best she could, but she was disappointed. And so she found other channels for her personal frustrations, between her seven pregnancies throwing herself into an enormous and ever more consuming workload of philanthropic work, hospital visiting and nursing, particularly during the wars of 1866 and 1870–1 into which Hesse was drawn.

Princess Alice had always mourned her father with an intensity and pain that were as private as her mother's were public, and spent much of her time—like her sister Vicky in Berlin—writing long, consoling letters focused on alleviating her mother's grief rather than her own. On the anniversary of Albert's death in 1872 it was still hard for her to find the right words: 'From year to year they can but express the same: the grief at the loss of such a father, such a man, grows with me, and leaves a gap and a want that nothing on earth can ever fill up.'[3] Alice's personal sense of grief was made far worse by the tragic death of her three-year-old haemophiliac second son, Frittie (Wilhelm Friedrich), in 1873, after he fell out of a window. Quite simply, it broke her heart and also much of her spirit. She never recovered, succumbing more and more to stress, headaches and insomnia. Her life in Darmstadt became stultifying and her relationship with Louis ever more estranged. She was weary and depressed. It was not Louis's fault, she told him, in a poignant and passionate letter written to him from Balmoral in October 1876:

I am bitterly disappointed with myself when I look back, and see that in spite of great ambitions, good intentions, and real effort, my hopes have nevertheless been completely ship-wrecked . . . Rain—fine weather—things that have happened—that is all I ever have to tell you about—so utterly cut off is my *real self*, my innermost life, from yours . . . I have tried again and again to talk to you about more serious things, when I felt the need to do so—but we never meet each other—we have developed separately . . . and that is why I feel true companionship is an impossibility for us—because our thoughts will never meet.[4]

By the following year, when Louis succeeded his uncle as Grand Duke Ludwig IV of Hesse and by Rhine, Alice was dreading having to take up the even more onerous responsibilities of Grand Duchess. And then another tragedy struck. In November 1878 her fifteen-year-old daughter Victoria fell ill with diphtheria. Within eight days four of her other children, Alix, May, Irene and Ernie—as well as her husband—all contracted it; the remaining unaffected child, Ella, was sent to stay with relatives.

Alice nursed her family devotedly, day and night, but her five-year-old daughter May—her adored little May-flower 'with her precious dimples and loving ways'—died on 15 November.[5] She bravely kept the news from her other sick children for as long as she could, dreading that her only son Ernie might die; it would kill her, she said, 'to have to give him up too'.[6] Against all the doctors' warnings of the risk of infection, she could not however restrain herself from comforting Ernie with a kiss when he was told the terrible news of his sister's death. And it was not long after she had seen May's tiny little coffin covered with white flowers off to its funeral that Alice herself felt the first symptoms of the disease. The attack, coming on 7 December, was very severe.

As soon as she heard the news at Windsor, Victoria repaired to 'that sad blue room where darling Alice and I watched together 17 years ago, on this day' and prayed.[7] She sent Dr Jenner out to assist in Alice's care, but by the 13th Alice could no longer swallow. A telegram came from Louis: 'my prayers are exhausted,' he said. With the spectre of those two terrible Decembers of 1861 and 1871 hovering over her, Victoria headed down the hill to the mausoleum to pray. She was met en route by a footman with a telegram warning that things were desperate. The diphtheria membrane had spread across Alice's windpipe and she was having difficulty breathing. Later that day she rallied, but it was the same false hope as the hope they had had the day before Albert died. 'I sat in my room writing, watching anxiously for every footstep, every door opening,' Victoria recalled.[8]

In Darmstadt on the 13th Alice read the two letters from her mother brought by Dr Jenner. Then she lay down: 'Now I will go to sleep again,' she said, but overnight her condition deteriorated. At half-past eight the following morning—14th December 1878, the seventeenth anniversary of her father's death—Princess Alice died, whispering the names of May and 'dear papa'.[9] She was thirty-five. It was John Brown who brought the telegram from

Louis to Victoria as she sat down to breakfast that morning: 'Poor Mama, poor me, my happiness gone, dear, dear Alice. God's will be done.'[10] Victoria took the news with extraordinary calm; all the old animosity between herself and Alice forgotten in an instant. Her dead daughter—'this dear, talented, distinguished, tender-hearted, noble minded, sweet child'—had now joined Albert in the pantheon of her personal saints. Victoria was convinced that it was an act of divine intervention, that God had called Alice away to be with her father, and she took great comfort in its terrifying logic. It was 'almost incredible and most mysterious'. Husband and daughter had both been 'for ever united on this day of their birth into another better world'.[11]

Queen Victoria ordered three weeks' public mourning for Princess Alice. She prayed often in the Blue Room over the days that followed and commissioned her favourite sculptor Boehm to make an effigy of Alice to join Albert's sarcophagus in the mausoleum.[12] Another Christmas in black loomed, as the public, who had long held the Princess in high regard for her dedicated nursing of her father and brother, responded with the same kind of grief-stricken loyalty as in 1861 and 1871. Princess Alice, Grand Duchess of Hesse—'the model of family virtue, as a daughter, a sister, a wife and a mother'—was elevated to a state of beatitude that was never to be shared by any of her siblings.[13] Once again the letters and telegrams of condolence streamed in to Windsor; Victoria meanwhile waited anxiously for letters from Louis giving her 'every detail' of Alice's final hours and the funeral ceremony. 'You must treasure her in your hearts as a *Saint*,' she told Alice's children and siblings: they should do as she herself had done for Albert and 'mourn for their lost sister and mother, *more* and *more*, if not for a lifetime then for many years to come'.[14]

Princess Alice's funeral was held in Darmstadt on the afternoon of 18 December 1878; later that evening, in biting winter wind, her coffin was conveyed by torchlight to the Hesse family mausoleum at Rosenhöhe. Bertie and Leopold were there to watch as Alice's coffin was placed alongside those of Frittie and May, draped with the Union Jack, for Alice had always said that she wanted 'to go with the old English colours above me'.[15] In England the rest of the royal family attended a private service in her memory at Windsor. Once again the muffled bells pealed out the solemn threnody of royal death, British churches were draped in black, and shopkeepers put up their shutters as the nation mourned its lost princess. It was, as Christmas approached, 'a strange dreadful time', a time of mourning instead of celebration, now made doubly melancholy by the tragedy of yet another death in the royal family on the same day.[16] The presents the Queen gave to her servants that year were framed photographs of Alice. On 28 December her letter to the nation was published, thanking them for 'the most touching sympathy shown to her by all classes of her loyal and faithful subjects'. It was, she said, 'most soothing' to see 'how entirely her grief is shared by her people'.[17]

The loss of Alice was, for Victoria, a terrible landmark: 'the first break in my circle of children'.[18] As bereaved mother, widow and Queen, her position was now unassailable; her sacred monopoly on grief transcended all criticism. But it was a heavy burden. On New Year's Eve 1878 Victoria sat down, as she had so religiously done for forty-five years now, to write the daily entry in her journal. But how to describe 'The last day of this terrible year' as it sadly ebbed away? It had been punctuated by so much tragedy:

the poor King of Italy, dying on Jan 8th, the Pope on the 23rd . . . the deaths of Ld Ailesbury and Ld Kinnaird . . . the awful loss of the 'Eurydice' . . . the first attempt on the Emperor William's life, the death of the poor Dss of Argyll of May 25th, the loss of the 'Grosse Kurfürst', the death of Lord Russell, the death of the King of Hanover on June 12th, and his funeral at Windsor on the 24th . . . the death of the poor young Queen of Spain, the illness and death of poor good Sir Thomas Biddulph, then the Affghan [sic] war, the awful illness at Darmstadt, dear little May's death on Nov 16th, the alarming account of dearest Alice, on the 8th, & the dreadful ending to her illness on the 14th![19]

Through the long years of her widowhood and the loss of so many she had loved, Queen Victoria had steadfastly held to the mantra she had chosen for herself, from the words written by Tennyson to commemorate Prince Albert in the Preface to *The Idylls of the King*: 'Break Not Oh Woman's Heart But Still Endure'. The dead would always be a necessary part of her, extending their lingering shadow over the unravelling of her own final mortal days. But she had found the courage to go on. And she had indeed endured. Yes, she had come through.

# APPENDIX

# *What Killed Prince Albert?*

Shortly after Prince Albert died, the registrar's office in Windsor town was notified by the Prince of Wales and a death certificate was issued, stating that the Prince had died from typhoid fever of a duration of twenty-one days.[1] Thus began 150 years of largely unchallenged thinking on the Prince Consort's final illness. One cannot know now what political or other pressures may have obliged the royal doctors to come up with this definitive diagnosis in the face of their undoubted and openly expressed uncertainty during the last month of the Prince's life. But the cause of death as given fell into line with their rather pat deduction that Albert's illness could be traced back to that day at Sandhurst on 22 November when he had got soaking wet and caught a chill.

The onset of the chill had, it was assumed, laid him open to infection by typhoid from contaminated drinking water or food—but not at Sandhurst for, feeling too unwell that day, the Prince ate and drank nothing while he was there. The logical conclusion to be reached was that he had contracted typhoid on his return to Windsor. By way of justification, in a front-page article on 28 December, the *Examiner* claimed that of late 'Her Majesty herself has been covering her nose on the way to the castle through the bad smells of the town', thanks to the supposed threat of 'Windsor Fever'. But this and similar reports in the press to the effect that there had recently been two or three cases of typhoid in the castle were later shown to be erroneous, and were rebutted by assertions elsewhere that 'the queen's household have been lately in the enjoyment of good health'.[2] Nevertheless the argument would not go away; some newspapers were quick to remind readers of an outbreak in 1858 in the town, which had carried off thirty-nine people, while others did the opposite and attempted to dampen claims that 'typhus fever or some similar disorder is raging at Windsor'. The town was 'in a very healthy condition', claimed the *Morning Star*, and in a long article on 21 December the *Medical Times and Gazette* presented a detailed discussion of the sanitation at Windsor, pointing out that the castle's drainage system was entirely independent of that in the town where the previous outbreak had occurred. Having conducted its own investigation, the paper asserted that it knew 'of no place where a more complete or more carefully worked system is to be found'. The only conclusion it could come to was that 'unless some dire and unsuspected source of danger should lurk in the royal apartments themselves—ample and well ventilated as they apparently are—the sewerage system of the castle must be acquitted of all share in the mischief, and the causes of the national calamity which we all deplore must be looked for elsewhere'.[3]

In 1860s Britain it was decidedly unfashionable for a prince consort to die of typhoid fever, and palace officials were clearly anxious to counter any public anxiety that the Queen and her family were at risk of infection. Typhoid fever was a disease that in the main decimated the poor—those who lived in squalid, urban areas where there was rudimentary sanitation and shared public water pumps. It is caused by the water-borne bacterium *Salmonella typhi* and is clinically and bacteriologically quite distinct from typhus, an illness that can only be spread from person to person by lice, through close contact in overcrowded slums or barracks. Although the bacterial cause of typhoid was not understood in the 1860s, its clinical distinction from typhus had been recognised by Albert's physician Dr Jenner a decade previously. In his 1850 study 'On the Identity or Non-Identity of Typhus and Typhoid Fevers', based on clinical and autopsy findings in sixty-six fatal cases, Jenner had applied the epithet 'typhoid', meaning 'typhus-like'. The association with poverty might explain the reluctance of the royal doctors to define the illness as such to the Queen and her entourage. Either way, they appear to have hedged their bets with regard to their diagnosis. If the Prince had indeed contracted typhoid fever at Windsor, then it would be expected (as a water-borne disease) that others in the castle sharing the same water supply would also have succumbed. But there is no record of anyone other than Prince Albert falling sick, and no evidence of him having come into contact with anyone suffering from the disease during the previous month.

The course of typhoid fever is a very emphatic one, with three clear stages: the first week (known as the invasive stage) is one of high temperature, agonising headache and extreme prostration. Also characteristic are muscular feebleness and tremor of the limbs with a low delirium, often accompanied by the involuntary passing of faeces and urine, as well as the accumulation of sordes (foul-smelling matter) around the lips and gums. In the first week of his illness Prince Albert, despite being clearly unwell and complaining of aches and pains and a furred tongue, was up and about and not displaying any of these extreme symptoms. The second week of the disease is marked by rising fever, tenderness, swelling and sometimes a gurgling sound in the abdomen, as well as diarrhoea and an enlarged spleen. Again, the intermittent symptoms Prince Albert was displaying of fever, occasional diarrhoea and wakefulness, accompanied by constant moving about, do not fit this scenario. In the third week and final stage—the point at which, on 8 December, the Prince finally took to his bed and became fitfully delirious and feverish—he should in fact, according to the classic typhoid pattern, have been moving into a slow and gradual recovery from temperature and other symptoms. With typhoid, however, relapses were often common and death from complications such as intestinal haemorrhage or perforation, or simply sheer physical exhaustion leading to pneumonia, often carried off patients who might otherwise have recovered.[4]

Medical knowledge in 1861 was in fact very limited in its ability to provide an accurate diagnosis of a whole range of gastroenteric fevers, irritation or inflammation, which have since been described and individually named. Prince Albert's typhoid-like symptoms may well have been a feature of acute deterioration of a chronic gastrointestinal inflammation (often referred to by Victorian doctors as 'catarrh of the stomach'), which had been developing over a long period of time. This would have been characterised by periods of remission during which he felt fairly well, followed by acute bouts or flare-ups, when the symptoms became very marked and at times intolerable. This might well account for Albert's frequent complaints about painful stomach cramps, vomiting and diarrhoea, as well as toothache or inflamed gums, which could well have been symptomatic of a chronic (meaning long-standing) condition. There seems little doubt that his poor health was aggravated by his excessive workload, his inability to sit still for long, eat properly without rushing his food or take adequate rest. Periods of stress in both his official life and his private one with the Queen— notably her bouts of post-natal depression and the excessive burden of her hysterical grieving when her mother died—would have made matters worse. Insomnia and worry, both of which Albert was plagued by, may have lowered not only his physical resistance, but also his mental state, leading to clear phases of apathy and depression. The only palliatives available for insomnia were ether-based proprietary drugs such as Hoffman's Drops—a popular, but highly addictive medication that was used for everything from coughs to croup and low fever.[5] They would have done nothing to relieve the Prince's symptoms, which collectively could be expected to exacerbate any underlying chronic condition. After the Prince caught a severe chill from his soaking on two consecutive days—inspecting the buildings at Sandhurst on 22 November 1861, followed by a day's shooting in the rain on the 23rd—the symptoms he complained of (chilliness, general aches and pains, waves of fever and sensations of cold running down the back alternating with bouts of heat) were all scrupulously noted by Queen Victoria. These are non-specific symptoms of infection, which could have been a predisposing factor to, or a feature of, a final and terminal deterioration in the insidious condition that had been present for at least the last four well-documented years of his failing health, and probably for much longer. Medical science knew even then that 'influenza opens the door to enteric fever so frequently that there would seem to be some relation between the two'.[6]

\* \* \*

Two days after Prince Albert died, the first intimations of disquiet among medical practitioners were sounded, suggesting that perhaps officials at Windsor had not been entirely honest with the public over the circumstances of the Prince's illness, its diagnosis or treatment. In a letter to *The Times* on 16 December, headed 'The Medical Treatment of the Late Prince Consort', the pseudonymous correspondent 'Medicus' asked:

When so valuable a life as the late Prince Consort's is taken by the particular disease stated, would it not be as well to publish for the satisfaction of the general body of the medical profession, as well as the public, an account of the treatment adopted by the acting responsible physicians who prescribed for and attended on his late Royal Highness from the commencement to the deplorable close of his illness?

387

It was a perfectly reasonable question and soon afterwards the *Morning Chronicle* reported that 'Information with respect to the fatal illness of the late Prince is being anxiously looked for, as well as the details of the medical treatment.' What is more, the medical profession, according to the paper, was divided in its opinion, although not for the first or last time. Doubt had been expressed 'in many quarters' that the Prince's treatment had been 'scarcely sufficiently vigorous, and that too much reliance was placed upon the previously sound constitution and temperate habits of the sufferer'. The paper was then bold enough—considering the Queen's deep sensitivity at the time—to express the one thought uppermost in every medical mind: 'The profession generally have been naturally anxious that a *post-mortem* examination should take place, but to such a proceeding Her Majesty expressed her decided unwillingness.'[7]

It is not surprising that the Queen resolutely refused to agree to such a thing, considering how traumatised she was by Albert's death, let alone the thought of his corpse being so horribly violated. This fact alone would have put pressure on the royal doctors to give a definitive diagnosis, for if any official doubts had been expressed about the cause of the Prince's death, a post-mortem might, legally, have been called for and would undoubtedly have sent the Queen into hysterics. It is possible of course that the doctors had indeed suspected something long-term or more deep-seated: if a post-mortem had proved this to be the case, they would also have been open to accusations of culpability through their perceived mismanagement or misdiagnosis of Albert's condition. In any event

*The Lancet* called for an official account of the Prince's illness to be published, given that the unexpected rapidity with which he had sickened and died had run so counter to official bulletins that had played down the seriousness of his condition. *The Lancet* also raised the question of 'the discrepancies and manifold imperfections' in those bulletins. It was therefore with some disappointment, early in 1862, that the journal was obliged to announce, 'We are officially informed that the authentic and coherent account of the illness of the late Prince Consort, for which the profession and the public have manifested an anxious desire, will for the present be withheld.' Once again the palace had blocked freedom of information on the subject. The British medical profession remained far from satisfied, with *The Lancet* again echoing the view of many practitioners that such an omission 'leaves open to various conjectures a matter on which there should rest no shadow of doubt'.[8] The demands for clarification were, however, short-lived and rapidly receded in the light of the Queen's extreme grief. To persist on this point was deemed insensitive and intrusive.

On the medical fringe, however, accusations of mismanagement rumbled on. In January 1862 the *British Journal of Homoeopathy* criticised the attendance of four medical practitioners, feeling that this may have prompted a compromise in the treatment methods chosen: 'Under this heavy infliction of medical advice, the Royal patient had hardly a chance of recovery; for it is scarcely to be supposed that an intelligent or intelligible plan of treatment would be pursued under the direction of so many, and perhaps such opposite opinions.' In summary, the journal could not imagine the Prince's death occurring under 'the mild and efficacious medication' of homoeopathy. The Temperance movement too had its own uncompromising opinions. In an article entitled 'Alcoholic Medication' in the *Irish Temperance Journal*, John Pyper strongly criticised the constant dosing of the Prince with brandy during the last six days of his life. When a system was weakened by fever, Pyper argued, it needed rest—not alcoholic stimulation. 'Stimulation is not nutrition and the stimulant in fact becomes a depressant.' In the Prince Consort's case, 'keeping a person up' was 'a sure method of sinking him down'. The alcohol had merely provoked a 'still greater expenditure and waste of vital power'. In Pyper's view, any physician administering alcoholic stimulation was committing 'a grave, and also a grave-filling error'. A strong, hale man such as the Prince should not have died of 'gastric fever'. The opinion was of course misguided, though shared by many medical commentators at the time. Not being privy to the Prince's long-standing physical decline, they would have expected him—like similar men of his age 'of vigorous and athletic frame, a moderate liver, and with every thing conducive to health around him'—to have recovered from a bout of typhoid fever.[9] Pyper concluded that the 'gastric fever' had been complicated in the final stages by pulmonary congestion. This is reasonable enough, but pulmonary congestion is a pre-terminal event in any fatal condition as the heart fails or pneumonia develops.

Concerns about the Prince's treatment were not only posthumous. It is clear that Baron Stockmar, the person who knew Prince Albert best of all (from both a personal and medical point of view) had been greatly alarmed by Albert's failing health and his increasing malaise when he had seen him in 1860. By the end of that year Albert had endured a two-month attack of sickness, diarrhoea and pain; when he fell ill again in November 1861 Stockmar had sent regular messages to Windsor enquiring anxiously about the Prince's health. He had found the replies that he received evasive and unsatisfactory. Knowing that the royal family's medicines were supplied by the pharmacist Peter Squire of Oxford Street, he wrote directly to Squire, asking for details of the medication being prescribed. Correspondence between them on this matter has sadly not survived, though Squire's prescription book for the period reveals supplies of the antispasmodic and anticholinergic belladonna, a popular remedy for gastrointestinal disorders. No details of the amounts prescribed survive, nor is there (among all the other medications) any real sense of a concerted therapeutic regime for a specific condition in November to December 1861.[10]

Stockmar could of course do nothing from a distance, but whether or not accusations of gross mismanagement of the Prince's illness can be levelled at the royal doctors is still subject to debate. Lord Clarendon had, throughout, been scathing in his assessment. 'Nothing shall convince me that the Prince had all the assistance that medical skill might have afforded,' he wrote. Doctors Holland and Clark, in his opinion, were 'not even average old women; and nobody who is really ill would think of sending for either of them'. As for Jenner, he was a 'book physician' who 'had had little practice and experience'. William Gladstone certainly had no faith in Jenner and said that if he were his own doctor, he would 'get rid of him at once'. The vigour of the invective against the royal doctors by members of the government is in striking contrast to the pallid criticism of them elsewhere, but strong opinions are often founded on uncertainty. At least, however (and at Palmerston's stubborn insistence), another practitioner—Dr Watson—had been called in. 'But Watson (who is no specialist in fever cases),' Lord Clarendon observed, 'at once saw that he came too late to do any good, and that the case had got too much ahead to afford hope of recovery.' Jenner was very much the *parvenu* at court and still on trial. He would by necessity have been obliged to kowtow to Dr Clark's perceived superior wisdom and experience after twenty years in the job as the senior royal physician. Albert's fatal illness was his baptism by fire as a royal physician and, whether or not he was certain of the typhoid diagnosis—and the evidence suggests that he was extremely *uncertain*—typhoid fever can be difficult to diagnose even today, since it can be mimicked by several other illnesses marked by fever.

The biggest scorn, perhaps inevitably, has been heaped on Sir James Clark: he was incapable of treating 'a sick cat', in Clarendon's view, and had not just a past history of misdiagnosis, but also a habit of predicting recovery shortly before a patient died. He managed this unwelcome achievement not only in the case of Prince Albert, but also during the final illnesses of the former Prime Minister Robert Peel, Queen Louise of the Belgians, and

Albert's secretary, George Anson. Queen Victoria's biographer, Elizabeth Longford, concluded that Clark 'erred on the side of optimism' out of an eagerness to please.[11] Yet when Victoria was sixteen he had nursed her through a severe attack of typhoid fever, so he was not unfamiliar with the disease. Clarendon put it all down to a matter of personalities and precedence: 'One cannot speak with certainty,' he added, 'but it is horrible to think that such a life *may* have been sacrificed to Sir J. Clark's selfish jealousy of every member of his profession.'[12] Whether he agreed with Clark's methods or not, Jenner was obliged to join in the misguided jollying along of Prince Albert by pandering to his restlessness, instead of sending him firmly to bed. Longford argues that by doing this Clark 'hoped to keep the sufferer going simply by refusing to let him lie down and die'—the continual dosing with brandy being a vain attempt to keep his pulse up (the alcohol's function being to dilate his blood vessels) and prevent him slipping into unconsciousness.[13] Whether or not the doctors concurred in the diagnosis of typhoid fever, it is clear that they remained highly reluctant to state its true nature, for fear of traumatising not only their patient, but also the Queen. Nebulous explanations therefore persisted: when Crown Prince Frederick arrived at Osborne on 19 December, the Queen told him that according to the doctors, Albert's disease in addition to its 'rheumatic character' had had 'a certain typhic element to it, without actually becoming typhus'. The confusion of typhus and typhoid here may well be the Queen's or Fritz's, or both—it was common enough at the time; but the following day, in a second letter, Fritz told Vicky

393

that he had spoken at length to Dr Jenner, who had 'attributed dear Papa's suffering to "an abdominal typhus"'—a rather contrived euphemism at best.[14]

*       *       *

The claim that typhoid fever killed the Prince Consort was not challenged in medical literature until 1993, but as early as 1977 historian Daphne Bennett offered alternative diagnoses in her biography of Prince Albert, *King without a Crown*.[15] In a brief discussion at the end of her book, Bennett suggested that perhaps the Prince had been suffering from a chronic wasting disease such as cancer, with the proviso that at that time doctors were unable to detect many of the deeper-seated or slow-growing cancers, relying largely on visual identification.[16] In his 1987 biography of Queen Victoria, the American historian Stanley Weintraub included a footnote regarding Albert's death in which he questioned the diagnosis of typhoid fever as the sole cause. He argued that Albert's frequent problems with sore and painful gums could have been caused by an oversecretion of hydrochloric acid in the stomach—caused perhaps by carcinoma of the stomach or a wasting disease such as a peptic ulcer, and arguing that perhaps he had been genetically predisposed to cancer (his mother died of cancer of the uterus at the age of thirty-one).[17] Another suggestion made to the author is that on the basis of known symptoms and their duration, stomach or bowel cancer is unlikely, but that Prince Albert might have been suffering from neuroendochrine tumours—or, more specifically, gastrinoma. This was accompanied by speculation that this rarer form of cancer could have been complicated by a secondary neuroendochrine tumour in the pituitary gland, which might have been responsible not just for Albert's increasing fatigue and weakness, but also for his distressed mental state—the irritability that Queen Victoria regularly commented on—and (though we have no way of knowing except by inference) a marked loss of libido. Gastrinoma is a type of malignant tumour that was first described in the 1950s; it usually arises in the pancreas or duodenum and grows slowly over many years, and is more common in men than women. Symptoms are often dramatic, since the tumour secretes gastrin, causing stomach ulcers, leading to intermittent stomach pain, vomiting and diarrhoea, all symptoms similar to those experienced by Prince Albert. In some cases gastrinomas metastasise in the later stages into the liver, causing it to become enlarged. Had this been the case with Prince Albert, it would not have escaped the notice of his Victorian physicians, who prided themselves on their clinical examination skills.

\*　　　\*　　　\*

In December 1861 *The Lancet* came close to what is probably the most accurate contemporary assessment, when it pointed out soon after the Prince's death that 'there was enough of suddenness in the immediate termination of the disease to raise the question whether it might not have been due to ulcerative perforation of the bowel', adding 'that regrettably no facts had been provided to confirm this'. Quoting an article in the French medical press

395

in January 1862, the *Medical Times and Gazette* supported this claim. The 'hints of "gastric fever" given by the first bulletin did not say much, and were anything but scientific'. But the account of the Prince's rapid decline and death suggested that 'a perforation of the intestines' had taken place.[18]

But what was the precise nature of the chronic, inflammatory condition of the gut that had led to this perforation and from which the Prince had suffered for so long? In 1993 J. W. Paulley was the first to suggest that Prince Albert may have been suffering from ulcerative colitis, or more probably a condition resulting from a fault in the immune system with which it is often confused: Crohn's disease.[19] The possibility of ulcerative colitis (first described in 1859, two years before Prince Albert's death) can be dismissed, since the cardinal feature of this condition is bloody diarrhoea and not recurrent abdominal pain, vomiting and fever. The problem with a diagnosis of Crohn's, in the view of some commentators, is that it tends to be a genetic condition, particularly prevalent in Jewish families. Such commentators misunderstand the condition, which is today commonplace and affects any race or creed. The diagnosis, however, inadvertently plays into arguments that Prince Albert was illegitimate and that his real father was a Jewish courtier, Baron von Meyer, who had an affair with his mother, Louise. But so far absolutely no substantive evidence in support of illegitimacy has come to light.[20] As it happens, only about 5 per cent of sufferers of Crohn's disease have an affected first-degree relative. Perhaps of more note is the predilection of Crohn's disease to affect the upper socio-economic groups, and it remains today much more common in the developed world than in developing countries.

One other possibility remains: that the Prince had contracted abdominal tuberculosis, which can appear years after initial exposure to the TB bacillus and cause symptoms clinically indistinguishable from Crohn's. In 1861 it would have been impossible for the royal doctors to have diagnosed TB with any accuracy. The cause (the bacillus *Mycobacterium tuberculosis*) and tissue diagnosis of it were only described by Robert Koch in 1882 (work for which he was awarded the Nobel Prize in 1905). Abdominal TB was at that time much more common than it is today; it can affect the lining of the abdomen (the peritoneum) and, when it does, fluid known as ascites accumulates in the abdominal cavity. It is possible, therefore, that Prince Albert was suffering from ascites due to abdominal TB, although the Victorian doctors should have been able to detect this clinically by percussing his abdomen, which would have been taut and uncomfortable.

The evidence, when carefully considered, would thus seem to favour a diagnosis of Crohn's disease. But such a diagnosis is, of course, entirely retrospective and anachronistic, for it was not described for the first time until 1913 (by a Scotsman, T. Kennedy Dalziel) and then again in 1932 by the Jewish-American gastroenterologist Burrill Crohn and colleagues. Nevertheless, Crohn's disease, which is gradually progressive and fluctuating in intensity, could explain the chronic, relapsing and remitting problems with his gut that Prince Albert had suffered from, undetected, over many years. It would have caused episodic partial obstruction in the bowel, which, if untreated, can be complicated by small perforations or abscess, leading to peritonitis, septicaemia and death. But only explorative abdominal surgery—at that time unavailable—would have revealed this. Crohn's disease is characterised in some patients by other, extra-intestinal problems that are quite independent of the activity of Crohn's itself, such as arthritis. It is conceivable that the Prince's frequent complaints of 'rheumatic' pain in his joints for much of his adult life, and which became so prominent in his final month, could also have been a manifestation of Crohn's disease. Such symptoms often persist even when the intestinal inflammation is inactive and are thus more compatible with this overall diagnosis. Like abdominal TB, Crohn's can be exacerbated by overwork and anxiety. A recent study by Charles Bernstein in Winnipeg has shown that the risk of relapse in Crohn's is almost doubled in those suffering high levels of perceived stress.[21] If this were true in Albert's case, then the ultimate irony is that Victoria's assertions that Bertie killed his father may in a way be true. Albert's extreme response to his son's escapade at the Curragh, and the excessive levels of anxiety and insomnia that followed, combined with a chill and overwork, may well have provoked a severe flare-up of his condition.[22]

In many respects, therefore, the natural history of Crohn's disease would fit the long-term pattern of Prince Albert's documented physical complaints: periodic diarrhoea due to inflammation of the gut, with abdominal pain and vomiting from intestinal obstruction, fluctuating between acute episodes marked by swinging fevers and periods of remission. The bouts of depression and lassitude that he latterly suffered are also highly characteristic of an abscess or chronic sepsis. A pink rash of spots detected by the doctors on his abdomen in early December—which they seemed to fix on, almost with relief, as a sure sign of typhoid fever—could have been a consequence of cutaneous vasodilation brought on by septicaemia.[23] One must bear in mind how desperate the royal doctors must have been in those final days: their most important patient (apart from the Queen) dying at a young age; the eyes of Her Majesty, their (envious) colleagues and the world upon them; and there they were, uncertain of their diagnosis.

The final three-week cycle of illness would thus fit the time-frame for Crohn's, complicated by an abdominal abscess, developing into a terminal event with the opportunistic onset of pneumonia ('pulmonary congestion') in the last two or three days.[24] Although it was not widely reported at the time, this latter view concurs with that of other medical practitioners: what in fact carried the Prince off was that age-old nemesis of the sick and vulnerable—pneumonia.[25] In the absence of solid clinical evidence, or detailed autopsy notes, we can only ever make informed guesses. Whatever it was that killed Prince Albert—and we must now lay the ghost of typhoid fever to rest—no antibiotics, steroids or abdominal surgery were then available to help him. To Prince Albert himself must go the final word; if his condition had not killed him in 1861, it is likely, as he told his stepmother, that the 'weak stomach with which I came into the world . . . I shall take with me to my grave'.[26]

# Notes

## Epigraphs

1. Prince Albert, letter to Baron Stockmar, 24 January 1854, Martin II: 559–60.
2. Rev. Norman Macleod, RA VIC/MAIN/R/2/28.
3. Queen Victoria, letter to King of Prussia, in Gernsheim and Gernsheim, *Queen Victoria:* p. 140.

## Prologue: Christmas 1860

1. For Christmas 1860, see Robert Chambers, *The Book of Days: A Miscellany*, vol. 2, 1878, pp. 760–1.
2. For descriptions and illustrations of the interior, see Girouard, *Windsor*, pp. 65–74; Hibbert, *The Court at Windsor*, pp. 207–8.
3. For descriptions of the Grand Corridor, see Stoney & Weltzien, *My Mistress the Queen*, pp. 40–1; Paget, *Embassies of Other Days*, vol. I, pp. 74–5.
4. Fulford, *Dearest Child*, p. 213; Hibbert, *Court at Windsor*, p. 107.
5. For the Queen's preferences for beech logs and gas lighting, see Girouard, *Windsor*, p. 72.
6. Martin, *Life of the Prince Consort* [hereafter Martin], I: 127.
7. Jagow, *Letters of the Prince Consort*, p. 134.
8. Moncure, Daniel Conway, *Memories and Experiences*, vol. I, New York: Houghton, Mifflin

& Co., p. 256.

9. RA VIC/MAIN/QVJ/1860: 23 December.
10. In the words of Colonel Francis Seymour, Groom of the Bedchamber to Prince Albert; RA VIC/ADDC10/44.
11. Dasent, *Delane*, p. 13.
12. Ibid., p. 14; Stoney & Weltzien, *My Mistress the Queen*, p. 42 re kitchens at Windsor.
13. RA VIC/MAIN/QVJ/1860: 24 December.
14. See entry for 'Christmas', in Rappaport, *Queen Victoria*, pp. 90–3; 'How the Christmas Tree came to the English Court', *The Times*, 22 December 1958; Hibbert, *Court at Windsor*, pp. 207–8. For descriptions of Christmas at Windsor in 1847 and 1851 by lady-in-waiting Eleanor Stanley, see Stanley, *Twenty Years at Court*, pp. 155–7 and 201–3.
15. Dasent, *Delane*, p. 15; RA VIC/MAIN/QVJ/1860: 24 December.
16. Dasent, *Delane*, p. 16.
17. Ibid.; RA VIC/MAIN/QVJ/1860: 24 December.
18. Ibid., 25 December.
19. Dennison, *Last Princess*, p. 22.
20. Dasent, *Delane*, p. 17.
21. RA VIC/MAIN/QVJ/1860: 27 December.
22. Dasent, *Delane*, p. 15.
23. Wake, *Princess Louise*, p. 23.
24. Stanley, *Twenty Years at Court*, p. 202.
25. Dasent, *Delane*, p. 15.
26. RA VIC/MAIN/QVJ/1860: 30 December. The anxieties expressed about Europe refer to the ongoing struggle for Italian unification.
27. Wyndham, *Correspondence of Sarah Spencer*, p. 401.

*Chapter 1: 'The Treadmill of Never-Ending Business'*

Title: Martin, V: 109–10.

1. Rhodes James, *Prince Albert*, p. 31.
2. In 1825 Duke Ernst succeeded his uncle, the Duke of Saxe-Gotha-Altenburg. The duchies shared with his estranged wife were reorganised and in 1826 Ernst assumed the new title of Duke of Saxe-Coburg & Gotha.
3. For a discussion of the unfounded rumours of illegitimacy, see James, *Prince Albert*, pp. 21–2; Hector Bolitho, who wrote extensively on Victoria and Albert, also scotched the rumours in a chapter, 'The Prince Consort's Mother', in his *A Biographer's Notebook*, pp. 102–22. For a recent argument in support of illegitimacy, see Richard Sotnick, *The Coburg Conspiracy*, London: Ephesus Publishing, 2008, esp. pp. 174–84.
4. Bolitho, *Prince Consort and His Brother,* p. 209.
5. Benson, *Queen Victoria*, p. 160; Ponsonby, *Mary Ponsonby*, p. 2.
6. Fulford, *Prince Consort*, p. 41.
7. Benson and Esher, *Letters of Queen Victoria 1837–1861*, II: 237 [hereafter Benson & Esher].
8. Jagow, *Letters of the Prince Consort*, p. 23.
9. Ibid., p. 24.
10. James, *Prince Albert,* p. 32.
11. Grey, *Early Years*, p. 200.
12. Duff, *Albert & Victoria*, p. 159.
13. Creston, *Youthful Queen Victoria*, p. 445.
14. Jerrold, *Heart of Queen Victoria*, p. 17.
15. Rosamund Brunel Gotch, *Maria Lady Callcott,*

London: John Murray, 1937, p. 295. The remark was made by the Queen's dresser, Marianne Skerrett.

16. Jagow, *Letters of the Prince Consort*, pp. 347–8.
17. John Jolliffe, ed., *Neglected Genius: The Diaries of Benjamin Robert Haydon 1808–1846*, London: Hutchinson, 1990, p. 203.
18. Hewett, '. . . *and Mr Fortescue*', pp. 25–6.
19. Warwick, *Afterthoughts*, p. 4.
20. Martin, I: 160.
21. Fulford, *Greville Memoirs*, p. 223.
22. Emden, *Behind the Throne*, p. 68.
23. RAVIC/MAIN/R/1/193. This anonymous account of the last hours of the Prince Consort was written by one of the royal governesses, Madame Hocédé.
24. Tisdall, *Queen Victoria's Private Life*, p. 22. Other nicknames were 'The Pauper Prince' and 'Lovely Albert'. Lord Clarendon would privately refer to the Queen and Albert in correspondence as 'Joseph and Eliza' (ibid., p. 42); Victoria was also referred to as 'Queen Albertine'.
25. Hewett, '. . . *and Mr Fortescue*', p. 25.
26. Emden, *Behind the Throne*, p. 99.
27. Crawford, *Victoria, Queen and Ruler*, p. 52.
28. Pound, *Albert*, p. 182.
29. Martin, II: 248.
30. Benson & Esher, III: 317.
31. Martin, II: 60.
32. Benson & Esher, III: 240.
33. Clark, *Sir Charles Lyell*, p. 354.
34. Fulford, *Prince Consort*, p. 117.
35. Pound, *Albert*, p. 261.
36. Benson & Esher, II: 362.
37. Fulford, *Dearest Child*, p. 215.
38. Hibbert, *Queen Victoria in Her Letters and*

*Journals* [hereafter *Letters and Journals*], p. 151; Bolitho, *Reign of Queen Victoria*, p. 147. For useful summaries of the Prince's health, see Duff, *Albert & Victoria*, pp. 24–5, and Bennett, *King Without a Crown*, pp. 239–44, 341–2, 352–4.

39. Jagow, *Letters of the Prince Consort*, p. 305.
40. James, *Prince Albert*, p. 211.
41. Stafford, *Henry Greville*, vol. 4, p. 227.
42. Bolitho, *Albert Prince Consort*, p. 166.
43. Magnus, *King Edward the Seventh*, p. 17; Strachey, *Queen Victoria*, p. 168.
44. Bennett, *King Without a Crown*, p. 360; Martin, V: 338–9; James, *Prince Albert*, p. 264.

Chapter 2: 'The First Real Blow of Misfortune'

1. Hibbert, *Letters and Journals*, p. 112.
2. Fulford, *Greville Memoirs*, p. 247. Downer, *Queen's Knight*, p. 104.
3. Corti, *English Empress*, p. 54.
4. Marie Louise, *My Memories of Six Reigns*, London: Evans Brothers, 1956, p. 113.
5. Fulford, *Prince Consort*, p. 25.
6. Phillipe Jullian, *Edward and the Edwardians*, London: Sidgwick & Jackson, 1967, p. 17.
7. Corti, *English Empress*, pp. 50–1; Pakula, *Uncommon Woman*, pp. 148–9.
8. Fulford, *Dearest Child*, p. 174.
9. Ibid, pp. 173–4.
10. Bennett, *King Without a Crown*, p. 341; Fulford, *Dearest Child*, p. 206.
11. Fulford, *Dearest Child*, p. 216.
12. Martin, IV: 500–1.
13. Ibid., 501–2.

14. Ibid., V: 109–10.
15. See Weintraub, *Uncrowned King*, pp. 393–4 ; Martin, V: 202–3; James, *Prince Albert*, p. 265; Jerrold, *Married Life of Queen Victoria*, p. 393.
16. Martin, V: 275; Bennett, *Uncrowned King*, p. 341.
17. Martin, V: 288.
18. See Robbins, 'The Missing Doctor', pp. 289–90.
19. *Zalkiel's Almanac* for 1861, London: George Berger, p. 19.
20. In 1850 Jenner published *On the Identity or Non-Identity of Typhoid and Typhus Fevers*, the result of two years' study of 'continued fever' at the London Fever Hospital. In it he defined the differences between the two fevers, typhoid being conveyed by contaminated food or water, typhus being carried by lice.
21. Fulford, *Dearest Child*, p. 309.
22. Martin, V: 292–4.
23. Ibid., 295–6.
24. Fulford, *Dearest Child*, p. 308.
25. Ibid., p. 310.
26. RA VIC/MAIN/QVJ/1861: 21 February.
27. Martin, V: 317–18. Martin's account of the Duchess's death is on pp. 316–19 and the quotations from the Queen's journal given in it differ from later published versions, in that these were used by Martin before the text was expurgated after the Queen's death.
28. Noel, *Princess Alice*, p. 70.
29. Wyndham, *Correspondence of Sarah Spencer*, pp. 338–9.
30. Martin, I: 202–3.
31. Benson & Esher, III: 6–7.
32. Fulford, *Dearest Child*, pp. 199–200, letter of 6 July 1859.

33. See K. D. Mathews and C. G. Reynolds, *Queen Victoria*, Oxford: Oxford University Press, pp. 50–1.
34. See Albert, *Queen Victoria's Sister*, chapter 9, and Fulford, *Dearest Child*, pp. 247, 249.
35. Strafford, *Henry Greville*, vol. 3, p. 33.
36. Fulford, *Dearest Child*, pp. 297–301.
37. Wallace, *Journal of Benjamin Moran*, p. 832.
38. For Victoria's response to seeing death for the first time, see her letter to Leopold of 26 March, in *Letters and Journals*, pp. 118–19. For the Duchess's funeral, see *The Times*, 26 March 1861.
39. Sarah Tytler, *Life of Her Gracious Majesty*, vol. 2, pp. 185–6.
40. For court mourning during these years, see Stanley, *Twenty Years at Court*, pp. 320–3, 376–7.
41. Kennedy, *My Dear Duchess*, p. 141; Wiebe, *Letters of Benjamin Disraeli*, vol. 8, p. 155, letter of Lord Henry Lennox, 18 December 1861.
42. See Lord Clarendon to the Duchess of Manchester, 3 April 1861, in Kennedy, *My Dear Duchess*, pp. 143–4.
43. See letters to King Leopold, 26 and 30 March, Benson & Esher, III: 436–7.
44. Windsor & Bolitho, *Letters of Lady Augusta Stanley*, p. 200. [Hereafter Windsor & Bolitho]
45. Albert, Queen Victoria's Sister, p. 189; Fulford, Dearest Child, p. 319.
46. Martin, V: 335.
47. Fulford, *Dearest Child*, p. 334.
48. RA LC/LCO/CER/MEMO, Drawing Room, St James's Palace, 19 June 1861.
49. Weintraub, *Uncrowned King*, p. 402.

1. Martin, V: 374.
2. Ibid.: 369.
3. Cooke, *Memoir of HRH Princess Mary Adelaide*, vol. 1, p. 364.
4. Ibid.
5. Magnus, *King Edward the Seventh*, p. 47.
6. RA VIC/MAIN/QVJ/1861: 26 August.
7. Duff, *Queen Victoria's Highland Journals*, pp. 96–100.
8. Fulford, Dearest Child, p. 354.
9. Duff, *Queen Victoria's Highland Journals*, p. 106.
10. Ibid., p. 110.
11. Ibid., p. 114. Victoria added the postscript when preparing her Highland journals for publication in 1867.
12. Benson & Esher, III: 461–2.
13. Martin, V: 407.
14. Letter to Queen Victoria, 22 October 1861, quoted in Fulford, *Prince Consort*, p. 249.
15. Fulford, *Dearest Child*, p. 356. Victoria was in fact alluding to a favourite sermon by the Roman Catholic convert, Henry Edward Manning, 'The Commemoration of the Faithful Departed', in which he alluded to 'the habitual consciousness of an unseen world'. She had this quotation copied into her 'Album Consolativum' after Albert's death. See BL Add. 62089, fo. 95; *Sermons of Henry Edward Manning*, London: James Burns, 1846, p. 326.
16. Martin, V: 415; Fulford, *Dearest Mama*, p. 30.
17. Katharine M. Lyell, ed., *Life, Letters and Journals of Sir Charles Lyell*, vol. 2, London: John Murray, 1881, p. 352.

18. See Strafford, *Henry Greville*, vol. 4, p. 226; Longford, *Victoria*, p. 313.
19. RA VIC/MAIN/R/1/193.
20. Branks, *Heaven our Home*, pp. 8, 6, 70, 52. Branks was a minister at Torphichen, West Lothian; his book tapped into the vogue for consolatory literature and homilies on death that proliferated after Albert died; it was in its eighth reprint by 1876. *Meet for Heaven* followed in 1862 and *Life in Heaven* in 1863—all three books selling in hundreds of thousands of copies in the UK and USA.
21. RA VIC/MAIN/Z/142: 9 November 1861. All comments by the Queen on Prince Albert's illness from this date to his death on 14 December are taken from her 'Account of My Beloved Albert's Last Fatal Illness from Nov. 9 to Dec. 14 1861'. Entries up to the 11 December were written at the time; those after were added in 1862 and 1872.
22. Royal Pharmaceutical Society: Queen Victoria's Account Book 1861–1869, which lists at the front the Queen's regular standing order for medical supplies, followed by monthly lists of additional supplies and their cost.
23. Martin, V: 411.
24. Longford, *Victoria RI*, pp. 292–3.
25. Fulford, *Dearest Child*, pp. 365–6.
26. Ibid., p. 367.
27. Wake, *Princess Louise*, p. 42; Jerrold, *Queen Victoria's John Brown*, p. 52.
28. Fulford, *Dearest Child*, p. 356.
29. Corti, *English Empress*, p. 72.
30. Hibbert, *Edward VII*, p. 40; St Aubyn, *Queen Victoria*, p. 279.

31. Bennett, *King Without a Crown*, p. 367; Scheele, *Prince Consort*, pp. 125–6.
32. Fulford, *Prince Consort*, p. 266.
33. RA VIC/MAIN/Z/141/94: 16 November 1861.
34. RA VIC/MAIN/Z/141/95: 20 November 1861.
35. Martin, V: 414.
36. RA VIC/MAIN/Z/142: 22 November.
37. Martin, V: 417; RA VIC/MAIN/Z/142: 23 and 25 November.
38. See Nightingale's letter to Mary Clarke Mohl, December 1861: 'Albert was really a Minister—this very few knew. Sir Robert Peel taught him'. Vicinus and Nergaard, *Ever Yours*, pp. 232–3
39. Martin, V: 412; James, *Prince Albert,* p. 270.
40. Martin, V: 417.
41. Benson & Esher, III: 468.
42. Martin, V: 417.
43. Wilson, *Life and Times of Queen Victoria*, vol. 2, p. 100. For an interesting medical article on the Windsor epidemic, see William Budd, 'On Intestinal Fever, *The Lancet*, vol. 1, 1860, pp. 390–1.
44. Martin, V: 417; Fulford, *Dearest Child*, pp. 369–70.
45. Ibid., 28 November.
46. Martin, V: 423.
47. Martin, V: 427.
48. Ball, *Queen Victoria: Scenes and Incidents*, p. 197.
49. Fulford, *Dearest Child*, p. 370; Corti, *English Empress*, p. 72.
50. *The Times*, 28 November 1861.
51. Fulford, *Dearest Child*, p. 370.
52. Bennett, *King Without a Crown*, p. 370.
53. Benson & Esher, III: 469.
54. Martin, V: 427.

55. RA VIC/MAIN/Z/142: 1 December.
56. For a detailed discussion of the Trent affair, see Weintraub, *Uncrowned King*, pp. 408–21.
57. Fulford, *Dearest Child*, p. 371.


*Chapter 4: 'Our* Most *Precious Invalid'*

Title: Queen Victoria to the King of the Belgians, 12 December 1861, in Benson & Esher III: 472.

1. RA VIC/MAIN/Z/142: 2 December 1861.
2. Ibid.
3. 'Descriptions of the death of the Prince Consort, 1861', Correspondence and Papers of Dean Stanley, Cheshire Archives, DSA 85.
4. RA VIC/MAIN/Z/142: 3 December.
5. RA VIC/Add MS/C/10/47: 2 December 1861.
6. RA VIC/MAIN/Z/142: 2 December 1861.
7. Connell, *Regina v. Palmerston*, p. 313.
8. RA VIC/MAIN/Z/142: 3 December.
9. Whittle, *Victoria and Albert*, pp. 106, 113.
10. Staatsarchiv Darmstadt: Briefe von Alice D24 Nr. 25/3–4 & 26/1: 3 December 1861; Windsor and Bolitho, p. 239.
11. Staatsarchiv Darmstadt: Briefe von Alice D24 Nr. 25/3–4 & 26/1: 3 December 1861.
12. See e.g. *Daily News* and *Morning Chronicle*, 4 December 1861.
13. RA VIC/MAIN/Z/142: 4 December.
14. Ibid; Benson & Esher, III: 470.
15. BL Add. MS 44325, Gladstone Papers vol. CCXL, letters from the Duchess of Sutherland; 19 December 1861.
16. RA VIC/MAIN/Z/142: 4 December.

17. Ibid.: 5 December.
18. Ibid.
19. Martin, V: 430. Excerpts from the Queen's account of Prince Albert's final days from 1 to 8 December as originally written by her can be found in Martin, V: 427–38. These original entries, published in 1880, differ slightly from their later edited transcription made after the Queen's death.
20. RA VIC/MAIN/Z/142: 6 December.
21. Ibid.
22. Benson & Esher, III: 470–1.
23. Fulford, *Dearest Child*, p. 372.
24. Connell, *Regina v. Palmerston*, pp. 313–14.
25. RA VIC/MAIN/Z/142: 7 December.
26. Martin, V: 431; Longford, *Victoria RI*, p. 296.
27. Ibid.
28. Ibid.
29. Connell, *Regina v. Palmerston*, p. 314.
30. RA VIC/MAIN/Z/142: 7 December.
31. Ibid.
32. Ibid.; Windsor & Bolitho, p. 240.
33. RA VIC/MAIN/R/1/193. Written on 23 December by Madame Hocédé to her family this letter was later, in all innocence, published by them in France, going against the Queen's demand for absolute discretion by members of the royal household. It appeared as a pamphlet, published by John Snow of Paternoster Row in 1864, and was syndicated in many journals as 'The Last Hours of Prince Albert'—see e.g. *Wesleyan-Methodist Magazine*, vol. 47, 1864, p. 906. Madame Hocédé had, by then, been quietly pensioned off for the additional indiscretion of encouraging the princesses to read 'unsuitable' books and went to

Paris, where she set up a school for Protestant English girls. Kenyon, *Scenes in the Life*, p. 78.

34. Ibid.
35. Ibid.
36. Staatsarchiv Darmstadt: Briefe von Alice D24 Nr. 25/3–4 & 26/1: 9 December 1861.
37. RA VIC/MAIN/Z/142: 8 December.
38. Ibid.
39. *The Times*, 9 December 1861.
40. RA VIC/MAIN/Z/142: 9 December.
41. Fulford, *Dearest Child*, p. 374.
42. Holland, *Notebooks of a Spinster Lady*, p. 177; Fulford, *Dearest Child*, p. 177.
43. Connell, *Regina v. Palmerston*, p. 315.
44. RA VIC/MAIN/R 1/12: 10 December.
45. RA VIC/MAIN/M/R/1/58/9 and 18.
46. Martin, V: 435.
47. RA VIC/MAIN/Z/142: 10 December.
48. Fulford, *Dearest Child*, p. 373.
49. Ibid.
50. RA VIC/MAIN/Z/142: 11 December; part of this entry was written by the Queen that day, the continuation on 24 December.
51. Martin, V: 435.
52. Benson & Esher, III: 472.
53. Fulford, *Dearest Mama*, p. 374; RA VIC/MAIN/Z/142: 11 December.
54. RA VIC/MAIN/Z/142: 11 December.
55. Ibid.
56. Strafford, Henry Greville, vol. 3, p. 420.
57. Malmesbury, *Memoirs of an Ex-Minister*, p. 550.
58. RA VIC/MAIN/R/1/19, 22: 11–12 December.
59. Walsh, *Religious Life and Influence of Queen Victoria*, p. 114.
60. See e.g. *Morning Chronicle, Daily News, The Times*

for 12 December 1861.
61. Walsh, *Religious Life and Influence of Queen Victoria*, p. 113.
62. RA VIC/MAIN/Z/142: 12 December.
63. Benson & Esher: III 472–3.
64. Connell, *Regina vs Palmerston*, p. 316; RA VIC/MAIN/M/R/1/58/19: 11 December.
65. Martin, V: 437.
66. RA VIC/MAIN/Z/142: 12 December.
67. Ibid.: 13 December, though the entry was actually written by the Queen on the 24th.
68. Windsor & Bolitho, p. 241.
69. Longford, *Victoria RI*, p. 299; Hibbert, *Letters and Journals*, p. 156.
70. RA VIC/MAIN/Z/142: 13 December.
71. Windsor & Bolitho, pp. 241–2.
72. RA VIC/MAIN/Z/142: 13 December.
73. Ibid., the remainder of this entry was written by the Queen on 27 March 1862; Windsor & Bolitho, pp. 241–2.
74. RA VIC/MAIN/Z/142: 13 December.
75. Connell, *Regina v. Palmerston*, pp. 316–17.
76. News International Archive, Delane Correspondence: TT/ED/JTD/10/131.
77. *Leeds Mercury*, 14 December.
78. *The Times*, 13 December; Walford, *Life of the Prince Consort*, p. 88; *Daily News*, 9 December; *Newcastle Courant*, 13 December.
79. Vicinus and Nergaard, *Ever Yours*, p. 232.
80. *The Times*, 14 December.
81. Downer, *Queen's Knight*, pp. 121–2.
82. 'Descriptions of the death of the Prince Consort, 1861'.

Title: written by Queen Victoria beneath a photograph of herself, Bertie, Helena and Vicky taken on 28 March 1862; Gernsheim & Gernsheim, *Queen Victoria*, p. 16.

1. Sala, *Life and Adventures*, vol. I, p. 373.
2. *North Wales Chronicle*, 14 December; *The Times*, 14 December.
3. *Glasgow Herald*, 14 December.
4. *The Times*, 14 December.
5. Dasent, *Delane*, vol. II, p. 38.
6. RA VIC/MAIN/Z/142: 14 December. This entry, not written by the Queen until February 1872, is preceded by this explanation: 'I have never had the courage to attempt to describe this dreadful day—but I will now at the distance of ten years . . . with the terrible facts imprinted on my mind as clearly as tho' they had occurred yesterday, and with the help of notes scrawled down at the time, try to describe it.'
7. Palmerston Papers, Broadlands Archive, quoted in Woodham-Smith, *Queen Victoria*, p. 428.
8. RA VIC/MAIN/Z/142: 14 December.
9. RA VIC/Add A/36/5: Henry Ponsonby to his mother, 14 December.
10. RA VIC/MAIN/Z/142: 14 December.
11. Ibid.
12. Staatsarchiv Darmstadt: Briefe von Alice D24 Nr. 25/3–4 & 26/1: 14 December, letter of Prince of Wales.
13. RA VIC/MAIN/Z/142: 14 December.
14. The children's governess, Sarah Hildyard, was another of the Queen's most loyal servants,

joining her in 1849. Known to Victoria as 'Tilla', she was forced to retire through ill health in 1867. Victoria found it a terrible wrench to lose her: 'I need not tell you how impossible it is to speak to you of your leaving us and indeed I will not call it by that name. It must be no real parting after 18 years . . . You have been a treasure to us.' Hildyard died in 1889. An album of photographs of the royal family collected by Sarah Hildyard can be found in the Raymond Richards Collection (M78), at Keele University Library, Special Collections. For extracts from Queen Victoria's letters written to Tilla, see *The Age* (Melbourne), 24 May 1956.

15. Ibid.
16. RA VIC/ADDC6, Lady Geraldine Somerset diaries: 14 December.
17. Villiers, *Vanished Victorian*, p. 309.
18. For the official bulletins issued from Windsor during 13 and 14 December, see Walford, *Life of the Prince Consort*, pp. 89–96.
19. *Medical Times and Gazette*, 14 December.
20. Pakula, *Uncommon Woman*, p. 159.
21. Walford, *Life of the Prince Consort*, p. 76.
22. Weintraub, *Uncrowned King*, p. 43.
23. Martin, V: 440.
24. RA VIC/MAIN/Z/142: 14 December; Walsh, *Religious Life*, p. 113.
25. Martin, V: 441.
26. Downer, *Queen's Knight*, pp. 122–3.
27. Aston, *Duke of Connaught*, p. 46; Downer, *Queen's Knight*, p. 123.
28. RA VIC/MAIN/Z/142: 14 December.
29. RA VIC/Add MS/4/25/819, diary of Howard Elphinstone: 14 December 1861.

30. Noel, *Princess Alice*, p. 78.
31. Windsor & Bolitho, p. 246.
32. Bodleian Library, Special Collections: MS.Eng. misc.d.472, Charles Pugh diary: 14 December 1861.
33. Martin, V: 441.
34. RA VIC/ADDU/416, account of Lady Winchester: 25 December 1861; RA VIC/ADDC6, Lady Geraldine Somerset diaries: 15 December 1861.
35. Windsor and Bolitho, p. 245; Noel, *Princess Alice*, p. 77.
36. RA VIC/ADDU/4, account of Lady Winchester: 25 December 1861.
37. Windsor & Bolitho, p. 245.
38. RA VIC/MAIN/Z/142: 14 December. A famous painting of the scene was later executed by William Walton, 'The Last Moments of HRH The Prince Consort', which slightly conflicts with some of the descriptions of where people were positioned in the room.
39. Battiscombe, 'Gerald Wellesley', p. 128; RA VIC/MAIN/Z/142; 'Descriptions of the death of the Prince Consort, 1861'.
40. The earliest source for this much-repeated, and possibly apocryphal, story of the shriek is Augustus Hare, *The Story of My Life*, vol. 2, London: George Allen, 1900.
41. RA VIC/ADDA8/377, letter from Miss Ella Taylor: 7 January 1872, p. 3.
42. Kuhn, *Henry and Mary Ponsonby*, p. 82.
43. RA VIC/ADDA25/819, diary of Howard Elphinstone: 14 December 1861.
44. 'Descriptions of the death of the Prince Consort, 1861'.
45. Stanley, *Twenty Years at Court*, pp. 388–9; Windsor

& Bolitho, p. 246; Tisdall, *Private Life*, p. 50;
Duff, *Shy Princess*, p. 10; RA VIC/MAIN/Z/142:
14 December.

46. RA VIC/MAIN/Z/142: 14 December. Martin's
account, V: 438–41, of the deathbed from the
Queen's journals has some slight variations,
because it was taken from her journal before
its later editing by Princess Beatrice. See n. 19
chapter 4 above.

47. RA VIC/ADDA8/377, letter from Miss Ella
Taylor: 7 January 1872, p. 3.

48. RA VIC/ADDA25/819, diary of Howard
Elphinstone: 14 December 1861; Downer, *The
Queen's Knight*, p. 125.

49. Thomas Catling, *My Life's Pilgrimage*, London:
John Murray, 1911, pp. 75–6.

50. Strafford, ed., *Leaves from the Diary of Henry
Greville*, vol. 3, p. 417.

51. Sheppard, *George Duke of Cambridge: A Memoir*,
p. 222.

52. Wilson, *Life and Times of Queen Victoria*, vol. 2,
p. 98.

53. Connell, *Regina v. Palmerston*, pp. 317–18.

54. Sala, *Life and Adventures*, vol. I, p. 374.

Chapter 6: *'Our Great National Calamity'*

Title: *British Mothers' Journal and Domestic
Magazine*, 1 January 1862.

1. Walford, *Life of the Prince Consort*, p. 125.
2. Philip Hedgeland, 'National Grief and Some of
its Uses' (sermon), Penzance, 1861, p. 3.
3. *Morning Star*, 16 December.

4. Hudson, *Munby*, p. 111; Pound, *Albert*, p. 350.
5. RA VIC/R2/112, letter of Adam Sedwick to Sir Charles Phipps: 10 February 1862.
6. *Leeds Intelligencer*, 21 December 1861.
7. Walford, *Life of the Prince Consort*, pp. 142–7; Wolffe, *Great Deaths*, p. 83.
8. Walford, *Life of the Prince Consort*, pp. 134–9; *The Times*, 16 December.
9. Nirad C. Chaudhuri, *Scholar Extraordinary: The Life of Professor the Right Honourable Friedrich Max Müller*, London: Chatto & Windus, 1974, p. 255.
10. Chomet, *Helena*, p. 17; House and Storey, *Letters of Charles Dickens*, vol. 9, p. 540.
11. Sheppard, *George, Duke of Cambridge*, vol. 1, p. 223.
12. 'Descriptions of the death of the Prince Consort, 1861'.
13. BL Add. MS 44325, Gladstone Papers, vol. CCXL, letters from the Duchess of Sutherland: ff. 266–73, 19 December 1861.
14. Cooke, *Princess Mary Adelaide,* vol. I, pp. 377.
15. RA VIC/ADDA8/376 p. 4 and RA VIC/ADDU/396/2, letter of Princess Mary Adelaide of Teck: 16 and 19 December 1861.
16. Maxwell, *Life and Letters of the 4th Earl of Clarendon*, p. 253.
17. RA VIC/ADDU/396, undated letter, c. 17 December, from the Hon. Victoria Stuart Wortley.
18. Windsor & Bolitho, p. 246; Fulford, *Dearest Child*, p. 375; Smith, *Life of Her Majesty*, p. 356.
19. RA VIC/R 1/51: 15 December 1861.
20. Walford, *Life of the Prince Consort*, pp. 152, 155.
21. Martin Duberman, *Charles Francis Adams,*

Stanford: Stanford University Press, 1968, p. 286.

22. Hibbert, *Court at Windsor*, p. 212.

23. Cooke, *Princess Mary Adelaide*, vol. I, p. 378.

24. C. E. Smith, *Journals and Correspondence of Lady Eastlake*, vol. 2, London: John Murray, 1895, p. 164.

25. 'Descriptions of the death of the Prince Consort, 1861'; Protheroe, *Dean Stanley*, p. 307.

26. Whittle, *Victoria and Albert*, p. 116; Dimond and Taylor, *Crown and Camera*, p. 23; Darby and Smith, *Cult of the Prince Consort*, pp. 4, 6; Fulford, *Dearest Mama*, pp. 27, 31.

27. Walford, *Life of the Prince Consort*, p. 130.

28. Louis Blanc, *Letters on England*, vol. 1, London: Sampson Low, 1866, p. 226.

29. *The Times, Morning Chronicle, Morning Post, Scotsman, Daily News*, 16 December 1861.

30. *Daily Telegraph*, 16 December 1861.

31. *London Gazette Extraordinary*, 16, 17 and 18 December 1861.

32. Chappell & Pollard, *Letters of Mrs Gaskell*, p. 671; diary of Charles Pugh, Bodleian Library, MS. Eng.misc.d 472.

33. RA VIC/R2/112, letter of Adam Sedgwick to Sir Charles Phipps: 10 February 1862.

34. *Leeds Mercury*, 17 December, 1861.

35. *Illustrated London News*, 28 December 1861.

36. PRO LC 1-90-005, 16 December 1861.

37. Wilson, *Life and Times of Queen Victoria*, p. 99; Walford, *Life of the Prince Consort*, p. 105.

38. Maxwell, *Life and Letters of the 4th Earl of Clarendon*, p. 253; Baroness Bloomfield, ed., *Extracts of Letters from Maria, Marchioness of Normanby*, London: Simson & Co., 1892, p. 424.

39. RA VIC/ADDU/32: 16 December 1861; Fulford,

*Dearest Mama*, p. 23.

40. *Daily Telegraph*, 17 December; RA VIC/ ADDU/396/1: undated letter, probably 17 December 1861.
41. *The Times*, 17 and 18 December; *London Review*, 21 December; Journal of John Rashdall, 22 December, Bodleian Library MS.Eng.misc.e 359.
42. *Illustrated London News*, 21 December 1861, p. 616.
43. *Glasgow Herald*, 17 December.
44. *The Times*, *Guardian* and *Telegraph*, 17 and 18 December. For a résumé of major press coverage, see Walford, *Life of the Prince Consort*, pp. 157–83. An extensive body of newspaper cuttings can also be found in RA VIC/MAIN/ M/64 and 66. Many press notices and magazine articles, as well as selected sermons and poetry, were collected by William Thomas Kime and published in a handsome large-format edition with embossed gold covers, as *Albert the Good: A Nation's Tribute of Affection to the Memory of a Truly Virtuous Prince*, London: J. F. Shaw & Co., 1862.
45. Vincent, *Disraeli, Derby and the Conservative Party*, p. 180. Cecil Y. Lang, ed., *Letters of Matthew Arnold*, vol. 2, Charlottesville: University Press of Virginia, 1996, p. 111; Wyndham, *Correspondence of Sarah Spencer*, pp. 422, 423.
46. 'Descriptions of the death of the Prince Consort, 1861'.
47. Ibid.
48. Maxwell, *Life and Letters of the 4th Earl of Clarendon*, p. 255; RA VIC/ADDC6, Lady Geraldine Somerset diaries: 15 and 16 December 1861.
49. Weibe, *Benjamin Disraeli Letters*, vol. 8, p. 156,

letter to Lady Londonderry, 19 December 1861.

50. Wake, *Princess Louise*, p. 45.
51. Dennison, *Princess Beatrice*, p. 26; Arkhiv der Hessischen Hausstiftung, Briefe 7.1/1-BA 3; letter of 19 December 1861.
52. Fulford, *Dearest Mama*, p. 23.
53. Ibid., pp. 24, 25.
54. Wake, *Princess Louise*, p. 45.
55. 'Descriptions of the death of the Prince Consort, 1861'.
56. Ibid; Longford, *Victoria RI*, p. 308.
57. Longford, *Victoria RI*, p. 308.
58. Jerrold, *The Widowhood of Queen Victoria*, p. 11.
59. Downer, *Queen's Knight*, p. 40; Tisdall, *Queen Victoria's Private Life*, p. 50.
60. Corti, *English Empress*, p. 77.
61. Benson & Esher, III: 473–4.
62. Smith & Howitt, *Cassells' Illustrated History of England*, p. 589.
63. *Daily Telegraph*, 19 December 1861.
64. Cowley, *Paris Embassy*, p. 228.
65. *Observer*, 16 December 1861.
66. Lyn MacDonald, ed., *Florence Nightingale's Theology*, Ontario: Wilfred Laurier University Press, 2002, p. 365.

## Chapter 7: 'Will They Do Him Justice Now?'

1. See Kate Williams, *Becoming Queen*, London: Hutchinson, 2008, pp. 116–23, and Schor, *Bearing the Dead*, ch. 6, 'A Nation's Sorrows', for an account of the mourning for Princess Charlotte. For royal funeral conventions, see Curl, *Victorian Celebration of Death*, pp. 224–5.

2. *Lady's Newspaper*, 21 December 1861.
3. The will is as quoted in Corti, *English Empress*, p. 77. In it Albert nominated Victoria as executrix and provided for the distribution of the extensive property he had acquired in the UK, but it was never lodged at the wills registry at Somerset House and probate was therefore never formally granted. The full details of its contents were never revealed, for the Queen refused to allow it to be published, prompting later rumbling accusations of Albert's avariciousness in his acquisition of wealth as consort.
4. See the Appendix to this book, 'What Killed Prince Albert?'
5. The practice of embalming royal corpses had been discontinued by the time of Albert's death, hence the prompt sealing-down of the coffin on the evening of the 16th. See RA LC/LCO/CER/ MEMO/Private Memoranda Ceremonials/93: Funeral of HRH the Prince Consort, Windsor, December 23rd 1861—Lord Chamberlain's Account. For the coffins, see Walford, *Life of the Prince Consort*, pp. 112–13.
6. PRO LC 1-90-007, 17 December 1861. Drugget was a thick felted fabric of wool and/or cotton used as a floor covering.
7. *Morning Post*, 21 December 1861. Banting had also made the state coffin for the Duke of Wellington in 1852. The firm of Thomas and William Banting was one of the most prosperous London undertakers. William (1796–1878), who succeeded his father, died a very rich man with an estate valued at around £70,000 (equivalent to £3.3 million today), and is also notable as the originator of probably the first Atkins-type high-

protein diet, which he devised to combat his own increasingly uncomfortable obesity. Published in 1863 as 'A Letter on Corpulence Addressed to the Public', it highlighted the dangers of excess sugar and fat in the diet and ran into four editions by 1869. Banting donated the profits to charity. The firm held the Royal Warrant for funerals until 1928; his sons organised Queen Victoria's funeral in 1901.

8. See Wolffe, *Great Deaths*, pp. 17–20, 194, 202–3.
9. RA LC/LCO/CER/MEMO/Private Memoranda Ceremonials/95: Funeral of HRH the Prince Consort, Windsor, December 23rd 1861—Lord Chamberlain's Account.
10. The accounts of the Prince's funeral were extensive, with many papers running syndications of those in *The Times* and the *Daily Telegraph* of 24 December, which are the most detailed and graphic. Sala's highly colourful, Gothic account for the *Telegraph* can also be found as Appendix II to Duff, *Albert and Victoria*, pp. 270–84.
11. Argyll, *Autobiography and Memoirs*, vol. 2, p.184; Hardman, *Mid-Victorian Pepys*, p. 69.
12. Information from Paul Frecker. See also *Photographic News*, 28 February 1862, pp 104, 108.
13. Hudson, *Munby*, p. 111.
14. Cooke, *Memoir of Princess Mary Adelaide*, p. 379; Smith & Howitt, *Cassells' Illustrated History of England*, p. 589.
15. Downer, *Queen's Knight*, p. 127.
16. Elvey, *Sir George Elvey*, p. 183. Croft's settings of the burial service were composed for the funeral of Queen Anne in 1714; both these chants or 'sentences' formed part of the funeral service for

Princess Diana at Westminster Abbey in 1997.

17. RA LC/LCO/CER/MEMO/Private Memoranda Ceremonials/93: Funeral of HRH the Prince Consort, Windsor, December 23rd 1861—Lord Chamberlain's Account.

18. Jerrold, *Widowhood of Queen Victoria*, p.11; Elvey, *Sir George Elvey*, pp. 183–4; *The Times*, 24 December.

19. *The Times*, 24 December; Dasent, *Delane*, p. 40.

20. Duff, *Hessian Tapestry*, p. 73.

21. Dasent, *Delane*, p. 40; Playfair, *Memoirs*, p. 190; Ashwell, *Life of the Right Rev Samuel Wilberforce*, vol. 3, p. 44; Prothero, *Life and Correspondence of Arthur Penrhyn Stanley*, p. 61.

22. Darby, *Cult of the Prince Consort*, p. 1; Hardman, *Mid-Victorian Pepys,* p. 70; *Bell's Life in London*, 29 December 1861.

23. O'Brien, *Correspondence of Lord Overstone*, vol. II, p. 980.

24. Wolffe, *Great Deaths*, pp. 84, 97–8.

25. RA VIC/MAIN/R/2/22.

26. RA VIC/MAIN/R/2/15; Wolffe, *Great Deaths*, p. 195.

27. *Jewish Chronicle*, 27 December; Loewe, *Diaries of Sir Moses and Lady Montefiore*, p. 13; John Purves, ed., *Letters from the Cape*, London: Oxford University Press, 1921, p. 68.

28. *Punch*, 21 December 1861.

29. Lee, *Queen Victoria*, vol. 2, p. 320; Wiebe, *Benjamin Disraeli Letters*, p. 164.

30. Stockmar, *Memoirs of Baron Stockmar*, vol.1, p. xviii; RA VIC/MAIN/M/64/28: letter of 9 January 1862. The existing German Confederation, created at the end of the Napoleonic Wars, consisted of thirty-eight states. They were finally

unified under Bismarck, ten years after Albert's death, in 1871.

## Chapter 8: 'How Will the Queen Bear It?'

1. Fulford, *Dearest Mama*, pp. 26, 28; Sheppard, *George Duke of Cambridge*, p. 223.
2. RA VIC/MAIN/R/1/181, Phipps to Lord Sydney: 22 December 1861; Sheppard, *George Duke of Cambridge*, vol. 1, p. 224.
3. RA VIC/MAIN/R/1/193: 23 December 1861— letter written by Madame Hocédé.
4. Arkhiv der Hessischen Hausstiftung, Briefe 7.1/1-BA 3; letter of 19 December 1861.
5. RA VIC/ADDA8/377, letter from Miss Ella Taylor, 7 January 1862, p. 5; Fulford, *Dearest Mama*, p. 27.
6. Noel, *Princess Alice*, p. 77; Arkhiv der Hessischen Hausstiftung, Briefe 7.1/1-BA 3: 20 December; RA VIC/MAIN/M/64/6: 22 December 1861.
7. Land and Shannon, *Letters of Alfred Lord Tennyson*, vol. II, p. 291; RA VIC/MAIN/R2/6: 24 December; Dyson and Tennyson, *Dear and Honoured Lady*, p. 54.
8. Dyson, *Dear and Honoured Lady*, pp. 66–7.
9. Jackman and Haasse, eds, *Stranger in the House*, p. 227, Letter to Lady Malet, 30 December 1861. Queen Sophie exchanged numerous gossipy letters at the time with those privy to the events close to the Queen and the royal household, including Lady Malet, the Duchess of Westmorland, Lady Ely, Lord Clarendon, the Duchess of Cambridge and Lady Cowley, but sadly none of their letters to her survive in the Royal Dutch Archives at The

Hague.
10. Fulford, *Dearest Mama*, p. 30.
11. Martineau, *Selected Letters*, pp. 196–7; Vincent, p. 181.
12. Benson & Esher, III: 476.
13. Ponsonby, *Mary Ponsonby*, p. 47.
14. RA VIC/ADDA8/376: letter of 19 December 1861, pp. 5–6.
15. Fulford, *Dearest Mama*, p. 27; RA VIC/MAIN/R/2/3: 24 December 1861.
16. Wake, *Princess Louise*, p. 4; News International Archive, TT/ED/JTD/A/022, Torrington Letters, c. 19 December; Wellesley, *The Paris Embassy*, p. 229.
17. Chapel & Pollard, *Letters of Mrs Gaskell*, p. 671, 26 December 1861; Moran, *Journal of Benjamin Moran*, vol. 2, p. 957, 24 December 1861.
18. *Morning Post*, 16 December; *Daily Telegraph*, 19 December; *Essex & West Suffolk Gazette*, 20 December; *Daily Telegraph*, 25 December.
19. *Daily News*, 25 and 26 December.
20. Russell, *My Diary*, p. 218.
21. *New York Times*, 5 January 1862; Maria Lydig Daly, *Diary of a Union Lady* 1861–65, New York: Funk & Wagnalls, 1962, p. 106.
22. Charles Reynolds Brown, *Lincoln, The Greatest Man of the Nineteenth Century*, New York: Little & Ives, 1922, p. 58.
23. Russell, *My Diary*, pp. 218–19. News that Mason and Slidell and their secretaries had been released and put on a steamer for Southampton did not reach the British press till 8 January 1862.
24. RA VIC/MAIN/M/58/4: 19 December 1861.
25. News International Archive, TT/ED/JTD/A/022, Torrington letters: c. 19 December 1861.

26. RA VIC/MAIN/M/58/16: 26 December 1861.
27. Watson, *Queen at Home*, p. 156.
28. *New York Times*, 5 January 1861; Martineau, *Selected Letters*, letter to Henry Reeve, Christmas Day 1861.
29. C. E. Byles, *The Life and Letters of R. S. Hawker*, London: John Lane, 1905, p. 353.
30. *Daily News*, 20 December; *Morning Post*, 16 December.

*Part Two: The Broken-Hearted Widow*

*Chapter 9: 'All Alone!'*

1. Windsor & Bolitho, p. 251; RA VIC/MAIN/QVJ: 1 January 1862.
2. RA VIC/MAIN/QVJ/1862: 1 January 1862.
3. 'Descriptions of the death of the Prince Consort, 1861'.
4. Ricks, *Poems of Tennyson*, vol. 2, p. 451.
5. Queen Victoria's 'Album Consolativum' appears to have been passed on to her daughter Vicky in Berlin after the Queen's death in 1901—perhaps to comfort the former Empress in her own terminal illness—she died of cancer seven months after her mother. The album is now in the British Library, BL Add. 62089; a second volume (62090) was started in 1872, but never completed.
6. Dasent, *Delane*, p. 48.
7. Bolitho, *Further Letters of Queen Victoria*, p. 118; RA VIC/ADDA8/390, Miss Ella Taylor's Reminiscences of HRH The Duchess of Cambridge, p. 51.
8. Longford, *Victoria RI*, p. 308.
9. Fulford, *Dearest Mama*, p. 47.

10. Jenni Calder, *Robert Louis Stevenson: A Life Study*, Oxford: Oxford University Press, 1980, p. 21; Wake, *Princess Louise*, p. 47.

11. RA VIC/ADDU/16, Lord Hertford's Account of Queen Victoria, Osborne, 1862, pp. 4–5.

12. Argyll, *Autobiography and Memoirs*, vol. 2, p. 188.

13. RA VIC/ADDA8/380: Miss Ella Taylor's Reminiscences of HRH The Duchess of Cambridge.

14. Erskine, *Twenty Years at Court*, p. 395.

15. Fulford, *Dearest Mama*, p. 47.

16. Buckle, *Letters of Queen Victoria* [hereafter Buckle], I: 9.

17. Kennedy, *My Dear Duchess*, p. 189; Dasent, *Delane*, p. 46.

18. Countess Blücher, née Madeline Dallas, was the daughter of the Lord Chief Justice. She married Count Gustavus Blücher von Wahlstadt in 1828. She was a close friend of Vicky in Berlin and attended the birth of her first child, Wilhelm, in 1859. The Countess died on 19 March 1870.

19. Sir Edwin Landseer said of Skerrett that 'If anything goes wrong in Buckingham Palace, Balmoral, or Windsor, whether a crowned head or a scullery maid is concerned, Miss Skerrett is always sent for to put it right.' Skerrett was the daughter of an officer who had served with distinction in the Peninsular War. See John Callcott Horsely, *Recollections of a Royal Academician*, London: John Murray, 1903, p. 128.

20. For an interesting discussion of Queen Victoria's ladies, see Reynolds, *Aristocratic Women*, pp. 212–17.

21. See Dulcie M. Ashdown, *Ladies-in-Waiting*, London: Arthur Barker, pp. 178–80.

22. The Duchess of Athole (1814–97) was widowed in 1864. Like Lady Jane Churchill (1826–1900), who remained with the Queen for forty-six years, Athole died still in service to Victoria. Lady Ely (1821–90) finally managed to retire in 1889 after thirty-eight years of devoted service.

23. Buckle, I: 12; RA VIC/MAIN/QVJ/1862: 21 January. Sadly, the spontaneous and more heartfelt expressions of popular support that must have been sent to the Queen from semi-literate, ordinary members of the public have not survived in the Royal Archives. The more formal tributes of monarchs and statesmen are, however, plentiful.

24. Kenyon, *Scenes in the Life of the Royal Family*, p. 224.

25. RA VIC/MAIN/Y/83/63: 1 February 1862.

26. Lily Wolpitz, ed., *The Diaries of John Rose of Cape Town 1848–1873*, Cape Town: Friends of South African Library, 1990, p. 97; Purves, *Letters from the Cape*, p. 47.

27. Purves, *Letters from the Cape*, p. 71; Orfeur Cavanagh, *Reminiscences of an Indian Official*, London: W. Allen, 1884, pp. 320–2; unpublished letter of Ra Haniraka, 3 March 1862, courtesy Ian Shapiro.

28. 'Address of the New Zealand Chiefs to Her Majesty, on the Death of the Prince Consort', forwarded by the governor of NZ, Sir George Grey, *Annual Register*, 1862, vol. 104, p. 503.

29. Buckle, I: 6.

30. Tooley, *Personal Life of Queen Victoria*, pp. 204–5.

31. Windsor & Bolitho, p. 257.

32. Another similar marble bust of Albert by Theed was completed in 1862 and two years later placed

in the entrance hall at Osborne. See Darby & Smith, *Cult*, p. 7.

33. Plunkett, *Queen Victoria: First Media Monarch*, p. 181.
34. See *Crown and Camera*, pp. 23–5, and Gere and Rudoe, *Jewellery in the Age* of *Queen Victoria*, pp. 56–7.
35. Zeepvat, *Prince Leopold*, p. 32.
36. A plaster cast of the statue was placed at the foot of the staircase at Balmoral that August and replaced with the marble version in October 1863. A massive bronze version of the statue, on a bust of rough stone, was later erected in the castle grounds for all the Queen's staff to see. See Darby & Smith, *Cult*, p. 11.
37. Bennett, *King without a Crown*, p. 376; Martin, II: 537. A statue was eventually raised in 1863, though in front of the Royal Albert Hall, not far from the Albert Memorial, rather than in the park.
38. Kennedy, *My Dear Duchess*, p. 199.
39. News International Archive, TT/ED/JTD/A/022, Torrington Letters.
40. *The Times*, 15 January 1862; *Temple Bar*, vol. IV, 1862, p. 575.
41. *Morning Post*, 13 August 1862; Kennedy, *My Dear Duchess*, p. 199.
42. Storey, ed., *Letters of Charles Dickens*, vol. 10, pp. 28 and 69: 1 February 1862 and 10 April 1862.
43. Dasent, *Delane*, pp. 44–5.
44. Fulford, *Dearest Mama*, p. 36.
45. Battiscombe, 'Gerald Wellesley', pp. 134–5; Darby & Smith, *Cult*, p. 23.
46. Kennedy, *My Dear Duchess*, pp. 189, 207.
47. Villiers, *Vanished Victorian*, p. 317.

48. Ibid., pp. 317, 319.
49. Connell, *Regina v. Palmerston*, p. 323; Maxwell, *Life of Letters of . . . 4th Earl of Clarendon*, p. 257.
50. *Annual Register*, vol. 104, p. 10; Wiebe, *Letters of Benjamin Disraeli*, vol. 8, p. 170.
51. RA VIC/MAIN/QVJ/1862: 26 February; Hibbert, *Court at Windsor*, p. 212.
52. Epton, *Queen Victoria and her Daughters*, p. 102; Corti, *English Empress*, p. 81.
53. RA VIC/ADDU/16, Lord Hertford's Account of Queen Victoria; Fulford, Dearest Mama, p. 40; Kennedy, My Dear Duchess; Villiers, *Vanished Victorian*, p. 315.
54. RA VIC/ADDU/16, Lord Hertford's Account of Queen Victoria.
55. Villiers, *Vanished Victorian*, p. 313.
56. Fulford, *Dearest Mama*, p. 56.
57. Buckle, I: 20.
58. Gladstone to the Duchess of Sutherland, 24 February 1862, BL Add. MS 44, 326 fos 44–5, and Sutherland to Gladstone, 26 February, fos 46–51. See also Reynolds, *Aristocratic Women*, pp. 215–16.
59. Vincent, *Disraeli, Derby*, p. 198; Storey, *Letters of Charles Dickens*, vol. 10, p. 54.
60. Whittle, *Victoria and Albert*, p. 118; Kennedy, *My Dear Duchess*, pp. 186, 188–9, 191; Darby & Smith, *Cult*, p. 11; Downer, *Queen's Knight*, p. 129.
61. Windsor & Bolitho, p. 262.
62. Kennedy, *My Dear Duchess*, p. 189; RA VIC/ MAIN/QVJ/1862: 15 March; Dasent, *Delane,* pp. 48–9.
63. Ricks, *Poems of Tennyson*, vol. 3, p. 263.

64. Dyson & Tennyson, *Dear and Honoured Lady*, p. 65.
65. Girouard, *Return to Camelot*, pp. 124–5.
66. Dyson & Tennyson, *Dear and Honoured Lady*, p. 124; Ricks, *Poems of Tennyson*, vol. 1, p. 207.
67. Dyson & Tennyson, *Dear and Honoured Lady*, p. 69.
68. 'On the bald street breaks the blank day', *In Memoriam*, canto VII, in Ricks, *Poems of Tennyson*, vol. 2, p. 326.
69. Dyson & Tennyson, *Dear and Honoured Lady*, pp. 69–70.
70. Ibid., p. 76.

## Chapter 10: 'The Luxury of Woe'

1. RA VIC/ADDA22/77; Staniland, *In Royal Fashion*, p. 156; *Illustrated London News*, 28 December 1861.
2. Staniland, *In Royal Fashion*, p. 156.
3. *Leeds Mercury*, 17 December 1861.
4. *Illustrated London News*, 28 December 1861.
5. George Frederick Pardon, *Routledge's Popular Guide to London and Its Suburbs*, London, 1862, front advertising.
6. King, *The Dying Game*, pp. 106–7; Morley, *Death, Heaven and the Victorians*, pp. 63–4. Courtaulds soon developed large-scale production of its own cheaper, coarser fabric—'Albert crape'—more durable and half the price, which during the 1870s was targeted at the burgeoning market among the lower middle and working classes.
7. Goldthorpe, *From Queen to Empress*, pp. 69–70. The expression the 'luxury of woe' or 'luxury of

grief' was a commonly used one at the time in poetry, philosophical writing; see e.g. *The Poetical Works of Thomas More*, 1826, Paris: Galignani, 1827, p. 246: 'Weep on, and as thy sorrows flow, I'll taste the luxury of woe'; Alison Adburgham, *Shops and Shopping*, London: Barrie & Jenkins, 1989, p. 66–7.

8. Christina Walkley, *Ghost in the Looking Glass*, London: Peter Owen, 1981, p. 29; Goldthorpe, *From Queen to Empress*, p. 76. A common complaint suffered by overworked seamstresses was temporary nystagmus, where the eye involuntarily flicks from side to side in rapid swinging motion and prevents the sufferer from fixing their gaze on an object. Kristine Hughes, *Everyday Life in Regency and Victorian Britain*, Cincinnatti: Writers Digest Books, 1998, pp. 217–18.

9. Staniland, *In Royal Fashion*, pp. 155–6.

10. RA VIC/MAIN/QVJ/1862: 1 July.

11. It was not until her Silver Jubilee of 1887 that the Queen was prevailed upon, thanks to the intervention of the Princess of Wales, to allow ladies at court to wear something other than jet. She agreed to silver and increasingly adopted it herself, thus sparking a new fashion and the further erosion of the jet trade.

12. Crawford, *Victoria, Queen and Ruler*, pp. 331–2.

13. The 1871 census listed 1,006 jet workers in the town. See Noreen Vickers, 'The Structure of the Whitby Jet Industry in 1871', http://www.localpopu lationstudies.org.uk/PDF/LPS38/LPS38 – 1987 –8–17.pdf

14. McMillan, *Whitby Jet Through the Years*, pp. 74–6, 211, 226. The Whitby jet trade began to decline

from the mid-1870s in the face of cheap foreign imports of imitation glass 'jet' from France, as well as vulcanite and poorer-quality jet from Spain. Thereafter trade in Whitby jet rapidly collapsed and the workforce shrank to 300.

15. RA VIC/ADDC6: 30 June 1862, diary of Lady Geraldine Somerset.
16. Fulford, *Dearest Mama*, p. 59.
17. Connell, *Regina v. Palmerston*, p. 327.
18. Argyll, *Autobiography and Memoirs*, vol. 2, p. 185, 187.
19. RA VIC/MAIN/QVJ/1862: 24 May; Fulford, *Dearest Mama*, p. 62.
20. Vincent, *Disraeli, Derby*, p. 187.
21. Bodleian Library Special Collections, Clarendon Papers, MS Eng.e.2122, Lady Katherine Clarendon diary for 3 February 1862; British Library, Add. MS 44289, Gladstone Papers, vol. CXCV: 16 March 1862.
22. Wyndham, *Correspondence of Lady Lyttleton*, p. 348.
23. RA VIC/MAIN/QVJ/1862: 20 June.
24. Noel, *Princess Alice*, p. 88.
25. Fulford, *Dearest Mama*, pp. 60, 83, 74.
26. Kennedy, *My Dear Duchess*, pp. 196–7.
27. Aston, *Duke of Connaught*, pp. 47–8.
28. RA VIC/ADDC6: 1 July 1862, Journal of Lady Geraldine Somerset.
29. Fulford, *Dearest Mama*, p. 85.
30. *Daily News*, 2 July 1862.
31. *Reynolds's Newspaper*, 6 July 1862.
32. A. MacGeorge, *Wm. Leighton Leitch Landscape Painter, A Memoir*, London: L. Blackie & Son, 1884, p. 63.
33. Fulford, *Dearest Mama*, p. 101.

34. Ibid., p. 102; the quotation is from Wisdom, chapter IV.
35. Anon, *Queen's Resolve,* p. 104.
36. Tisdall, *Queen Victoria's Private Life*, pp. 66–8.
37. Kennedy, *My Dear Duchess*, p. 201.
38. Connell, *Regina vs. Palmerston*, p. 331.
39. RA VIC/ADDA/25/85: 4 October 1862, letter to Howard Elphinstone; Connell, *Regina v. Palmerston*, p. 332.
40. RA VIC/MAIN/QVJ/1862: 22 July.
41. Fulford, *Dearest Mama*, p. 130; Windsor & Bolitho, pp. 272, 273.
42. RA VIC/ADDA/8/384: 'Miss Ella Taylor's Reminiscences of HRH The Duchess of Cambridge', p. 2.
43. Fulford, *Dearest Mama*, pp. 138, 139, 142.
44. RA VIC/MAIN/QVJ/1862: 14 December 1862.
45. Ashwell & Wilberforce, *Life of Bishop Wilberforce*, p. 72.
46. Fulford, *Dearest Mama*, p. 148.
47. Walsh, *Religious Life and Influence of Queen Victoria*, p. 116.
48. Fulford, *Dearest Mama*, p. 153.
49. *Belfast News-letter*, 1 December 1862.

*Chapter 11: 'A Married Daughter I* Must *Have Living with Me'*

1. Dasent, *Delane*, p. 64.
2. Hudson, *Munby*, p. 152.
3. Strafford, *Henry Greville*, p. 106.
4. Fulford, *Dearest Mama*, pp. 98, 126.
5. Ibid., pp. 172, 165.
6. Morier Family Papers, Balliol College, Oxford,

K1/4/4, Queen Victoria, letter to General Peel, 25 January 1864.

7. Bailey, *Diary of Lady Frederick Cavendish*, p. 154; Greville, *Leaves*, vol, 4,. p. 109.

8. Cooke, *Princess Mary Adelaide*, vol. 1, p. 407; Wiebe, *Letters of Benjamin Disraeli*, vol. 8, p. 261.

9. Fulford, *Dearest Mama*, p. 180.

10. Hibbert, *Edward VII*, p. 62; Windsor & Bolitho, p. 308.

11. The wedding was extensively described in the newspapers and in journals such as *The Times, Telegraph, Daily News, Morning Chronicle*, etc. for 11 March. The Queen's own account can be found in Hibbert, *Letters and Journals*, pp. 172–4; the account of Disraeli is in Wiebe, *Letters of Benjamin Disraeli*, vol. 8, pp. 412–13; Windsor & Bolitho, pp. 281–8, 306–12; Lord Clarendon, in Kennedy, *My Dear Duchess*, pp. 210–15; Bailey, *Diary of Lady Frederick Cavendish*, pp. 154–7; Battiscombe, *Princess Alexandra*, pp. 43–50. Munby's vivid description of the crowds in London is in Hudson, *Munby*, pp. 149–53.

12. Hibbert, *Letters and Journals*, p. 172.

13. Hudson, *Munby*, p. 153.

14. Frederick Pollock, *Personal Reminiscences of Sir Frederick Pollock*, vol. 2, London: Macmillan, 1987, pp. 110–11.

15. Strafford, *Henry Greville*, vol. 4, p. 110.

16. Fulford, *Dearest Mama*, pp. 192, 193.

17. Hibbert, *Letters and Journals*, p. 177.

18. Chomet, *Helena*, p. 17.

19. Bailey, *Diary of Lady Frederick Cavendish*, vol. 1, pp. 199, 214.

20. Fulford, *Dearest Mama*, pp. 226, 209, 212.

21. Ibid., pp. 235, 213.

22. Hibbert, *Letters and Journals*, p. 178.
23. Elphinstone, *Queen Thanks Sir Howard*, p. 64; Fulford, *Dearest Mama*, p. 245.
24. *The Times*, 12 October 1863.
25. Fulford, *Dearest Mama*, p. 273.
26. *Morning Post*, 15 October 1863.
27. Ibid.
28. *The Times*, 12 October 1863.
29. Wake, *Princess Louise*, p. 75; Hibbert, *Letters and Journals*, p. 178.
30. Hibbert, *Letters and Journals*, p. 179; Windsor & Bolitho, p. 294.
31. Magnus, *Gladstone*, p. 160; Arengo Jones, *Queen Victoria and Switzerland*, p. 21.
32. Wake, *Princess Louise*, p. 74.
33. Arengo Jones, *Queen Victoria and Switzerland*, p. 18.
34. Hibbert, *Letters and Journals*, p. 178.
35. Fulford, *Dearest Mama*, pp. 205–6.
36. Hibbert, *Letters and Journals*, p. 181.
37. Connell, *Regina v. Palmerston*, p. 352.
38. Hibbert, *Letters and Journals*, pp. 184, 185.
39. Ibid., p. 185.
40. *Manchester Examiner*, 19 March 1864; Tisdall, *Queen Victoria's John Brown*, pp. 86–7.
41. *Saturday Review*, 26 March 1864.
42. Bailey, *Diary of Lady Frederick Cavendish*, p. 207; E. F. Benson, *As We Were*, London: Longman's, Green & Co., 1930, p. 38.
43. Watson, *Queen at Home*, p. 166; Tooley, *Personal Life*, p. 212.
44. Maxwell, *Life and Letters of 4th Earl Clarendon*, vol. II, p. 293.
45. Vincent, *Disraeli, Derby*, pp. 209, 210.
46. Ibid., p. 211.

47. Dasent, *Delane*, vol. II, pp. 108, 110.
48. Ibid., p. 130.
49. McMillan, *Whitby Jet Through the Years*, p. 212.
50. *The Times*, 15 December 1864.
51. *Morning Post*, 16 December 1864.
52. Balliol College Oxford, Morier Family Papers, K/ Box 2/1, letter of 19 August 1864.
53. Vincent, Disraeli, Derby, p. 214.

Chapter 12: 'God Knows How I Want So Much to be Taken Care Of'

Title: Queen Victoria to Vicky, 5 April 1865, in Fulford, *Your Dear Letter*, p. 22.

1. House and Storey, eds, *The Letters of Charles Dickens*, vol. 10, p. 425.
2. *Civil Engineer and Architect's Journal*, vol. 37, January 1864, p. 27.
3. Wiebe, *Letters of Benjamin Disraeli*, vol. 8, p. 270.
4. *Art Journal*, 1866, vol. 5, p. 203; *Tomahawk*, vols 4–5, 3 April 1869, p. 148. This was indeed the case. By the time Foley's statue was finally positioned under the canopy in 1875 the monument was already blackened by ten years of London soot.
5. *Pall Mall Gazette*, 11 September 1865.
6. Hibbert, *Letters and Journals*, p. 196; Fulford, *Your Dear Letter*, p. 109; *Punch*, 15 December 1866, p. 238; *Morning Post*, 1 December 1866; *Illustrated London News*, 8 December 1866.
7. *Ladies' Companion*, vol. 28, 1865, p. 324.
8. *Friend of India*, 15 October 1865, no. 1605.
9. Fulford, *Your Dear Letter*, p. 22; Hibbert, *Letters and Journals*, p. 187.

10. Lamont-Brown, *John Brown*, p. 79.
11. Hibbert, *Letters and Journals*, p. 189; Fulford, *Your Dear Letter*, p. 29.
12. In his travels through England in 1869 and published in 1870, Daniel Joseph Kirwan, a reporter for the *New York World*, painted a vivid and idiosyncratic portrait of the Queen, gleaned from his conversations with people at Windsor and elsewhere, as a result of which he felt compelled to 'lift the veil' on the true reason for the Queen's continuing seclusion. It was, Kirwan claimed, due in part to her serious 'fondness for liquor', a fact that was 'continually hinted at obscurely in the more liberal organs'. What is more, Kirwan had it on good authority that the Queen 'was in the habit of drinking half a pint of raw liquor per day'. The fact that the Queen had found comfort in the bottle in her widowhood is no real surprise; it is an acknowledged fact that she enjoyed whisky, and entirely plausible that her need for its anaesthetising effect to counter the pain of grief may have grown in her widowhood. It would also explain the physical changes noted by many—of her increased weight (partly the result of a voracious appetite that she soon recovered) and her reddened and puffy face. But in the absence of further substantiating evidence, we only have Kirwan's word for it. See Daniel Joseph Kirwan, *Palace and Hovel or Phases of London Life*, reprinted by Abelard-Schuman in New York, 1963. See also Charles Morris & Murat Halstead, *Life and Reign of Queen Victoria*, International Publishing Society, 1901, p. 223.
13. Longford, *Victoria RI*, p. 325. Rumours abounded during the Queen's reign and after her death

that Brown had acted as a spiritualist medium in séances held in the Blue Room, during which the Queen had made contact with Albert on the other side. Despite exhaustive research, Victoria's biographer Elizabeth Longford found no evidence of either the Queen's indulgence in spiritualist practices or of Brown's role in them, nor did she of a sexual relationship between them. But unsubstantiated gossip and rumour—going so far as allegations of a morganatic marriage having taken place—persist to this day. No supporting evidence, however, survives in the Queen's journals—if it was ever there—though these were edited and bowdlerised by her daughter Beatrice after her death. Nor is there a mention of it in her thousands of uncensored letters to Vicky. All of the Queen's letters to Brown and his to her, as well as his diaries, which might have provided an answer one way or the other, were destroyed after the Queen's death, on the orders of Edward VII. See Rappaport, *Queen Victoria*, entries on John Brown, pp. 75–81, and the Paranormal, pp. 285–8; also Longford, *Victoria RI*, pp. 334–9; Cullen, *Empress Brown*, pp. 97–9; 'Victoria and John Brown' in Thompson, *Queen Victoria*, pp. 61–86; Lamont Brown, 'Queen Victoria's "Secret Marriage"', in *Contemporary Review*, December 2003, available online at http://findarticles.com/p/articles/mi m2242/is 1655 283/ai 112095011/ Perhaps the best summary of Victoria's relationship with John Brown, and one that clearly defines it in personal and social terms, comes in a letter she wrote to Viscount Cranbrook after Brown's death in 1883 and which recently came to light. In it she wrote,

'Perhaps never in history was there so strong an *attachment*, so warm and loving a *friendship* between the sovereign and *servant*' (my italics). Those three words—'attachment', 'friendship' and 'servant'—define a close romantic friendship built on trust and mutual respect, but one that was nevertheless contained within the parameters of Victoria's own very clear understanding of class difference. She was right to feel 'that life for the second time is become most trying and sad' after Brown's death. She had lost a friend, and true friends were a rare thing indeed to a lonely monarch, isolated by her position. Nevertheless some commentators appear to have totally misread this statement as alluding to Brown having taken the place, sexually and maritally, of Albert. Victoria in fact totally disapproved of the remarriage of widows. See Bendor Grosvenor, 'Dear John', *History Today*, January 2005, pp. 2–3.

14. For a discussion of Victoria's chronic grief, see Parkes, *Recovery from Bereavement*, pp. 129–31, 134–5; Jalland, *Death in the Victorian Family*, ch. 16, 'Chronic and Abnormal Grief', pp. 318–22.

15. Sylvain Van de Weyer died in 1874. Madame Van de Weyer (who died in 1878), was formerly Elizabeth Bates, daughter of a Barings banker, and had with her husband been a very particular friend of Victoria and Albert since 1840 and, with their close links to Uncle Leopold, were favourites at court. Victoria was godmother to their first child and after her widowhood frequently visited Madame Van de Weyer at her home, New Lodge, four miles from Windsor. Written evidence of their relationship is, however, extremely scant. See Paul Bishop, *Synchronicity and Intellectual*

*Intuition in Kant, Swedenborg and Jung*, New York: Ewin Hellen Press, 2000, p. 314; *Spiritual Notes*, 1993, p. 52; Stanislaw Przybyszewski, *Erinnerungen an Berlin und Krakau*, 119, p. 123.

16. Crawford, *Queen Victoria*, pp. 327–8; Whittle, *Victoria and Albert at Home*, p. 142.

17. Longford, *Victoria RI*, p. 321.

18. Fulford, *Your Dear Letter*, p. 48; Thompson, *Queen Victoria*, p. 76.

19. *Morning Post*, 9 April 1866.

20. Lamont-Brown, *John Brown*, p. 69.

21. Hibbert, *Letters and Journals*, p. 191.

22. Justin G. Turner, ed., *Mary Todd Lincoln—Her Life and Letters*, New York: Knopf, 1972, p. 230.

23. Fulford, *Your Dear Letter*, p. 66.

24. Ibid., pp. 90–1.

25. Fulford, *Dearest Mama*, p. 211; Fulford, *Your Dear Letter*, pp. 56–7.

26. Hibbert, *Letters and Journals*, p. 193.

27. Hudson, *Munby*, p. 218.

28. Crawford, *Queen Victoria*, p. 328.

29. Russell, *Amberley Papers*, vol. 1, p. 466.

30. Crawford, *Queen Victoria*, p. 319.

31. Conway, David Moncure, *Autobiography, Memories and Experiences of Daniel Moncure Conway*, vol. 2, London: Cassell & Co., 1904, p. 65.

32. Ibid.

33. Crawford, *Queen Victoria*, p. 320.

34. Buckle, I: 299.

35. Longford, *Victoria RI*, pp. 348–9.

36. Arengo-Jones, *Queen Victoria in Switzerland*, p. 21.

37. Russell, *Amberley Papers*, vol. 1, p. 515; *Pall Mall Gazette*, 24 May 1865.

38. *Punch*, 7 July 1866; Tisdall, *Queen Victoria's John Brown*, pp. 105–6.
39. See, for example, *Examiner*, 7 September 1867.
40. *The Light Blue: A Cambridge University Magazine*, vol. 2, 1867, p. 330.
41. *Tomahawk*, 11 May 1867.
42. Ibid., 30 May 1868.
43. Martineau, *Selected Letters*, p. 212.
44. Cullen, *Empress Brown*, pp. 94–6.
45. Kuhn, *Henry and Mary Ponsonby*, p. 98.
46. Tisdall, *Queen Victoria's John Brown*, p. 109.
47. Ibid., p. 111.
48. Hibbert, *Letters and Journals*, p. 197; Fulford, *Your Dear Letter*, p. 120.
49. Kuhn, *Henry and Mary Ponsonby*, p. 97; Bailey, *Diary of Lady Frederick Cavendish*, vol. 2, p. 10.
50. *Tomahawk*, 8 June 1867; *Huddersfield Chronicle*, 30 June 1866; Russell, *Amberley Papers*, vol.1, p. 515; Cullen, *Empress Brown*, p. 94.
51. Longford, *Victoria RI*, p. 374; Tooley, *Personal Life of Queen Victoria*, pp. 217–18.
52. Cullen, *Empress Brown*, p. 113.
53. Hibbert, *Letters and Journals*, p. 198.
54. Cullen, *Empress Brown*, p. 104; Jerrold, *Widowhood of Queen Victoria*, p. 97.
55. *Daily News*, 13 June 1867; *Reynolds's Newspaper*, 21 July 1867.
56. Arengo-Jones, *Queen Victoria in Switzerland*, p. 24.
57. Downer, *Queen's Knight*, p. 170; Vincent, *Disraeli, Derby*, p. 242; Wake, *Princess Louise*, p. 75.
58. Fulford, *Your Dear Letter*, pp. 169, 51.

1. Fulford, *Dearest Mama*, p. 219.
2. For a detailed discussion of the extent of the Queen's involvement in the compilation of *The Early Years*, see Homans, *Royal Representations*, pp. 115–31.
3. *Medical Times and Gazette*, 3 August 1867.
4. *Quarterly Review*, 1867–8, vol. 29, pp. 199, 304, 280.
5. *Medical Times and Gazette*, 3 August 1867.
6. Fulford, *Your Dear Letter*, p. 166.
7. Lee, *Queen Victoria*, p. 410.
8. Victoria, *Leaves from the Journal*, p. 106.
9. *The Times*, 10 January 1868.
10. Fulford, *Your Dear Letter*, p. 169.
11. Vineta and Robert Colby, *The Equivocal Virtue: Mrs Oliphant and the Victorian Literary Market Place*, Hamden: Archon Books, 1966, p. 117.
12. Gail Turley Huston, *Royalties: The Queen and Victorian Writers*, Charlottesville: University Press of Virginia, 1999, pp. 148, 142. In a study entitled 'Queen Victoria: A Personal Sketch', published in 1900 after her own death, Oliphant was less equivocal. In literary matters, the Queen was, she argued, 'no student of style, nor does she ever, we imagine, ponder and wait for the best word'. See also entry on Margaret Oliphant in Rappaport, *Queen Victoria*, pp. 271–3.
13. *Fraser's Magazine,* vol. LXXVII, February 1868, p. 154; *North British Review*, vols 5–6, 1868, p. 196.
14. *Daily Telegraph*, 10 January 1868.
15. *Tomahawk*, 18 January 1868.
16. *Chronicle* quoted in *York Herald*, 25 January 1868.
17. *Reynolds's Newspaper*, 19 January 1868.

18. Fulford, *Your Dear Letter*, p. 172.
19. Ibid., p. 171; Helps, *Correspondence of Sir Arthur Helps*, pp. 265–6.
20. Fulford, *Your Dear Letter*, p. 169; Hudson, *Munby*, p. 249.
21. Martin, *Queen Victoria As I Knew Her*, p. 28; Fulford, *Your Dear Letter*, p. 169.
22. Georgina Battiscombe, *Shaftesbury A Biography of the 7th Earl*, London: Constable, 1974, p. 298.
23. Cullen, *Empress Brown*, p. 128.
24. Windsor & Bolitho, p. 65.
25. Helps, *Leaves from the Journal*, p. 128.
26. Richard Altick, *The English Common Reader: A Social History of the Mass Reading Public 1800–1900*, Columbus: Ohio University Press, 1998, p. 388.
27. Tooley, *Personal Life of Queen Victoria*, p. 236.
28. Fulford, *Your Dear Letter*, p. 178.
29. Windsor & Bolitho, p. 73. For a detailed discussion of *Leaves from the Journal*, see Homans, *Royal Representations*, pp. 131–52.
30. Fulford, *Your Dear Letter*, p. 173.
31. Martin, *Queen Victoria as I Knew Her*, p. 29.
32. Ibid., pp. 38–9.
33. Fulford, *Your Dear Letter*, pp. 173, 171.
34. Hibbert, *Letters and Journals*, p. 90.
35. Fulford, *Your Dear Letter*, pp. 174, 175, 176.
36. Moneypenny & Buckle, *Life of Disraeli*, vol. II, p. 389; Fulford, *Your Dear Letter*, p. 174.
37. Helps, *Correspondence of Sir Arthur Helps*, pp. 264–5.
38. Nevill, *Under Five Reigns*, p. 177.
39. Bailey, *Diary of Lady Frederick Cavendish*, vol. 2, p. 49.
40. Hibbert, *Letters and Journals*, p. 205.

41. Ibid.
42. Arengo-Jones, *Queen Victoria in Switzerland*, pp. 29–30.
43. *The Times*, 20 May 1868.
44. Wake, *Princess Louise*, p. 81.
45. Arengo-Jones, *Queen Victoria in Switzerland*, p. 32.
46. Ibid., p. 43.
47. Duff, *Queen Victoria's Highland Journals*, p. 141.
48. Guedalla, *Queen and Mr Gladstone*, vol. I, p. 47.
49. Kennedy, *My Dear Duchess*, p. 248.
50. Arengo-Jones, *Queen Victoria in Switzerland*, p. 26.
51. Benson & Esher, I: 213.
52. Magnus, *Gladstone*, p. 200; Weintraub, *Queen Victoria*, pp. 351–2.
53. Magnus, *Gladstone*, p. 199.
54. Wake, *Princess Louise,* pp. 86–7; Bailey, *Diary of Lady Frederick Cavendish*, vol. 2 , p. 69.
55. *The Times*, 6 November 1870.
56. Dasent, *Delane*, p. 252.
57. Hibbert, *Letters and Journals*, p. 209.
58. *Morning Post*, 6 November 1869.
59. Martin, *Queen Victoria as I Knew Her*, pp. 39–40.
60. Fulford, *Your Dear Letter*, p. 263.
61. *National Reformer*, 18 September 1870.
62. Williams, *Contentious Crown*, p. 37.
63. Magnus, *Gladstone*, p. 111
64. Ramm, *Political Correspondence of Mr Gladstone*, p. 170.
65. Hibbert, *Letters and Journals*, p. 212.
66. *Reynolds's Newspaper*, 25 December 1870.
67. Hudson, *Munby*, p. 292.
68. Hibbert, *Queen Victoria*, p. 332.

1. Tisdall, *Queen Victoria's Private Life*, pp. 106–7; Kuhn, 'Ceremony and Politics', pp. 160–1; Ponsonby, *Henry Ponsonby*, p. 71.
2. Ponsonby, *Henry Ponsonby*, p. 71.
3. Ibid., p. 72.
4. This accusation was entirely unfounded. Any monies saved from the Queen's Civil List income were returned to the Exchequer and did not go into the royal privy purse. Ponsonby, *Henry Ponsonby*, p. 76. See also Kuhn, 'Ceremony and Politics', pp. 138–40.
5. Charles Bradlaugh, 'The Impeachment of the House of Brunswick', 1871, quoted in Thompson, *Queen Victoria*, p. 106.
6. For an exhaustive account of the ceremony, see for example *Daily News*, 30 March 1871.
7. Cullen, *Empress Brown*, p. 135.
8. Hibbert, *Queen Victoria*, p. 339, and Pakula, *Uncommon Woman*, p. 293.
9. It is possible that the abscess under Victoria's arm had been caused by germs spreading from her severely inflamed throat. No official diagnosis was ever announced, though it has since been suggested by Weintraub (*Queen Victoria*, p. 363) that she was suffering from quinsy.
10. Magnus, *Gladstone*, p. 209.
11. Longford, *Victoria RI*, p. 382; for Henry Ponsonby's memorandum on the Queen's seclusion in 1871, see Ponsonby, *Henry Ponsonby*, pp. 73–6.
12. Ponsonby, *Henry Ponsonby*, p. 75.
13. The loyal Emilie Dittweiler finally retired in 1892,

after thirty-five years' service; Annie Macdonald remained with the Queen for an equal length of time, till her death in 1897. Both women were commended by the Queen in *More Leaves from the Journal of Our Life in the Highlands, from 1862 to 1882,* published in 1884.

14. Weintraub, *Queen Victoria*, p. 366; Longford, *Victoria RI*, pp. 384–5; Cullen, *Empress Brown*, p. 140.
15. Cullen, *Empress Brown*, p. 141; Jalland, *Death in the Victorian Family*, p. 320.
16. G. T. Wrench, *Lord Lister, His Life and Work*, pp. 227–8. See also Godlee, *Lord Lister,* pp. 305–6. Lister was honoured by the Queen with a baronetcy in 1893 and a peerage in 1897 for his pioneering medical work.
17. Godlee, Lord Lister, p. 306. The use of India-rubber drainage tubes for wounds had first been described in France in 1859, but Lister was the first to apply them in the UK. He finally described his procedure on the Queen in *The Lancet*, 1908, vol. I, p. 1815.
18. Longford, *Victoria RI,* p. 385.
19. Ponsonby Papers quoted in Cullen, *Empress Brown*, p. 143.
20. Hibbert, *Letters and Journals,* p. 226.
21. See *The Times,* 9 November, and *Newcastle Weekly Chronicle*, 11 November 1871; the speech was subsequently published as 'The Cost of the Crown'. For Dilke's accusations, see also Kuhn, 'Ceremony and Politics', pp. 140–3; Jerrold, *Widowhood*, p. 162–3.
22. *Pall Mall Gazette*, 9 November 1871.
23. Fulford, *Darling Child,* p. 29; Ramm, *Political Correspondence of Mr Gladstone*, vol. 2, p. 264.

24. One of the other guests, Lord Chesterfield, as well as Bertie's groom, Charles Blegg, contracted the disease. Both of them died.
25. Hibbert, *Letters and Journals*, p. 213. In addition to extensive newspaper coverage of the Prince's illness, the best first-hand accounts are to be found in the Queen's journals and in the letters of Alix's lady-in-waiting, Lady Macclesfield, written from Sandringham at the time, to be found at RA VIC/ADDMSS/C/18. See also Sheppard, *George Duke of Cambridge*, vol. 2, pp. 302–5.
26. Windsor & Bolitho, p. 148.
27. RA VIC/ADDC18, Lady Macclesfield letter: 8 December 1871.
28. Hibbert, *Queen Victoria*, p. 343.
29. Windsor & Bolitho, p. 149.
30. Hibbert, *Letters and Journals*, p. 213.
31. Sheppard, *George Duke of Cambridge*, vol. 2, p. 304.
32. Hibbert, *Letters and Journals*, p. 213.
33. Buckle, II: 177; Tisdall, *Unpredictable Queen*, p. 111.
34. Henry James Jennings, *Chestnuts and Small Beer,* London: Chapman & Hall, 1920, p. 81.
35. Hudson, *Munby*, p. 300.
36. Hibbert, *Letters and Journals*, p. 214.
37. See 'The Royal Fever and Our Feverish Constitution', *Reynolds's Newspaper*, 10 December 1871.
38. *Daily Telegraph* quoted in Cullen, *Empress Brown*, p. 156.
39. Morris, 'Illustrated Press', p. 118.
40. Reid, *Memoirs of Sir Wemyss Reid,* p. 157.
41. Hibbert, *Letters and Journals*, p. 214.

42. Cullen, *Empress Brown*, p. 157; Sheppard, *George Duke of Cambridge*, vol. 2, pp. 301–11.
43. Fulford, *Darling Child*, p. 20.
44. Sheppard, *George Duke of Cambridge*, vol. 2, p. 307.
45. Fulford, *Darling Child*, p. 20.
46. Tisdall, *Unpredictable Queen*, p. 113.
47. Kuhn, *Henry and Mary Ponsonby*, p. 155; Magnus, *Gladstone*, p. 211.
48. RA VIC/ADDC18, Lady Macclesfield letter: 29 November 1871.
49. Lant, *Insubstantial Pageant*, p. 29.
50. Weintraub, *Victoria*, p. 400.
51. Battiscombe, *Queen Alexandra*, p. 120.
52. For details of the fraught discussions with Gladstone over the arrangements, see Kuhn, *Democratic Royalism*, pp. 39–47.
53. Kuhn, 'Ceremony and Politics', pp. 153–4; Lant, *Insubstantial Pageant*, pp. 28–9.
54. Windsor & Bolitho, p. 151.
55. For discussion of the Thanksgiving Service, see e.g. *The Times, Daily News, Daily Telegraph*, 28 February 1872. It was also exhaustively reported in the popular weeklies, notably the *Illustrated London News*, which produced some thirty engravings depicting the celebrations over four issues between 24 February and 16 March. A useful summary of the press response is 'Epitome of Opinion in the Morning Journals', in *Pall Mall Gazette* for 28 February. See also, Lant, *Insubstantial Pageant*, pp. 26–33; Kuhn, 'Ceremony and Politics'.
56. Bailey, *Diary of Lady Frederick Cavendish*, vol. 2, p. 127.
57. Cullen, *Empress Brown*, pp. 159–61; Reid,

*Memoirs of Sir Wemyss Reid*, p. 190; Morris, 'Illustrated Press', p. 120. The limited number of police on duty that day were totally unable to marshal the vast crowds surging forward to catch sight of the Queen, particularly at Ludgate Hill and Temple Bar—at which latter three people were suffocated to death in the crush. *Reynolds's* claimed that six people in all were killed that day and a hundred seriously hurt, with 227 being hospitalised. See issue for 3 March 1872: 'Tuesday's Tomfoolery' and 'Accidents at the Thanksgiving'.

58. Hibbert, *Letters and Journals*, p. 216.
59. *Reynolds's Newspaper*, 3 March 1872.
60. Gavard, *A Diplomat in London*, pp. 96–7.
61. Ibid., p. 97; Hudson, *Munby*, p. 305.
62. Hudson, *Munby*, p. 305; Bailey, *Diary of Lady Frederick Cavendish*, vol. 2, p. 127.
63. Buckle, II: 195.
64. Hibbert, *Letters and Journals*, p. 216.
65. Reid, *Memoirs of Sir Wemyss Reid*, p. 190; Hudson, *Munby*, p. 305.
66. *Reynolds's Newspaper*, 25 February 1872.
67. Fulford, *Darling Child*, p. 31.
68. *The Times*, 28 February 1872.
69. Ibid.; *Lloyd's Weekly* and *Reynolds's Newspaper*, 3 March 1872.
70. Hibbert, *Letters and Journals*, p. 227.
71. Ibid.; Bailey, *Diary of Lady Frederick Cavendish*, vol. 2, p. 128.
72. *The Times*, 20 March 1872.
73. Bailey, *Diary of Lady Frederick Cavendish*, vol. 2, p. 129; Cullen, *Empress Brown*, p. 156.

1. Williams, *Contentious Crown*, pp. 49–50: *National Reformer*, 21 January and 25 February 1872.
2. Hibbert, *Letters and Journals*, p. 228.
3. Ibid., pp. 228–9.
4. Tisdall, *Queen Victoria's Private Life*, p. 105.
5. See e.g. Williams, *Contentious Crown*, p. 209.
6. Parkes, *Recovery from Bereavement*, contains a fascinating case study of the Queen's grief. See especially pp. 129–31, 134–5, 138–42.
7. Tennyson, *In Memoriam*, Canto IX, in Ricks, *Poems of Tennyson*, vol. 2, p. 328.
8. Hibbert, *Letters and Journals*, p. 229.
9. Ibid.
10. Parkes, *Recovery from Bereavement*, p. 153.
11. Mallet, *Life With Queen Victoria*, p. 52.
12. Ibid., p. 122.
13. Ibid., p. 44.
14. See 'The Widow at Windsor', in Rappaport, *Queen Victoria*, pp. 407–11.
15. Craik, *Fifty Golden Years*, p. 45.
16. 'Letter from the Queen to Her People' on the occasion of her Jubilee, 24 June 1887, published in *Lloyd's Weekly News*, 26 June 1887.
17. Tennyson, *In Memoriam*, Canto XC, in Ricks, *Poems of Tennyson*, vol. 2, p. 408; A. S. Byatt, 'The Congugial Angel', in *Angels and Insects*, London: Vintage, 1995, p. 177.
18. H. G. Wells, *An Experiment in Autobiography: Discoveries and Conclusions of a Very Ordinary Brain (since 1866)*, vol. 1, London: Victor Gollancz, 1934, p. 46.
19. Percy Lubbock, *Shades of Eton*, London: Jonathan Cape, 1929, pp. 122–3.

20. Fulford, *Your Dear Letter*, p. 121
21. Tennyson, *In Memoriam*, Canto CVI, in Ricks, *Poems of Tennyson*, vol. 2, p. 427.
22. The Royal Mausoleum, open to the public once a year on the nearest Wednesday to Queen Victoria's birthday of 24 May, is now, sadly, closed indefinitely to the public, due to structural problems.
23. Weintraub, *Victoria*, p. 324.
24. For a detailed description of the many later memorials to Albert, see Darby & Smith, *Cult of the Prince Consort*. See also entries on Albert Memorial; Frogmore; Royal Albert Hall; Victoria and Albert Museum in Rappaport, *Queen Victoria: A Biographical Companion*.
25. Stanford, *Recollections of Sir Gilbert Scott*, pp. 263, 264, 267.
26. Gavard, *Diplomat in London*, pp. 36–7.
27. 'Mark Twain's 1872 English Journal', in Lin Salamo and Harriet Elinor Smith, eds, *Mark Twain's Letters, 1872–1873*, Berkeley: University of California Press, 1997.
28. E. Beresford Chancellor, *Life in Regency and Early Victorian Times*, London: Batsford, 1926, p. 46. For a full account of the restoration project, see Chris Brooks, *The Albert Memorial: The Prince Consort National Memorial, Its History, Contexts and Conservation*, New Haven: Yale University Press, 2000.
29. Strachey, *Queen Victoria*, pp. 187–8.
30. See Williams, *Contentious Crown*, pp. 126–7. Criticism of the extent of Stockmar's influence over Albert and the levels of the Prince's interference in government foreign policy during the Crimean War was prompted by revelations in

the third volume of Martin's biography. See 'The Crown and the Cabinet: Five Letters on the Biography of the Prince Consort', published pseudonymously in *The Times* by Henry Dunckley as 'Verax' in 1878.

31. Warwick, *Afterthoughts*, pp. 3–4.
32. Aronson, *Grandmama of Europe*, p. 12. Victoria assumed the Latin title after 1876.
33. Henry James, *Portraits of Places*, Boston: James Osgood & Co., 1883, p. 310–11.
34. Williams, *Contentious Crown*, p. 210.
35. Grey, *Early Years of the Prince Consort*, p. 322.
36. Flora Thompson, *Lark Rise to Candleford*, Harmondsworth: Penguin, 1973, p. 295.

## *Epilogue: Christmas 1878*

1. Noel, *Princess Alice*, p. 120.
2. Bennett, *Queen Victoria's Children*, p. 63.
3. *Alice, Princess of Great Britain*, p. 125.
4. Noel, *Princess Alice,* pp. 224–5.
5. *Alice, Princess of Great Britain*, p. 37. An account of the illness of Princess Alice and her children, written by her close friend Miss McBean, is on pp. 32–44.
6. Ibid., p, 41.
7. RA VIC/MAIN/QVJ/1878: 12 December.
8. Buckle, III: 653–4.
9. *Alice, Princess of Great Britain*, p. 44.
10. RA VIC/MAIN/QVJ/1878: 14 December.
11. Ibid.
12. The exquisite effigy of a recumbent Alice clasping her dead daughter May was executed in white marble by Boehm and was placed near her father's

sarcophagus in the Royal Mausoleum at Frogmore, in time for the first anniversary of Alice's death in 1879.

13. *The Times*, 17 December 1878.
14. Richard Hough, *Advice to a Grand-Daughter: Letters from Queen Victoria to Princess Victoria of Hesse*, London: Heinemann, 1975, p. 10
15. Epton, *Victoria and Her Daughters,* p. 155.
16. RA VIC/MAIN/QVJ/1878: 19 December.
17. *The Times,* 28 December 1878.
18. Buckle, *Life of Disraeli*, vol. I, p. 341. Two more of Victoria's children died during her lifetime: Leopold in 1884 and Affie in 1900. Vicky outlived her mother only by seven months, dying of cancer in August 1901. A further tragic family death from diphtheria followed soon after Alice's, in April 1879, when Vicky's fourth son, Waldemar, died of the disease. The birth, in 1896, of Prince Albert, the future George VI, on the same day— 14 December—would add to the talismanic significance of the date for the royal family. Five months after Alice's death Queen Victoria took it into her head to try to marry Princess Beatrice off to Alice's widower, Louis, so that she could mother her dead sister's children, for the most part in England. She even persuaded Disraeli to try and get the law changed, permitting marriage with a sister-in-law, but it was thrown out by the House of Lords. See Mary Lutyens, ed., *Lady Lytton's Court Diary,* London: Rupert Hart-Davis, 1961, p. 47.
19. RA VIC/MAIN/QVJ/1878: 31 December. Victor Emmanuel II of Italy died on 9 January 1878; Pope Pius IX died on 7 February 1878. HMS *Eurydice*, a British training frigate, sank in a storm

off the Isle of Wight on 24 March 1878; her crew of 376 drowned. In 1878 two assassination attempts were made in quick succession against Emperor Wilhelm of Prussia: on 11 May and 2 June. The German armoured frigate *Grosse Kurfürst* was damaged in a collision and sunk off Folkestone during manoeuvres on 31 May 1878; 284 of her crew drowned. George V of Hanover—the only son of the Queen's cousin, Ernest Augustus, Duke of Cumberland—died on 12 June 1878. María de las Mercedes d'Orléans, Queen Consort of Spain, died on 26 June 1878, of tuberculosis aged eighteen. The Second Anglo-Afghan War broke out in September 1878 and lasted till 1880.

## *Appendix: What Killed Prince Albert?*

1. Fulford, *Prince Consort,* p. 270.
2. Walford, *Life of the Prince Consort,* p. 106
3. *Morning Chronicle*, 19 December; *Medical Times and Gazette*, 21 December, pp. 640–2.
4. For medical thinking on typhoid in the Victorian period, see: Alexander Duane, ed., *A Dictionary of Medicine and the Allied Sciences*, 3rd edn, New York: Leah Brothers, 1900, pp. 610–11; and Dr Montague Murray, ed., *Quain's Dictionary of Medicine,* rev. edn, London: Longman's, Green & Co., 1902, pp. 1764–7. Anne Hardy, *The Epidemic Streets: Infectious Disease and the Rise of Preventive Medicine,* 1856–1900, Oxford: Clarendon Press, 1993, has useful background on the incidence of typhoid fever in the 1860s.
5. Woodham-Smith, *Queen Victoria*, p. 424.

6. Murray, ed., *Quain's Dictionary of Medicine*, p. 1766.
7. *Morning Chronicle,* 20 December 1861.
8. *The Lancet,* 28 December 1861 and 11 January 1862.
9. *Irish Temperance Journal*, 1863, vol. 1, pp. 57–8; *British Journal of Homoeopathy*, 1862, vol. 20, pp. 174–5.
10. For Stockmar's communication with the royal pharmacist Peter Squire, see Dr G. C. Williamson, *Memoirs in Miniature: A Volume of Random Reminiscences*, London: Grayson & Grayson, 1933, pp. 253–4; Weintraub, *Uncrowned King*, pp. 426, 456. Thanks to the recommendation of Dr James Clark, Squire & Son had been appointed royal chemists on the Queen's accession in 1837. Squire's prescription and account book containing details of his supplies to the royal family for 1861–9 is in the archive of the Royal Pharmaceutical Society. It lists both regular monthly supplies and additional, variable orders, but unfortunately does not specify for whom particular medicines were intended. After Albert's death a large consignment of twenty bottles of smelling salts was sent by Squire's on 17 December, no doubt to deal with the flood of exhausted feelings among the ladies of the royal household at the Prince's death.
11. Longford, 'Queen Victoria's Doctors', p. 83.
12. Villiers, *Vanished Victorian*, p. 311; Cowley, *Paris Embassy* p. 229.
13. Longford, 'Queen Victoria's Doctors', pp. 85–6.
14. Arkhiv der Hessischen Hausstiftung: Briefe 7.1/1-BA 3: letters from Crown Prince Frederick, 19 and 20 December 1961.

15. In the medical press the following articles appeared concurring on the diagnosis of typhoid: Kevin Anderson, 'Death of a Prince Consort', *Medical Journal of Australia*, 9 November 1968, pp. 865–7. A. G. W. Whitfield, in his 'The Last Illness of the Prince Consort', *Journal of the Royal College of Physicians*, vol. 12, no. 1, 1977, pp. 96–102, offers a loose argument for typhoid, but with no compelling evidence. Michael Robbins in 'The Missing Doctor: An "If" of Victorian Medical History', *Journal of the Royal Society of Medicine*, vol. 90, March 1997, pp. 163–5, argues that had Albert's talented new physician Dr William Baly not been killed in an accident in January 1861, the course of the Prince's treatment—demanding complete bed rest and the removal of all stress, including the demands of the Trent affair—might have been different. For an interesting overview of Queen Victoria's relationship with Dr Clark, see Longford, 'Queen Victoria's Doctors'.

16. See Bennett, *King without a Crown*, pp. 371, 381–2.

17. Weintraub, *Victoria*, pp. 295–301, and Weintraub, *Uncrowned King*, pp. 435, 456.

18. *The Lancet*, 21 December 1861; *Medical Times and Gazette*, 11 January 1862. The French source for the latter article would appear to be *L'Union médicale,* 7 January 1862, vol. 13, no. 2, p 17.

19. J. W. Paulley, 'The Death of Albert Prince Consort: The case against typhoid fever', *Quarterly Journal of Medicine*, vol. 86, 1993, pp. 837–41.

20. See Sotnik, *The Coburg Conspiracy*, London: Ephesus Publishing, 2008, Ch. 18, 'Albert's Paternity'.

21. Charles N. Bernstein, Sunny Singh, Lesley A.

Graff, John R. Walker, Mary S. Cheang. 'A prospective population-based study of triggers of flares of IBD', *Gastroenterology*, 2009; 136 suppl 1: A1106.

22. After Albert's death Victoria found a comment in his diary in which he said he had not slept for 14–16 days, as she later told Lord Clarendon—see Clarendon Papers, Bodleian Library Special Collections, Ms Eng. e. 2123, 5 February 1862.

23. Charlot, *Victoria, the Young Queen*, p. 421.

24. For further discussion of Crohn's, see: S. P. L. Travis and N. Mortensen, 'Anorectal and Colonic Crohn's Disease', in J.-C. Givel, N. C. Mortensen and B. Roche, eds, *Anorectal and Colonic Diseases: A Practical Guide to Their Management* (3rd edn), London: Springer, 2010, pp. 501–12.

25. Both the temperance and the homoeopathic medicine movements took a particular interest in the circumstances of the Prince's death, which provided them with an occasion for critiques of conventional allopathic methods. The *Water-Cure Journal* of 1865 (vols 39–40, p. 140) boldly stated that 'Alcoholic medication killed the Prince Consort'.

26. Letter to the Dowager Duchess of Coburg, 9 April 1857, in James, *Albert*, p. 254.

# Bibliography

## Archives

Arkhiv der Hessischen Hausstiftung, Schloss Fasanerie, Eichenzell:
Briefe Kronprinz Wilhelm von Preussen an Kronprinzessin Victoria, 1861, 7.1/1-BA 3

Balliol College, Oxford:
Morier Family Papers, K1/4/4, 1866–72, Queen Victoria's letters to General Peel

Bodleian Library Special Collections:
Diaries of Lady Katherine Clarendon, Clarendon Papers, MSS Eng. e. 2122–5
Diary of Charles Pugh, MS.Eng.misc.d472
Journal of John Rashdall, MS.Eng.misc.e 359

British Library:
Gladstone Papers, vol. CCXL, Add. MSS 44325 and 44326, letters from the Duchess of Sutherland; vol. CXCV Add. MS 44289
Queen Victoria's 'Album Consolativum', Add. MSS 62089, 62090

Cheshire Archives:
Correspondence and Papers of Dean Stanley, DSA 85

Public Record Office, Kew:
Lord Chamberlain's papers, PRO LC 1-90-005

Royal Archives, Windsor:
Letters and journals of Queen Victoria, Prince Albert and members of the royal household; memoranda from the Lord Chamberlain and

Comptroller of the royal household [itemised in detail in the Notes]

Royal Pharmaceutical Society of Great Britain Collections:
Peter Squire, pharmacist: Queen Victoria's Account book, 1861–1869

Ian Shapiro collection:
Diaries of Sir John Cowell, 1861–2; letter of Ra Haniraka, 3 March 1862

Staatsarchiv Darmstadt:
Briefe von Prinzessin Alice, 1861, D24 Nr. 25/3–4 and 26/1

*The Times* Newspapers Limited Archive, News International Archive:
TT/ED/JTD/A/022, Lord Torrington letters to Delane
TT/ED/JTD/10–13, Delane Correspondence

### Newspapers and Journals

British national and regional newspapers digitised in the online resource, 19th Century British Library Newspapers, available at the British Library, London, and other libraries and repositories. Major papers consulted:

*Belfast News-letter*
*Daily News*
*Daily Telegraph*
*Leeds Mercury*
*Lloyds Weekly Newspaper*
*London Gazette*
*Morning Chronicle*

*Morning Post*
*Pall Mall Gazette*
*Reynolds's Newspaper*

*The Times* Digital Archive 1785–1985

*New York Times* Article Archive 1851–1980

Magazines and journals digitised in 19th Century UK Periodicals, British Library, London (availability as per the newspaper archive):

*Illustrated London News*
*The Lancet*
*Medical Times and Gazette*
*Punch*
*Tomahawk*

## Primary Published Sources

*Alice, Princess of Great Britain, Grand Duchess of Hesse: Letters to Her Majesty the Queen*, New and Popular Edition with a Memoir by HRH Princess Christian, London: John Murray, 1897.

Anon., 'The Last Hours of Prince Albert', in *Wesleyan-Methodist Magazine,* vol. 47, 1864, p. 906; published in pamphlet form as 'The Last Hours of HRH Prince Albert of Blessed Memory', London: John Snow, 1864.

Arengo-Jones, Peter, *Queen Victoria in Switzerland*, London: Hale, 1995.

Bailey, John, ed., *Diary of Lady Frederick Cavendish*, 2 vols, London: John Murray, 1927.

Bennett, Daphne, *King without a Crown,* London:

Heinemann, 1977.

Benson, A. C. and Viscount Esher, eds, *The Letters of Queen Victoria, 1837–61*, 1st series, 3 vols, London: John Murray, 1911.

Bolitho, Hector, *Albert, the Good*, London: Cobden-Sanderson, 1932 [revised in 1970 as *Albert, Prince Consort*].

—— *The Prince Consort and his Brother: Two Hundred New Letters*, London: Cobden-Sanderson, 1933.

—— *Victoria and Albert*, London: Cobden-Sanderson, 1938.

—— *Further Letters of Queen Victoria from the Archives of the House of Brandenburg-Prussia*, London: Thornton Butterworth, 1938.

Buckle, George Earl, ed., *Letters of Queen Victoria 1862–85*, 2nd series, 3 vols, London: John Murray, 1926–8.

Connell, Brian, *Regina v. Palmerston: The Correspondence between Queen Victoria and her Foreign and Prime Minister*, London: Evans Brothers, 1962.

Corti, Egon, *The English Empress*, London: Cassell & Co., 1957.

Downer, Martin, *The Queen's Knight*, London: Bantam Press, 2007.

Erskine, Mrs Stewart, ed., *Twenty Years at Court: From the Correspondence of the Hon. Eleanor Stanley*, London: Nisbet & Co., 1916.

Fulford, Roger, *Dearest Child: Letters Between Queen Victoria and the Princess Royal, 1858–61*, London: Evans Brothers, 1964.

—— *Dearest Mama: Letters between Queen Victoria and the Crown Princes of Prussia, 1861–64*, London: Evans Brothers, 1968.

—— *Your Dear Letter: Private Correspondence of Queen Victoria and the Crown Princess of Prussia, 1863–71*, London: Evans Brothers, 1971.

—— *Darling Child: Private Correspondence of Queen Victoria and the German Crown Princess, 1871–78*, London: Evans Brothers, 1976.

—— *Beloved Mama: Private Correspondence of Queen Victoria and the German Crown Princess, 1878–85*, London: Evans Brothers, 1981.

Grey, Hon. Charles, *The Early Years of HRH The Prince Consort*, London: Smith, Elder & Co., 1867.

Helps, Arthur, ed., *The Principal Speeches and Addresses of HRH The Prince Consort*, London: John Murray, 1862.

Hibbert, Christopher, *Queen Victoria in Her Letters and Journals*, London: Viking, 1984.

Hobhouse, Hermione, *Prince Albert: His Life and Work*, London: Hamish Hamilton, 1983.

Hough, Richard, *Advice to a Grand-daughter: Letters from Queen Victoria to Princess Victoria of Hesse*, London: Heinemann, 1975.

Jagow, Kurt, *Letters of the Prince Consort, 1831–1861*, London: John Murray, 1938.

James, Robert Rhodes, *Albert Prince Consort: A Biography*, London: Hamish Hamilton, 1983.

Kime, William Thomas, ed., *Albert the Good: A Nation's Tribute of Affection to the Memory of a Truly Virtuous Prince*, London: J. F. Shaw & Co., 1862.

Longford, Elizabeth, *Victoria RI*, London: Weidenfeld & Nicolson, 1998 [1964].

—— ed., *Darling Loosy: Letters to Princess Louise, 1856–1939*, London: Weidenfeld & Nicolson, 1991.

Lorne, Marquis of, *VRI: Her Life and Empire*,

London: Eyre and Spottiswood, 1901.

Martin, Sir Theodore, *The Life of HRH The Prince Consort*, 5 vols, London: Smith, Elder & Co., 1875–80.

—— *Queen Victoria as I Knew Her*, Edinburgh: William Blackwood & Son, 1908.

Pound, Reginald, *Albert: A Biography of the Prince Consort*, London: Michael Joseph, 1973.

Rappaport, Helen, *Queen Victoria: A Biographical Companion*, Santa Barbara: ABC-Clio, 2003.

Sell, Karl, ed., *Alice Grand Duchess of Hesse, Princess of Great Britain and Ireland, Biographical Sketch and Letters*, London: John Murray, 1884.

'Services Held in Windsor Castle on the Anniversary of the Lamented Death of the Prince Consort', London: privately printed, 1862.

Sheppard, Edgar, *HRH George, Duke of Cambridge, A Memoir*, vol. I 1819–1871, London: Longman's, Green & Co., 1906.

Victoria, Queen of Great Britain, *Leaves from the Journal of Our Life in the Highlands from 1848–1861*, ed. Arthur Helps, London: Smith, Elder, 1868.

Wake, *Jehanne, Princess Louise: Queen Victoria's Unconventional Daughter*, London: Collins, 1988.

Walford, Edward, *The Life of the Prince Consort*, London: Routledge, Warne & Routledge, 1862.

Weintraub, Stanley, *Victoria, Biography of a Queen*, London: Unwin Hyman, 1987.

—— *Albert, Uncrowned King*, London: John Murray, 1997.

Windsor, Dean of and Hector Bolitho, eds, *Letters of Lady Augusta Stanley: A Young Lady at Court 1849–1863*, London: Gerald Howe, 1927.

—— *Later Letters of Lady Augusta Stanley*

*1864–1876*, London: Jonathan Cape, 1929.

Woodham Smith, Cecil, *Queen Victoria: Her Life and Times,* vol. 1, 1819–1861, London: Hamish Hamilton, 1972.

Wyndham, Hon. Mrs Hugh, ed., *Correspondence of Sarah Spencer, Lady Lyttleton 1787–1870*, London: John Murray, 1912.


## Secondary Published Sources

Airplay, F. (pseud.), 'Prince Albert, Why is He Unpopular?', London: Saunders & Otley, 1856.

Albert, Harold, *The Life and Letters of Princess Feodore: Queen Victoria's Sister,* London: Robert Hale, 1967.

Allan, Oswald, 'Worthy a Crown?', London: Head & Meek, 1876.

—— 'The Vacant Throne', London: E. Head, 1877.

Ames, Winslow, *Prince Albert and Victorian Taste*, London: Chapman & Hall, 1967.

Anon., *The Private Life of Queen Victoria: By One of Her Majesty's Servants,* London: C. Arthur Pearson, 1897.

Argyll, George Douglas Campbell, Duke of, *Autobiography and Memoirs*, vol. 2, London: John Murray, 1906.

Aronson, Theo, *Grandmama of Europe: The Crowned Descendants of Queen Victoria*, London: Cassell, 1973.

Ashwell, Arthur Rawton, ed., *Life of the Right Reverend Samuel Wilberforce*, 3 vols, London: John Murray, 1880–2.

—— and Reginald Garton, *The Life of Bishop*

*Wilberforce*, London: John Murray, 1881.

Aston, Sir George, *HRH The Duke of Connaught and Strathearn*, 2 vols, London: George C. Harrap, 1929.

Auchinloss, Louis, *Persons of Consequence: Queen Victoria and her Circle,* London: Weidenfeld & Nicolson, 1979.

Ball, T. Frederick, *Queen Victoria: Scenes and Incidents of her Life and Reign,* London: S. W. Partridge, 1886.

Battiscombe, Georgina, 'Gerald Wellesley: A Victorian Dean and Domestic Chaplain', in 'St George's Chapel Annual Report to 31st December', 1963.

—— *Queen Alexandra,* London: Constable, 1969.

Bayley, Stephen, *The Albert Memorial*, London: Scholar Press, 1981.

Bell, George Kennedy, *Randall Davidson, Archbishop of Canterbury*, London: Oxford University Press, 1952.

Bellows, John, 'Remarks by J. Bellows on Certain Anonymous Articles Designed to Render Queen Victoria Unpopular', Gloucester, 1864.

Bennett, Daphne, *Queen Victoria's Children,* London: Gollancz, 1980.

Benson, E. F., *As We Were: A Victorian Peep-Show*, London: Longman's, Green & Co., 1930.

—— *Queen Victoria*, London: Longman's, Green & Co., 1935.

Bolitho, Hector, *Victoria the Widow and Her Son*, London: Cobden-Sanderson, 1934.

—— *Victoria and Albert*, London: Cobden-Sanderson, 1938.

—— *Romance of Windsor Castle,* London: Evans Brothers, 1948.

—— *The Reign of Queen Victoria*, London: Collins, 1949.

—— *A Biographer's Notebook*, London: Longman's, Green & Co., 1950.

Branks, William, *Heaven our home, or Memorials of Sarah Craven, gathered chiefly from her own letters*, London: Wertheim, Mackintosh & Hunt, 1859.

Brown, Raymond Lamont, *John Brown: Queen Victoria's Highland Servant,* Stroud: Sutton, 2000.

—— *Royal Poxes and Potions: The Lives of the Court Physicians, Surgeons and Apothecaries*, Stroud: Sutton, 2001.

Bullock, Rev. Charles, *The Home Life of the Prince Consort*, London: 'Home Words' Publishing Office, 1861.

—— *The Queen's Resolve 'I Will Be Good': with Royal Anecdotes and Incidents*, London: 'Home Words' Publishing Office, 1887.

Cannadine, David, The Context, Performance and Meaning of Ritual: The British Monarchy and the Invention of Tradition, c. 1820–1977 in Eric Hobsbawm and Terence Ranger, eds, *The Invention of Tradition*, Cambridge: Cambridge University Press, 1983.

Cartwright, Julia, ed., *The Journals of Lady Knightley of Fawsley (1856–1884),* London: John Murray, 1915.

Chaple, J. A. V., and Pollard, Arthur, *Letters of Mrs Gaskell*, Manchester: Manchester University Press, 1966.

Charlot, Monica, *Victoria, the Young Queen*, Oxford: Blackwell, 1991.

Chomet, S., *Helena, A Princess Reclaimed,* New York: Begell House, 1999.

Clark, John Willis, ed., *Life, Letters and Journals*

*of Sir Charles Lyell*, vol. 2, London: John Murray, 1881.

Cook, Edward, *Delane of the Times*, London: Constable, 1915.

Cooke, Clement K., *Memoir of HRH Princess Mary Adelaide, Duchess of Teck*, 2 vols, London: John Murray, 1900.

Cowley, H. R. C., Duke of Wellington, *The Paris Embassy During the Second Empire*, London: T. Butterworth, 1928.

Craik, D. M., *Fifty Golden Years: Incidents in the Queen's Reign.* London: n.p., 1887.

Crawford, Emily, *Victoria, Queen and Ruler*, London: Simpkin, Marshall, 1903.

Creaton, Heather, *Victorian Diaries, The Daily Lives of Victorian Men and Women* London: Mitchell Beazley, 2001.

—— *Unpublished London Diaries,* London: London Record Society, 2003.

Creston Dormer, *The Youthful Queen Victoria: A Discursive Account*, London: Macmillan, 1952.

Cullen, Tom, *The Empress Brown: The Story of a Royal Friendship*, London: Bodley Head, 1969.

Dafforne, James, *The Albert Memorial Hyde Park: Its History and Description*, London: Virtue & Co., 1877.

Darby, Elisabeth and Nicola Smith, *The Cult of the Prince Consort*, New Haven: Yale University Press, 1983.

Dasent, Arthur, *John Thadeus Delane, Editor of 'The Times': His Life and Correspondence*, vol. 2, London: John Murray, 1908.

De-La-Noy, Michael, *Windsor Castle: Past and Present*, London: Headline, 1990.

Dennison, Matthew, *The Last Princess: The Devoted*

*Life of Queen Victoria's Youngest Daughter*, London: Weidenfeld & Nicolson, 2007.

Dimond, Frances, and Taylor, Roger, *Crown and Camera: The Royal Family and Photography*, Harmondsworth: Penguin, 1987.

Duff, David, *The Life Story of HRH Princess Louise, Duchess of Argyll*, Bath: Cedric Chivers, 1940.

—— *The Shy Princess: The Life of HRH Princess Beatrice*, London: Evans Brothers, 1958.

—— *Hessian Tapestry*, London: Macmillan, 1967.

—— *Victoria Travels: Journeys of Queen Victoria between 1830 and 1900*, London: Frederick Muller, 1970.

—— *Albert & Victoria*, London: Tandem, 1972.

—— , ed., *Queen Victoria's Highland Journals*, London: Webb and Bower, 1980.

Dyson, Hope and Tennyson, Charles, eds, *Dear and Honoured Lady: The Correspondence between Queen Victoria and Alfred, Lord Tennyson*, London: Macmillan, 1969.

Ellis, S. M., *A Mid Victorian Pepys: The Letters and Memoirs of Sir William Hardman*, London: Cecil Palmer, 1923.

Elvey, Lady Mary Savory, *Life and Reminiscences of Sir George Elvey*, London: Sampson, Low, Marston, 1894.

Emden, Paul, *Behind the Throne*, London: Hodder & Stoughton, 1934.

Epton, Nina, *Victoria and Her Daughters*, London: Weidenfeld & Nicolson, 1971.

Eyck, Frank, *The Prince Consort: A Political Biography*, Bath: Cedric Chivers, 1975.

Frankland, Noble, *Witness of a Century: the Life and Times of Prince Arthur Duke of Connaught 1850–1942*, London: Shepheard-Walwyn, 1993.

Fulford, Roger, ed., *The Greville Memoirs,* London: B. T. Batsford, 1963.

—— *The Prince Consort*, London: Macmillan, 1966.

Gardiner, A. G., *The Life of Sir William Harcourt*, 2 vols, London: Constable & Co., 1923.

Gavard, Charles, *A Diplomat in London: Letters and Notes 1871–77*, New York: Henry Holt & Co., 1897.

Gernsheim, Helmut and Gernsheim, Alison, *Queen Victoria: A Biography in Word and Picture,* London: Longman's, Green & Co., 1959.

Girouard, Mark, *The Return to Camelot: Chivalry and the English Gentleman*, New Haven: Yale University Press, 1981.

—— *Windsor, the Most Romantic Castle*, London: Hodder & Stoughton, 1993.

Guedalla, Phillip, ed., *The Queen and Mr Gladstone, 1845–1898*, vol. 1, 1845–1879, London: Hodder & Stoughton, 1933.

Handley, C. S., *An Annotated Bibliography of Diaries Printed in English*, 4 vols, Aldeburgh: Hanover Press, 1997.

Hardie, Frank, *The Political Influence of Queen Victoria 1861–1901*, London: Oxford University Press, 1938.

Hedley, Owen, *Windsor Castle*, London: Robert Hale, 1967.

Helps, Edmund A., ed., *The Correspondence of Sir Arthur Helps*, London: John Lane, 1917.

Hewett, Osbert, ed., *'. . . and Mr Fortescue': A selection of the diaries from 1851 to 1862 of Chichester Fortescue, Lord Carlingford*, London: John Murray, 1958.

Hibbert, Christopher, *The Court at Windsor: A Domestic History,* London: Longman's, Green &

Co., 1964.

—— *Edward VII: A Portrait*, London: Allen Lane, 1976.

—— *Victoria: A Personal History*, London: HarperCollins, 2000.

Holland, Caroline, *Notebooks of a Spinster Lady*, London: Cassell & Co., 1919.

Homans, Margaret, *Royal Representations: Queen Victoria and British Culture 1837–1876*, Chicago: University of Chicago Press, 1998.

—— and Munich, Adrienne, *Remaking Queen Victoria*, Cambridge: Cambridge University Press, 1997.

Hough, Richard, *Victoria and Albert: Their Love and Their Tragedies*, London: Richard Cohen, 1996.

House, Madeline and Storey, Graham, eds, *The Letters of Charles Dickens*, vol. 9, 1859–1861, and vol. 10, 1862–1864, Oxford: Clarendon Press, 1998.

'How the Christmas Tree Came to England', *The Times*, 22 December 1958.

Hudson, Derek, *Munby: Man of Two Worlds*, London: Abacus, 1974.

Jackman, S. W. and Haasse, Hella, eds, *Stranger in the House: Letters of Queen Sophie of the Netherlands to Lady Malet, 1842–1877*, London: Duke University Press, 1989.

Jerrold, Clare, *The Heart of Queen Victoria: True Anecdotes of Her Majesty's Life*, London: Jarrold, 1897.

—— *The Married Life of Queen Victoria*, London: Eveleigh Nash, 1913.

—— *The Widowhood of Queen Victoria*, London, Eveleigh Nash, 1916.

Kennedy, A. L., *My Dear Duchess: Social and*

*Political Letters to the Duchess of Manchester 1858–1869*, London: John Murray, 1956.

Kenyon, Edith C., *Scenes in the Life of the Princess Alice (Grand Duchess of Hesse)*, London: W. Nicholson & Sons, 1887.

—— *Scenes in the Life of the Royal Family*, London: W. Nicholson & Sons, 1887.

Kharibian, Leah, *Passionate Patrons: Victoria & Albert and the Arts*, London: Royal Collection Publications, 2010.

Kiste, John van Der, *Sons, Servants and Statesmen: The Men in Queen Victoria's Life*, Stroud: Sutton, 2006.

Kuhn, William M., 'Ceremony and Politics: The British Monarchy 1871–2', *Journal of British Studies*, vol. 26, 1987, pp. 133–62.

—— *Democratic Royalism: The Transformation of the British Monarchy, 1861–1914*, Basingstoke: Macmillan, 1996.

—— *Henry and Mary Ponsonby*, London: Duckworth, 2002.

Lant, J. L., *Insubstantial Pageant: Ceremony and Confusion at Queen Victoria's Court*, London: Hamish Hamilton, 1979.

Lee, Sydney, *Queen Victoria, A Biography*, London: Smith, Elder & Co., 1904.

'Letter to the Queen on Her Retirement from Public Life', by one of Her Majesty's most loyal subjects, London: Samuel Tinsely, 1875.

Lindsay, W. A., *The Royal Household*, London: K. Paul, Trench, Trübner & Co., 1898.

Loewe, Louis, ed., *Diaries of Sir Moses and Lady Montefiore*, vol. 2, London: Griffith Farran Okeden & Welsh, 1890.

Longford, Elizabeth, 'Queen Victoria's Doctors',

in Martin Gilbert, ed., *A Century of Conflict 1850–1950*, London: Hamish Hamilton, 1966.

—— *The Pebbled Shore: The Memoirs of Elizabeth Longford*, Stroud: Sutton, 2004.

McClintock, Mary Howard, *The Queen Thanks Sir Howard*, London: John Murray, 1945.

Macleod, Donald, *Memoir of Dr Norman Macleod*, vol. 2, London: Belford Brothers, 1876.

Magnus, Philip, *Gladstone: A Biography*, London: John Murray, 1963.

—— *King Edward the Seventh*, London: John Murray, 1964.

Mallet, Victor, ed., *Life with Queen Victoria: Marie Mallet's Letters from Court, 1887–1901*, London: John Murray, 1968.

Malmesbury, Lord, *Memoirs of an Ex-Minister*, 2 vols, London: Longman's, Green & Co., 1884.

Marie Louise, Princess, *My Memories of Six Reigns*, Harmondsworth: Penguin, 1961.

Maxwell, Sir Herbert, ed., *Life and Letters of the 4th Earl of Clarendon*, 2 vols, London: Arnold, 1913.

Millar, Delia, *Queen Victoria's Life in the Scottish Highlands*, London: Philip Wilson Publishers, 1985.

Moneypenny, William F. and Buckle, G. E., eds, *The Life of Benjamin Disraeli, Earl of Beaconsfield*, London: Smith, Elder & Co, 1910–20.

Morris, Frankie, 'The Illustrated Press and the Republican Crisis of 1871–1872', *Victorian Periodicals Review*, vol. 25, Fall 1992, pp. 114–26.

Munich, Adrienne, *Queen Victoria's Secrets*, New York: Columbia University Press, 1996.

Nevill, Barry St John, *Life at the Court of Queen Victoria: Selections from the Journals of Queen Victoria*, Stroud: Sutton, 1997.

Nevill, Lady Dorothy, *Under Five Reigns*, London: Methuen, 1910.

Nicholls, David, *The Lost Prime Minister: A Life of Sir Charles Dilke*, London: Hambledon Press, 1995.

Noel, Gerald, *Princess Alice: Queen Victoria's Forgotten Daughter*, London: Constable, 1974.

O'Brien, D. P., ed., *Correspondence of Lord Overstone*, vol. 2, Cambridge: Cambridge University Press, 1971.

Packard, Jerrold, *Victoria's Daughters*, New York: St Martin's Press, 1998.

Paget, Lady Walburga, *Embassies of Other Days*, vol. I, London: Hutchinson, 1923.

Pakula, Hannah, *An Uncommon Woman: The Empress Frederick, daughter of Queen Victoria*, London: Weidenfeld & Nicolson, 1996.

Ponsonby, Arthur, *Henry Ponsonby, Queen Victoria's Private Secretary: His Life from his Letters*, London: Macmillan, 1942.

Ponsonby, Frederick, *Side Lights on Queen Victoria*, London: Macmillan, 1930.

—— *Recollections of Three Reigns*, London: Eyre & Spottiswoode, 1951.

Ponsonby, Magdalen, ed., *Mary Ponsonby: A Memoir, Some Letters and a Journal*, London: John Murray, 1927.

Protheroe, Rowland E., *Life and Letters of Dean Stanley*, London: Thomas Nelson, 1893.

Purves, John, ed., *Letters from the Cape—Lady Duff Gordon*, London: H. Milford, 1921.

Ramm, Agatha, *The Gladstone–Granville Correspondence*, Cambridge: Cambridge University Press, 1998.

Rappaport, Helen, *Queen Victoria: A Biographical*

*Companion*, 2 vols, Santa Barbara: ABC-Clio, 2003.

Reid, Stuart J., ed., *Memoirs of Sir Wemyss Reid 1842–1885*, London: Cassell & Co., 1885.

Reid, T. Wemyss, ed., *Memoirs and Correspondence of Lyon Playfair*, London: Cassell, 1899.

Reynolds, K. D., *Aristocratic Women and Political Society in Victorian Britain*, Oxford: Clarendon Press, 1998.

Richardson, Joanna,*Victoria and Albert: A Study of a Marriage*, London: Dent, 1977.

Rickman, John Godlee, *Lord Lister*, Oxford: Clarendon Press, 1924.

Ricks, Christopher, ed., *The Poems of Tennyson*, vols 2 and 3, London: Longman's, 1987.

Robbins, Michael, 'The Missing Doctor: An "if" of Victorian history', *Journal of the Royal Society of Medicine*, vol. 90, March 1997, pp. 163–5.

Russell, Bertrand and Russell, Patricia, eds, *The Amberley Papers: Diaries and Letters of Lord and Lady Amberley*, 2 vols, London: Hogarth Press, 1937.

Russell, William Howard, *My Diary: North and South*, vol. 1, London: Bradbury & Evans, 1863.

St Aubyn, Giles, *Queen Victoria: A Portrait*, London: Sinclair Stevenson, 1991.

Sala, George Augustus, *Life and Adventures,* vol. 1, London: Cassell & Co., 1895.

Sanders, Valerie, ed., *Harriet Martineau: Selected Letters*, Oxford: Clarendon Press, 1990.

Scott, Gilbert, *Personal and Professional Recollections*, Stamford: Paul Watkins, 1995.

Smith, G. Barnett, *The Life of Her Majesty Queen Victoria: Compiled from All Available Sources*, London: G. Routledge, 1887.

Smith, J. F. and Howitt, W., eds, *John Cassell's Illustrated History of England*, vol. 8, London: W. Kent & Co., 1864.

Stockmar, Ernest et al., *Memoirs of Baron Stockmar*, vol. 1, London: Longman's, Green & Co., 1873.

Stoney, Benita and Weltzien Heinrich C., eds, *My Mistress the Queen: The Letters of Frieda Arnold, Dresser to Queen Victoria 1854–9*, London: Weidenfeld & Nicolson, 1994.

Strachey, Lytton, *Queen Victoria*, Harmondsworth: Penguin, 1971 [1921].

Strafford, Alice, Countess of, ed., *Leaves from the Diary of Henry Greville*, London: Smith Elder & Co., 3rd series [1857–61] 1904 and 4th series [1862–72] 1905.

Thompson, Dorothy, *Queen Victoria: Gender and Power*, London: Virago Press, 2001.

Tinling, James Forbes, *Lessons from the Life and Death of the Princess Alice*, London: S. Bagster & Sons, 1879.

Tisdall, E. E. P., *Queen Victoria's John Brown*, London: Stanley Paul, 1938.

—— *Restless Consort: The Invasion of Albert the Conqueror*, London: Stanley Paul, 1952.

—— *Unpredictable Queen: The Intimate Life of Queen Alexandra*, London: Stanley Paul, 1953.

—— *Queen Victoria's Private Life*, London: Jarrolds, 1961.

Tooley, Sarah, *Personal Life of Queen Victoria*, London: Hodder & Stoughton, 1896.

Tyack, Geoffrey, 'The Albert Memorial', in *Victorian Studies*, vol. 44, no. 2, Winter 2002, pp. 293–5.

Underwood, Peter, *Queen Victoria's Other World*, London: Harrap, 1982.

Van Der Kiste, John, *Queen Victoria's Children*, Stroud: Sutton, 2003.

Villiers, George, *A Vanished Victorian, Being the Life of George Villiers, 4th Earl of Clarendon 1800–1870*, London: Eyre & Spottiswoode, 1938.

Vincent, John, ed., *Disraeli, Derby and the Conservative Party: The Journals and Memoirs of Edward Henry, Lord Stanley*, Hassocks: Harvester Press, 1978.

Wallace, Sarah Agnes, ed., *The Journal of Benjamin Moran 1857–1865*, vol. 2, Chicago: University of Chicago Press, 1949.

Walsh, Walter, *The Religious Life and Influence of Queen Victoria*, London: Swann Sonnenschein, 1902.

Warwick, Frances, Countess of, *Afterthoughts*, London: Cassell, 1931.

Watson, Vera, *A Queen at Home: An Intimate Account of the Social and Domestic Life at Queen Victoria's, Court*, London: W. H. Allen, 1952.

Weibe, Mel et al., eds, *Benjamin Disraeli Letters*, vol. 8, 1860–1864, Toronto: University of Toronto Press, 2009.

Weintraub, Stanley, *Victoria*, London: John Murray, 1996.

Wheatcroft, Andrew, *The Tennyson Album: A Biography in Original Photographs*, London: Routledge & Kegan Paul, 1980.

'Where the Prince Consort Died', *The Times*, 13 December 1961.

Whittle, Tyler, *Victoria and Albert at Home*, London: Routledge & Kegan Paul, 1980.

Williams, Richard, *Contentious Crown: Public Discussions of the British Monarchy in the Reign of Queen Victoria*, Aldershot: Ashgate, 1997.

Wilson, Robert, *The Life and Times of Queen Victoria*, 2 vols, London: Cassell & Co., 1891–3.

Wrench, G. T., *Lord Lister, His Life and Work*, London: Unwin, 1913.

Zeepvat, Charlotte, *Prince Leopold: The Untold Story of Queen Victoria's Youngest Son*, Stroud: Sutton, 1998.

*Sources for grief and bereavement, mourning dress and jewellery*

Adburgham, Alison, *Shops and Shopping 1800–1914*, London: Barrie & Jenkins, 1989.

Arnold, Catharine, *Necropolis: London and Its Dead*, London: Simon & Schuster, 2006.

Behrendt, Stephen C., *Royal Mourning and Regency Culture: Elegies and Memorials of Princess Charlotte*, Basingstoke: Macmillan, 1997.

Bland, Olivia, *The Royal Way of Death*, London: Constable, 1986.

Bower, J. A., 'Whitby Jet and its Manufacture', *Journal of the Society of Arts*, vol. 22, 19 December 1873, pp. 80–7.

Bowlby, Richard, *Attachment and Loss*, Harmondsworth: Penguin, 1991.

Cooper, Diana and Battershill, Norman, *Victorian Sentimental Jewellery*, Newton Abbott: David & Charles, 1972.

Curl, James, *The Victorian Celebration of Death*, Stroud: Sutton, 2000.

Dawes, Ginny Redington, *Victorian Jewelry*, Ann Arbor: University of Michigan Press, 1991.

'Fashions for January', *Illustrated London News*, 28 December 1861.

Freud, Sigmund, 'Mourning and Melancholia', in *The Future of an Illusion*, London: Penguin, 2008.

Garlick, Harry, *The Final Curtain: State Funerals and the Theatre of Power*, Amsterdam: Editions Rodopi B.V., 1999.

Gere, Charlotte and Rudoe, Judy, *Jewellery in the Age of Queen Victoria*, London: British Museum Press, 2010.

Goldthorp, Caroline, *From Queen to Empress: Victorian Dress 1837–1877*, New York: Metropolitan Museum of Art, 1989.

Hayden, Ilse, *Symbol and Privilege: The Ritual Context of British Royalty*, Tucson: University of Arizona Press, 1987.

Jalland, Pat, *Death in the Victorian Family,* Oxford: Oxford University Press, 1996.

Kendall, Hugh P., *The Story of Whitby Jet: Its Workers from Earliest Times,* Whitby: Whitby Literary & Philosophical Society, 1988.

King, Melanie, *The Dying Game,* Oxford: Oneworld, 2008.

Kontou, Tatiana, *Spiritualism and Women's Writing from Fin de Siecle to the Neo-Victorians,* Basingstoke: Palgrave, 2009.

Kübler-Ross, Elizabeth, *On Death and Dying*, London: Tavistock Publications, 1970.

Luthi, Ann Louise, *Sentimental Jewellery*, Princes Risborough: Shire, 1998.

McMillan, Mabel, *Whitby Jet through the Years,* Whitby: privately published, 1992.

Morley, John, *Death, Heaven and the Victorians*, London: Studio Vista, 1971.

Muller, Helen, *Jet Jewellery and Ornaments*, Aylesbury: Shire Publications, 1980.

—— and Muller, Katy, *Whitby Jet*, Oxford: Shire

Publications, 2009.

Parkes, Colin Murray, *Bereavement: Studies in Grief in Adult Life*, London: Penguin, 1996.

—— *Love and Loss: The Roots of Grief and Its Complications*, London: Routledge, 2006.

—— and Hinde, Joan Stevenson, *The Place of Attachment in Human Behaviour*, London: Tavistock Publications, 1982.

—— and Weiss, Robert S., *Recovery from Bereavement*, New York: Basic Books, 1983.

Powles, William E. and Alexander, Mary G., 'Was Queen Victoria Depressed?', *Canadian Journal of Psychiatry*, vol. 32, February 1987, pp. 14–19.

Puckle, Bertram S., *Funeral Customs: Their Origin and Development*, London: T. Werner Laurie Ltd, 1926.

Ramchandani, Dilip, 'Pathological Grief: Two Victorian Case Studies', *Psychiatric Quarterly*, vol. 67, no. 1, Spring 1996, pp. 75–84.

Schor, Esther, *Bearing the Dead: The British Culture of Mourning from the Enlightenment to Victoria*, Princeton: Princeton University Press, 1994.

Staniland, Kay, *In Royal Fashion: The Clothes of Princess Charlotte of Wales and Queen Victoria, 1796–1901*, London: Museum of London, 1997.

Taylor, Lou, *Mourning Dress—A Costume and Social History*, London: Allen & Unwin, 1983.

Walter, Tony, 'Royalty and Public Grief in England', in Tony Walter, *The Mourning for Diana*, Oxford: Berg, 1999.

Whaley, Joachim, ed., *Mirrors of Mortality: Studies in the Social History of Death*, London: Europa Publications, 1981.

Wheeler, Michael, *Heaven, Hell and the Victorians*, Cambridge: Cambridge University Press, 1994.

Wolffe, John, *Great Deaths: Grieving, Religion and Nationhood in Victorian and Edwardian Britain*, Oxford: Oxford University Press, 2000.